POLITICS IN WIRED NATIONS

POLITICS IN WIRED NATIONS

Selected Writings of
Ithiel de Sola Pool

edited, and with an introduction by
Lloyd S. Etheredge

Transaction Publishers
New Brunswick (U.S.A.) and London (U.K.)

Copyright © 1998 by Transaction Publishers, New Brunswick, New Jersey.

All rights reserved under International and Pan-American Copyright Conventions. No part of this book may be reproduced or transmitted in any form or by any means, electronic or mechanical, including photocopy, recording, or any information storage and retrieval system, without prior permission in writing from the publisher. All inquiries should be addressed to Transaction Publishers, Rutgers—The State University, 35 Berrue Circle, Piscataway, New Jersey 08854-8042.

This book is printed on acid-free paper that meets the American National Standard for Permanence of Paper for Printed Library Materials.

Library of Congress Catalog Number: 97-51703
ISBN: 1-56000-344-8
Printed in the United States of America

Library of Congress Cataloging-in-Publication Data

Pool, Ithiel de Sola, 1917–
    Politics in wired nations : selected writings of Ithiel de Sola Pool / edited, and with an introduction by Lloyd S. Etheredge.
        p. cm.
    Includes bibliographical references and index.
    ISBN 1-56000-344-8 (alk. paper)
    1. Telecommunication—Social aspects. 2. Telecommunication—Technological innovations. 3. Communication in politics. 4. Information technology—Social aspects. I. Etheredge, Lloyd S. II. Title.
HE7631P658   1998
303.48'33—dc21   97-51703
                                                                CIP

To the memory of Ithiel de Sola Pool

Contents

List of Tables

List of Figures

Preface

Across forty years Ithiel de Sola Pool wrote, co-authored, or edited more than two dozen books and several hundred articles. He contributed to the development of the social sciences and to almost every field within political science. This volume brings together selections from his work concerning communication systems, and especially the social and political impact of communications technology.

I have many debts. The responsibility for the final selections is my own, but many of Ithiel's former colleagues and students gave advice, and they deepened my knowledge of the development of social science. I especially want to thank Jean Pool, who helped at each step. And to express my appreciation to Jonathan Pool who facilitated the scanning of publications and other logistics, and to the archives at the University of Chicago, at Yale University (for access to the Harold Lasswell papers) and at MIT where Helen Samuels has helped to organize the papers of Ithiel Pool and Ed Davy checked the preliminary bibliography. Also to the holders of the original copyrights who generously granted permission to reprint these selections.

Beyond selecting papers of enduring value, I have applied two other tests:

First, from each selection, was something being communicated of wider benefit, a sense of becoming more in contact with reality and a broader perspective? Would a reader learn something not just about the American Congress and a foreign trade bill, but a way of seeing a communication system that could apply to other cases?

Second, was there something ahead of its time? Did it bear rereading not only as a classic introduction to its subject, but also because a fresh look in a new historical context allows ideas, emphases, or turns of mind to emerge? Did it contribute, in conversation with the other selections in this volume, to a wider vision and set of current implications? In an introduction to each section I have suggested where I think this is true.

Lloyd S. Etheredge
February 1997

Acknowledgments

"Political Communication: Introduction" by Ithiel de Sola Pool. Reprinted with permission of Macmillan Reference USA, a Division of Simon & Schuster, from *International Encyclopedia of the Social Sciences*, David L. Sills, editor, vol. 3, pp. 90–96. Copyright © 1968 by Crowell Collier and Macmillan, Inc. Copyright renewed (c) 1996.

"Contacts and Influence" by Ithiel de Sola Pool and Manfred Kochen. Reprinted from *Social Networks: An International Journal of Structural Analysis*, vol. 1, no. 1, pp. 5–51, with kind permission from Elsevier Science—NL, Sara Burgerhartstraat 25, 1055 KV Amsterdam, The Netherlands.

"Trends in Content Analysis Today: A Summary" by Ithiel de Sola Pool from *Trends in Content Analysis*. Copyright © 1987 by the Board of Trustees of the University of Illinois. Used with permission of the University of Illinois Press.

"Foresight and Hindsight: The Case of the Telephone" by Ithiel de Sola Pool. Reprinted with permission from *The Social Impact of the Telephone*, 1977, pp. 127–57. Copyright (c) 1977 MIT Press.

"Communication Technology and Land Use" by Ithiel de Sola Pool from *Annals of the American Academy of Political and Social Science*, vol. 451, pp. 1–12. Copyright (c) 1980. Reprinted by Permission of Sage Publications, Inc.

"Tracking the Flow of Information" by Ithiel de Sola Pool. Reprinted with permission from *Science*, vol. 221, no. 4611, 1983, pp. 609–13. Copyright (c) 1983 American Association for the Advancement of Science.

"Citizen Feedback in Political Philosophy" by Ithiel de Sola Pool. Reprinted with permission from *Talking Back: Citizen Feedback and Cable Technology*, 1973, pp. 237–26. Copyright (c) 1973 MIT Press.

"Communication and Integrated Planning" by Ithiel de Sola Pool from *Media Asia*, vol. 8, no. 3, pp. 152–55. Reprinted by permission of Media Asia.

"Policies for Freedom" from *Technologies of Freedom* by Ithiel de Sola Pool. Copyright © 1983 by the President and Fellows of Harvard College. Reprinted by permission of Harvard University Press.

Introduction

"Most movements that are self-described as radical are highly urbanistic, or nationalistic, or oriented to obsolete class structures, or to central bureaucratic planning. The changes that we can see on the horizon are much more drastic than that.... People who think about social change in traditional political terms cannot begin to imagine the changes that lie ahead. Conventional reformers cast their programs in terms of national policies, or in terms of laws and central planning. But in the end, what will shape the future is a creative potential that inheres in the new technologies."[1]

—Ithiel de Sola Pool (1983)

Ithiel de Sola Pool was one of the most original thinkers in the development of the social sciences and a distinguished scholar of the political process. For thirty years he directed the Research Program on Communications at the Massachusetts Institute of Technology. *Politics in Wired Nations* presents a selection of his pioneering work that explores different communication systems in society and politics and especially the impact of new communications technologies.

Among the classic studies included in this volume are:

- The first study of trends to a global information society.
- The first study of social networks and the "small world" phenomenon that creates new relationships and routes of informal influence and political power, domestic and international.
- The politics of foreign trade and the influence of businessmen on foreign policy.
- A historical study of forecasting, testing whether the methods used to predict the impact of earlier technology are successful.
- Four "unnatural institutions" of the modern world (e.g., bureaucracies, mega-cities, nation-states) that will change because of the new capacities, lower costs, and the user control of new technologies.
- Policy choices for freedom, the battlegrounds ahead, and the risks of government and United Nations involvement in the regulation of new telecommunication technologies, even for good purposes.

1

Inevitably, a diminishing portion of the readers who consult this volume will know the major events of the twentieth century at first hand. Ithiel de Sola Pool's research responded to these events. I believe that it will assist the reader to place his work in the context of Pool's life and this history. Next, I will place them in the context of his commitment to freedom and the framework that his research was developing to assess the exponential changes in telecommunications technologies that are underway.

A Brief Biography

Ithiel de Sola Pool was born in New York City in 1917, the son of two distinguished parents: Rabbi David deSola Pool (Heidelberg, Ph.D.), an Englishman and the spiritual leader of the Sephardic Congregation in New York City; and Tamar Hirshenson (Hunter College, the Sorbonne), the daughter of a rabbi. He attended the University of Chicago of the 1930s (B.A., 1938; M.A., 1939; Ph.D., 1952) amid the tumult and political passions of the Depression and was a passionate Trotskyite and student leader. The University of Chicago, in this era of President Robert Hutchins, the political scientist Charles Merriam, and others, was the birthplace of social science and Ithiel was one of the first recruits.

During World War II, Ithiel Pool joined two of his young teachers, Harold Lasswell and Nathan Leites, in Washington, D.C. to apply the new quantitative methods of social science to research Nazi and communist propaganda. Next, he moved to Stanford University (to study the effects of symbols, revolution, and revolutionary elites) and, in the early 1950s, to MIT, where he spent the next thirty years.

Ithiel Pool initially moved to MIT's new Center for International Studies to direct a research program on communication technology and its effects on global politics. He continued his earlier role of leadership, helping to create and build the new Political Science Department at MIT into one of the best in the world. He organized international teams of scientists and collaborated widely to develop the understanding of global political change, especially in the years after World War II.

Ithiel Pool's early work applied quantitative methods to traditional academic sources (e.g., speeches, editorials, newspaper stories). However, at MIT the growth of the Political Science Department was part of the post-World War II increase of Cambridge-based academic involvement in international and domestic policy.[2] And as part of this new role of social science, Ithiel Pool and his colleagues were frequent advisers to governments and there were remarkable opportunities to travel and conduct well-funded field research in other countries: in Ithiel's case this included India and Japan (especially) but also Vietnam, Turkey, and Egypt. In these decades, new communication technologies (e.g., print, radio) were penetrating the world's traditional societies (including former colonies that were achieving independence) and bringing new ideas, passionate efforts at nation-building, and revolutionary (especially communist-linked) ferment around the world. The study of political development—reflected in these selections—was one of the specialties of the MIT Political Science Department.

Two team-written books from this period remain classic empirical studies in political science: Bauer, Pool, and Dexter's *American Business and Public Policy: The Politics of Foreign Trade* (1963) explored the new internationalism of American business and trade policy and created a refined image of Congress and the process of political influence that has been of continuing value. Pool's basic sympathies lay with the Democrats and, when the opportunity presented itself to apply the new capacities of mainframe computers and attitude surveys to advise President Kennedy's 1960 election campaign, he and several colleagues (Abelson, Pool, and Popkin 1964) built the first computer simulation model of the American electorate to draw upon such data, predicting the outcome of the election, state-by-state, as the interplay of issues with 480 types of voters.[3]

From his youthful engagement as a political radical in the 1930s, and his research, Ithiel Pool came to believe, as did others of his generation, that many self-described revolutionary leaders used idealistic language and images but established restrictive regimes. He was a member of the Council on Foreign Relations and advised the U.S. government during the Cold War in several capacities, for example, through a long-standing association with RAND Corp.; research to understand communication systems in totalitarian societies and improve the work of Radio Free Europe/Radio Liberty in fostering political change in Eastern Europe and the Soviet Union; as a public defender of the Vietnam War and an organizer of major research projects in Vietnam that sought to change how it was fought.

As a scientist, Ithiel Pool continued to grow and pioneer new areas. In the early 1970s he organized and edited a distinguished *Handbook of Communication* (1973) which defined the field and summarized its early scientific accomplishments. Next, it was clear that a new era was beginning, with the growth of communication satellites, computer technology, cable television, packet switched networking, fiber optic cable, and other inventions. He began to develop a framework to assess the effects of these new telecommunication technologies, integrating his early work on mass communications (e.g., Nazi propaganda) and the modernization of peasant societies, to forecast the road ahead and identify key policy choices. Many of the selections in this volume are drawn from this work, which continued until his death in 1984.

During this period he developed a steady, cumulative research program to assemble the components needed for the task: Among other projects, he studied earlier forecasting methods, began the measurement of trends (e.g., the original studies of movement toward a global information society), reviewed the earlier debates and court decisions that justified control of communication innovations (e.g., licensing of television and radio), and analyzed (in *Technologies of Freedom* [1983]) whether the earlier justifications remained valid in the emerging era of new telecommunication technologies. There is a growing excitement in this work as he begins to see its implications—a subject that I discuss in the next section.

Freedom and the Road Ahead

These selections are united by Ithiel Pool's belief that first-rate social science can strengthen citizen decision making and advance freedom. There are two ways in which this is so: First, a perception, widely shared by pioneering social scientists, of the inherent value of an independent scientific framework; second, a more powerful logic to Ithiel Pool's own cumulative research program.

Concerning the traditional belief of social scientists: recently, it has become fashionable for deconstructionists and other practitioners of literary criticism in communication studies to emphasize that social and political reality is created, and to portray themselves as liberators (e.g., from being entrapped in a reality that is socially constructed by communicators). The implied contrast is to early social scientists, measuring an allegedly "objective" reality with mathematical models and fixed coefficients, who are naively entrapped, not as primarily committed to freedom, or misdirecting their energies to technocratic enthusiasms.

The appropriate response is brief: as these selections illustrate, Ithiel Pool and other founders of social science *knew* that social and political reality was created. And that men were manipulated, entrapped, and limited in their images of themselves and of the possibilities open to them; and by the flows of communications that maintained traditional societies or that were programmed by governments. These claims were not presented with verbal flourishes and rebellious poses because to a generation that saw a world in flames (millions of troops marching at the behest of Nazi propaganda, the passions of nationalist and communist revolutionary movements) they were axiomatic. And they believed that social science could be liberating by providing an independent, steadier, truer, and more realistic alternative to the frameworks and choices that the political world provided.

Concerning the more powerful claim about social science and freedom, quoted at the beginning of this introduction, that pertains to the road ahead: Pool's argument is that social science can provide a unique and powerful guidance to augment freedom (given the exponential changes in telecommunications technology and computers that can be forecast) *and* that *"people who think about social change in traditional political [even radical] terms cannot begin to imagine the changes that lie ahead."* That is, specifically, when applied to the study of communication systems, social science *does* pay off and *does* provide an independent, steadier, truer, and more realistic alternative to the frameworks and choices that the political world provides.

Pool's claim, if true, is important. There are (limited) implications for government and (many) implications for other institutions (e.g., foundations, professional and scientific societies, universities, religious and cultural institutions, nongovernmental organizations (NGOs), corporations) and individuals (e.g., inventors, students, activists, citizens) in all countries: if you wish a world that works better, and must choose between: (a) traditional political activities and a focus on government policy, and (b) the thoughtful development and application of these new technologies, shift toward b.

Pool's full case is made by implication, as he did not live to pull together all of the pieces. The selections allow the reader to see where he was coming from, and how the cumulative force of research leads to his conclusion. I will discuss the argument more fully in the introduction to the third section of readings.

Notes

1. The quotation is from "Four Unnatural Institutions..." reprinted in this volume and drawn from the essay in Aida, 1983 cited in the bibliography.

2. The Center for International Studies was created at MIT to strengthen American research capacity when James Killian from MIT was science adviser to President Eisenhower.

3. Pool and Kessler (1965) was the first computer simulation of crisis decision making. An assessment of early contributions to the development of social science credited Ithiel Pool with a pioneering role in three areas: the quantitative analysis of communications content, the study (during his Stanford period) of ruling elites, and these computer simulation projects: Karl W. Deutsch, J. Platt, and D. Senghaas, "Conditions favoring major advances in social science." *Science* 171 (1971): 450–59.

Part I

Political Communication

Editor's Introduction

The first selection, Ithiel Pool's "Introduction to Political Communication" from the *International Encyclopedia of the Social Sciences* (1968), begins with a brief comment that might be overlooked as an aside. However Pool's view that "The domain of the study of communication can thus legitimately be the entire domain of the social sciences" is an entrance to his work and to this volume.

Specifically, a group of wide-ranging pioneers (Harold Lasswell, Nathan Leites, Ithiel Pool, and Karl Deutsch, among others) saw communication systems with the same vividness that economists see economic systems. This framework is unique and seemed to permit them, with apparent effortlessness, to think (e.g., in Pool's case) usefully about subjects as disparate as the modernization of peasant societies, nuclear deterrence, how Congress works, the computer simulation of American voting behavior, and many other topics.

This "communication studies" framework is rarely taught and it differs from a typical academic major that might have a similar name. It is not a designation for a diffuse and limited education but a framework that is recommended if one wants to make a commitment to integrate insights and methods ("the entire domain") of all the social sciences. The understanding of a particular communication system requires detailed field work: as Bauer, Pool and Dexter wrote in their multiyear study of Congress (pp. 91–117 in this volume): "[C]ommunications is one input into a complex sociopsychological system. The effect of the communication on that system is, to a greater degree than is usually acknowledged, a function of the structure of that system.... [T]he study of communications in real-life situations is a study of complex structural facets of society. It is not enough to examine a message flow between the black boxes. One needs to know the transforming characteristics of the black boxes." They carefully studied five sets of black boxes.

Images and Influence

Changing Images: Communication in the Process of Modernization,
Newsmen's Fantasies, Audiences and Newswriting, Deterence
as an Influence Process

The next three selections reflect a greater depth that emerges in Pool's research after his personal experience with psychoanalysis. (It also was a common sensibility in his circles early in his professional life: Lasswell and Leites were pioneers in the application of psychoanalytic sensibilities and methods.) I have included them because of the subjects which they illuminate, and also because the emphasis upon imagery remains ahead of its time; social scientists have developed more quickly the measurement of attitudes toward an external reality [Does the subject agree or disagree with a particular expression of opinion, and how strongly, using a seven-point scale] than the measurement of images. Yet the altered images—in political modernization, in psychoanalysis, in social science research itself—are often the pathway for change or learning: an "image Congress" (real enough in the imagination) becomes, after a multiyear field study, a different Congress. The reality of American capacity to destroy the Soviet Union with nuclear weapons can be distinguished from the "image America" that impinges on the mind of Soviet leaders—and one may want (for example) this "image America" to convey strength and resolve, but to keep the menace in the background.

If Pool is right, the impact of communications on images is a key to predict one set of major social and political effects of new telecommunications technology.

Concerning the paper on nuclear deterrence: for several decades, MIT and Harvard trained defense analysts (for example, in graduate seminars where students had rotary slide rules calibrated in megadeaths—a theory of how to make nuclear deterrence rational.) Ithiel Pool spent his post-World War II professional life surrounded by these questions of nuclear weapons and nuclear deterrence. His "Deterrence as an Influence Process" sought to create a productive discussion between two opposing camps that seldom spoke to one another. It was highly regarded in the Cambridge arms control community and prescient. (A student of the period might find it insightful to read the paper as an implicit commentary on the work of a Harvard economics professor of the era, Thomas Schelling, who was brilliant, innovative, influential, and [by implication] not always reliable in some of his ideas about nuclear deterrence.[1])

Networks and Power

Contacts and Influence

"Contacts and Influence" may become Ithiel Pool's most original single contribution to theory and research, with special value for the decades ahead as the verb "to network" increasingly characterizes behavior.

The original version was drafted in the late 1950s when the organizing imagery of American politics (and indeed, world politics) was still group-based. A minuet of organized political parties and formal interest groups bargained, lobbied, brokered public opinion and campaign contributions, and decided political outcomes. National governments set the agendas and made decisions through formal institutions and representatives. As a contrast, Pool looked at *personal* communication systems and networks of potential influence from a global perspective and, with his co-author, sought to estimate the probabilities that any two persons selected at random might share a common contact. Or (to extend the question) how many steps or degrees of separation would there be between any two people on the planet, selected at random? Or between a randomly selected American voter and a president or congressman?[2]

Both Pool and Kochen worked on the paper (Kochen, especially, on the formal mathematics which is not reprinted here.) Subsequent researchers earned the label "the small world phenomenon" for this line of work.[3] The title of a play and movie, *Six Degrees of Separation*, was based on the ideas in the paper.

The Pool and Kochen paper lays a groundwork for monitoring and predicting new routes of influence and power as new communication technologies extend the capacities of personal two-way communication systems on a global scale.

Congress and Its Constituents

If [early social science research has] shown that, for good or ill, the ordinary man does not conform to Rousseauian prescriptions of citizenship, what we have done here is to say a similar thing about his political betters. They, too, fulfill their roles while uninformed, preoccupied, and motivated by adventitious private goals. If such facts disqualify men for a role in affairs of state, it is difficult to say who would be qualified. We believe we have shown that, the rush of events being what it is and the limitations of time and energy being what they are, no leading politician could meet the test. A political theory that expects a statesman to act with that degree of delib-eration on all issues which he might at best achieve for one issue at a time is clearly unrealistic.... [M]ost existing literature portrays the policy decision-process in what we came to feel was an overly intellectualized way. (p. 111, below)

We find that the notion that big business interferes rudely and violently with the democratic process needs qualification. This notion is based on a long historical stream of writings, but, so far as our reporting goes, it was not true on the tariff in the period since 1953. (p. 113, below)

In the calculations of self-interest that occurred continuously among our [busi-nessmen] subjects, the aspects of the conception that varied included *whose* self-interest, in the light of *which facts*, and *over what time periods*. (p. 98)

Bauer, Pool, and Dexter's *American Business and Public Policy: The Politics of Foreign Trade* (1963) from which this selection is drawn, remains the best case study of a political communication system and congressional decision making. Each of the three quotations above il-lustrates a finding that affected the understanding of Congress, public opinion, and the role of businessmen. For example, a standard arm-chair analysis of political behavior is that businessmen pursue their self-interest in politics: the study determined three critical ingredients (cited above) that needed resolution before self interest was defined. And, Bauer, Pool, and Dexter found, big businessmen often did not know—in this framework—on which side of these issues their rational self-interest was to be found.[4]

Trends in Content Analysis

Stir the human mind with a word, an idea, or an action, and ripples of thought and feeling will billow across the world...[5]

An example of an analysis which uses the representational element in highly ma-nipulated communications is *Movies*, by Wolfenstein and Leites. It is a content analysis designed to identify national myths in one of the most calculated of the mass media. Movies are made for the box office. Every shot is designed to appeal to an imagined audience. It does not represent the aesthetic taste or the emotional states of the authors or directors in any immediate way. Individual idiosyncrasies are ironed out in the collective process of production. Yet in the very process of collectively producing an expression of what the producers conceive to be the fantasy life of their audience, they are representing something about their own image of the culture in which they live. In that lies the creative element in the making of a movie, which emerges despite the influence of box-office consider-ations. There are choices to be made which express the character and environ-ment of the chooser. There is a story to be thought up, pieces to be put together; there is room for associations to float, controlled of course by one's image of the audience's associations. And in this process the fantasies and values of the culture somehow get expressed. There is thus room for analysis of movies, not only in terms of the instrumental calculations which go into them but also as representations of their makers. (Pp. 134–35, below)

The first generation of social scientists was captivated by the idea of monitoring the flow of mass communications in different countries and using new quantitative methods to draw inferences. The work was done by hand. One study in which Ithiel Pool participated (with Daniel Lerner and Harold Lasswell) hand-coded 19,553 editorials, a sample from five prestige newspapers in the U.S., Great Britain, Russia, France, and Germany across sixty years, for 416 symbols.

Eventually, they stopped. The work was fiercely time consuming. They recognized that it needed to wait for better technology, both for the mechanics and, especially, for any analysis of the data that could answer the more sophisticated questions they wanted to ask. This technical summary symposium in 1959, from which Ithiel Pool's selection is drawn, was a message in a time capsule to future generations who could pick up the work. Today, with scanning technology and the expanded capacities of computers, the time is arriving when renewed progress may be possible.[6]

Concerning more advanced questions: one of the fascinations in Ithiel Pool's circle was to analyze public communications in each country with a psychoanalytic-like (but more rigorous and structured) sensibility to describe and infer the "operational code" of the country or culture. The pioneer was Nathan Leites, whose monumental *Study of Bolshevism* (Glencoe, IL: Free Press, 1953) and briefer *Operational Code of the Politburo* (New York: McGraw-Hill, 1951) fascinated his associates.[7]

Ithiel Pool began a similar project in India to infer the operational code that made Indian culture, politics, and behavior uniquely Indian. Among his papers is a trunk, filled with hundreds of careful note cards detailing classic Indian texts and folk stories of monkey kings, arguments from Indian philosophers about how Indian categories of logic differ from Western categories, and puzzled letters about Indian movies (whose plots and conclusions he could not predict, and whose great popularity with Indian audiences partly eluded him.)

The movies produced by Indian culture illustrate the research problem: India produces more motion pictures than any other country and Indian audiences love these motion pictures. But there is virtually no market outside of India. Why not? (By contrast, the market for movies generated by American culture is global and extraordinary.)

In the end, Ithiel never figured out the answer. The problem may be another "ahead of its time" challenge. The methods that can provide a general solution to the distinctiveness of each culture would be insightful for studying the spread of cultures in coming decades.[8]

Notes

1. The extended series of case studies and books by Pool's contemporary, Alexander George, also can be read as an implicit critique of Schelling, although both authors characteristically make external reality, rather than other academic theorists, the focus of their published work.
2. The discussion of Congress in the paper (pp. xx–xx) may put the formal academic literature concerning public opinion more in touch with reality. Congressmen can be extraordinarily sensitive to the action moods and concerns of the people who elect them and the Pool and Kochen analysis suggests a plausible process (i.e., letter writing and telephone calls, which represent a minute fraction of constituents, aside) by which political discussions in personal networks link together to give 500 elected representatives a degree of workable feedback system from 200,000,000 people.
3. See Manfred Kochen (ed.). *The small world: a volume of recent research advance commemorating Ithiel de Sola Pool, Stanley Milgram, Theodore Newcomb*. Norwood, NJ: Ablex Publishing Corp., 1989.
4. Concerning the influence of business: the interested reader may wish to pursue the comments along these lines in Pool's review of Charles Lindblom's *Politics and markets*, which ignored the results of this empirical work. The essay is "How powerful is big business?" in *Does big business rule America?* edited by Hessen, Robert. Washington, DC: Ethics and Public Policy Center, 1981, pp. 23–34.
5. This is the opening sentence of the Advisory Committee *Report* on international communications research, which led to the founding of the MIT Research Program in Communications. Ithiel Pool was secretary of the committee. An abridged version of the report is Hans Speier et al. "A plan of research in international communication." *World Politics* 6, no. 3 (April 1954): 358–77.
6. As a companion to Pool's edited volume and his essay (from which this excerpt is drawn) anybody interested in content analysis should consult an excellent book by Ole R. Holsti, *Content analysis for the social sciences and humanities*. Reading, MA: Addison-Wesley Pub. Co., 1969. The stress (tension) indicators discussed by Pool continued to develop and have provided valuable insight into foreign policy decision making in crises. See M. Hermann's review, "Indicators of stress in policymakers during foreign policy crises," *Political Psychology* 1, no. 1 (1979): 27–46.
7. Alexander George, Ole Holsti, and others attempted to infer "operational codes" of different decision makers. The task was analogous to inferring the key elements of a computer simulation that would, with appropriate changes in parameters, generate the distinctive decisions and sentences of a selected American president or secretary of state or foreign leader.
8. Good indicators would help to prevent hasty generalizations by people thinking in traditional political categories. For example, Samuel Huntington's *The clash of civilizations and the remaking of world order*. New York: Simon & Schuster, 1996. Huntington's categories of cultures and analysis (e.g., Islamic culture v. Western culture) overlook trends that are readily recognized by monitoring global communications. (In addition to the worldwide popularity of American movies, MTV has became a global channel, serving a global teenage culture.)

1

Introduction to Political Communication

Just as the economist focuses his antenna on exchange relations (either in the particular institution, the market, where such relations are most active or, alternatively, as a way of conceptualizing any or all of social life), and just as the political scientist focuses his antenna on power relations (either solely in the state or as a way of conceptualizing any or all of social life), so too the student of communication may use the exchange of messages either as an index by which to describe institutions (such as the press) that are specifically set up for the purpose of message dissemination or may use the universal social act of communicating as a powerful index for describing any and all aspects of social life. The domain of the study of communication can thus legitimately be the entire domain of the social sciences.

If one takes the communications approach to the study of society as a whole, then the study of political communication becomes just one particular approach to the study of all of politics.

Some Classical Contributions

One can document the breadth of the topics that may be analyzed as political communication by reviewing some of the classical contributions to the field. Among works prior to 1914 that a student of communication would have to consider as major contributions to his field would be Plato's *Gorgias*, which considers morality in propaganda; Aristotle's *Rhetoric* and Mill's *System of Logic*, which analyze the structure of persuasive argumentation; Machiavelli's *The Prince* and Lenin's *What Is to Be Done?* which are handbooks of political communication for the securing of power; Milton's *Areopagitica* and Mill's *On Liberty*, which consider the systemic effects of permitting individual variation

From *International Encyclopedia of the Social Sciences* (1968).

in the flow of political messages; Dicey's *The Development of Law and Opinion in England in the Nineteenth Century*, which considers the effects of the ideological context on public actions; and Marx's *German Ideology*, Sorel's *Reflections on Violence*, and Pareto's *The Mind and Society*, which distinguish the social function from the true value of beliefs.

Propaganda and Persuasion

The study of political communication underwent a major efflorescence after World War I. A number of factors stimulated that growth. The Allies, particularly after Wilson's Fourteen Points, had undertaken a substantial psychological warfare effort against Germany (Lasswell 1927).[1] The German ultra-right, unwilling to admit the facts of defeat, perpetrated the myth that the German soldier had been undefeated on the field of battle but had had victory snatched away by an Allied propaganda *Schwindel* that fooled Germany into giving up. This myth was expressed in a large body of German literature that overestimated the power of propaganda (Thimme 1932).[2]

Such illusions about the vast powers of the "hidden persuaders" (Packard 1957)[3] were in the same period reinforced in the United States by the growth of advertising and public relations. The men in these new businesses, eager to win clients, overstated their own powers over the public mind. They acted as propagandists for propaganda.

While the illusion that clever propagandists with the aid of the mass media could achieve great manipulation of the public became widespread, both research and experience were showing how painfully hard it was to educate the public to preferred civic attitudes. Notable was the National Opinion Research Center's study (1948)[4] of a large-scale United Nations week in Cincinnati, which despite Herculean efforts affected an almost unnoticeable segment of the population. Such observations of the ineffectuality of propaganda led students of political communication to seek by field and experimental studies to understand the conditions under which persuasion does change attitudes and the conditions under which it does not.

Among the field studies perhaps the most notable were the studies by Lazarsfeld, Berelson, and others, of the impact of election campaigns. They demonstrated that relatively few minds are truly changed by a campaign but that a campaign serves other important functions; it may define the issues and mobilize interest and partisanship.

Communication has many effects besides that of persuading people of the thing said. It also affects attention, information, interest, and action. It often does so without causing a person to decide that what he previously thought to be false is true, or vice versa (Lerner 1951; Pool et al. 1956)[5] Nonetheless, a large part of the sociological and psychological literature on political communication has dealt with the conditions of persuasion.

Laboratory studies, most notably those of Carl Hovland and his associates at Yale, have shed substantial light on the conditions under which messages persuade. Certain individuals show a general tendency to be more easily persuaded than others. Informed and intelligent persons are more apt to be persuaded permanently by a presentation that refutes the arguments on the other side as well as presenting its own arguments, while uninformed and unintelligent persons are moved more by a one-sided presentation. Threatening communications, where circumstances permit, are apt to be disregarded and forgotten more than communications that present encouraging information. Arguments on matters of attitude (not fact) when presented to persons already predisposed to accept the arguments are apt to have more effect on the hearer's attitude after a passage of time than they did immediately after the presentation. Factual information and also attitudinal material that goes against the hearer's predisposition lose part of their impact with time (Hovland 1959).[6]

Psychological experiments have also shown that when a person's opinion structure is dissonant or unbalanced, his opinions are apt to change. If a person simultaneously believes two things that are hard to reconcile, and if circumstances force attention to this imbalance, then a person is apt to change an attitude or redefine the situation to avoid such imbalance (Abelson & Rosenberg 1958; Brown 1962; Festinger 1964; Attitude Change 1960).[7] The classic political case is cross-pressure in an election campaign, when a voter favors a candidate in one respect and dislikes him in another (Berelson et al. 1954).[8] Balance may be restored by deciding that only one of those aspects is important, or by forgetting one of them, or by reversing one of the perceptions of the candidate, or by changing one's own evaluation on one of the points.

However, the results of laboratory studies of attitude change, as Hovland pointed out (1959),[9] diverge from the results of field surveys in one important respect. In the laboratory the messages communicated usually have an effect on the subject; in the field the usual finding is that propaganda makes little discernible difference in any democratic, that is, competitive communication situation. That is because the paid or otherwise controlled subject in the laboratory is in a forced communication situation. In real life, on the other hand, exposing oneself to communication is generally a voluntary act. Persons listen and read selectively, and they do not readily expose themselves to communications that will change their minds. In politics voters attend primarily to their own candidate. They seldom listen to the opposition and even when they do so may selectively misperceive or forget things that are said that they disagree with. So, in real-life situations the directly persuasive effects of political communication are much less cogent than they are in the laboratory. A book that summarizes comprehensively and well what social scientists know about the impact of communications on their receivers is Joseph Klapper's *The Effects of Mass Communication* (1960).[10]

Contents of Communications

Political scientists have long been interested in effects of communications other than their immediate persuasive power over their receivers. They have often been interested in describing, for example, the contents of the information flow permeating a society. Dicey's study of the spread of collectivist ideas in England is a classic example. Perhaps the foremost contemporary exponent of such studies is Harold Lasswell, who has either made or instigated the most systematic attempts to provide surveys of the social distribution of attention. In the 1930s he initiated the use of content analysis to compare the political propaganda output at different times and places (Lasswell & Blumenstock 1939), an effort expanded at the Library of Congress during World War II. The studies at the Hoover Institute, originated by him, produced comparisons of the political symbols used in editorials in major papers in five countries over a sixty-year period (Lasswell et al. 1952; Pool et al. 1952).[11]

A study of the contents of political communications in a country may be motivated by purely descriptive purposes. It is interesting to note, for example, the growth of attention to world affairs in the United States or the decline of attention to economics in political campaigns as the Great Depression has receded into the past. But study of the distribution of attention in society can have more than just descriptive interest. Content analysis of political media can be useful both for intelligence purposes and for social scientific purposes.

During World War II content analysis of enemy broadcasts was effectively used by both British and American agencies to decipher Nazi military plans (George 1959).[12] Kremlinology is a present version of the same technique (Griffith 1963; Rush 1958).[13] The order in which leaders are named, the disappearance of one formula and the appearance of another, or the allusion to some past analogical event may provide clues to major political developments. Needless to say, this kind of analysis is superfluous when a political movement is willing to engage in free discussion of its problems and precluded when it can afford total silence.

The deciphering of Aesopian meanings becomes important when a political group feels simultaneously obliged to communicate and constrained not to communicate frankly. That happens under a variety of circumstances. It happens when dissidents attempt to express their views in ways that will avoid repression by the powers that be. It happens when elites wish to communicate to fellow cognoscenti without revealing their hand to naive hearers. It happens when a politician wishes to convey a message without unduly disturbing established conventions.

Historical examples of such Aesopian political communication have been analyzed most extensively by Leo Strauss (1948).[14] The logic of such analysis has been most fully dissected by Alexander George (1959).[15] Actual analyses of Soviet covert debates are many, but little careful attention has been given to just why it is that the Soviets choose to engage in a mode of political communication that is probably no longer well adapted to their needs. It reveals much that they would like to keep secret, while making the conduct of their policy discussions inefficient. Various relevant factors may be adduced to account for their discussion of policy questions in covert but revealing ways in their major public organs. Among these are the heritage of an illegal revolutionary past, but also a past full of ideological debate; the heritage of the authoritarian tsarist past; and an irrational reaction-formative preoccupation with secrecy in the Russian culture. There is also the need to give directives to thousands of middle-echelon persons on how to behave, for a complex society, even a centralized planned one, must find a way to have millions of independent decisions made in a socially functional way. Finally, informal communications are so severely hampered by Soviet fear of uncontrolled social action that discussion in major media often becomes just as easy as more private kinds of informal discussion. For example, only one central mimeograph facility is allowed in each major department, all stencils are numbered, and a card on the use of each kept by the police authorities.

Effects of Political Communication

The ways in which Aesopian political material can provide insights into a political system may also demonstrate how the distribution of communication content can be a matter of interest to social scientists concerned with the effects of communication. Clearly, there are both systemic and individual consequences to the distribution of attention, quite different from the persuasive consequences of individual messages.

One example is the emergence of political alienation when the contents of communications in the official and the mass media do not correspond to the perceptions and the interest of their audiences (Kris & Leites 1947; Levin 1962).[16] Modern totalitarian societies, unlike historical authoritarian ones, are very public-opinion conscious and put out vast amounts of political communication to the public. The publics, however, may learn to consider such communications unreliable, often trusting more to rumor (Bauer et al. 1956);[17] they then become less involved in political matters and devote minimum attention to the mass of material thrown at them. But the depolitization is, of course, never complete, and people who are given highly censored versions of the news acquire great skill at reading between the lines and become quite energetic at seeking information by such means as listening to foreign broadcasts. The non-Asian communist countries are now virtually covered by short-wave radios (about twenty million in the Soviet Union); and listening to foreign broadcasts is fairly universal. A very different situation exists, of course, in some underdeveloped countries, where large parts of the public do not know about major outside world events and trends. Nowadays, since every major nation broadcasts internationally the latest trends in culture, art, and popular music, political matters too become universally known, among interested persons, without much delay. The political consequences of such a change in the attention situation have already been profound and may be accentuated as communication satellites make international communication even easier.

Practicing propagandists are generally aware that it is much easier to change people's distribution of attention than to change their values and attitudes. Virtually all propaganda efforts serve only to focus people's attention on certain issues rather than to reverse their previous views on those issues. Advertisers seldom seek to change the desires of the public; they try to convince the public that their product meets those desires. Successful psychological warriors do not try to convert the enemy nationals into rejecting their own fatherland and joining in the cause of the propagandists. They succeed only when their target forces are falling apart anyway and they can simply focus the attention of the enemy troops on that fact and inform them how to save themselves (Lerner 1949; Shils & Janowitz 1948).[18] In general, it may be said that persuasion as such is only a small part of political communication. Most of it consists of modifying the information on which people will act, given their own values and preferences.

The Mass Media

The growth of the mass media has had a major impact on the conduct of political activity. In the United States, for example, radio and, even more, television have significantly reduced the power of the local political machine and drastically reduced the use of rallies and mass meetings. Since Franklin Roosevelt's fireside chats on radio in the 1930s it has been possible for the president or the presidential candidate to establish a direct campaign relationship with every individual voter. In a presidential campaign this relationship is far more significant than the remarks of a local politician. Television, of course, adds an extra element of visibility and probably some extra impact. There is some evidence that different political personalities are more effective on radio than on television, but this has not been much investigated (Pool 1959).[19] Both media certainly give an opportunity for the exercise of political charisma.

Furthermore, the cost-effectiveness of the mass media is likely to be greater than that of more individualized campaign methods, at least in terms of spreading information. Expensive as television time may be, it is apt to be cheap per person reached. This is true even if one disregards the mammoth audiences reached on such special occasions as the Kennedy-Nixon debates in the 1960 presidential campaign.

However, it would be a mistake to make any simple comparative statement about the relative political effectiveness of the mass media versus face-to-face organization. They serve different functions and for maximum effectiveness they must be linked together. That is a principle that skillful political organizers have generally understood. In *What Is to Be Done?* Lenin developed the notion of a disciplined party of professional revolutionists, but in the same pamphlet he also strongly advocated the establishment of an all-Russian newspaper to serve as a "collective organizer." Even today in the Soviet Union, the several million oral agitators are serviced by a special magazine, *Bloknot agitatora* (The Agitator's Notebook).

Indeed, the growth of political parties and the growth of the press went hand in hand in most countries of the world until recent decades. One of the difficulties of establishing effective party systems in some of the newly emerging nations is that the newer mass media, particularly radio, cannot meet the needs of the small partisan group as well as the revolutionary newspaper put out in a small print shop.

A number of major social science studies have dealt with the relationship of word-of-mouth communication to the mass media. It has been fairly well established in a variety of cultures that whereas the mass media serve effectively to diffuse information, people seldom act on that information without confirming their impulse by checking with an opinion leader with whom they are in face-to-face contact (Katz & Lazarsfeld 1955; Rogers 1962; Pool 1963).[20] In India, for example, villages in which people listened to agricultural broadcasts in groups and then discussed them were compared with similar villages that received the same broadcasts but had no organized listening groups. In both sets of villages learning of the information was comparable, but only where there were organized listening groups with face-to-face discussion was there any significant amount of adoption of the new practices that were learned (Mathur & Neurath 1959).[21] The implications for the complementarity of the mass media and political organization are clear.

Notes

1. Lasswell, Harold D. *Propaganda technique in the World War*. New York: Smith, 1938 (1927).
2. Thimme, Hans. *Weitkrieg ohne waffen: Die propaganda der westmächete gegen Deutschland*. Stuttgart: Cotta, 1932.
3. Packard, V. *The hidden persuaders*. New York: McKay, 1957.
4. National Opinion Research Center. *Cincinnati looks again*. Report 37A. Unpublished manuscript.
5. Lerner, Daniel. *Propaganda in war and crisis: Materials for American foreign policy*. New York: Stewart, 1951. Pool, Ithiel de Sola; Keller, Suzanne; Bauer, Raymond. "The influence of foreign travel on political attitudes of American businessmen." *Public Opinion Quarterly* 20, no. 1, pp. 161–75.
6. Hovland, C. "Reconciling conflicting results derived from experimental and survey studies of attitude." *American Psychologist* 14, no. 1, pp. 8–17.
7. Abelson, Robert, Rosenberg, M. J. "Symbolic psycho-logic: A model of attitudinal cognition." *Behavioral Science* 3, pp. 1–13; Brown, Roger. "Models of

attitude change." In Brown, Roger et al. *New directions in psychology*. New York: Holt, 1962; Festinger, Leon. *Conflict, decision, and dissonance. Stanford Studies in Psychology*, no. 3. Stanford, CA: Stanford University Press, 1964; Attitude Change. *Public Opinion Quarterly* 24 (1960): 163–365.

8. Berelson, B.; Lazarsfeld, Paul F.; McPhee, William N. *Voting: A study of opinion formation in a Presidential campaign*. Chicago: University of Chicago Press, 1954.

9. Hovland, C. "Reconciling Conflicting Results."

10. Klapper, Joseph. *The effects of mass communication*. Glencoe, IL: Free Press, 1960.

11. Lasswell, Harold D.; Blumenstock, Dorothy. *World revolutionary propaganda: A Chicago study*. New York: Alfred A. Knopf, 1939. Pool, Ithiel de Sola et al. *The "prestige papers": A survey of their editorials*. Stanford, CA: Stanford University Press, 1952.

12. George, Alexander L. *Propaganda analysis: A study of inferences made from Nazi propaganda in World War II*. Evanston, IL: Row, Peterson, 1959.

13. Griffith, William E. *Albania and the Sino-Soviet rift*. Cambridge, MA: MIT Press, 1963; Rush, Myron. *The rise of Khrushchev*. Washington, DC: Public Affairs Press, 1958.

14. Strauss, Leo. *On tyranny: An interpretation of Xenophon's "Hiero."* Glencoe, IL: The Free Press, 1948.

15. George, Alexander L. *Propaganda Analysis*.

16. Kris, Ernst; Leites, Nathan. "Trends in twentieth century propaganda. " In Berelson, Bernard; Janowitz, Morris (eds.). *Reader in public opinion and communication*. Enlarged edition. Glencoe, IL: The Free Press, 1953 (1947).

17. Bauer, Raymond; Inkeles, Alex; Kluckhohn, Clyde. *How the Soviet system works*. Cambridge, MA: Harvard University Press, 1956.

18. Lerner, Daniel. *Sykewar: Psychological warfare against Germany, D-Day to VE-Day*. New York: Stewart, 1949; Shils, E.; Janowitz, M. "Cohesion and disintegration in the Wehrmacht in World War II." *Public Opinion Quarterly*. 12:3, pp. 280–315.

19. Pool, Ithiel de Sola. "TV: A new dimension in politics." In Burdick, Eugene, Brodbeck, Arthur J. (eds.). *American voting behavior*. Glencoe, IL: The Free Press, 1959.

20. Katz, Elihu, Lazarsfeld, Paul F. *Personal influence: The part played by people in the flow of mass communications*. Glencoe, IL: The Free Press, 1955; Rogers, Everett M. *Diffusion of innovations*. New York: The Free Press, 1962; Pool, Ithiel de Sola. "The mass media and politics in the modernization process." In Conference on Communication and Political Development. Dobbs Ferry, NY: 1961. Pye, Lucian (ed.). *Communications and political development*. Princeton, NJ: Princeton University Press, 1963, pp. 234–53.

21. Mathur, Jagdish Chandra; Neurath, Paul M. *An Indian experiment in farm radio forums*. Paris: UNESCO, 1959.

2

Changing Images:
The Role of Communications in
the Process of Modernization

The process of modernization is, very largely, the process of acquiring new images. For example, there is the image of life as subject to deliberate change. The peasant who perceives the failure of his crops as resulting from the operation of a jealous purposeful fate against which man is impotent can acquire, instead, the image of events as subject to technical manipulation through knowledge and organization.

Another image is that of the possibility of economic growth. Malayan communists, as described by Pye, had acquired a rudimentary image of modern life; they had not yet perceived the available good things as being essentially limitless because subject to creation. They saw a static consumption economy in which there were a certain number of good things—most of them possessed by the West. Communism was a way to distribute the wealth by taking from those who had and giving to those who had not. Modernization means, among other things, the acquisition of an image of limitless progress and growth as the normal character of life.

A third image is of what it is to be cultured and educated. This has reached millions of young men and women, and has filled them with the aspiration to be literate, to know the names of the great writers and artists, to practice the marvels of science, to work as professionals and intellectuals.

The sectors of the world not yet modernized have an image of the modernized portion of the world. The "revolution of rising expectations" is the phrase most often used to describe the awareness, reach-

From *Industrialization and Society* (1963) edited by Bert Hoselitz and Wilbert E. Moore.

ing all the world's peoples, that diseases can be cured, that people can drive automobiles, etc. The point is frequently made that knowledge of technological possibilities comes on the wings of the mass media and vastly outdistances people's willingness to do the things necessary to achieve these possibilities. Essentially, this is what we are trying to say here—in forming images, the media reach right down and change the people directly; action comes only by the more tortuous processes of social organization.

Identification with the objects whose images the mass media convey does not follow automatically. It is a somewhat more complex phenomenon than imagery itself. It clearly depends in part on interpersonal leadership, but not so much as action does. People do learn to identify with characters whom they have met only through the media. The little world of friends and relatives who are the subjects of village gossip is replaced by the world of film stars and party leaders encountered through the mass media. The media audience member puts himself into their places and begins to consider what he would do in their circumstances. He approves of some of the new members of his circle of experience and is against others. Psychically, he has become part of the great society before he is asked to participate actively in it.

The psychic initiation of vast numbers of people is an essential step in the process of modernization. The modernizing actions which any developing society must call upon people to take are so many and so varied that they cannot be prescribed by central authority alone. Punctuality, good work habits, investment, readiness to change to improved methods, confidence about manipulating machinery, moving to new residences, adopting personal hygiene, tolerating new liberties by one's wife and children, etc., are all acts which millions of individuals must perform in billions of specific circumstances. The experience must be psychically rehearsed many times before the acts can be performed. Personal leadership is often required as the final impetus to such actions; but it can operate only after the media have first made these actions familiar and understandable.

That is why the development of a modern communication system is an important part of a well-conceived development plan. Many things are needed. Among them are expanding the manufacture of newsprint, the building of movie theaters, the promotion of literacy. Radio and television are particularly important because they bypass literacy. The government of Malaya has wisely waived tariffs on low-cost receivers. It would be good to see the production and wide diffusion of a four- or five-dollar, long-lived battery radio or of a comparable, though some-what more expensive, television set. Technologically, such sets are fea-sible if manufactured in large quantities.

Measures to raise the professional status of mass media personnel would also be helpful to modernization. One cannot expect the cast-offs of better-paid professions—frequently unemployed intellectuals, men without security—to provide a constructive, responsible national voice. The values, aspirations, and quality of media personnel will be translated into the character of a nation's development process.

Modernization would also be facilitated by a mass media system which consciously set out to raise the level and knowledge of the popu-lace, by means of advertisements, exhortations, education, and pur-poseful effort.

The media have a great responsibility, and one which they cannot fulfill by preaching alone. The mass media system must be linked with the face-to-face organization of the population. Listening groups, clubs, village workers, cooperatives, etc., cannot be replaced by the mass media nor can they be substitutes for them. The two kinds of communication must parallel and reinforce each other.[1]

Let us close by noting one contribution which the world's mass me-dia can make to the democratic modernization of a country. As the limits of a people's awareness grow to include foreign countries, and especially the industrialized ones, the people become curious about the ways other nations view them. Indeed, universally, the foreign news which interests people most is foreign news about themselves. Each of us likes to read about others' attitudes toward ourselves.

Thus, the world view of a nation's performance becomes a signifi-cant sanction toward good and progressive performance. During the blockade, the Berliners needed, for their morale, assurance that the world was watching them and understood the sacrifices that they were mak-ing in the cause of freedom.[2] So, too, when a new country holds its first election, and millions of people go to the polls peaceably and responsi-bly to choose their own government, the approving attention of the world can provide an important reinforcement to democracy. Every nation wants to be recognized as modern and advanced. Shame is an important factor in undermining many deep-rooted customs which run counter to modern values—for example, customs in the treatment of women, in denying equality on the basis of social origin, in the use of magic, and so on. Shame is felt also for the very fact of poverty or for lack of political order. Pride is felt in development plans, in new schools and hospitals, in steel mills (the temples of industry), and in the emergence of the arts of culture and progress. A very positive contribution can be made to modernization if foreign peoples turn their spotlights on the admirable and forward-moving steps which a modernizing country takes, and if the mass media inform people how much and with what respect others are watching their successes.

Note

1. For further development of this point, see this author's "Mass media and their interpersonal social function in the process of modernization" in Pye, Lucian (ed.). *Communications and political development*. Princeton, NJ: Princeton University Press, 1963.

3

Newsmen's Fantasies, Audiences, and Newswriting

with Irwin Shulman

Most studies of communication address themselves to the problem of how the message affects the audience. In the communication process, however, effects go both ways: the audience also affects the communicator. The messages sent are in part determined by expectations of audience reactions. The audience, or at least *those audiences about whom the communicator thinks,* thus play more than a passive role in communication. The present study concerns this feedback.

What we are here describing is a reference group phenomenon. "Imaginary interlocutors,"[1] who may also be described as reference persons, enter the author's flow of associations at the time of composition and influence what he writes or says.[2]

In an earlier article our associates Claire Zimmerman and Raymond A. Bauer showed that the character of the audience one expects to address affects what one remembers of the materials available for a speech. Facts which were perceived as incongruent with the attitudes of the prospective audience were often forgotten over a period of one week; approximately twice as many facts were remembered and thus available to be communicated when the audience was expected to be favorable to them.[3] A replication by Wilbur Schramm and Wayne Danielson has confirmed these results.[4] In those experiments, however, there was not direct evidence of how the subjects were thinking about audiences;

From *Public Opinion Quarterly* (1959).

one audience was experimentally induced. It was assumed that this would, as it did, have some impact on the subjects.

In the present study we sought to ascertain empirically something about the population of reference persons who actually flowed into the consciousness of a communicator as he communicated (rather than assume that we had induced a particular audience) and also to ascertain whether those spontaneously produced images influenced a communication in the way that we know an experimentally induced audience does.

The study proceeded in three phases. First we conducted thirty-three exploratory interviews with newsmen. On the basis of the hypotheses formed in the interviews, we constructed a controlled experiment in which the subjects were journalism students. The final phase, two years later, was a re-interview with some of the newsmen.

The interviews, after the first few, proceeded in a standardized fashion. Mr. Shulman would arrive at a newspaper office by previous appointment at a time when the newsman to be interviewed was still working on some copy. He would wait until the story was finished and begin the interview immediately thereafter. (The absence of a time gap is crucial to the success of the interviewing technique we developed.) Shulman would then go through the text paragraph by paragraph, asking the reporter to recall in detail all the persons who at the time of writing had come to his mind. Respondents varied greatly in the extent to which they could produce recall. However, enough material was gathered to enable us to sense certain recurrent patterns. Let us examine what these were, for they provided the hypotheses we tested in the experiment.

Supporters and Critics

Single interviews generally showed consistency in the kind of image produced. A defensive respondent might deny that he thought of anyone but the characters in the story; another respondent would mention a whole series of persons threatened by ill fate whom he would like to help; while a third might list "fakers" and "crooks" whom he would like to punish.

The variable in the writer's flow of associations which appeared to influence most markedly what he wrote was the affective relationship that he conceived to exist between himself and his imaginary interlocutors. Some respondents thought about persons who were disliked, critical, or hostile; others thought of persons who were liked, supportive, or friendly. Thus, for most of our respondents, the act of writing seemed to provide one of two alternative kinds of gratification. For some, writing provided the opportunity to bestow pleasure on readers, who would reward them for it by admiration and affection. For others, the gratification came from awareness of the weapon of words which they had in their hands and the damage that it could do to the "bad guys."

Both the gratification of winning affection and the gratification of aggression are predicated upon the power of the printed word. They involve a fantasy of someone's reading the text and being strongly moved by it. The reporter himself may be a shy man, but behind the protective moat that separates him and his piece of paper from the world, he can indulge in fantasy about overcoming all sorts of toils and troubles and ending up either with love or with triumph.[5]

The two sets of fantasies are in part opposed and in part similar. They both presuppose danger and hostility, but they meet it in the one case by denial and ingratiation and in the other by counterattack. Our overall hypothesis was that newswriters would be better able to communicate stories which fit their particular strategy of self-enhancement than stories which did not.

Some Illustrative Quotations from the Interviews

It might be well at this point to examine quotations from some typical interviews of both kinds. A columnist who had just written a story on muscular dystrophy stated that he had "an intense desire to write and write entertainingly." He saw his readers as "people with a sense of humor.... If I stopped a man in the street and told him what I wanted to write, if he said, 'What do you want to do that for?' I would probably drop it .... You'd be dead if you didn't know what is interesting. If it's read, it's a success." "If I can humanize a person who is generally regarded as stiff and formal, I may create a warm attitude toward that person." "I have to please widely." "I try not to ridicule even a person like X.... [That] would make people mad." "Readers like to relax.... I get a fair amount of mail and phone calls, most of it enthusiastic." The columnist was aware of restraining himself from mentioning directly that muscular dystrophy might be hereditary because of the effect on families with a history of the ailment. But then he did allude to it and explained that the family without it "would say 'how lucky *we* are.' I felt it might cause some people to think 'We haven't very much but we are pretty lucky.'" With regard to a passage quoting a patient as saying he would not get better, "I had some pretty disquieting feelings about this.... This might be a little cruel." "The [paper] didn't say it; he did.... I expected people to be mad or disagree with him."

In that interview the gratification of the writer was revealed to be the fantasy of people reading what he writes with pleasure. In his eyes if you don't please them you are "dead"; people would get mad. If you do they will be enthusiastic. This interview also illustrates what happens when such a writer has to deal with incongruent material—material which could make his readers uncomfortable and unhappy. By his own admission that material gave him disquieting feelings and made him hesitate to say certain things. It made him put things in quotes which he might otherwise have said directly, and it made him rationalize the "cruel" things he did say by thinking of the people who would be happy that they had been spared. Perhaps the fact that this man is a columnist and specializes in rosy human interest stories is a result of these emotional predispositions, for he himself says that he would not make a good "hard-driving" reporter.

Let us look at two other cases, interviews with newsmen whose professional role has not become specialized on writing to keep people happy and who nevertheless show the same motivation strongly. The first was a foreign affairs specialist of the press and radio who had just finished writing on the Hungarian and Suez crises, which were then taking place. The lead referred to "wanton massacres." The writer indicated he was having second thoughts about the accuracy of the dispatches on the actual size of the massacres: "I started the lead about the political situation, then discarded it, a thing I rarely do." He thought another passage "would have a potentially unsettling effect on the listener." About another passage: "I was also aware that this would relieve some isolationist fears." He felt that the reference to Dulles' illness might not hurt Republican chances; it would remove from the scene an unpopular man. Once again we have a writer who has hesitations about including items which might cause or suggest harm and who wants to include items which will reassure.

Our other example of reporters of this type was a general assignment reporter. He had just written a piece concerning a missing Army machine gun. "I thought of the potential danger to the public...someone using the gun with reckless abandon...people being mowed down by bullets." But the missing gun was defective, and he was very aware of wanting to stress this fact, reassuring readers that the gun was not dangerous. He had no desire to increase the impact of the story, or to scare people. "I wanted to make sure the readers would not be...unduly alarmed—this was calculated to reassure the readers." He hated guns, knew nothing about them, and did not want to know anything about them. He had recently won an award for a series of articles on safety and expressed concern at road death statistics. He said about the reporter who had phoned in the facts on the machine gun: "He's a good newspaperman, but I felt he was being extra-long-winded." Here we have a story which our man, with his fear of violence, would himself have played down, so he felt some conflict with the importance another reporter gave it. He strove to reassure his readers: indeed, the first two words of the lead labeled the gun as defective, even before noting that it was missing.

Now let us turn to some interviews where the other common pattern of gratification is illustrated. These are interviews with writers who think not of persons they wish to please and protect but of hostile persons toward whom they, too, feel hostile. Such writers are ruminating on the power of their pen to destroy.

For example, a general assignment reporter who had written a story on a suicide was not concerned to spare anyone from pain. "The first thing that came into my mind...was that the boy was from Xtown. I thought of his classmates from Xtown who might read this, and I made sure to refer to Xtown in the lead.... I thought I would call his father if there was any more to the story—and I thought of his father in a negative way, how to avoid having to do this." (It should be emphasized here that, as we noted above, having an aggressive fantasy does not at all mean that the reporter is willing to perform the aggressive act in person; the aggression may be confined to the privacy of his writing desk. He thinks of calling the father but shies away from really doing so. It is the aggressive fantasies and their effect on writing with which we are here concerned.) "I know when there are these problems you can usually pin it down to the parents." He continued with his fantasy of the bad news hurting people. "Every senior at the high school he attended would be cognizant; the news would spread by word of mouth; the teachers there would know about it." Then, talking about himself, he indicated some awareness of his tenseness, saying that he would not feel happy "sitting in front of a TV set with a bottle of beer."

Another general assignment reporter had just finished three short crime stories. The first was on the conviction of a public housing official. "I thought the story would be of interest to the thousands of people who live in housing projects.... I thought [laughter] that it would reinforce their beliefs that everyone who works for a public housing project has his hand in the till. But actually before I got to that stage, the first thought that was in my mind was why X (a fellow reporter who had supplied the material) didn't write his own damn copy properly.... The man did not go to jail; either he has political pull or a hell of a big family or something like that." Story two concerned a killer who did go to jail. Our respondent said, "[If the killer] could have afforded the lawyers that other people could have...he might have gotten off with less than five years.... There is a lot of injustice in justice." As to readership of the story: "Some people may read this one accidentally while they're looking for the comics or the obituaries." The third story concerned shoplifting. "The police claimed the women were part of a ring...while actually all the women were accused of was a $100 theft. Actually, I believe that the story of the ring is probable, though. I think that shoplifting goes on on a tremendous scale.... The stores could stop it if they really wanted to.... no sympathy for the stores...public has to pay for these goods indirectly when they buy something else."

Each of the stories written by our last respondent had only one or two short paragraphs. They followed highly conventional journalistic format. It is hard to see how the writer's personality and fantasies affected the copy in any way. This instance helps us to make an important point. The author's private fantasies are clearly not the only things that affect the character of what be writes. An experienced professional newsman will have acquired great facility in turning out a standard product for each of the many kinds of routine story of which so much of the news consists. The more experienced, the more professionally skillful, a newsman, the less important may be his own fantasy life in determining much of what he writes. The role of fantasy grows with every factor that gives greater freedom to the writer. In the above illustration, a longer text would have done so. Other factors would be more unusual stories, the greater latitude of format provided by the feature story, or a less well organized and professionalized newspaper.

Let us turn to one last example in which the reporter's desire to mete out punishment apparently did affect the distribution of emphasis in the article. This story concerned level crossings, and the point which received unusual stress was a finding that both the railroad and the town were at fault in a series of accidents. "I thought immediately of prospective readers in the town of X.... I know that what happens at the crossings is the people's own fault as well as the railroad.... I thought that the residents of the town of X would find some impact in learning

'We were at fault too.'" "I didn't have any concepts of bereaved relatives or anything of that sort.... Mrs. Y (who was killed) had another woman in her car,...they were probably talking, and...she had been oblivious." Then, speaking of the railroad's spokesman: "He is a man subject to the foibles of most humans." Clearly, our respondent took the opportunity here to hand out blame, stressing that theme over other aspects of the story.

The interviews, of which the above were examples, suggested an hypothesis, namely, that reporters who have supportive images in mind would have trouble reporting unpleasant facts, and that reporters who have hostile images in mind would have trouble reporting pleasant facts. The interviews we have just described suggested this, but in field interviews it is not possible to determine the direction of causality. The kind of story written by a reporter might have determined his images, or the images the kind of story, or both might be a function of the man's career assignment, and that in turn might be influenced by his personality. In order to separate out some of these influences we designed an experiment to be conducted with journalism students under controlled classroom conditions.

The Experiment

Four sets of facts were drafted, each providing the material for a news story. Within each set the facts were then scrambled so as to require rewriting to constitute a good story. Two of the stories described events which our subjects would presumably find pleasing; we shall call these "good news." Two of the stories described "bad news." In each pair, one of the stories concerned events at Boston University, where our subjects were enrolled, and one of the stories concerned events overseas.[9] The topics were a blindness cure discovered at B.U., a successful Asian good-will baseball trip by the Brooklyn Dodgers, a tuition raise, and the Suez crisis.

The subjects, assembled in their regular class hour, had a mimeographed set of facts distributed to them as a class assignment and were given twenty minutes to rewrite it. Each student received only one of the four sets of facts, the distribution being made in a random fashion. The total number of subjects was 132, or thirty-three students writing on each story.

As soon as he had finished writing his story, each subject turned to a questionnaire. The first question asked the subject to list all the persons who had happened to come to mind while he was writing the story. The directions emphasized that the respondent should list everybody he thought of, not just persons relevant to the story. The mean number of images listed was seven. The subject was then asked a number of questions about himself and about each image person he had listed. Most importantly, he was asked to check on a six-inch scale ranging from "very approving" to "very critical" each of the persons he had listed. The specific instruction was: "Try to reconstruct very carefully how you felt, as you were writing the story, about the extent of agreement or disapproval expressed by the people you thought of toward what you were writing." This scale permitted us to compute for each subject the mean degree of approval or criticism of him which he conceived his image persons to feel.

Hypothesis and Evidence

1. The first hypothesis confirmed by this experiment was that persons writing about good news tend to produce supportive images, while persons writing about bad news tend to produce more critical ones. This is in a sense the obverse of the hypothesis which interests us. It is concerned not with the effect which free associations, as an independent variable, may have on what is written, but rather with the effect of the material about which one is writing (as an independent variable) on the mood and thoughts of the writer.[7] We find, as we might expect, that bad news produces dysphoric associations, good news euphoric ones. The only interest in this result is that bad news not only produces images of persons who are less well liked (we asked that, too) but also of persons who are viewed as being more often critical of the author, a conclusion which is not completely obvious. The data supporting this result are contained in table 3.1, which is based on 129 usable questionnaires.

2. We turn now to the more significant question, whether there is also a reverse direction of effect: If we hold constant the effect of the stimulus materials, do the images which a particular person produces predict what he will write? Clearly, even though bad news tends in general to elicit critical images, there will be some individuals who produce strongly supportive images despite the fact that they are handed bad news to write about, while others given the same assignment will produce even more than the usual quota of critical images. So, too, with good news; the mean of the images will be supportive, but there

TABLE 3.1
Mean Scores of Subjects on Approving or Critical Character
of Their Images for Each Assigned Story

	Mean Score*
"Good news: stories:	
Close event	1.4
Overseas event	1.6
"Bad news" stories:	
Close event	2.3
Overseas event	2.5

*The scores represent distance along the 6-inch scale from 0, very approving, to 6, very critical.

will be a distribution. Our procedure was to take the distribution for each of the four stories and divide it by natural breaking points into three segments: the modal individuals, those whose images were more supportive than normal for that story, and those whose images were more critical than normal for that story. The result was the assignment of the subjects to three groups, namely, twenty-three persons who produced unusually supportive images, eighty-six modal persons, and twenty persons who produced unusually critical images. The question to be answered was whether the stories written by the twenty-three persons who produced unusually supportive images would be more accurate on good news and less accurate on bad than those written by the twenty persons who produced unusually critical images.

The stories written by the forty-three deviant individuals were subjected to content analysis. The analysis was designed to explore a highly subjective matter, how far the writer, in writing the story, had distorted or modified the facts given him. In order to make this evaluation of the stories reasonably objective, we did two things. We broke down the judgment of distortion into three separate judgments, and we had the judgments made independently by two expert judges (former practicing newspaper reporters who had returned to graduate study in the behavioral sciences). We asked each judge to indicate for each story (1) whether there had been significant rearrangement of the order of the facts given; (2) whether any significant information had been added to that given; and (3) whether any significant information had been omitted.

One judge was considerably stricter than the other, which permitted the construction of a three-point scale of change in the story instead of the usual dichotomy, changed-unchanged. On a highly changed story both would agree that it was changed; on a slightly changed story A would call it changed, and B would call it the same (the direction of disagreement being almost always the same); on a still less changed story both would call it unchanged. Unreliability would consist of a reversal of the direction of disagreement in the middle category. Let us illustrate by reference to deletions. Of the forty-three analyzed stories, both judges agreed with regard to eleven that there had been significant deletions, and both agreed with regard to seventeen that there had been none. Thus they disagreed on fifteen stories. But of these fifteen stories there was only one instance in which the usual direction of disagreement between the two judges was reversed, that is, there was only one coding discrepancy regarding deletions. There were five regarding additions and four regarding changes in order.

The three-level scale of change allows for greater sensitivity of the scale and greater confidence in our assessment of the extreme cases than would a dichotomy. We shall label changes which both judges agreed were significant (++), those one judge thought significant (+0), and those both agreed were not significant (00).

We want to compare the amount of change under two experimental conditions which we shall label congruent and incongruent. We have, it will be recalled, segregated those individuals who produced an unusual preponderance of supportive images (given the story event on which they were writing) from those who produced an unusual weight of critical ones. These two groups of persons were not simply responding in an average way to the facts of the story, but were giving expression to some autonomous tendencies of their own. A congruent situation is one in which the story event and this autonomous tendency reinforce each other. Thus the two congruent situations are the one in which a story concerns good news and the images are unusually supportive and the one in which the story concerns bad news and the images are unusually critical. The two incongruent situations are the one in which supportive images are produced despite bad news and the one in which critical images are produced despite good news. As table 3.2 shows, we have fifteen instances of congruent behavior and twenty-eight of incongruent.

Table 3.3 provides the evidence for our major hypothesis: *Where a person's images are incongruent with the character of the event being described, his accuracy in reporting is reduced.* More precisely, persons who have supportive images in their flow of associations do a more straightforward job of reporting good news and a less precise job of reporting bad news than do persons who have critical images in their

TABLE 3.2
Congruent and Incongruent Cases

	Congruent	Incongruent	Total
Bad news	7	15	22
Good news	8	13	21
	15	28	43

TABLE 3.3
Accuracy of Reporting in Congruent and Incongruent Cases

	Definitely Changed (++)	Intermediate Change (+0)	Unchanged (00)
Changes in order of facts*	22	12	9
Congruent situation	4	5	6
Incongruent situation	18	7	3
Additions†	13	14	16
Congruent situation	2	5	8
Incongruent situation	11	9	8
Deletions‡	11	15	17
Congruent situation	1	5	9
Incongruent situation	10	10	8

*$x^2 = 6.95$ $p = .015$ (one tail test).
†$x^2 = 4.23$ $p = .06$ (one tail test).
‡$x^2 = 5.68$ $p = .024$ (one tail test).

associations. Those persons with predominantly critical images in their associations do a more straightforward job of reporting bad news and a less precise job of reporting good news than do persons who have supportive images. It is important to emphasize that accuracy of reporting turns out to be a function of the relation between the image flow and the events being described, not just a function of the image flow. Plausible hypotheses that thinking about critics or thinking about supportive characters in and of itself produces more accurate reporting turn out not to be sustained. The important point is the congruence between the character of the news event and of the images in the flow of association.

Table 3.4 indicates that the above hypothesis does indeed hold up for both good and bad news. In short, the results summarized in table 3.3 are not an artifact arising from the presence of a massive effect in one

TABLE 3.4
Accuracy of Reporting in Congruent and Incongruent Cases,
Bad and Good News Separately

	Definitely Changed (++)	Intermediate Change (+0)	Unchanged (00)
Changes in order of facts:*			
Bad news	14	3	5
Congruent	3	0	4
Incongruent	11	3	1
Good news	8	9	4
Congruent	1	5	2
Incongruent	7	4	2
Additions:†			
Bad news	8	9	5
Congruent	2	3	2
Incongruent	6	6	3
Good news	5	5	11
Congruent	0	2	6
Incongruent	5	3	5
Deletions:‡			
Bad news	7	7	8
Congruent	1	1	5
Incongruent	6	6	3
Good news	4	8	9
Congruent	0	4	4
Incongruent	4	4	5

*For comparison of bad news total with good news total, $x^2 = 4.72$.
†For comparison of bad news total with good news total, $x^2 = 4.06$.
‡For comparison of bad news total with good news total, $x^2 = 0.92$.

of the two types of situation and not in the other. Of course, the numbers in table 3.4 are generally too small to attain independent significance. What is important, however, is that they all are in the direction required by the main hypothesis. Our explanatory discussion must therefore take account just as much of the fact that it was hard for subjects thinking of critics to be accurate about good news as that it was hard for subjects thinking about supportive characters to be accurate about bad. The familiar hypothesis that people distort unpleasant facts is not an adequate explanation of the findings. Our explanation must also take account of the discovery that some of our respondents had a tendency against accurately reporting pleasant facts.

There is, it is true, a definite, though not always statistically significant, tendency for bad news to be more extensively distorted than good news (compare the total in the Definitely Changed column of table 3.4). That is hardly surprising. The surprising result is the stronger tendency for either kind of news to be distorted when not congruent with the individual's image flow.

Implications of the Findings

Our data have revealed three tendencies to be simultaneously and independently operating in the writing process: (1) Good news tended to elicit images of supportive persons, bad news, images of critics. (2) Where the images elicited were congruent with the kind of news, the reporting was more accurate than where the images were incongruent. Good news was more accurately reported in the presence of supportive images, bad news in the presence of critical ones. (3) Good news was more accurately reported than bad. Proposition 2 is the novel one, and the one which interests us here. It is also the one that was suggested by our interviews.

How can we explain the fact that accuracy of reporting is low on good news and bad news alike when the news is incongruent with the tone of the reporter's fantasies? Let us consider some possible explanations.

Reference group theory, at least in simple form, does not fully explain what we found. The simple reference notion is that persons behave in ways which will be approved by those whom they value highly. But for many of our respondents negative reference groups were controlling. Their communication behavior was designed to punish and offend individuals they disliked; it was not designed to win approval from those they liked.

A reference phenomenon was indeed in operation. The potential effects of the communicator's behavior were tested by him by fantasy reference to people's expected reactions. But the process was more dynamic than simply following imaginary leaders. It involved adopting dissonance reduction strategies to sustain an established mental picture of the world. Each respondent had a basic fantasy which related him to the world, either as a recipient of rewards from it or as a battler against it. His actions as a communicator sought to sustain this image.

But dissonance reduction alone is not an adequate explanation of our results either. There could be an infinity of mental dramas relating a communicator to his imaginary reference audiences, and just as many ways for him to distort his communication so as to make his behavior consonant with the point of each drama. We found, however, only two main types of mental drama arising in the newswriting situation: (1) winning of favor from the reader and (2) verbal aggression to demolish him. These patterns correspond to what one might expect from familiar political science hypotheses such as those developed by Lasswell from Freudian notions. The newswriting situation, like political oratory, is an instance of one-way communication to a secondary audience. The gratifications arising from such activities are largely deference and power, either real or fantasied. The communicator is the teacher, instructor, guide, that is, the authority figure over a passive audience. And since the audience consists of secondary contacts, at best, notions of power and deference replace and symbolize more tangible and intimate rewards. Thus one result of our study is that the fantasies of our writers as they write are polarized around the power which their pen gives them, power to command affection, or power to destroy.

Bringing together these various strands of theory we are led to a possible, though admittedly speculative, picture of what may have been going on as reporters accurately or inaccurately relayed good or bad news. A reporter with a flow of unusually supportive imaginary interlocutors may have great need for support from reference persons. In a wish-fulfilling fashion, he may regard his act of bringing good news as performing a favor which will be rewarded by gratitude and affection. He may fear that bringing bad news will alienate him, and he may therefore distort it, either to soften its edge or because anxiety engendered by having to report it makes him less efficient.

Conversely, a person with a flow of unusually critical imaginary interlocutors may be engaged in a mental debate in which he aggresses against and triumphs over his critics by giving them bad news unblunted. News is a weapon in his hands. He may report good news inaccurately, for it does not serve the purpose of his fantasies.

One more empirical finding is relevant to the above speculations. It is the consistency over time of a man's imaginary interlocutors. How far are the persons thought about a matter of mood and how far a matter of personality? Our reinterview with the newsmen two years later was designed to throw some light on this matter. With the attrition over two years from an already small sample, the numbers become very low. However, the repetition of the same procedure with the same individuals suggests that temperament may be a more important factor than mood. Respondents tended to display the same image patterns in both interviews, even though they rarely remembered what the earlier interview was about and the stories they were writing were, of course, always somewhat different. If that is so, then the most plausible explanation of the results we obtained would treat the population of interlocutors in the writer's mind as a personality variable.

Our results could conceivably have practical implications, but these depend upon some of the unanswered questions on which we have been speculating. Could one, for example, increase the accuracy of reporting by deliberately drawing attention to certain kinds of audience figures? It is not clear from our results that that is the case. A person who spontaneously thinks of critical images may be a better reporter for bad news, but it is not clear that subjecting to critical images a person who by temperament (if it is a temperamental matter) spontaneously thinks of supportive images will improve his accuracy. Such a manipulation might frighten him and thus reduce his accuracy. Our results, however, suggest that there is an important area here for exploration, and one which might possibly have practical implications.

One should also keep in mind that what we have been describing here as accurate reporting is not always a result to be desired. If all our results could be restated in terms of imaginativeness rather than accuracy, the overtones of what we have said would be reversed. The persons who handed back exactly the facts that had been handed to them, and in much the same way, were conforming to one set of values particularly important in journalism—straightforwardness or accuracy of reporting—but they were failing to meet another set of preferred values concerning creative writing—originality and imagination. Possibly incongruity of the events described with the structure of the author's image flow promotes the latter qualities.

These are questions which have heretofore been largely neglected by scientific students of public opinion. Except on the psychiatrist's couch, the flow of mental images has not been extensively used in research. The simple instrument of asking respondents to name who or what had just come into their minds, while obvious in the light of its use in psychiatry, has not been in the standard battery of techniques of behavioral science research. Perhaps a reason has been that the content of free associations seemed relatively inaccessible to careful experimentation. A subject's report of his associations cannot be independently validated, and he has many obvious motivations for distorting them. We have no illusions that the reports of free associations which we received are either very reliable or complete. Whatever the shortcomings, however, the successful use of such data in this study seems to show that at least a portion of the image flow can be recaptured even on a questionnaire and a sufficient portion to give useful results on at least some topics.

Notes

1. A term used by Cooley, Charles Horton. *Human nature and the social order.* New York: Scribners, 1902.
2. The importance of such reference persons in communication is suggested by a great deal of recent social science research. Stouffer, Samuel A. et al. *The American soldier.* Princeton, NJ: Princeton University Press, 1949; Shils, Edward A.; Janowitz, Morris. "Cohesion and disintegration in the Wehrmacht." *Public Opinion Quarterly,* 12 (1948): 300–6, 308–15; Berelson, B.; Lazarsfeld, Paul F.; McPhee, William N. *Voting: A study of opinion formation in a Presidential campaign.* Chicago: University of Chicago Press, 1954; Katz, Elihu; Lazarsfeld, Paul, *Personal influence.* Glencoe, IL: The Free Press, 1955; Pool, Ithiel de Sola; Keller, Suzanne; Bauer, Raymond. "The influence of foreign travel on political attitudes of American businessmen." *Public Opinion Quarterly* 20, no. 1, pp. 161–75; Coelho, George. *Changing images of America: A study of Indian Students' Perceptions.* Glencoe, IL: The Free Press, 1958; Isaacs, Harold. *Scratches on our minds.* New York: John Day, 1955; Lerner, Daniel. *The passing of traditional society.* Glencoe, IL: The Free Press, 1958; Rogers, Everett M.; Neal, George M. *Reference group influence in the adoption of agricultural technology.* Ames: Iowa State College Press, 1958; Ryan, Bryce; Gross, Neal C. "The diffusion of hybrid seed corn in two Iowa communities." *Rural Sociology* 8 (1943): 697–709, have all shown that those groups whose opinions are important to a person and whose respect he wants influence his communications in a very direct fashion. Such studies fall into two groups: those which ask direct questions about personal influence, for example, whose opinions do you respect, whom would you consult, etc., and those which attempted to infer the importance of a reference group from the fact that an individual's behavior approximates the modal behavior of the group, for example, in the voting studies it was found that the friends of most Republicans are Republicans, the friends of most Democrats, Democrats. But neither of these previous approaches nails down evidence on whom respondents actually thought about as they reached a decision, and how much difference that made.
3. Zimmerman, Claire; Bauer, Raymond A. "The effect of an audience on what is remembered." *Public Opinion Quarterly* 20 (1956): 238–48.
4. Schramm, Wilbur; Danielson, Wayne. "Anticipated audiences as determinants of recall." *Journal of Abnormal and Social Psychology* 56 (1958): 282–83.
5. Swanson, Guy. "Agitation through the press: A study of the personalities of publicists." *Public Opinion Quarterly* 20 (1956): 441–56.
6. The authors wish to thank Dr. David White of the Journalism Department of Boston University for his help with this project.
7. The reader may desire a fuller census of the kinds of images which our subjects reported as having come to mind. The students listed 247, or 28 percent of all images, as possible readers. In the interviews with newsmen 17 percent of the 510 images were of readers. Of the 580 identifiable persons listed on the student questionnaire study, 107 were characters in the story (12 percent) and 242 were

personally known (29 percent of classifiable), including 31 family members, 129 others known well, and 82 others known more casually.

The largest group as yet unaccounted for are those who are not actually characters in the story but are persons who have been involved in related situations. For example, the Suez Canal story did not mention Nasser, but he might easily come to mind. The preponderance of such related persons may be indexed by the correlation of the location of the story and the locale of the images, as shown in the following table:

Locale of Images by Locale of Story

	Locale of Story	
Locale of Image	*University*	*Foreign*
University	107	10
Local	47	11
United States	125	124
Foreign	15	229
	294	364

4

Deterrence as an Influence Process[1]

A theoretical discussion which is designed to foster a broader-than-usual approach to deterrence theory. Deterrence has usually been attributed to the nature of military preparations but is here defined as a special case of influence. Various nonmilitary modes of influence are proposed, including modifying what comes to the adversary's attention and providing information to the adversary.

Deterrence is a special case of influence. We know a fair amount about pressure, persuasion, propaganda, bargaining, fear, and other mechanisms of influence. An extensive literature treats of the processes whereby human beings influence each other. Clearly, any theory of deterrence should be either congruent with existing theories of influence or should specify the reasons for its divergence.

There are many complex ways in which one human system may influence another. It is well to distinguish these different modes of influence, though in life they overlap. These modes of influence are:

1. Generating trust and positive affect
2. Generating fear
3. Modifying what comes to the influencee's attention
4. Modifying the salience of different things to him
5. Providing information
6. Modifying certainty
7. Providing a behavioral model to the influencee
8. Changing the objective environment
9. Changing the influencee's resources

From *Theory and Research on the Causes of War* (1969) edited by Dean G. Pruitt and Richard C. Snyder.

Generating Trust

The influencing of people by generating confidence and good relations has been abundantly studied by social psychologists, particularly those in the fields of human relations and group dynamics. Such psychologists, living in a democratic society and generally having liberal predispositions, have focused on persuasion in relatively noncoercive environments such as those of voluntary associations, social cliques, and classrooms. There they have found that constructive and stable changes are produced under conditions of positive reinforcement, low tension levels, equalitarian relationships, and democratic leadership.

These are important findings. They apply to environments which all of us would like to see prevailing throughout the world. They apply to environments which actually do exist through a large part of human life and not only in the democratic West.

With due allowances for cultural differences, the principles of group behavior can be usefully applied by a foreman in Japan, India, or Russia as much as in the United States. Even in the most totalitarian society, much of life consists of courteous human interaction among friends, neighbors, co-workers, and so on. Democratic and equalitarian principles are at least in part valid interpretations of universal human nature. With proper qualifications, psychological insights about persuasive relations in informal groupings may have relevance to dealing with Soviet diplomats or even with Khrushchev. The question at issue is what are the proper qualifications, and this has been very little studied.

One obvious qualification is that the principles for generating trust have been derived in situations where a modicum of affection or trust is found in the group already. The family, for example, though not voluntary, shares strong bonds of affection. Even arbitrarily chosen subjects from a sophomore class approach each other with the assumptions of civility common to secondary contacts in a free society. Such subjects are not in a state of terror of each other. In that situation, identifications result from pleasantness, not aggression. Contrast this to the situation in a concentration camp where Bettelheim found the victims identifying with the aggressors.[2]

In short, while the principles of how to persuade by trust are important, we need to know more about their limitations (1) in extreme environments and (2) where institutional structures demand distrust and competition. We must avoid assuming that the principles of democratic human relations are applicable before we give due consideration of their interaction with other modes of influence.

Generating Fear

We have just noted that most psychological experiments seem to show fear to be a relatively ineffectual force for persuasion. People repress or deny unpleasant facts. But practical experience seems a better guide here than do research results achieved under quite limited or artificial circumstances. Commonsense evidence includes the experience that men at war quickly learn how to protect themselves when live bullets start coming. Or one might cite the penal system. Fear of "cops" does lower driving speeds. Or, turning to strategic matters, American policy has certainly been affected by our assessment of Soviet strength. Two years ago, when we believed a missile gap existed, there was much more urgency at high governmental levels about disarming and controlling nuclear weapons than there is now when (rightly or wrongly) we believe ourselves to have overwhelming strategic superiority. If at some point in the future we again become convinced that the Russians could destroy us, we may become much more receptive to difficult compromises.

The entire peace movement is a reflection of the persuasive power of fear. The disarmers may feel that the public is blind in not being as anxious as they. But the fact that thousands of persons have taken an antinuclear position is evidence of the impact of fear.

It is only a platitude, however, that fear influences people. The important question is how, when, and under what circumstances. The research literature is not too helpful here, so let us spell out some speculative hypotheses.

1. Fear will be effective when the danger is seen as certain to face one in a finite time period. If the danger is only a possibility, then one may use the mechanism of denial. Unless the worst is seen as certain to occur, one can hope for the best and defer worrying about the worst until it happens.

2. Fear will be effective upon people whose role it is to concern themselves with the danger. If one has a job as a fireman, or doctor, or undertaker, or policeman, or strategic planner, one will develop an objective way of taking account of the danger; whereas if one has no such responsibility to force one to think about it, one may indulge in denial.

3. Fear will be effective if it has been present in the background for some time, and if the persuader's short-run action is to give relief. Thus, police

interrogators have long known that a way to get a confession is suddenly to be kind to a man after terrorizing him for a long period.

4. Fear will be effective if the intimidated person is allowed to establish good rationalizations for yielding.

If these principles are valid, then the American deterrent posture of building a large ballistic missile force without indulging in threats is a very good one. The message conveyed by that force-in-being is addressed to professional diplomats, statesmen, and soldiers who are not likely to miss its import. It provides a background against which to act in a generous or friendly fashion at some future time. If force is overwhelming, no psychic energy will be given to fruitless seeking of ways to safely disarm it by surprise instead of accepting its intended message. If the force is not verbally brandished (as it was in an unfortunate Stewart Alsop *Saturday Evening Post* article), the foe can invent many good reasons for not feeling defeated by it.[3]

So regarding one mode of influence—generating fear—the American posture has much to commend it. It uses fear in a fairly effective way. But fear is only one mode of influencing an enemy. Before we accept the present posture as optimal we must consider what it does in each other mode of influence. But before we change our posture we must also consider how such changes would affect the use of this mode of influence.

Modifying what Comes to the Influencee's Attention and Modifying the Salience of Different Things to Him

These two modes of influence are so much alike that they can be discussed together.

Along with the dissemination of information, the most frequent result of propaganda campaigns is to change attention and saliency. Propaganda is sometimes described as an attempt to change attitudes, but that is something it seldom achieves. Studies of voter behavior have demonstrated how, in American electoral campaigns, few people get converted in their views; but many are redirected in their attention or have the saliency of different issues changed for them, and this affects their actions.

It is the same in world politics. Khrushchev turns the Berlin heat on and off without changing any American belief about communism or about Berlin or about anything; but the result is marked changes in American actions, such as mobilizing or demobilizing reserves. An agricultural problem drastically reduces both the Chinese and Russian proneness to foreign adventure. The Israeli-Franco-British adventure in Suez saved the Russians many of the embarrassing international consequences of their actions in Hungary and vice versa.

A deterrence policy characteristically seeks certain changes in saliency and attention. It seeks to reduce the saliency to an enemy of those objectives which are of maximum salience to us. If a vital goal for us is to deter any Soviet attack on Western Europe, then it is helpful to us to keep Europe relatively unimportant to Russia, for example, by keeping the Sino-Soviet conflict acute. Similarly, it is helpful to focus political rivalry on the race for economic development.

Note that these two examples of how to deemphasize a Soviet focus on Europe included one that used antagonistic actions and one that sublimated hostility. Both routes are possible. Naturally, one prefers to find "the moral equivalent of war" in constructive activities such as the science race. But it is also perfectly possible to lower the salience of conflict in one area by creating conflict in another. Thus, in this sense, we defend Laos and South Vietnam against Communist China insofar as we keep the situation in the Formosa Straits unstable.

Providing Information

Changes in the perception of the external environment can change the conclusion of means-ends calculation without changing the calculator's goals or values one whit.

For example, as long as the United States did not have accurate and complete information about the number and types of Soviet missiles, we had to assume the worst and build up our forces accordingly. The acquisition of reliable intelligence now allows us to confine our program to appropriate levels. At any time the Soviets could have restrained the American arms program by releasing credible information on the size of their stockpile and on their development program. They chose instead to work a bluff, exaggerating their forces. American policy responded to facts as misperceived due to the bluff. Successful intelligence ultimately broke the bluff and permitted a modified policy. Note that in all of these changes there was no change in basic American goals or values. The only changes were in perceptions of the facts.

The provision of information—and for similar reasons the focusing of attention—is a mode of influence particularly suitable to deterring Soviet aggression. There are reasons why:

1. Information is something people accept even from a hostile source. The experiments of Hovland and others on the "sleeper effect" have shown that, while initially people accept or reject information according to their attitude to the informant, with the passage of time, the source tends to be forgotten and the information acquires a life of its own.[4]

2. The Soviet elite are avid consumers of foreign information. Their doctrine discourages receptiveness to friendly gestures or overt verbal persuasion by the capitalist foe. It also steels them against threats. But on the other hand it requires them to take realistic account of changed circumstances and balances of forces. They pride themselves on cold realism in assessing the objective facts. This claim is valid, but only partly, because the facts the Soviet leaders attend to are so thoroughly screened. Ideology, censorship, and conformism mean that information—whether pleasant or unpalatable—is likely to be noted only if it is credible in terms of their world view.

Aside from a substantial body of theory on the conditions of credibility, social science research on persuasion by information suggests rather forcefully that facts do not speak for themselves. A fact is capable of many interpretations. Its significance is seldom unambiguously conveyed unless made explicit. A fact plus an explanation of its significance are more likely to communicate than either the fact alone or the interpretative generalization alone.

Deterrent information may fail if it does not conform to that principle. If it consists only of a warning statement or only of a particular weapons action each unlinked to the other, it may not communicate as intended.

A common instance of a military fact that does not communicate without interpretation is the first move in a planned series. A Soviet move to assume a larger role in a Southeast Asian guerrilla area could be either a move to forestall the Chinese or a move to step up pressure against us; yet we would not know which. An American buildup of conventional NATO forces or of mobile retaliatory forces could be a first step toward a later reduction of more provocative forces, but unless unambiguously labeled, it could be interpreted as an overall force buildup.

This is a point which cannot be overstressed since, to the actor who knows his total plan, the significance of the first moves may seem glaringly obvious. It is hard for him to avoid overestimating how much he is communicating. Redundance and more redundance is usually necessary.

Modifying Certainty

It is well to introduce a distinction between two kinds of information communicated in the course of an influence process: namely, the distinction between the substantive facts themselves and estimates of their probable occurrence. For the statistically inclined the distinction can be expressed as the difference between communicating the first moment of a distribution and communicating its second moment. The Russians deterred us from more vigorous action in Laos by somehow communicating to us that they did not want to push to the limit there. But that information was ambiguous. They had two separate decisions to make: first whether to give us the information that compromise was possible, and second what degree of certainty to provide us with on that matter. They chose, and probably skillfully, to give us the information in such a fashion that we could never be sure whether it was real or whether we were being mousetrapped.

We are blurring a further distinction here, the distinction between degree of probability and degree of certainty. The relation of these concepts is one of the profoundest and most controversial in the philosophy of science. We prefer to avoid such issues here. Both those things, in whatever way they are related, are manipulable, and apart from the content of the information.

A large part of the art of deterrence, as of influence in general is the manipulation of certainty rather than the manipulation of the substance of the facts. Certainty is often much easier to affect than net conclusions. Our net image of the Soviet regime is that it is hostile to us. Their occasional good-will maneuvers are not likely to change our net judgment, but these maneuvers do have the effect of causing some doubt as to whether our assumptions are right and thus generate confusion. They reduce American confidence in our understanding of them and leave us without a sense of easy predictability. On this matter the situation is largely symmetrical. We probably also have a wider latitude of influence on their certainties than on their net conclusions.

The literature on the psychology of decision making under uncertainty is extensive. Learning from consistent stimuli is much faster than learning from stochastic ones. But the problem in deterrence is only partly that of teaching. It is also one of maintaining certain motivational states. It is important in planning deterrent strategy to be clear which objective is being served, teaching facts or affecting confidence. Raising certainty may help if the objective is to teach a conclusion; lowering it may help if the objective is to compel caution and indecision.

Providing a Behavioral Model to the Influencee

All the facts in the world do not tell a person how to act. He needs to be guided by the example of how some ego-ideal acts when faced with similar facts.

Oddly enough, the United States is to a considerable extent such a model for the Soviet Union and indeed for the whole world.

The Soviet Union is essentially an imitative society. All the vital ideas in the socialist world are imports from the West. Marxism is itself a radical version of popular democratic doctrines that permeated Europe in the first half of the nineteenth century. With one partial exception, the changes which the Russians have introduced are either also Western importations or they are failures. The one partial exception is Bolshevik party organization. The notion of the disciplined political machine which Lenin introduced was his adaption of American and European party machines and bureaucratic organization, but it was an extreme version, and unfortunately it worked. Since this 1905 idea, Bolshevism has produced no interesting innovations. Stalin transformed central planning into the key concept of communism, but the idea of a planning board with a development plan was a completely Western notion discussed in detail by all wings of opinion in England and Germany in the 1920s. When Khrushchev defined socialism to Sukarno as "calculation, nothing but calculation," he underlined that Russian communism has been nothing but a way of introducing a Western industrial society.

Whatever the Soviets have tried to add that is non-Western has failed. There are three such elements, any one of which if it had succeeded would have made the "Soviet experiment" something other than perverted Westernization. The first was total control over man—Stalin's attempt at creating a society well characterized by Orwell and Milosz. But the total police state is a failure, hated by everyone in the bloc and verbally repudiated in Khrushchev's secret speech, in the "thaw," and in Polish and Yugoslav revisionism. The "new Soviet man" has not appeared.

The Soviet Union is still a totalitarian tyranny, but one thing has become clear: Totalitarianism is not a successful stable system of human organization. It is preserved with great effort against continuous resistance. It shows no prospect of becoming a new historic form of civilization capable of lasting for hundreds of years. It is a fragile system unable to get human beings to internalize its values in "1984" fashion.

The second novel and non-Western attempt of Soviet communism was aimed at the destruction of religion. That too has failed, with religion still continuing to attract many young Russians.

The third great leap out of the Western tradition was the attempt to substitute communal living for peasant farming—the collective farms in Russia and, in an even more extreme form, the communes in China. This has been the greatest failure of all. To the extent that collectivism has been pushed, the farm problem has been made insoluble.

While the few original Soviet ideas have been unsuccessful, communism in Russia has been effective as a way of rapid Westernizing. The goal is admittedly to overtake the U.S. Admiration for American achievements has always permeated the Soviet elite. And it has been Western ideas, be they jazz or abstract art, or input-output analysis, or survey research, which have excited Russian intellectuals.

Even in the military field, Russian strategic thinking has, to a substantial degree, followed American strategic thinking, generally with a one- or two-year time lag. The Americans developed the doctrine of deterrence. The Russians learned it. We recognized the importance of hardening. The Russians are beginning to see it. We developed a mobile Polaris system. The Russians are moving toward it.

Providing the Russians with ourselves as a model is one more way in which we influence Soviet behavior. Whatever major commitments we make are likely to be partial models for the Russians. It would be nonsense to say that everything we do will be copied. The imitation is partial and selective. But anything we do in a major and successful way creates a pressure within the Soviet Union to try the same.

Changing the Objective Environment

We have already noted how dependent any set of calculations is on the perceptions of the real world which go into it. Changing the facts is obviously a way to change perceptions of them. Making a deterrent invulnerable, adding strength at any level, or changing force structures are obvious ways of affecting the opponent's calculations.

Changing the Influencee's Resources

One kind of change in the objective environment needs special treatment. That is the denial to the opponent of resources to carry out undesirable actions. The American economy is sufficiently larger than the Soviet economy so that an arms race in one area may serve to deny to the Soviets the resources they need in another. It is hard for the Soviets to sustain a full-scale moon program, conventional forces, missile hardening and mobility, and passive defense. Pushing our opponents into preferred ones of these programs is a realistic measure against their adopting others.

Summary

While the practice of deterrence has been relatively sophisticated, the literature about it has tended to look at it in very oversimplified ways. Among the many mechanisms involved in influence, it has tended to look at but one at a time. Indeed, the writings about deterrence by psychologists have tended to look at only one mode of influence, namely, generating trust, while the writings of some strategic writers have considered only the influence of threats. Unfortunately, it is often true that what has a desired action in one mode of influence is damaging in another. That is further complicated by considerations of timing.

It is necessary to distinguish short-run and long-run results of each mechanism and to consider feedback. Fear today may be a condition of trust tomorrow. A model may be copied only after a time lag.

So whenever we consider a proposed deterrent action, we should test it against the gamut of ways in which it may operate:

1. What does it do to the development of the adversary's trust in us and in our intentions?
2. What does it do in causing them to fear undesired courses of action, and is that fear so managed as to maximize its constructive consequences?
3. To what topics does it shift whose attention and interest and with what action effects?
4. What added information does it provide to the adversary, and how will that information be used in his calculations?
5. How does it affect his confidence in his own estimates of the situation?
6. What effect will our action have by way of example, if and to the extent that we are taken as a model by the adversary?
7. In what way does the action change the environment; and will the adversary, in taking account of those changes, act in ways we like?
8. Does the action deny to the adversary any resources for acting in undesired ways?

Notes

1. An extensive set of footnotes, including many references, are included in an original version of this article, of the same name, available as a technical publication, TP 3879 of the U. S. Naval Ordnance Test Station, China Lake, California, November, 1965.
2. Bettelheim, B. "Individual and mass behavior in extreme situations." *Journal of Abnormal and Social Psychology* 38 (1943): 417–52.
3. Alsop, S. "Kennedy's Grand Strategy." *Saturday Evening Post* 235 (March 1962): 11–16.
4. Hovland, C.I.; Janis, I.; Kelley, H.H. *Communication and persuasion.* New Haven, CT: Yale University Press, 1953.

5

Contacts and Influence

with Manfred Kochen

This essay raises more questions than it answers. In first draft, which we have only moderately revised, it was written about two decades ago and has been circulating in manuscript since then. (References to recent literature have, however, been added.) It was not published previously because we raised so many questions that we did not know how to answer; we hoped to eventually solve the problems and publish. The time has come to cut bait. With the publication of a new journal of human network studies, we offer our initial soundings and unsolved questions to the community of researchers which is now forming in this field. While a great deal of work has been done on some of these questions during the past twenty years, we do not feel that the basic problems have been adequately resolved.

1. Introduction

Let us start with familiar observations: the "small world" phenomenon, and the use of friends in high places to gain favors. It is almost too banal to cite one's favorite unlikely discovery of a shared acquaintance, which usually ends with the exclamation, "My, it's a small world!" The senior author's favorite tale happened in a hospital in a small town in Illinois where he heard one patient, a telephone lineman, say to a Chinese patient in the next bed: "You know, I've only known one Chinese before in my life. He was from Shanghai." "Why that's my uncle," said his neighbor. The statistical chances of an Illinois lineman know-

From *Social Networks* (1978–79).

ing a close relative of one of (then) 600,000,000 Chinese are minuscule; yet that sort of event happens.

The patient was, of course, not one out of 600,000,000 random Chinese, but one out of the few hundred thousand wealthy Chinese of Westernized families who lived in the port cities and moved abroad. Add the fact that the Chinese patient was an engineering student, and so his uncle may well have been an engineer too—perhaps a telecommunications engineer. Also there were perhaps some geographic lines of contact which drew the members of one family to a common area for travel and study. Far from surprising, the encounter seems almost natural. The chance meetings that we have are a clue to social structure, and their frequency an index of stratification.

Less accidental than such inadvertent meetings are the planned contacts sought with those in high places. To get a job one finds a friend to put in a good word with his friend. To persuade a congressman one seeks a mutual friend to state the case. This influence is peddled for 5 percent. Cocktail parties and conventions institutionalize the search for contacts. This is indeed the very stuff of politics. Influence is in large part the ability to reach the crucial man through the right channels, and the more channels one has in reserve, the better. Prominent politicians count their acquaintances by the thousands. They run into people they know everywhere they go. The experience of casual contact and the practice of influence are not unrelated. A common theory of human contact nets might help clarify them both.

No such theory exists at present. Sociologists talk of social stratification; political scientists of influence. These quantitative concepts ought to lend themselves to a rigorous metric based upon the elementary social events of man-to-man contact. "Stratification" expresses the probability of two people in the same stratum meeting and the improbability of two people from different strata meeting. Political access may be expressed as the probability that there exists an easy chain of contacts leading to the power holder. Yet such measures of stratification and influence as functions of contacts do not exist.

What is it that we should like to know about human contact nets?

- For any individual we should like to know how many other people he knows, that is, his acquaintance volume.
- For a *population* we want to know the distribution of acquaintance volumes, the mean and the range between the extremes.
- We want to know what kinds of people they are who have many contacts and whether those people are also the influentials.

- We want to know how the lines of contact are stratified; what is the structure of the network?

If we know the answers to these questions about individuals and about the whole population, we can pose questions about the implications for *paths* between pairs of individuals.

- How great is the probability that two persons chosen at random from the population will know each other?
- How great is the chance that they will have a friend in common?
- How great is the chance that the shortest chain between them requires two intermediaries; that is, a friend of a friend?

The mere existence of such a minimum chain does not mean, however, that people will become aware of it. The surprised exclamation "It's a small world" reflects the shock of discovery of a chain that existed all along.[1] So another question is:

- How far are people aware of the available lines of contact? A friend of a friend is useful only if one is aware of the connection. Also a channel is useful only if one knows how to use it. So the final question is, what sorts of people, and how many, try to exert influence on the persons with whom they are in contact: what sorts of persons and how many are opinion leaders, manipulators, politicists (de Grazia 1952; Boissevain 1974; Erickson and Kringas 1975)? [2]

These questions may be answered at a highly general level for human behavior as a whole, and in more detail for particular societies. At the more general level there are probably some things we can say about acquaintanceship volume based on the nature of the human organism and psyche. The day has twenty-four hours and memory has its limits. There is a finite number of persons that any one brain can keep straight and with whom any one body can visit. More important, perhaps, there is a very finite number of persons with whom any one psyche can have much cathexis.

There are probably some fundamental psychological facts to be learned about the possible range of identifications and concerns of which a person is capable (Miller 1956).[3]

These psychic and biological limits are broad, however. The distribution of acquaintanceship volumes can be quite variable between societies or social roles. The telephone makes a difference, for example. The contact pattern for an Indian villager *sans* radio, telephone, or road to his village is of a very different order from that of a Rotarian automobile dealer.

There is but little social science literature on the questions that we have just posed.[4] Even on the simplest question of the size of typical acquaintanceship volumes there are few data (Hammer, n.d.; Boissevain 1967).[5] Some are found in anecdotal descriptions of political machines. In the old days there was many a precinct captain who claimed to know personally every inhabitant of his area. While sometimes a boastful exaggeration, there is no doubt that the precinct worker's success derived, among other things, from knowing 300–500 inhabitants of his neighborhood by their first names and family connections (Kurtzman 1935).[6] At a more exalted level too, the art of knowing the right people is one of the great secrets of political success; James Farley claimed 10,000 contacts. Yet no past social science study has tested how many persons or what persons any politician knows. The estimates remain guesswork.

There exists a set of studies concerning acquaintanceship volume of delinquent girls in an institutional environment: J. L. Moreno and Helen Jennings asked girls in a reform school (with 467 girls in cottages of twenty-three or twenty-four apiece) to enumerate all other girls with whom they were acquainted (Jennings 1937).[7] It was assumed they knew all the girls in their own cottage. Computed that way, the median number of acquaintances was approximately sixty-five. However, the range was tremendous. One girl apparently knew 175 of her fellow students, while a dozen (presumably with low IQs) could list only four or fewer girls outside of their own cottage.

These figures have little relevance to normal political situations; but the study is valuable since it also tested the hypothesis that the extent of contact is related to influence. The girls were given sociometric tests to measure their influence. In each of two separate samples, a positive correlation (0.4 and 0.3) was found between contact range and influence.

One reason why better statistics do not exist on acquaintanceship volume is that they are hard to collect. People make fantastically poor estimates of the number of their own acquaintances (Killworth and Russell 1976).[8] Before reading further, the reader should try to make an estimate for himself. Define an acquaintance as someone whom you would recognize and could address by name if you met him. Restrict the definition further to require that the acquaintance would also recognize you and know your name. (That excludes entertainment stars, public figures, etc.) With this criterion of acquaintance, how many people do you know?

The senior author tried this question on some thirty colleagues, assistants, secretaries and others around his office. The largest answer was 10,000; the smallest was fifty. The median answer was 522. What is more, there seemed to be no relationship between the guesses and reality. Older or gregarious persons claimed no higher figures than young or relatively reclusive ones. Most of the answers were much too low. Except for the one guess of 10,000 and two of 2,000 each, they were all probably low. We don't know that, of course, but whenever we have tried sitting down with a person and enumerating circles of acquaintances it has not taken long before he has raised his original estimate as more and more circles have come to mind: relatives, old school friends, merchants, job colleagues, colleagues on former jobs, vacation friends, club members, neighbors, and so on. Most of us grossly underestimate the number of people we know for they are tucked in the recesses of our minds, ready to be recalled when occasion demands.

Perhaps a notion of the order of magnitude of acquaintanceship volume can be approached by a *gedankenexperiment* with Jennings' data on the reform school. The inmates were young girls who had not seen much of the world; they had but modest IQs and memories; they had come from limited backgrounds; and in the recent past they had been thoroughly closed off from the world. We know that the average one knew sixty-five inmates. Is it fair to assume that we may add at least twenty teachers, guards, and other staff members known on the average? Somewhere the girls had been in school before their internment. Perhaps each knew forty students and ten teachers from there. These girls were all delinquents. They were usually part of a delinquent gang or subculture. Perhaps an average of thirty young people were part of it. They had been arrested, so they knew some people from the world of lawyers, judges, policemen, and social workers. Perhaps there were twenty of them. We have not yet mentioned families and relatives; shall we say another thirty? Then there were neighbors in the place they had lived before, perhaps adding up to thirty-five. We have already reached 250 acquaintances which an average girl might have, based solely on the typical life history of an inmate. We have not yet included friends made in club or church, nor merchants, nor accidental contacts. These might add another fifty. Nor have we allowed for the girls who had moved around—who had been in more than one school or neighborhood or prison. Perhaps 400 acquaintances is not a bad guess of the average for these highly constricted, relatively inexperienced young girls. Should we not suspect that the average for a mature, white collar worker is at least double that?

Perhaps it is, but of course we don't know. All we have been doing so far is trying to guess orders of magnitude with somewhat more deliberation than was possible by the respondents to whom we popped the question "How many people do you know?" There has been no real research done to test such estimates.

It could be done by a technique analogous to that used for estimating a person's vocabulary. In any given time period during which we observe, a person uses only some of the words he knows and similarly has contact with only some of the people he knows. How can we estimate from this limited sample how many others are known to him? In each case (words and friends) we can do it by keeping track of the proportion of new ones which enter the record in each given time period. Suppose we count 100 running words. These may contain perhaps sixty different words, with some words repeated as many as six or seven times, but most words appearing once. Adding a second 100 running words may add thirty new ones to the vocabulary. A third hundred may add twenty-five new ones, and so on down. If we extrapolate the curve we reach a point where new words appear only every few thousand running words, and if we extrapolate to infinity we have an estimate of the person's total vocabulary. In the same way, on the first day one may meet thirty people. On the second day one may meet another thirty but perhaps only fifteen of them are new, the other fifteen being repeaters. On the third day perhaps the nonrepeaters may be down to ten, and so on. Again by extrapolating to infinity an estimate of the universe of acquaintances may be made.

Extrapolation to infinity requires strong assumptions about the number of very rarely seen acquaintances. If there are very many who are seen but once in a decade, then a much longer period of observation is required. If the number of people seen once in two decades is not significantly smaller than the number seen in a shorter period, then there are methodological difficulties in estimation.

Two further cautions are necessary. It turns out that the lumpiness in the schedules of our lives makes this technique unusable except over long periods. Perhaps we start on Thursday and go to work. Friday we go to work and see almost the same people. Saturday we go to the beach and have an entirely new set of contacts. Then Monday, perhaps, we are sent on a trip to another office. In short, the curves are highly irregular. Long and patient observation is called for.

Also note that at the end of a lengthy experiment (say after one year), it is necessary to check back over the early lists to determine who are forgotten and no longer acquaintances. Just as new persons enter the acquaintanceship sphere, old ones drop out of it. In one record, for example, a subject recorded 156 contacts in five successive days, with 117 different persons whom he then knew. Two years and ten months later, though still working in the same place, he could no longer recall or recognize thirty-one of these, that is, eighty-six (or 74 percent) were still acquaintances.

It is important to collect more such empirical information. Section 2 of this paper describes some empirical findings that we have obtained. But before we can decide what to collect we need to think through the logical model of how a human contact net works. We shall do that roughly and nonmathematically in this introduction. Section 3 of the paper deals with it more formally.

One question that quite properly is raised by readers is what do we mean by acquaintanceship, or friendship, or contact. For the mathematical model, the precise definition of "knowing" is quite irrelevant. What the mathematical model gives us is a set of points each of which is connected with some of the other points. As we look away from our model to the world for which it stands, we understand that each point somehow represents a person, and each connection an act of knowing. The model is indifferent to this, however. The points could stand for atoms, or neurons, or telephones, or nations, or corporations. The connections could consist of collisions, or electric charges, or letters written, or hearing about, or acquaintanceship, or friendship, or marriage. To use the model (and satisfy ourselves that it is appropriate) we shall have to pick definitions of person (i.e., point) and knowing (i.e., connectedness) related to the problem at hand. But we start with a model that is quite general. We do indeed impose some constraints on the points and on their connections. These constraints are the substance of our theory about the nature of human contacts.

One simplification we make in our model is to assume that the act of knowing is an all-or-none relationship. That is clearly not true and it is not assumed by Hammer (n.d.), Gurevich (1961) and Schulman (1976).[9] There are in reality degrees of connectedness between persons. There are degrees of awareness which persons have of each other, and there are varied strengths of cathexis. But we cannot yet deal with these degrees. For the moment we want to say of any person, A, that he either does or does not know any given other person, B.

The criterion of human acquaintanceship might be that when A sees B he recognizes him, knows a name by which to address him, and would ordinarily feel it appropriate that he should greet him. That definition excludes, as we have noted, recognition of famous persons, since as strangers we do not feel free to greet them. It excludes also persons whom we see often but whose names we have never learned, for example, the policeman on the corner. It is, however, a useful operational definition for purposes of contact net studies, because without knowing a name it is hard to keep a record.

Alternatively, the criterion might be a relationship which creates a claim on assistance. In politics, that is often the important kind of knowing. One might well find that a better predictor of who got a job was a man's position in the network of connections defined by obligation than his position in the network of mere acquaintance connections.

For some anthropological studies the connection with which we are concerned might be kinship. As many societies operate, the most important fact in the dealings of two persons is whether they are kin or not. Kinship creates obligations and thus provides a protection of each by the other. Blood kinship is a matter of degree fading off imperceptibly; we are all ultimately related to everyone else. But society defines the limit of who are recognized as kin and who are unrelated. This varies from society to society, and sometimes is hard to establish. In many societies, Brazil and India for example, the first gambit of new acquaintances is to talk about relatives to see if a connection can be established. For such societies kinship is clearly an important criterion of connectedness.

Another criterion of connectedness, of considerable relevance in the United States, is the first-name index. This makes a sharp distinction between levels of knowing, just as does *Sie* and *du* in German or *vous* and *tu* in French.

Whatever definition of knowing we choose to use, our model proceeds by treating connectedness as an all-or-none matter. In short, we are trying to develop not a psychological model of the knowing relationship, but a model for treating data about knowing relationships (however defined) which can be applied using whatever knowing relationship happens to be of interest.

The political scientist, using an appropriate definition, may use a contact net model to study influence (Gurevich and Weingrod 1976).[10] He asks the number of "connections" of a political kind a person has. The sociologist or anthropologist, using an appropriate definition, may use such a model to study social structure. He asks what kinds of persons are likely to be in contact with each other. The communications researcher may use such a model to study the channels for the flow of messages. Psychologists may use it to examine interrelationships within groups.

So far we have imposed only one restriction on the knowing relationship in our model, namely, that it be all-or-none. There are a few further things we can say about it. When a mathematician describes a relationship he is apt to ask three questions about it: Is it reflexive? Is it symmetric? Is it transitive? The "equals" (=) relationship is reflexive, symmetric, and transitive.

The knowing relationship about which we are talking is clearly not an equality relationship. Anything equals itself, that is, the equals relation is reflexive. Acquaintanceship is reflexive or not as one chooses to define it. The issue is a trivial one. One could say that by definition everyone knows himself, or one could say that by definition the circle of acquaintances does not include oneself. (We have chosen in our examples below to do the latter and so to define the knowing relation as nonreflexive.)

There is no reason why the knowing relation has to be symmetric. Many more people knew the film star Marilyn Monroe than she knew. If we use the definition of putting a face together with a name then, clearly, persons with good memories know persons with bad memories who do not know them. Similarly, it has been found in some studies that persons are more apt to know the names of persons with higher than lower social status. Thus, privates know each others' names and the names of their officers. Officers know each others' names and the names of those they serve, but not necessarily those of privates. Those served may only know servants categorically as, for example, "the tall blond waitress." All in all, to define any knowing relationship as a symmetric one is a great constraint on reality, but it is one which simplifies analysis enormously. It helps so much that for the most part we are going to make that assumption in the discussion below. And, for many purposes, it is largely correct. A kinship relationship is clearly symmetric; if A is a kin to B, B is a kin to A. Also the recognition relationship is mostly symmetric. Most of the time if A can recognize and greet B, B can recognize and greet A. It is generally convenient in our model to define away the minority of cases where this does not hold.

On the other hand, the assumption of transitivity is one that we cannot usefully make. If A knows B, and B knows C, it does not follow that

A knows C. If it did follow, then all of society would decompose into a set of one or more cliques completely unconnected with each other. It would mean that everyone you knew would know everyone else you knew, and it follows that you could not know anyone who was outside the clique (i.e., not known to all your friends).[11] Clustering into cliques does occur to some extent and is one of the things we want to study. We want to measure the extent to which these clusters are self-contained, but they are not that by definition.

Thus one useful model of a contact network consists of a set of individuals each of whom has some knowing relationships with others in the set of a kind which we have now defined: all-or-none, irreflexive, symmetric, not necessarily transitive.

We would like to be able to describe such a network as relatively unstructured or as highly structured. Intuitively that is a meaningful distinction, but it covers a considerable variety of strictly defined concepts. Figure 5.1 describes three hypothetical groups of eight people each, in which each individual has three friends. In the first there are no cliques, in the third there are two completely disjoint cliques, and the second group is intermediate. In the first any two people can be connected by at most one intermediary; in the second some pairs (e.g., A and E) require two intermediaries to be connected; in the third some individuals cannot be connected at all. We are inclined to describe the third group as the most stratified or structured and the first as least so, and in some senses that is true. But, of course, the first graph is also a rigid structure in the sense that all individuals are alike. In general, however, when we talk of a network as showing more social stratification or clustering in this paper, we mean that it departs further from a random process in which each individual is alike except for the randomness of the variables. The clustering in a society is one of the things which affects who will meet whom and who can reach whom.[12] Any congressman knows more congressmen than average for the general populace; any musician knows more musicians.

The simplest assumption, and one perhaps to start with in modelling a large contact net, is that the number of acquaintances of each person in the population is a constant. We start then with a set of N persons each of whom knows n persons from among the N in the universe; n is the same for all N persons.

If in such a population we pick two persons at random and ask what is the probability that they know each other, the answer can quickly be given from knowing N and n (or, if n is a random variable, the mean n).

FIGURE 5.1
Networks of Different Structuredness

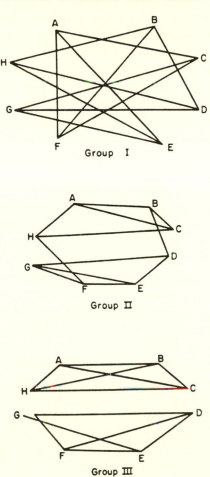

We know nothing about A and B except that they are persons from a population of size N each of whom on the average knows n other persons in that population. The probability that B is one of the n persons in the circle of acquaintances of A is clearly n/N. If we were talking of a population of 160,000,000 adults and each of them knew, on the average, 800 persons, the chances of two picked at random knowing each other would be one in 200,000.

Suppose we pick A and B who do not know each other, what is the probability of their having an acquaintance in common? The answer to that question, even with random choice of A and B, no longer depends just on n and N. The results now depend also on the characteristic structure of interpersonal contacts in the society, as well as on the size of the population and the number of acquaintances each person has. To see the reason why, we turn to an example which we outline diagrammatically in figure 5.2. This figure represents parts of two networks in which n = 5, that is, each person knows five others in the population. We start with A; he knows B, C, D, E, and F; this is his circle of acquaintances. Next we turn to B; he also knows five people. One of these, by the assumption of symmetry, is A. So, as the acquaintanceship tree fans out, four persons are added at each node.

However, here we note a difference between the structured and the unstructured population. In a large population without structure the chance of any of A's acquaintances knowing each other is very small (one in 200,000 for the U.S. figures used above). So, for a while at least, if there is no structure the tree fans out adding four entirely new persons at each node: A knows five people; he has twenty friends of friends, and eighty friends of friends of friends, or a total of 125 people reachable with at most two intermediaries. That unstructured situation is, however, quite unrealistic. In reality, people who have a friend in common are likely to know each other (Hammer, n.d.). That is the situation shown in the slightly structured network on the left side of figure 5.2. In that example one of D's acquaintances is B and another is E. The effect of these intersecting acquaintanceships is to reduce the total of different people reached at any given number of steps away from A. In the left-hand network A has five friends, but even with the same n only eleven friends of friends.

So we see, the more cliquishness there is, the more structure there is to the society, the longer (we conjecture) the chains needed on the average to link any pair of persons chosen at random. The less the acquaintanceship structure of a society departs from a purely random process of interactions, in which any two persons have an equal chance of meeting, the shorter will be the average minimum path between pairs of persons.[13] Consider the implications, in a random network, of assuming that n, the mean number of acquaintances of each person, is 1,000. Disregarding duplications, one would have 1,000 friends, a million $(1,000^2)$ friends-of-friends, a billion $(1,000^3)$ persons at the end of chains with two intermediaries, and a trillion $(1,000^4)$ with three. In such a

FIGURE 5.2
Structure in a Population

Structured
Population

Unstructured
Population

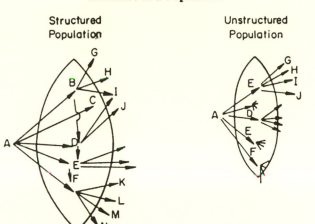

random network two strangers finding an acquaintance in common (i.e., experiencing the small-world phenomenon) would still be enjoying a relatively rare event; the chance is one million out of 100 or 200 million. But two intermediaries would be all it would normally take to link two people; only a small minority of pairs would not be linked by one of those billion chains.

Thus, in a country the size of the United States, if acquaintanceship were random and the mean acquaintance volume were 1,000, the mean length of minimum chain between pairs of persons would be well under two intermediaries. How much longer it is in reality because of the presence of considerable social structure in the society we do not know (nor is it necessarily longer for all social structures). Those are among the critical problems that remain unresolved.

Indeed, if we knew how to answer such questions we would have a good quantitative measure of social structure. Such an index would operationalize the common sociological statement that one society is more structured than another. The extent to which the mean minimum chain of contacts departs from that which would be found in a random network could be a convenient index of structuredness.

FIGURE 5.3
Effect of Structure

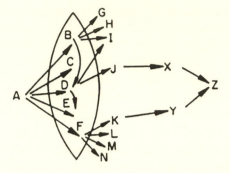

There are all sorts of rules for the topology of a network that can make its graph depart from random linkages. Perhaps the simplest and most important structure is that of triangular links among a given person's friends. If two persons both know person A, the odds are much better than otherwise that they will know each other; if they do know each other the acquaintanceship links form a triangle. For an example see figure 5.3. Disregarding the symmetric path (i.e., A knows B so B knows A), let us ask ourselves how many links it takes to go from A out to each of his acquaintances and back to A via the shortest path. If we start out on the path from A to B, we can clearly return to A via a triangle, A,B,D,A. We can also return by a triangle if we go from A to D or A to E. On the other hand, there is no triangle which will take one back if one starts on the path from A to F. Sooner or later there will be a path back, in this instance a path of eight links. (The only instance in which there would be no path back would be if the society were broken into two cliques linked at no point (see figure 5.1), or at only one point.) Clearly, the number of triangles among all the minimum circular chains is a good index of the tightness of the structure, and one that is empirically usable. It is perfectly possible to sample and poll the acquaintances of A to estimate how many of them know each other. That figure (which measures the number of triangles) then provides a parameter of the kind for which we are looking (Hammer, n.d.; Wasserman 1977).[14]

The fact that two persons have an acquaintance in common means that to some extent they probably move in the same circles. They may live in the same part of the country, work in the same company or profession, go to the same church or school, or be related. These institutions provide a nucleus of contacts so that one acquaintance in common is likely to lead to more. One way to describe that situation can be explained if we turn back to figure 5.3. Suppose we inquire of a person whether he knows A. If the answer is yes, then the chances of his knowing B are better than they would otherwise have been. Conversely if the answer is no, that reduces the chances of his knowing B. If he has told us that he does not know either A or B the chances of his knowing C are still further reduced. And so on down the list. This fact suggests that a second measure of structuredness would be the degree to which the chance of knowing a subsequent person on the list of acquaintances of A is reduced by the information that a person does not know the previous person on the list. In a society that is highly segmented, if two persons have any acquaintances in common they will have many, and so each report of nonacquaintanceship reduces more markedly than it otherwise would the chances of finding one common acquaintance on the list.

We require a measure, such as one of those two we have just been discussing, of the degree of clusteredness in a society, to deal with the question with which we started a few pages back, namely, the distribution of length of minimum contact chains: how many pairs of persons in the population can be joined by a single common acquaintance, how many by a chain of two persons, how many by a chain of three, and so on?

The answer depends on three values: N, n, and a parameter measuring structuredness. Increased social stratification reduces the length of chains between persons in the same stratum and at the same time lengthens the chains across strata lines. Thus, for example, two physicians or two persons from the same town are more likely to have an acquaintance in common than persons who do not share such a common characteristic. While some chains are thus shortened and others are lengthened by the existence of clusters within a society, it seems plausible to conjecture that the mean chain averaged over pairs of persons in the population as a whole is lengthened. Two persons chosen at random would find each other more quickly in an unstructured society than in a structured one, for most of the time (given realistic values of N, n, and clustering) persons chosen at random will not turn out to be in the same strata.

We might conjecture, for example, that if we had time series data of this kind running over the past couple of decades, we would find a decline in structuredness based on geography. The increased use of the long-distance telephone (and in the future of computer networks), and also of travel, probably has made acquaintanceship less dependent on geographic location than ever in the past.

In the final section of this paper we turn to an exploration of some of the alternative ways of modelling a network of the kind just described. The central problem that prevents an entirely satisfactory model is that we do not know how to deal with the structuredness of the population. Because of its lovely mathematical simplicity, there is an almost irresistible tendency to want to assume that whenever we do not know how the probability of acquaintanceship within two pairs of persons differs, we should treat it as equal; but it is almost never equal (Hunter and Shotland 1974; White 1970a).[15] The real-world population lives in an n-dimensional space distributed at varying social distances from each other. But it is not a Euclidean space. Person A may be very close to both B and C and therefore very likely to know them both, but B and C may be very far from each other.

In the hope of getting some clues as to the shape of the distribution of closeness among pairs in real-world populations, we undertook some research on the actual contact networks of some twenty-seven individuals. These data we shall describe in section 2 of this paper. While we learned a lot from that exercise, it failed to answer the most crucial questions because the most important links in establishing the connectedness of a graph may often be not the densely travelled ones in the immediate environment from which the path starts, but sparse ones off in the distance. How to go between two points on opposite sides of a river may depend far more critically on where the bridge is than on the roads near one's origin or destination. The point will become clear as we examine the data.

2. Empirical Estimates of Acquaintanceship Parameters

One is awed by the way in which a network multiplies as links are added. Even making all allowances for social structure, it seems probable that those whose personal acquaintances range around 1,000, or only about 1/100,000 of the U.S. adult population, can presumably be linked to another person chosen at random by two or three intermediaries on the average, and almost with certainty by four.

We have tried various approaches to estimating such data. We start with gedankenexperiments, but also have developed a couple of techniques for measuring acquaintance volume and network structure.

Consider first a rather fanciful extreme case. Let us suppose that we had located those two individuals in the U.S. between whom the minimum chain of contacts was the longest one for any pair of persons in the country. Let us suppose that one of these turned out to be a hermit in the Okefenokee Swamps, and the other a hermit in the northwest woods. How many intermediaries do we need to link these two?

Each hermit certainly knows a merchant. Even a hermit needs to buy coffee, bread, and salt. Deep in the backwoods, the storekeeper might never have met his congressman, but among the many wholesalers, lawyers, inspectors, and customers with whom he must deal, there will be at least one who is acquainted with his representative. Thus each of the hermits, with two intermediaries reaches his congressman. These may not know each other, though more likely they do, but in any case they know a congressman in common. Thus the maximum plausible minimum chain between any two persons in the United States requires no more than seven intermediaries.

This amusing example is not without significance. Viewed this way, we see Congress in a novel but important aspect, that of a communication node. The Congress is usually viewed as a policy-choosing, decision-making instrument, which selects among preexisting public opinions which are somehow already diffused across the country. Its more important function, however, is that of a forum to which private messages come from all corners, and within which a public opinion is created in this process of confrontation of attitudes and information. Congress is the place which is quickly reached by messages conveying the feelings and moods of citizens in all walks of life. These feelings themselves are not yet public opinion for they are not crystallized into policy stands; they are millions of detailed worries concerning jobs, family, education, old age, and so on. It is in the Congress that these messages are quickly heard and are revised and packaged into slogans, bills, and other policy formulations. It is these expressions of otherwise inchoate impulses that are reported in the press, and which become the issues of public opinion. Thus the really important function of the Congress, distinguishing it from an executive branch policy making body, is as a national communication center where public reactions are transformed into public opinion. Its size and geographically representative character puts it normally at two easily found links from everyone in the country. Its members, meeting with each other, formulate policies which express the impulses reaching them from outside. Through this communication node men from as far apart as the

Okefenokee Swamps and the north woods can be put in touch with the common threads of each other's feelings expressed in a plank of policy. A body of 500 can help to weld a body of 100,000,000 adults into a nation.

While thinking about such matters has its value, it is no substitute for trying to collect hard data. Empirical collection of contact data is possible but not easy. First of all, people are not willing to reveal some or all of their contacts. Second, it is hard to keep track of such massive and sequential data. Third, because contacts run in clusters and are not statistically independent events, the statistical treatment of contact data is apt to be hard.

Reticence is probably the least serious of the difficulties. It is certainly no more of a problem for studies of contacts than for Kinsey-type research or for research on incomes or voting behavior, all of which have been successfully conducted, though with inevitable margins of error. As in these other areas of research, skill in framing questions, patience, proper safeguards of confidence, and other similar requirements will determine success, but there is nothing new or different about the difficulties in this field. Reticence is less of an obstacle to obtaining valid information about contacts than are the tricks played by our minds upon attempts at recall.

Indeed it is usually quite impossible for persons to answer questions accurately about their contacts. We noted above the bewilderment which respondents felt when asked how many people they knew, and how most gave fantastic underestimates. Over one day, or even a few hours, recall of contacts is bad. Given more than a very few contacts, people find it hard to recall whom they have seen or conversed with recently. They remember the lengthy or emotionally significant contacts, but not the others. The person who has been to the doctor will recall the doctor, but may neglect to mention the receptionist. The person who has been to lunch with friends may forget about contact with the waiter. In general, contacts which are recalled are demonstrably a highly selected group.

Most importantly, they are selected for prestige. A number of studies have revealed a systematic suppression of reports of contacts down the social hierarchy in favor of contacts up it (Warner 1963; Festinger et al. 1950; Katz and Lazarsfeld 1955).[16] If one throws together a group of high status and low status persons and later asks each for the names of the persons in the group to whom he talked, the bias in the outcome is predictably upward. Unaided recall is not an adequate instrument for collecting contact data except where the problem requires recording only of emotionally meaningful contacts. If we wish to record those, and only those, we can use the fact of recall as our operational test of meaningfulness. Otherwise, however, we need to supplement unaided recall.

Some records of contacts exist already and need only be systematically noted. Noninterview sources of contact information include appointment books, committee memberships, and telephone switchboard data. The presidential appointment book is a fascinating subject for study.

Telephone switchboard data could be systematically studied by automatic counting devices without raising any issues of confidence. The techniques are already available and are analogous to those used for making load estimates. They could have great social science value too. A study, for example, of the ecology of long-distance telephone contacts over the face of the country would tell us a great deal about regionalism and national unity. A similar study of the origin and destination of calls by exchange could tell us a great deal about neighborhoods, suburbanism, and urbanism in a metropolitan region. This would be particularly interesting if business and residential phones could be segregated. The pattern of interpersonal contact could be studied by counting calls originating on any sample of telephones. (What proportion of all calls from any one phone are to the most frequently called other phone? What proportion to the ten most frequently called others?) How many different numbers are called in a month or a year? Would the results on such matters differ for upper and lower income homes, urban and rural, etc.?

In similar ways mail flows can tell us a good deal (Deutsch 1956, 1966).[17] The post office data are generally inadequate, even for international flows, and even more for domestic flows. Yet sample counts of geographic origins and destinations are sometimes made, and their potential use is clear.

Not all the information we want exists in available records. For some purposes interviews are needed for collection of data. Various devices suggest themselves for getting at the range of a person's contacts. One such device is to use the telephone book as an aide-memoire. We take a very large book, say the Chicago or Manhattan book. We open it to a page selected by a table of random numbers. We then ask our respondent to go through the names on that page to see if they know anyone with a name that appears there or a name that would appear there if it happened to be in that book. Repeat the operation for a sample of pages. One can either require the subject to think of all the persons he knows with such names, which is both tedious and, therefore, unreliable, or assume that the probability of a second, third, or fourth known person appearing on a single page is independent of the previous appearance of a known name on the page. Since that is a poor assumption we are in a dilemma. Depending on the national origins of our respondent, he is apt to know more persons of certain names; he may know more Ryans, or Cohens, or Swansons according to what he is. Nationality is a distorting factor in the book, too. The Chicago phone book will contain a disproportionate number of Polish names, the Manhattan phone book a disproportionate number of Jewish ones. Also if the subject knows a family well he will know several relatives of the same name. In short, neither the tedious method of trying to make him list all known persons of the name, nor the technique in which one simply counts the proportion of pages on which no known name occurs (and uses that for p, 1–p = q, and then expands the binomial), gives a very satisfactory result. Yet with all those qualifications, this technique of checking memory against the phone book gives us a better estimate of approximate numbers of acquaintances than we now have.

One of the authors tried this technique on himself using a sample of thirty pages of the Chicago phone book and thirty pages of the Manhattan phone book. The Chicago phone book brought back names of acquaintances on 60 percent of the pages, yielding an estimate that he knows 3,100 persons. The Manhattan phone book, with 70 percent of the pages having familiar names, yielded an estimate of 4,250 acquaintances. The considerations raised above suggested that the estimate from the Manhattan phone book should be higher, for the author is Jewish and grew up in Manhattan. Still the discrepancy in estimates is large. It perhaps brings us closer to a proper order of magnitude, but this technique is still far from a solution to our problem.

To meet some of these problems we developed a somewhat better method which involves keeping a personal log of all contacts of any sort for a number of sample days. Each day the subject keeps a list (on a pad he carries with him) of all persons whom he meets and knows. The successive lists increasingly repeat names which have already appeared. By projecting the curve one hopes to be able to make estimates of the total size of the acquaintanceship volume, and from the lists of names to learn something of the character of the acquaintances.

The rules of inclusion and exclusion were as follows:

1. A person was not listed unless he was already known to the subject. That is to say, the first time he was introduced he was not listed; if he was met

again on a later day in the 100 he was. The rationale for this is that we meet many people whom we fail to learn to recognize and know.

2. Knowing was defined as facial recognition and knowing the person's name—any useful name, even a nickname. The latter requirement was convenient since it is hard to list on a written record persons for whom we have no name.

3. Persons were only listed on a given day if when the subject saw them he addressed them, if only for a greeting. This eliminated persons seen at a distance, and persons who the subject recognized but did not feel closely enough related to, to feel it proper to address.

4. Telephone contacts were included. So were letters written but not letters received. The rationale for the latter is that receiving a letter and replying to it is a single two-way communication such as occurs simultaneously in a face-to-face contact. To avoid double counting, we counted a reply as only half the act. Of course, we counted only letters written to people already known by the above criterion.

5. A person was only listed once on a given day no matter how often he was seen. This eliminated, for example, the problem of how many times to count one's secretary as she walked in and out of the office.

The task of recording these contacts is not an easy one. It soon becomes a tedious bore. Without either strong motivation or constant checking it is easy to become forgetful and sloppy. But it is far from impossible; properly controlled and motivated subjects will do it.

The data on twenty-seven persons were collected mostly by Dr. Michael Gurevich (1961) as part of a Ph.D. dissertation which explored, along with the acquaintanceship information itself, its relation to a number of dependent variables.[18] As table 5.1 shows us, the respondents, though not a sample of any defined universe, covered a range of types including blue collar, white collar, professional, and housewives.

Among the most important figures in the table are those found in the right-hand column. It is the ratio between the number of different persons met and the number of meetings. It is what psychologists call the type-token ratio. It is socially very indicative, and is distinctive for different classes of persons.

Blue-collar workers and housewives had the smallest number of different contacts over the 100 days. They both lived in a restricted social universe. But in the total number of interpersonal interactions the blue-collar workers and housewives differed enormously. Many of the blue collar workers worked in large groups. Their round of life was very repetitive; they saw the same people day in and day out, but at work they saw many of them. Housewives, on the other hand, not only saw

TABLE 5.1
100–Day Contacts of Respondents

Sex	Job	Age	(a) No. of different persons seen in 100 days	(b) No. of contact events	Ratio b/a
Blue collar					
M	Porter	50–60	83	2946	35.5
M	Factory labor	40–50	96	2369	24.7
M	Dept. store receiving	20–30	137	1689	12.3
M	Factory labor	60–70	376	7645	20.3
M	Foreman	30–40	510	6371	12.5
F	Factory labor and unemployed	30–40	146	1222	8.4
White collar					
F	Technician	30–40	276	2207	8.0
F	Secretary	40–50	318	1963	6.2
M	Buyer	20–30	390	2756	7.1
M	Buyer	20–30	474	4090	8.6
M	Sales	30–40	505	3098	6.1
F	Secretary	50–60	596	5705	9.5
Professional					
M	Factory engineer	30–40	235	3142	13.5
F	T.V.	40–50	533	1681	3.2
M	Adult educator	30–40	541	2175	3.8
M	Professor	40–50	570	2142	3.1
M	Professor	40–50	685	2142	3.1
M	Lawyer–politician	30–40	1043	3159	3.0
M	Student	20–30	338	1471	4.4
M	Photographer	30–40	523	1967	4.8
M	President*	50–60	1404**	4340**	3.1**
Housewives					
F	—	30–40	72	377	5.2
F	—	20–30	255	1111	4.4
F	—	20–30	280	1135	4.0
F	—	30–40	363	1593	4.4
F	—	30–40	309	1034	3.3
F	—	50–60	361	1032	2.9
Adolescent					
M	Student	10–20	464	4416	9.5

*Data estimated from Hyde Park records.
**Record for 85 days.

few different people, but they saw few people in the course of a day; they had small type-token ratios. They lived in isolation.

In total gregariousness (i.e., number of contact events) there was not much difference among the three working groups. Blue-collar workers, white collar workers, and professionals all fell within the same range, and if there is a real difference in the means, our small samples do not justify any conclusions about that. But in the pattern of activity there was a great difference. While blue-collar workers were trapped in the round of a highly repetitive life, professionals at the other extreme were constantly seeing new people. They tended to see an average acquaintance only three or four times in the hundred days. One result of this was that the professionals were the persons whose contacts broke out of the confines of social class to some extent. They, like the others (see table 5.2) tended to mix to a degree with people like themselves but, to a slightly greater degree than the other classes, they had a chance to meet people in other strata of society.

The tendency of society to cluster itself as like seeks like can also be seen in tables on contacts by age, sex, and religion (see tables 5.3, 5.4, and 5.5). These data reflect a society that is very structured indeed. How can we use the data to estimate the acquaintanceship volume of the different respondents? We found that over 100 days the number of different persons they saw ranged between seventy-two for one housewife and 1,043 for one lawyer-politician. Franklin Roosevelt's presidential appointment book, analyzed by Howard Rosenthal (1960),[19] showed 1,404 different persons seeing him. But that leaves us with the question as to what portion of the total acquaintance volume of each of these persons was exhausted.

One of the purposes of the data collection was to enable us to make an estimate of acquaintance volume in a way that has already been described above. With each successive day one would expect fewer people to be added, giving an ogive of persons met to date such as that in figure 5.4. In principle one might hope to extrapolate that curve to a point beyond which net additions would be trivial.

Fitting the 100-day curve for each subject to the equation (acquaintanceship volume) $= At^x$ gave acquaintanceship volumes over twenty years ranging from 122 individuals for a blue-collar porter in his fifties to 22,500 persons for Franklin Roosevelt.

However, that estimation procedure does not work with any degree of precision. The explanation is that the estimate of the asymptote is sensitive to the tail of the distribution (Granovetter 1976).[20] Such a large pro-

TABLE 5.2
Number of Acquaintances by Occupation

Acquaintances' occupation	Subject's occupation				
	Blue collar (%)	Housewife (%)	White collar (%)	Professional (%)	Entire group (%)
Professional	11	24	20	45	24
Managerial	9	7	19	14	14
Clerical	13	7	13	7	11
Sales worker	5	6	19	4	11
Craftsman, foreman	15	5	6	5	7
Operative	25	1	3	5	8
Service worker	9	2	2	1	3
Laborer	4	1	1	—	1
Housewife	4	35	10	12	13
Student	2	3	1	5	3
Farmer	—	—	—	—	—
Don't know	4	10	8	3	6
	100*	100*	100*	100*	100*

*Figures may not add up to 100% because of rounding.

TABLE 5.3
Subject's Age Compared with his Acquaintance's Age

Acquaintance's age	Subject's age			
	20–30 (%)	31–40 (%)	41–50 (%)	Over 50 (%)
Under 20	7	2	2	1
20–30	21	19	11	15
31–40	30	39	33	20
41–50	21	22	27	32
Over 50	21	19	27	33
	100*	100*	100*	100*

*Figures may not add up to 100% because of rounding.

portion of the respondent's acquaintances are seen only once or twice in 100 days that any estimate which we make from such data is very crude. Table 5.6 shows the figures. Except for blue collar workers, half or more of the acquaintances were seen only once or twice in the period.

TABLE 5.4
Sex of subject and sex of acquaintance

Subject	Acquaintances		
	Male (%)	Female (%)	Total (%)
Blue collar			
Male	83	17	100
White collar			
Male	65	35	100
Female	53	47	100
Professional			
Male	71	29	100
Housewife			
Female	45	55	100

TABLE 5.5
Religion of Subject and Religion of Acquaintance

Subject's religion	Acquaintance's religion				
	Protestant (%)	Catholic (%)	Christian (didn't know denomination) (%)	Jewish (%)	Religion known (%)
Protestant	46	25	25	4	100*
Catholic	15	57	23	4	100*
Jewish	9	16	27	47	100*

*Figures may not add up because of rounding and omission of other religions.

One may think that the way around this problem would be to rely more heavily on the shape of the curve in its more rugged region where contact events are more frequent. The problem with that is that the nature of the contacts in the two parts of the curve are really quite dissimilar. To explain that perhaps we should look more closely at a single case; we shall use that of one of the author's own contact lists.

In 100 days he had contact with 685 persons he knew. On any one day the number of contacts ranged from a low of two other persons to a high of eighty-nine, the latter in the Christmas season. The mean number of acquaintances with whom he dealt on a day was 22.5. The median number was nineteen. There were several discreet typical patterns

FIGURE 5.4
Acquaintanceship Ogives

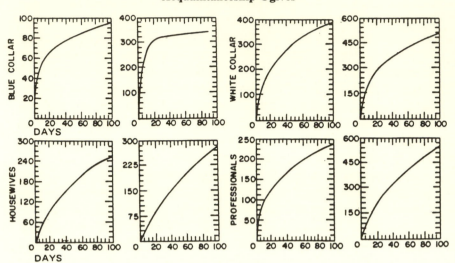

of days, resulting in a multimodal distribution. There was one type of day, including most weekend days, when he would typically meet seven to nine people, another type of day with typically around seventeen contacts, and a third type of day of highly gregarious activity which involved dealing with about thirty people.

Only about half of the 685 persons were seen more than once in the 100 days. The mean frequency was 3.1 times per person. The distribution, however, is highly skewed (table 5.7).

These figures, however, are somewhat misleading. It seems that we are actually dealing with two distributions: one which includes those persons living in the author's home and working in his office whom he saw during his regular daily routine, and the other including all his other acquaintances in the seeing of whom all kinds of chance factors operated. All individuals seen nineteen or more times are in the former group; so are all but two individuals seen thirteen or more times. Removing fifty-one such family members and coworkers gives us the data that are really relevant to estimating the large universe of occasional contacts, but in that sample more than half the persons listed were seen only once and 91 percent five times or less. No easily interpretable distribution (such as Poisson which would imply that there is no structure among these contacts) fits that distribution, and with such small frequencies the shape of the distribution is unstable between respondents. It is possible that the projection of the 100-day data for this author to a year's time could come out at anywhere between 1,100 and 1,700 persons contacted. That is not a very satisfactory estimate, but it is far better than the estimates we had before.

This estimate is way below our telephone book estimates, which it will be recalled ranged from 3,100 to 4,250 acquaintances. The discrepancy is more revealing than disturbing. It suggests some hypotheses about the structure of the universe of acquaintances. It suggests that there is a pool of persons with whom one is currently in potential contact, and a larger pool in one's memory, which for the senior author is about two to three times as large. The active pool consists of acquaintances living in the areas which one frequents, working at the activity related to one's occupation, belonging to the groups to which one belongs. Random factors determine in part which persons out of this pool one happens to meet, or even meet several times during any set period. But in one's memory there are in addition a considerable number of other persons whose names and faces are still effectively stored, but who are not currently moving in the same strata of contacts as oneself. These are recorded by the telephone book measure; they will not appear in the record of meetings except for the rarest kind of purely chance encounter. Needless to say, these two pools are not clearly segregated, but merge into each other. Yet, our data would suggest that they are more segregated than we would otherwise have suspected. The probabilities of encounter with the two types of persons are of quite different orders of magnitude.

We have now established plausible values for some of the parameters of the contact net of one of the authors. He typically deals with about twenty people in a day. These are drawn from a set of some 1,500 persons whom he actively knows at the present time. At the same time he remembers many other persons and could still recognize and name perhaps 3,500 persons whom he has met at some point in the past. (Incidentally, he has never regarded himself as good at this.)[21]

TABLE 5.6
Frequency Distribution of Contacts with Acquaintances

Frequency of contact over 100 days	Blue collar group				
	Case A (%)	Case B (%)	Case C (%)	Case D (%)	Case E (%)
1	4.8	23.9	29.0	9.3	23.5
2	2.4	11.4	11.6	5.0	10.7
3	—	4.1	6.5	3.9	8.4
4	—	4.1	4.3	3.4	4.7
5	1.2	3.1	3.6	3.4	4.9
6–10*	2.4	0.4	1.7	3.4	2.2
11–20*	0.8	0.5	1.2	2.1	1.3
21–30*	1.0	0.6	1.0	1.3	1.0
31–40*	1.8	0.6	0.6	0.9	0.7
41–50*	1.7	0.3	0.5	0.5	0.4
51–60*	1.7	1.4	0.1	0.4	0.2
61–70*	0.6	1.1	—	0.7	0.1
71–80*	0.1	0.1	0.07	—	0.02
81–90*	—	—	—	—	—
01–100*	0.2	0.2	0.07	0.05	0.02
	100%	100%	100%	100%	100%

Frequency of contact over 100 days	White collar group					
	Case G (%)	Case H (%)	Case I (%)	Case J (%)	Case K (%)	Case L (%)
1	43.4	44.3	27.2	30.8	47.7	37.7
2	11.5	16.9	20.0	12.4	13.1	12.9
3	7.9	7.5	10.7	9.0	6.5	7.5
4	4.3	3.7	6.1	6.9	7.1	4.5
5	3.2	3.4	6.1	4.0	3.2	3.0
6–10*	1.9	1.8	2.3	2.8	1.9	2.3
11–20*	0.7	0.8	0.7	1.1	0.6	0.9
21–30*	0.4	0.3	0.4	0.4	0.2	0.3
31–40*	0.3	—	0.2	0.2	0.2	0.3
41–50*	0.5	0.09	0.1	0.2	0.1	0.3
51–60*	0.1	0.1	0.2	0.2	0.1	0.4
61–70*	—	0.2	—	0.1	0.06	0.1
71–80*	—	—	—	—	—	—
81–90*	—	—	—	—	—	—
90–100*	0.04	0.03	0.03	0.02	0.02	0.02
	100%	100%	100%	100%	100%	100%

TABLE 5.6 (continued)
Frequency Distribution of Contacts with Acquaintances

Frequency of contact over 100 days	Professional Housewives						
	Case M (%)	Case O (%)	Case P (%)	Case Q (%)	Case V (%)	Case W (%)	Case X (%)
1	39.5	53.0	43.4	49.6	56.0	54.6	47.9
2	7.7	12.3	17.5	18.5	18.8	18.9	16.5
3	4.3	7.5	12.2	10.9	7.8	7.8	8.8
4	3.9	4.2	5.9	4.7	1.5	3.2	6.8
5	3.0	3.6	5.2	3.8	3.9	2.5	4.4
6–10*	1.2	2.3	1.8	1.3	1.1	1.3	1.6
11–20*	1.6	0.4	0.5	0.3	0.3	0.4	0.3
21–30*	0.4	0.09	0.07	0.09	0.04	0.04	0.2
31–40*	0.4	0.07	0.02	0.06	0.08	0.04	0.03
41–50*	0.3	0.05	0.05	0.01	0.04	—	0.1
51–60*	0.7	0.07	0.02	0.01	0.08	0.1	—
61–70*	0.1	—	—	—	—	—	—
71–80*	—	—	—	—	0.04	0.07	—
81–90*	—	—	—	—	—	—	0.03
91–100*	0.1	0.02	0.02	0.01	0.08	0.04	0.03
	100%	100%	100%	100%	100%	100%	100%

*The percentages in each entry are average percentages for a single day, not for the 5- or 10-day period.

TABLE 5.7
Contact Frequency Distribution for One Person

Number of days on which contact was had during the 100 days	Number of persons with that frequency of contact	Days	Persons	Days	Persons
1	335	11	4	24	1
2	125	12	4	26	2
3	74	13	1	30	1
4	32	14	2	33	2
5	26	15	4	34	1
6	12	16	2	36	1
7	16	18	1	45	1
8	5	19	1	51	1
9	8	20	4	92	1
10	4	23	2		

The remaining parameter which we would wish to estimate is the degree of structuredness in this acquaintanceship universe. The indicator that we proposed to use was the proportion of the acquaintances of the list-keeper who knew each other, that is, the proportion of triangles in the network graph. When the 100-day data collection was finished, we took the lists of some of the respondents and turned them into a questionnaire. To a sample of the people who appeared on the respondent's list of contacts, we sent a sample of the names on the list and asked, regarding each, "Do you know that person?". This provided a measure of the degree of ingrowth of the contact net. It can be expressed as the percentage of possible triangles that are completed (Wasserman 1977).[22] The values for five subjects from whom we got the data ranged from 8 to 36 percent, and we would speculate that a typical value lies toward the low end of this range.

We have indicated above that the degree of structure affects how much longer than chance the minimum chain between a pair of randomly chosen persons is apt to be. We can go no further in specifying the effect of structure on the chains in this qualitative verbal discussion. Any more precise conclusion depends on the treatment of this subject. in a much more formal mathematical way. We turn, therefore, to a restatement of our presentation in a mathematical model...

Notes

1. In the years since this essay was first written, Stanley Milgram and his collaborators (Milgram, S. "The small world problem." *Psychology Today* 22 [1967]: 61–67; Travers, J.; Milgram, S. "An experimental study of the small world problem." *Sociometry* 32 [1969]: 425–43; Korte, C.; Milgram, S. "Acquaintanceship networks between racial groups: Application of the small world method." *Journal of Personality and Social Psychology* 15 [1970]: 101–8) have done significant experiments on the difficulty or ease of finding contact chains. It often proves very difficult indeed. [The interested reader also should consult Kochen, Manfred (ed.) *The small world: A volume of recent research commemorating Ithiel de Sola Pool, Stanley Milgram, and Theodore Newcomb.* Norwood, NJ: Ablex Publishing Company, 1989—L.E.]
2. de Grazia, A. *Elements of political science.* New York: Free Press, 1952; Boissevain, J. *Friends of friends: Networks, manipulators, and coalitions.* New York: St. Martin's Press, 1974; Erickson, B.; Kringas, P. "The small world of politics, or, seeking elites from the bottom up." *Canadian Review of Sociology and Anthropology* 12 (1975): 585–93.
3. Miller, G. "The magic number seven plus or minus two." *Psychological Review* 63 (1956): 81–97.
4. In the last few years, however, the literature on human networks has started proliferating. There are articles dealing with information and help-seeking networks in such fields as mental health: Saunders, J., Reppucci, N. "Learning

networks among administrators of human service institutions." *American Journal of Community Psychology* 5 (1977): 269–76; Horowitz, A. "Social networks and pathways to psychiatric treatment." *Social Forces* 56 (1977): 81–105; McKinlay, J. "Social networks, lay consultation and help-seeking behavior." *Social Forces* 51 (1973): 275–92. There is also some anthropological literature on networks in different societies: Nutini, H., White, D. "Community variations and network structure in social functions of Compradrazgo in rural Tlaxcala, Mexico." *Ethnology* 16 (1977): 353–84; Mitchell, J. C. (ed.). *Social networks in urban situations—analysis of personal relationships in central African towns.* Manchester: University Press, 1969; Jacobson, D. "Network analysis in East Africa: the social organization of urban transients." *Canadian Review of Sociology and Anthropology* 7 (1970): 281–86.

5. Hammer, M. *Social access and clustering of personal connections.* Unpublished, n.d.; Boissevain, *Friends of friends.*

6. Kurtzman, D. H. *Methods of controlling votes in Philadelphia.* Philadelphia, PA: University of Pennsylvania, 1935.

7. Jennings, H. "Structure of leadership—development and sphere of influence." *Sociometry* 1 (1937): 131.

8. Killworth, P.; Russell, B. "Information accuracy in social network data." *Human organization* 35 (1976): 269–86.

9. Hammer, M. *Social access*; Gurevich, M. *The social structure of acquaintance-ship networks.* Cambridge, MA: MIT Press, 1961; Schulman, N. "Role differentiation in urban networks." *Sociological Focus* 9 (1976): 149–58.

10. Gurevich, M.; Weingrod, A. "Who knows whom—contact networks in Israeli national elite." *Megamot* 22 (1976): 357–78; idem. *Human organization* (n.d. To be published).

11. Most sociometric literature deals with "liking" rather than "knowing." Preference relationships do tend to be transitive (Hallinan, M.; Felmlee, D. "An analysis of intransitivity in sociometric data." *Sociometry* 38 [1975]: 195–212).

12. A growing literature exists on structures in large networks: Boorman, S.; White, H. "Social structures from multiple networks." *American Journal of Sociology* 81 (1976): 1384–1446; Lorrain, F. *Social networks and classification.* Unpublished manuscript, 1976; Lorrain, F.; White, H. "Structural equivalence of individuals in social networks." *Journal of Mathematical Sociology* 1 (1971): 49–80; Rapoport, A.; Horvath, W. "A study of a large sociogram." *Behavioral Scientist* 6 (1961): 279–291; Foster, C. et al. "A study of large sociogram II: elimination of free parameters." *Behavioral Science* 8 (1963): 56–65; Foster, C., Horvath, W. "A study of a large sociogram III: reciprocal choice probabilities as a measure of social distance." *Behavioral Science* 16 (1971): 429–35; Wolfe, A. "On structural comparisons of networks." *Canadian Review of Sociology and Anthropology* 7 (1970): 226–44; McLaughlin, E. "The power network in Phoenix: An application of the smallest space analysis." *The Insurgent Sociologist* 5 (1975): 185–95; Lundberg, C. Patterns of acquaintanceship in society and complex organization: a comparative study of the small world problem." *Pacific Sociological Review* 18 (1975): 206–22; Alba, R.; Kadushin, C. "The intersection of social circles: a new measure of social proximity in networks." *Sociological Methods and Research* 5 (1976): 77–102.

13. Let us state this more carefully for a network of n nodes and m links, in which $n!$ $\gg m$, but all nodes are reachable from all nodes. In that case, m pairs know each other. The question is what structure will minimize the average number of steps between the $n!—m$ remaining pairs. Whenever the m pairs who know each other are also linked at two steps, then the two-step connection is wasted. The same is

true for pairs linked by more than one two- step route. Such wastage occurs often when there are dense clusters of closely related nodes in a highly structured network. It happens rarely (because $n! \gg m$) in a random network structure—but it does happen. The minimum average chain would occur not in a random structure, but in one designed to minimize wasted links. However, when $n! \gg m$, the random structure will depart from that situation only to a small extent.

14. Hammer, M. *Social access*; Wasserman, S. "Random directed graph distributions and the triad census in social networks." *Journal of Mathematical Sociology* 5 (1977): 61–86.
15. Hunter, J., Shotland, R. L. "Treating data collected by the small world method as a Markov process." *Social Forces* 52 (1974): 321–32; White, H. "Search parameters for the small world problem." *Social Forces* 49 (1970): 259–64.
16. Warner, W. L. *Yankee city*. New Haven, CT: Yale University Press, 1963.
17. Deutsch, K. "Shifts in the balance of communication flows." *Public Opinion Quarterly* 20 (1956): 143–60; and idem. *Nationalism and social communication*. Cambridge, MA: MIT Press, 1966.
18. Gurevich, M. *The social structure*.
19. Rosenthal, H. *Acquaintances and contacts of Franklin Roosevelt*. Unpublished B. S. thesis, MIT.
20. Granovetter, M. *Getting a job: A study of contacts and careers*. Cambridge, MA: Harvard University Press, 1974.
21. The $n = A t^x$ fitted curve for this author's ogive reached that level in just five years, but without taking account of forgetting.
22. Wasserman, S. "Random directed graph distributions."

6

American Politics:
Congress and Its Constituents

with Raymond Bauer and Lewis Dexter

Most of this study has been devoted to establishing the facts on the information and attitudes that were present and how they were distributed among the population. We have examined who believed and who said what. The sources from which they acquired such information have often been a matter in which we have relied on inference, the effects of it almost always so. As we now sum up our conclusions, it is to these inferences that we turn. We wish in the closing pages not so much to review the facts as to take note of patterns in the effects of communications and most particularly of those patterns which probably apply wherever men are reaching national decisions under the impact of persuasive messages from a multitude of global sources.

A New Look at Communication

Perhaps the most important thing we learned is that individual communications act on people more as triggers than as forces. Students of communication working in psychological laboratories have experimented with the interrelations of several variables, for example, the contents of a communication, the characteristics of the experimental subjects who hear it, and the response of these subjects to the message in it. That kind of analysis lends itself to metaphorical description as a vector model. The direction of behavior observed in the experiment is

From *American Business and Public Policy: The Politics of Foreign Trade* (1963), by Raymond Baver, Ithiel de Sola Pool, and Lewis A. Dexter.

FIGURE 6.1
The Vector Model of Persuasion

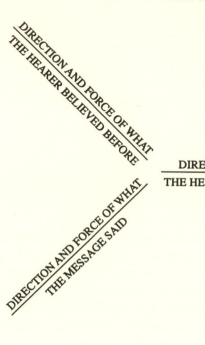

DIRECTION AND FORCE OF WHAT
THE HEARER BELIEVED OR DID AFTER

treated as a resultant of the attitudes of the subject beforehand and of the contents of the message stimulus.

That vector model is not necessarily naive. It does not treat propaganda as all-powerful, as do some popular writers on persuasion these days. The model allows appropriate weight to inertia against change rooted in the hearer's prejudices and made effective by mechanisms of psychological defense.

Our data add one more to the large number of case studies in which mechanisms of selective exposure and perception have been documented. As others have before us,[1] we, too, found that persons read and heard expositions of the views they already believed. Protectionists attended to protectionists, liberal traders to liberal traders.[2] That finding can be fitted into the vector model; it characterized the vectors which impinge upon one another.

The vector model also encompasses findings as subtle as the "sleeper effect," in which the fact that messages come from disapproved sources is gradually forgotten, while their contents come to be accepted. The vector pattern which expresses that finding shifts through time, so that vectors which were earlier opposed to each other come to be seen as having the same direction.

What phenomena do not fit this vector model of communication effects? Let us take a situation we noted early in the volume. There, we found that, among the general population, liberalism on foreign trade was highly correlated with education and social studies. The lower in the social spectrum one looked, the more latent protectionists one found and also the more people unaware of the foreign trade issue. Under such conditions, any propaganda campaign which increased popular attention to the issue would probably thereby increase manifest protectionist sentiment by bringing otherwise apathetic persons, who tended to have a disproportionate number of latent protectionists among them, into the area of discourse. That would be true whether the campaign which alerted the public was conducted on behalf of protection or conducted, as by the League of Women Voters, on behalf of freer trade. The direction of the stimulus in such a situation matters little. What matters more is that the reservoir of uninformed protectionism at the bottom of the cultural ladder is apt to be tapped by any campaign sufficiently vigorous to catch the attention of the whole public. Any sort of popular propaganda on foreign trade matters could trigger the protectionist potential.

We have cited another example of a situation where the metaphor of a trigger releasing a fixed potential (in determining the character of which the trigger plays no part) seems more relevant than the metaphor of vectors. Republican electoral campaigning in 1954, whether the contents were free trade or protectionist served to strengthen protectionist efforts, for a Republican majority in Congress would have served to bring some of the most powerful and protectionist congressman into leading positions on the appropriate committees. In a local constituency contest between a protectionist Democrat and a free trade Republican, protectionists would have been well advised to vote for the free trader, and free traders for the protectionist, not only with an eye to close committee votes, but also to the power which the leadership of a Congressional committee may have on the molding of public opinion.

In both these examples, the reversal of the stimulus content in the response content is the result of a social mechanism. In neither case is the vector model of individual behavior denied. In the first example, League of Women Voters propaganda, for instance, might make each individual more liberal than he was before, but have the effect of activating a larger number of slightly modified protectionists than of slightly accentuated free traders. A similar thing may also happen within the psyche of a single individual if that psyche contains several discrete and not fully consonant attitudes.

Take, for example, the New Anglia businessman who believed in protection in principle but for whom the immediate problem is that he was using imported residual fuel oil at the same time of the Simpson bill discussion. Protectionist literature from the National Coal Association on the cost difference between coal and imported fuel oil designed to show why coal needs protection could well mobilize his awareness of his interests in cheap imported fuel oil. He might well be stimulated by the propaganda to express general protectionism in the occasional context of civic discussions, but in his office he is organized to act on the concrete business problem. The office mechanisms are geared so that a stimulus supporting his general views would, as its primary effect, mobilize action on matters of specific business importance. If these happen to require that he go contrary to his own generalized attitudes and those of the stimulus communication, no matter. Furthermore, since the action of advocating one side of an issue generally tends to shift the actor toward belief in the views on behalf of which he acts, the net effect of propaganda on its recipient's attitudes may be indeterminate in those instances where it causes him to act contrary to the persuasive message of the stimulus material.

Specific action by a businessman or politician contrary to his overall views was a common phenomenon. It is not clear to us whether a majority of letters to Congress from our generally antiprotectionist survey-respondents were anti- or protectionist. Since they were more apt to write on specific business problems than on their more general views, the net weight of their correspondence may have been to undercut their general views.

What we have been saying does not deny the vector image of communication. It merely adds some important complications. First, there lies latent in individuals a great collection of traces of previous communications. Any new communication may serve to change this massive structure only imperceptibly, but it may at the same time set it into action in directions determined by the structure itself more than by the trigger stimulus.

Second, the event triggered within the system may itself have more effect on the system than does the original stimulus. Arguing for one's own views in reply to a challenge may have more effect on one than does the challenge.

Third, within an individual many latent attitudes may be simultaneously present. The structure of social controls and social relations may make some of them easier to express than others. Thus, even stimuli which have a persuasive effect on a man's thought may trigger opposite expressions.

Fourth, where a stimulus is addressed to a population of individuals, structural determinants may result in its mobilizing different proportions of those who agree and those who disagree with it. If it mobilized more of those who disagree, the stimulus may boomerang.

The image of the communications process with which we emerged from this and other studies is that communication is one input into a complex sociopsychological system. The effect of the communication on the system is, to a greater degree than is usually acknowledged, a function of the structure of that system. The impact of a given communication is of itself essentially indeterminate. Effects can be predicted only if one has quite detailed knowledge of the state of the system into which the communication is being fed.

Thus, the study of communications in real-life situations is a study of complex structural facts of society. It is not enough to examine a message flow between the black boxes. One needs to know the transforming characteristics of the black boxes.

We looked inside five sets of black boxes which constituted the system of foreign trade discussion: (1) the individual businessman as reader, traveler, communicator; (2) the business firm, small, medium, and large; (3) the communities in which the businessman lives; (4) trade associations and lobbies; and (5) Congress. What we have learned about the behavior of each of those as it finds itself in complex transactions involving its own purposes and the environment of the outside world—global, national, and local?

To the individual businessman, knowledge of the outside world came in a number of ways. It came in part through the printed word, but what came that way was surprisingly general and unfocused. Our respondents read *Time, Business Week, The Wall Street Journal, The New York Times,* and other such journals. They read a great deal. They also do research in published sources. They read what the editors chose to provide. Even men with wide foreign business did not read publications from the places where they carried on that business. Knowledge of foreign economic affairs came either from the most general new sources or, more vividly, from correspondence and personal experience.

In the interpersonal communication network on which businessmen rely for making specific decisions, knowing a man who knows is more important than knowing of a source that has the information. The mails, the telegraph, and the telephone bring knowledgeable men from anywhere in the world into an effective businessman's immediate contact net. By translating the percentages of men exposed to various communications into a rough time series measure, we can get a picture of what volume of communications on the specifics of foreign trade comes to the average business leader. Such a translation of percentages into frequencies is, we must emphasize, only a presentational device, for it is subject to statistical fallacies. We make this rough translation in order to arrive at a partially postulated ideal type. Every few days, an American businessman will spot some item on foreign trade policy as he skims in a cursory way through his newspaper or news magazine. Ninety percent of the big businessmen and 16 percent of the small had heard of the Randall Commission report: 74 percent of the big businessmen and 59 percent of the small had heard of President Eisenhower's message on foreign economic policy, both of these being recent events. But it is only about half a dozen times a year that a big business executive will read an article or listen to a speech specifically on that topic, and the head of a firm with only 100 to 1,000 employees will seriously inform himself in that way perhaps twice a year. Once a year, the typical big business executive will also attend a meeting at which the topic is foreign business. The smaller businessman may do that only once every three years. About as often again, each of these men will find himself at another meeting at which this topic is part of the business. In addition, about twice a year, the business executive of either size of firm finds himself in a discussion of this topic with some acquaintance who is not a business associate. Four times a year, the big businessman will have a similar conversation with a business associate outside his firm, the small businessman will also discuss these matters with his foreign trade manager; this is a less typical event for a small businessman. Every few months, the big businessman also has a discussion of such matters with some other official of his firm, something which the typical smaller businessman does about twice a year. All in all, purposive communication activities going beyond a review of the day's news and dealing with foreign trade and related matters are engaged in by an ideal-type head of a major American business firm about once every two weeks. A similar head of a smaller firm may engage in such communication less than once a month. About two-thirds of these communication events are conversations.

Of all channels of information about the world abroad, one of the most significant was travel. The heads of firms whom we studied are a highly traveled group of men. They go abroad an average of once every two years. And, what is more important, those who frequently travel abroad behave quite differently from those whose horizons have not risen above their provincial environment.

Those who do not travel much behave to a certain extent as some critics of our study told us all businessmen would. "Tell me what a man makes and I will tell you where he stands on foreign trade," is what we were told. For those businessmen who have not traveled abroad, one can do that fairly well. They answer questions on national policy in the role of a spokesman for a particular firm. But not so the men who had traveled. For them, prediction from product to viewpoint was less feasible. In the course of their experience, they had changed their frame of reference. It was not that they had acquired the foreign views with which they came into contact. On the contrary, travel placed them in the role of spokesmen for America in a foreign environment. In that broadened role, they learned to speak for a self-interest that went beyond their particular industry. They became more internationalist in the sense that they took more foreign facts into account in their calculations, but in another sense, they became more nationalist. They came to answer questions in the light of what seemed to them the interests of America in the world, not the interest of one firm in America.

The Concept of Self-Interest

One way to describe this book is as an attempt to relate the study of communication to the study of economic man.

The world of social service has been divided between users of two different models of man. In most of psychology and sociology, including the study of communication, men are seen as subject to influence. They are the objects of action by causal forces. Conditioning stimuli, punishments and rewards, persuasive devices produce predictable attitudes and behavior in them. Economics had proceeded by a different model. Men are seen as rational, maximizing animals, and the scientist attempts to deduce what a maximizer ought to do to live up to the maximizing postulates. Sometimes maximizing theories assume that what he ought to do is what he will do.

In this study, we have tried to make the empirical-influence model and the teleological-maximizing model meet. The student of communications will describe the formation of attitudes in a businessman as the result of propaganda stimuli to which he is subjected. The student of the economic man will see his actions as determined by his economic goals. Which way is it? Are the economic views of businessmen myths which their culture has instilled in them or are they rational calculations?

The answer is that these two alternatives are not opposed. In fairly complex ways, they are interrelated. The influence model and the maximizing mode are simultaneously true for the behavior of businessmen.

Businessmen do, indeed, follow their own self-interest. They do it consciously and continuously. It is a rare businessman who says, "My business would be helped by protection, but the national interest calls for freer trade. I yield before higher considerations than my pocketbook." That happened a few times in our sample of observations. More often, rationalization justified the pursuit of self-interest. By that statement, however, we do not mean that each man started with a fixed self-interest and that such other considerations as his views of the national interest yielded to it. On the contrary, it is our conviction that a man's self-interest is as vague a concept as is that of national interest. Self-interest, too, can be redefined. Rationalization means viewing what is self-serving and what is good as identical. That satisfying state is sometimes achieved by changing the image of the good to confirm to perceived self-interest. But the identity can as well be established by changing one's beliefs as to what is self-serving.

To say that a man's goal is promotion of his self-interest is a purely formal and tautological assertion. A man's interest lies in the achievement of whatever it is he desires. Interest, in that respect, is like the Aristotelian concept of the good as an end or the economic concept of utility. That which is sought is the good; that which is desired has utility. The statement that men seek their self-interest asserts a truth about behavior, but the truth is only that men seek that which they seek. The truth asserted is that behavior is purposeful. What can be conceived of as self-interest is as varied as are men.

In the calculations of self-interest that occurred continuously among our subjects, the aspects of the conception that varied included *whose* self- interest, in the light of *which facts*, and *over what time periods*.

Consider, first, whose self-interest is maximized. Certainly, it is seldom the interest of the physically individual human animal. The executives we interviewed viewed themselves merely as agents of groups. Corporation presidents like to comment that they are only hired hands. Their proper goal is not personal enrichment from the treasury of the company, but the advancing of a collectivity which is designated as "the firm."

But "the firm" is a vague concept. Is it the stockholders only, or is it also employees, management, and customers? We recall the case of the protectionist firm which stood to benefit from a reversal of American liberal trade policies if its balance sheet were taken as the criterion of self-interest. But the firm in question happened to be controlled by British investors. Where did the self-interest of the firm lie? Was it in an improved balance sheet at the expense of an American economic policy which would have adverse economic consequences for British business, or was it in the acceptance of a poorer return on this one investment under an economic policy of clear advantage to the alien majority but not to all of the stockholders? For the sake of the historical record, we may mention that it never even occurred to the American management of the firm to take account of the fact that the major stockholders were British. The immediate balance sheet of the American firm was the sole criterion they used. That is a fact of communications and ideology which helped define what "the firm" meant and what its self-interest meant in this instance.

Consider, also, the cases where a man's self-identification was as a manufacturer and not as a merchant, or where his feeling for his employees prescribed his conception of self-interest. A lace manufacturer had all the merchandising outlets required to do well in selling either his own lace or lace bought abroad. But the very suggestion that he close his plant and be an importer brought fury. It would be at the cost of the jobs of his men. And, besides, he said with pride, "We are manufacturers, not merchants." He too was protecting the self-interest of a firm, but a firm conceived as a certain body of men or even as a physical plant, not as undifferentiated sum of financial capital which could be used in whatever way would make the most money. The balance sheet did not define the firm for him.

Perhaps one might also say that our lace manufacturer was serving a self-interest that was measured in pride and respect and that went beyond money. The point is too obvious to labor. Not only must we ask whose self-interest is to be maximized, but, also, what are the social values in terms of which it is measured?

Then there is the matter of time discounts. Is it a short of long run goal that the maximizer seeks? What is the trade-off between a relatively likely small short-run loss and a possible large long-run gain? These are at least two time discounts operating; one for waiting and one for the uncertainty that the future introduces. What these discount rates are for any individual is something not for maximizing theory but for a theory of personal psychology to explain.

The time discounts which we found operating, particularly in smaller firms, were remarkably large. One of the great weaknesses of the liberal trade side was that a clearly predictable short-run loss to foreign competition was far more productive of vigorous business action than a possible much larger ultimate gain in foreign business from a liberal policy. The long-run prospect of gain was too indirect, too "iffy," to be a basis of action for men with an American business psychology.

In very large firms, that was less true. A giant firm might aim, not at maximizing immediate profit, a policy which might only call antitrust action down on its head, but rather at securing a stable 6 to 8 percent return. Plans in such firms are often made on a twenty-year basis.

We have so far considered three aspects of the formal concept of self-interest which help make concrete this otherwise highly abstract concept. They are: who is the self, what value does he maximize, and over what time period? The answers given by any person to these questions are obviously subject to the operation of influence. By changing businessmen's notions about these matters, communications change policies without in the least modifying the formal feature—that action remains the pursuit of business interests.

All this is even more clearly true of a fourth concretizing aspect of purposive behavior—information. To have knowledge about a market for a product may justify entering it. A man without such information would be following his business interest by refraining from investment. Indeed, one of the greatest weaknesses of the liberal trade side was the prevailing ignorance among American businessmen about foreign markets and the cost to them of acquiring such information. Over and over we were told that "the American market is our primary one." Foreign opportunities might exist, but they were not worth the trouble of learning about them. There is a wide dissatisfaction in the American business community with the available means of acquiring information about foreign markets and foreign opportunities for investment. U.S. commercial attaches are widely dismissed by businessmen as "incompetents who never met a payroll." Published sources are, as we have noted, not well used. Specialized consulting services are only now beginning to function widely. The best information source, in the eyes of most businessmen, is to go abroad and to talk there to trusted business colleagues.

Under such conditions, foreign investments and promotions occur partly by chance. The presence within the management of a firm of a man with experience in a particular country is the most important factor in leading the firm into that country. In the absence of such contracts, an aura of uncertainty blocks action. It is not only uncertainty about the facts, but also uncertainty about whether it is worth the effort to get the facts. The calculation of self-interest depends both on the stock of knowledge already at hand and on a guess about which unknown facts might be worth acquiring. These are clearly social facts about the existing system of communications.

If the picture is, indeed, as we have just described it, then we can disregard as irrelevant and naive most arguments about the relative role of ideology and economics in influencing public policy decisions. The formal acts of economic calculation acquire their concrete content only through acts of communication and social influence. Conversely, economic calculation is one of the processes which occur inside the black boxes into which communications are fed. Neither a simple study of influence processes nor a simple study of economic interests without their interactions could have yielded much understanding of the behavior of our business respondents.

Structural Factors in Communication and Decision Making

We have looked thus far at the businessman as an individual and how structural facts about his life and role interact with the messages he receives to determine the decisions he makes.

But the businessman acts within the framework of the business firm. That framework is not uniform. In almost all our survey results, the most dramatic statistical differences were not those which interested us originally. They were differences between the large, medium, and small firms. These represent differing ways of life for their chief officers.

The head of a small firm, especially one with under 400 employees, is essentially a manager of operations. His look is inward, to problems of production, or, if outward, it is toward problems of marketing. He has few men in specialized staffs around him. In contrast, the head of a giant corporation deals most of the time with such staffs. Production has long since slipped from his immediate attention. He works with people, statistics, and memoranda, and not with things. The heads of large and small firms differ, too, in sociological characteristics: ethnic background, rural-urban origins, education, and the like. Thanks to their competence but even more to their staffs, the big businessman read more, know more, and do more, particularly with respect to the external environment.

On foreign economic matters, the heads of big firms are far better informed and more apt to be interested. On the other hand, they are likely to have conflicting interests in the various sectors of their companies. The heads of small firms are more often not at all interested in foreign economic issues. However, in the rare cases where foreign trade affects them, it can be a life-or-death matter.

The administrative structure of American corporations has some significant effect on their export-mindedness, and often unfavorably to liberal trade policies. In the first place, Canadian sales are generally under the sales manager, not under the export manager, and are not included in foreign trade calculation. Top management, when it quotes export figures, generally quotes export-department figures, disregarding Canada, the largest foreign customer. Second, the export manager, even in large firms where he heads a department, is not usually a vice president. He is apt to report to the president through the vice president of sales, the very man who is most concerned with foreign competition. Furthermore, since the United States levies import duties and not export duties, the effects of American tariffs on the problems of the export department are only indirect. Congressional action never threatens to tax export sales directly. At worst, tariff increases create a situation in which world markets might deteriorate, foreign countries might retaliate, or domestic costs might increase. But, since all these effects are still only possibilities, the export manager worries about them indecisively. Finally, the purchasing department, which might have the interest in tariff reduction, seldom even knows how much tariffs have contributed to the prices it pays. It usually has no competitive concern with duties. If a tariff results in higher price for a raw material or component part, it raises it for domestic industrial consumers alike, and this increase can be passed on in increased prices. Unless the firm's product faces the competition from foreign manufacturers or from functionally equivalent but not identically made products, a uniform price increase in the domestic market does it little harm. In that respect, there is no symmetry between the injury done the sales department by a cheap foreign import and that done the purchasing department by an expensive one.

All these structural facts deeply affect what American business leaders hear from within their firms and in turn what they say to the world. What they say is in large part said for them by others. Our study therefore moved from the businessman to the lobbies and associations which talk for them.

Here, once more, we found important structural facts influencing the message flow. The association must maintain a quasi-unanimity within themselves. Multipurpose organizations are hampered by fear of saying things which would offend some of their members. The focus of such organizations becomes internal morale-building activities instead of external representation.

The single-purpose organization does not suffer this limitation; it may become an aggressive lobby. But none of the lobbies we observed were the powerful monsters they are reputed to be. Under financed, they had to spend much of their time recruiting members and raising funds. Poorly staffed and overworked, they generally became effective, not as lobbies persuading public officeholders, but as service bureaus auxiliary to the efforts of those public servants.

Indeed, in many instances, and the most important ones, the relation between officeholder and lobby is exactly the reverse of what the public thinks. The protectionist leadership in the United States clearly lay inside the United States Congress. Congressmen Richard Simpson and Cleveland Bailey and Senators Malone and Eugene Millikin were far more important defenders of a waning ideology than were the more or less inert American Tariff League or the clamorous but relatively unsophisticated Strackbein committee. The business interests that sought protection were, of course, an essential ingredient in the picture, since congressmen for whom protection was a major platform plank greeted every business request as one more piece of evidence of the need for protection and one more opportunity to gain political supporters. It was the congressman, however, who opened the path to business pleas, and it was he who stimulated and guided the protectionist lobbies in their every effective move. The lobby became the congressman's publicity bureau. Indeed, without a congressman working with it, a lobby found it difficult to do anything the press would consider newsworthy.

On the liberal trade side, it was only slightly different. There, the lobby spoke largely for the White House. It was organized at the White House's request. It tried to act as the White House's private arm. Without White House support, it would have been a mere shell, were it to have existed at all. Indeed, its frustration and relative failure in 1953–1955 was very largely because the White House and Clarence Randall, the president's special aide, adhered to the letter and spirit of the law against executive lobbying. Randall had scruples against covert manipulation of a private lobby. He waited frustrated for the private lobby to start a tidal wave of public opinion which would push upon him.

It rarely happens that way. It never happened in the events we studied. The time the Coleman committee became effective in the 1953–1955 period was when Senator Albert Gore launched a legislative drive and called on the committee to provide staff, publicity, and contracts. Then, with a public figure to lead them, their staff and technical skills became meaningful.

What we have said about lobbies already indicates our view of the role of Congress. Congressmen have a great deal more freedom than is ordinarily attributed to them. The complexities of procedure, the chances of obfuscation, the limited attention constituents pay to any one issue, and the presence of countervailing forces all leave the congressman relatively free on most issues. He may feel unfree because of the great demands on his time, but, consciously or unconsciously, by his own decisions as to what he chooses to make of his job he generates the pressures which impinge upon him. He hears from voters about those things in which he himself chooses to become involved.

The great decisions a congressman must make are not so much those determining the position to take on individual bills, but rather decisions as to what kind of congressman to be, what sorts of things to specialize in, how to allocate time, and how to project himself into a role of leadership.

A congressman needs issues in the public eye. He needs people who want favors from him. His stock in trade is his power to take action on things citizens care about. If there were no clamorous demands giving him the opportunity to show his worth, he would have to create them. And that, indeed, is what he habitually does.

Congress is not a passive body, registering already-extant public views forced on its attention by public pressures. Congress, second only to the president, is, rather, the major institution for initiating and creating political issues and projecting them into a national civic debate. Congressmen are often the leaders in that debate.

To say, as we are doing, that congressmen create public opinion is not to deny that they must also attend to it closely. But the attention a congressman pays to what his constituents think is a complex matter. Constituents seldom come to clear conclusions on technically feasible steps within the congressman's competence early enough to urge action that could affect legislation. Public opinion is more often a reaction when the decision process is all over; it likes or dislikes the result. The intelligent congressman looks to his constituents, not for instructions, but for clues as to what their reactions might be in future, hypothetical circumstances. The congressman listens, not only to actual constituents conveying injunctions to him, but also to constituents whom his imagination anticipates and to their reactions to future events which he can foresee better than they can.

There is, then, no straight-line process in which businessmen receive messages about foreign economic affairs, respond by messages to their trade associations, which in their turn respond by messages to congressmen, who to some measure respond by action. The low saliency of foreign trade matters and the competition of other matters for time means that at every level there is only a limited amount of actual communication and a great deal of speculative imagination of what each relevant group must be thinking and feeling. The flow of information is going both ways. For example, the messages about foreign economic affairs often start with the congressman or the trade association and are spread via domestic media. Except by means of foreign travel, little substantial foreign information comes directly to the businessman. The people who most actively frame the issues to be discussed and debated are the symbolic leaders in Congress and the executive. They generate the public concern which come back as pressures on them.

Decision Making as a Social Process

One way or another, decision making is much talked about by academics and by practical men of affairs, much observed, and sometimes even achieved. The predominant tendency is to regard it as an intellectual process which usually proceeds according to a certain formal order, such as definition of the problem, consideration of alternate courses of action, data gathering, and selection of the most appropriate course of action. This is far from what happens. Not only do these intellectual steps fail to exhaust the factors which determine decision, but they falsify even what takes place on the strictly intellectual level. But consideration of the intellectual aspects of problem solving is a digression. What most impressed us was the extent to which decision making is a social process and embedded in a stream of social processes.

In one respect, the assertion that decision making is a social process is more or less self-evident. In business organizations or in Congress, certain social units—committees or officers—are formally designated to deal with such a matter as tariff legislation. The composition of such groups, their formal mandate in the larger organization, and the type and volume of other business such a group has assigned to it all affect the outcome of any single issue. We have already discussed at some length how structural features of American business firms, of the business community, and of Congress affected the outcome of the events we studied.

In addition, we learned that we could not isolate foreign trade policy as an issue with anything like the ease that we expected. What a man said about foreign trade policy was very much a function of his involvement in other issues. General Motors and DuPont could well have been more active than they were, had it not been for the antitrust suit in which they figured. The delegation of farmers in the Midwest did not raise the issue of foreign trade policy with Representative Stubborn because they chose to expend their finite resources of good will on issues which they had a chance of influencing him.

In 1954, the Ways and Means Committee of the House failed to hold hearings on the Reciprocal Trade Act for a variety of reasons which bore mainly on other issues: the committee, and especially its chairman, Congressman Reed, were tired from the long tax hearings, and the White House was reluctant to put pressure on Reed, in part because of its desire to maintain good relations with the conservative wing of the Republican Party.

Any given issue must compete with other issues for those scarce resources which determine the outcome: time, energy, attention, money, manpower, and good will. Where a given issue stands in priority affects not only the fight for resources but also the whole manner of its handling. If a matter has very low priority, it gets no attention, and nature is left to take its course. This was true of certain members of the general public (about 50 percent) who did not know that a fight over trade legislation existed. Or an issue such as the Reciprocal Trade Act may be accorded a status of second priority. This not only affects who handles the problem—second-rank officers rather than the top business brass—but also which courses of action may be attempted. In a fight of second priority, one must be careful not to take actions which would jeopardize higher-priority objectives.

An issue not merely consumes resources, but is often also an opportunity for creating them. Some congressmen went along with the leadership on foreign trade solely to generate good will which they could expend on objectives of higher priority to them. The skillful operator is alert to these opportunities to obtain resources. He may, for example, place a supplicant in his debt by pretending to be coerced into doing what he wants to do in the first place.[3]

In general, an issue of relatively low priority is likely to be used to generate resources for use on issues of higher priority. But, since priority is itself a relative matter, we cannot assess the priority given any one issue except by reference to all issues which compete or might compete for position.

We have already spoken of good will as one of the resources that affect the outcome of issues. Good will is but an aspect of the large problem of maintaining effective social relationships. Since virtually every decision involves working with or through other people, whether in business, in the public arena, or within Congress, it is necessary for each actor to zealously guard his relations to these others. What he will guard depends somewhat on his own style. He may prefer to use fear rather than good will in order to influence others to go his way. But, whatever mode of relationship he prefers, he must apply himself to keeping it in working order. This means that only on very occasional issues of highest priority can he act as a truly free agent. In all other instances, he must take care to keep his supply of good will, respect, fear, and the like, at an adequate level and, furthermore, to act in a sufficiently patterned manner so that others will know what to expect of him and that they can count on him. This does not mean that he will always do what is predictable, but that he will do so in such situations and to such an extent that others will continue to respond as he wishes them to. Thus, he cannot often violate agreements, or others will stop making agreements with him; nor can he fail to carry through on threats, or others will lose fear of his threats.

In such respects, the social aspects of decision making constrain a man's freedom of action. But, for the knowledgeable man, the social aspect of decision making also offers opportunities. We have mentioned how a congressman may make it virtually impossible for his constituents to know how he stood on a given issue. The business administrator can and does do the same thing. How did DuPont stand on protection? It seems impossible to be certain. An important officer, Frederick G. Singer, was active in the American Tariff League in 1953–1955, but the company per se took no stand. It could be maintained, and quite possible correctly—that Singer was acting as a private citizen, even though many knowledgeable people thought of him as acting for the company.

It often seemed to us that the term "decision making" was a misnomer. What we saw did not often warrant so intellectual-sounding a label. At some point, it was possible to say that an issue existed, though how it arose was not always clear. For example, in tracing the history of the Committee for a National Trade Policy, we identified several streams of influence. Several people were trying to organize several different things. It might be possible to specify when and under what circumstances the question was first posed: "Should we form just such a committee?" But people were working on the matter long before that idea came to exist as one alternative about which to decide.

Not only may the formulation of a problem not have taken place deliberately, but the decision, also, may not have been deliberate. Under the pressure of circumstances, a man does something that seems small, and suddenly he finds himself committed to something much larger than he envisioned. He may give a small speech and suddenly find himself a spokesman. Or the actions of subordinates may create conditions which determine his line of action. His decision is to recognize the inevitable.

We have pointed out that in 1954–1955 the CNTP became more of an educational society than the hard-bitten lobbying group it had set out to be. Was this the result of a decision? Decisions were made about fund raising which failed to produce the funds thought necessary for the original plan of action. Decisions were made to hire certain personnel. At a later date, as a result of those decisions, the CNTP existed as an organization with personnel and funds of types which determined what it did. Was there a decision about debating versus lobbying?

In any study such as ours, the question of whether a decision has been made at all should be regarded as a moot point. It is an issue that could be settled on empirical grounds in each instance. The label "decision making" probably cannot be abandoned entirely, but it is necessary to call attention to how far this phrase fails to describe what happens in a social group between the time that an issue is recognized and the time that one or more persons are committed to a course of action.

Sometimes, the length of time between these steps may itself be so compressed that a person may first realize that he is confronted with an issue when he finds himself already committed to a course of action. A congressman may make a routine commitment to support a given piece of legislation and find only afterward that one or more of his constituents are adversely affected by it. In such instances, the retrievability of a decision becomes a crucial issue in its own right.

One of the ways is which the usual model of decision making differs from the model which emerged from this study is its assumption of much more clear-cut outcomes than apparently occur in many situations. The passage of the Reciprocal Trade Act in 1955 proved not to be the culmination of a fight. It turned out to be but one phase of an ongoing controversy and an ongoing process of Congressional activities. While we in designing our study were looking forward only to the final vote on the act, the members of Congress were setting their sights on other legislation coming up in that session of Congress and also on the next time when the Reciprocal Trade Act and other foreign trade legislation would be considered. In the end, both sides claimed victory, and even outside observers were not in agreement as to which side had won. It would be difficult to prove that any decision was actually made on trade liberalization in 1955. The passage of the bill was a decision only about procedures to be followed in the future conduct of the controversy. The same thing could be said of the 1962 law, the operation of which was bound to depend heavily on the policies of the Common Market. The 80 percent provision, allowing some tariffs to be cut to zero, will affect a significant number of commodities only if Great Britain joins the EEC. That was still an imponderable at the time of the bill's passage. The Reciprocal Trade Act and the Trade Expansion Act are sets of directives and licenses to the executive branch. The directives were unclear, the licenses varied. There was no way of knowing for certain just how the Tariff Commission, the president, and other parts of the executive branch would interpret the provisions of this legislation. Such indeterminacy is not equally present in all legislation, but it is widespread.

We said previously that it should be regarded as a moot point whether a decision has in any meaningful sense been made. Even when, as in the case we studied, some decision has been made in a meaningful sense, it still does not mean that the decision should be regarded as the terminal phase of a sequence of events. The decision may be a workable formula designed to keep the decision-making apparatus operating on this and related issues. It may be something between a resolution of conflict and a tabling of issues, with perhaps a little bit of passing the buck involved.

Social Science and the Political Process

Any study of political matters, and especially a study of the relationship of business to politics, is likely to be interpreted as in itself a political document. Ideas are weapons, and, even where the analyst or scholar protests his neutrality and loyalty to the facts, other people are likely to handle his ideas and reports and findings as weapons—weapons which they can use, weapons directed against themselves, or weapons helpful in parlor games for the entertainment of themselves and friends. "Scientific inquiry," in other words, "has latent as well as realized functions, inadvertent as well as intended results. This dual and uncontrollable quality of scientific inquiry…"[9] is sometimes, perhaps usually, influential in determining how a report is written and what its authors emphasize. We have found ourselves in preliminary versions of this book accused of forging weapons for purposes which we did not have in mind.

Ideas are weapons, not only for or against relatively specific legislative proposals, but, regardless of the intentions of the scientist or scholar, for supporting or upsetting habitual ways of looking at the segment of reality which is under discussion. A report which suggests that reality operates in a manner differing from the reader's expectations engenders more or less discomfort. And, depending on his previous expectations, a reader is likely to interpret the report, if it deals with political matters, as having a conservative or a liberal orientation.

Our experience is that readers tend to feel that our orientation is conservative. We have found objection not so much to our findings as to the fact that the findings might be correct. There are those who would prefer that the facts we report not be so.

We have reflected on the unhappy reaction from some of our professional colleagues. As a matter of fact and intention, our work is not, so far as we can see, conservative in any traditional sense of the term, nor is it liberal. But, for the case which we have studied, it tends to cast doubt on the stereotype of pressure politics, of special interests effectively expressing themselves and forcing politicians either to bow to their dictates or to fight back vigorously. Our presentation of the congressman as one who is part of a transactional process, who can himself signal what communications he wants, and who has a good deal of latitude in those which he heeds is not precisely in accord with the stereotyped picture. Nor do we portray the lobbyist and the business interest conventionally when we show them faced by many priorities, often deliberately restrained in exerting pressure or woefully ignorant of where pressure could be profitable exerted.

What we believe we are doing is extending and qualifying certain insights recently ably restated by V. O. Key in his *Public Opinion and American Democracy*[5] and earlier by Bernard Berelson in *Voting*[6] and still earlier by Walter Lippmann in *Public Opinion*[7] and the *The Phantom Public*.[8]

Those authors compared a popular version of the theory of democracy with facts of democratic politics.

> What Mr. Lippmann did was to destroy a straw man. He did it thoroughly. He refused the more extravagant beliefs about the role of the average man in self governance...demolished whatever illusion existed that "the public" could be...equipped to decide the affairs of the average man...exhausted his energies earning a livelihood...looked at the comics rather than attempting to inform himself.... Even if he were willing to devote his spare time to the study of public issues, the information available to him was both inadequate and unenlightening.[9]

Public opinion pollsters, by showing how many issues do not in fact get much public attention, and political behavior specialists, by showing how many issues are decided by a relatively small in-group, have confirmed this picture many times over.

But it was only with Berelson's concluding chapter in *Voting* that due recognition was given to positive functions that are served when voters behave as human beings, not as stereotypes of good citizenship. A society where no one was apathetic about any issue, Berelson showed, would be chaos, indeed. The citizens of a democracy may not behave as some theorists wish they would, but it is thanks to the ways that they do behave that democracy functions.

If Lippmann, Berelson, Key, and others have shown that, for good or ill, the ordinary man does not conform to Rousseauian prescriptions of citizenship, what we have done here is to say a similar thing about his political betters. They, too, fulfill their roles while uninformed, preoccupied, and motivated by adventitious private goals. If such facts disqualify men for a role in affairs of state, it is difficult to say who would be qualified. We believe we have shown that, the rush of events being what it is and the limitations of time and energy being what they are, no leading politician could meet the test. A political theory which expects a statesman to act with that degree of deliberation on all issues which he might at best achieve for one issue at a time is clearly unrealistic.

We have often asked ourselves why it is that most existing literature portrays the policy decision process in what we came to feel was an overly intellectualized way. Certainly it is not because previous writers were less aware that we of the complexity of reality or because they failed to note how often policymakers depart from norms of orderly action. Rather than failure of knowledge, we feel that it is an urge by writers to make the descriptions of events neat and satisfying which accounts for the way decision processes have been described.

Most political behavior studies have, for example, tended to concentrate on the cases where someone made a purposeful decision or was thought to have done so, not the cases where there was nothing to say or report because of inaction, indifference, or ignorance. And, in general, students of political science ask questions in such a way that people are encouraged to report something happening, rather than inattention, indifference, unconcern, ignorance. American social science has tended to show business as an active, aggressive agent, always taking part in politics for its own purposes. Such studies as A. Eugene Staley's *War and the Private Investor,*[10] which present a different picture, have attracted too little attention and been almost forgotten.

Now, our methods of interviewing focused on communication, and we were as much interested in non communication as in communication, in what did not happen as in what did. Accordingly, we found that, in a number of instances where something could have happened, where a special interest could have been effective, where a politician might have been under pressure, inaction or ignorance seemed to prevail. We found businesses leaning over backward not to exert pressure; we found politicians discounting or utterly unaware of pressure campaigns directed against them; we found politicians inviting, rather than resisting, pressures. In other words, we think we differ from most previous reporters of pressure group behavior in that we asked what did not happen, as well as what did.

Another consideration that shaped the earlier literature is the appeal of melodrama. We have suggested that pressure is sometimes a phantom or at least weak and ineffective. That is not what political scientists generally observe nor what lobbyists, journalists, and congressmen themselves report. Why? A journalist can make a much more interesting and credible story about heavy pressure than about the tepid sort of relationship presented in our chapters. A congressman, eager either to build himself up or denigrate his opponents, can castigate the special interests and wicked lobbyists on the other side. A good many lobbyists have obvious enough self-serving reasons for building themselves up and, what is not generally realized, much stronger reasons for building up the forces of evil on the other side. We have sacrificed drama by stressing complexities and qualifications.

In a carefully restricted and precisely defined sense, the introduction of complexities and qualifications into a simple picture may be regarded as conservative. But, of course, this is not the major basis for the objections which we have experienced. Social scientists do not generally object to complexities!

A more important source of discomfort is that we are questioning cherished notions in the conventional criticism of society.

We have said that pressure groups which we observed were more inept than we had anticipated. This will presumably be interpreted as a defense of such groups, since it implies that pressure groups taken individually are not as dangerous as they have been made out to be. It could, however, be taken as a criticism of the people who run these groups, and we expect that some of them will be irritated with us for our judgment of them.

We have minimized the role of such factors as evil intentions, crookedness, and cynicism. We have conveyed the impression that most of the men with whom we were in contact were convinced of the rectitude of their positions. This may also be taken as a defense of them, for it denies the easy assumption that the men on the other side are cynical opportunists. But almost every issue is sufficiently complicated for arguments to be made on both sides.

We have also suggested that the picture of congressmen as influenced by pressure groups is not always valid. The people supposed to make decisions, officeholders, often really do make decisions. Congress as a body can to a great extent be its own boss. This means that the notion that the special interests decide, a qualification some adopted to the notion that the people decide, in its turn needs qualification.

Furthermore, we have made statements which will be taken as a defense of big business as against small business. We find that the notion that big business interferes rudely and violently with the democratic process needs qualification. This notion is based on a long historical stream of writings, but, so far as our reporting goes, it was not true on the tariff in the period since 1953.

We also picture the heads of large firms as active in public affairs, well-informed, with a broad perspective. (For most American readers of books like this one, these are positively valued statements and will be taken as praise.) In general, it may be said that, the larger the firm is, the more concern its chief officers must have for the interaction of their own behavior and that of the economic, social, and political environment in which they operate. For one thing, their own actions may have predictable second-order consequences back on themselves via the economy as a whole. Also, once a business reaches a certain size, it acquires a good deal of social visibility. Because it can have an effect on the economy as a whole, public agencies keep an eye on it. This does not necessarily mean that every head of a large organization develops a social conscience. But he must at least acquire a sensitivity to the reactions of politicians who may capitalize on the social conscience of others.

The head of a big business firm has great potential for influencing public policy in the direction which he prefers. But, particularly in the past few decades, he has seen a growth of forces acting to constrain him from doing so and impelling him to be subtle in his political behavior. We know of no evidence that would enable us or anyone else to answer the questions of how these two opposing tendencies relate to each other summatively. But it is our suspicion that the relative power of big business in American politics has declined in the past fifty years and that the manner in which power is exercised has become more responsible. We believe it to be beyond controversy that the new situation of big business in American society demands qualities of mind on the part of the leaders of these big firms that make them generally closer in attitude and thinking to the intellectual community than are the heads of smaller firms. In general, the larger the firm, the more the head of the firm is forced by his role to think in broad economic, political, and social terms. This does not mean that he becomes a theorist, a term which many of them despise, but that he must attend to the same set of variables as do academic theorists.

There are certain trends in American social science—naturalism, functionalism, and transactionism—which are at present making themselves felt in the analysis of political phenomena. Each of them serves as a source of irritation to the reformer and the moralist, since they appear to be defenses of the status quo. Naturalism is simply a disposition to study phenomena in a non normative fashion. It is no more than the application of the scientific precept that one understands prior to evaluating. Functionalism[11] is a mode of social analysis that takes as its point of departure the notion that various social phenomena may be useful in the larger social context in ways that would not immediately strike the eye. Transactionism, among other things, obscures the direction of causality by stressing the interdependence of events that were once viewed more simply. An example would be our proposition that the congressman determines the sort of letters that come to him just as certainly as the sort of letters that come to him determine the behavior of the congressman.

Those trends in social analysis could lead toward conservatism. For instance, our contention that pressure groups are not as effective as sometimes alleged could lead to complacency. The notion that congressmen lead pressure groups as much as pressure groups influence congressmen could have a similar effect. The discovery of latent functions for a given phenomenon may be taken as a justification of that phenomenon. Thus, our proposition that many legislators find pressure groups to be useful sources of information might be interpreted as a justification of them. There is no more necessity for this conclusion that there is for interpreting the law of gravity as a reason for letting little old ladies fall into manholes. If things tend to fall to the earth at a given speed under given conditions, this knowledge is an excellent resource in our attempts to keep from falling those things that we wish not to fall. Similarly, our naturalistic knowledge of political and social phenomena can serve a normative purpose.

Another reason why our report may be interpreted as conservative is that we appear to approve, and certainly make no objection to, the political processes which we describe.

There are, indeed, values associated with the stability of any existing and tolerably benign political process. It can be argued that political processes are more important than specific political decisions. This notion is best exemplified in the Anglo-American legal tradition that the courts should operate according to due process of law, regardless of any extrinsic factors which lead judges and juries to feel subjectively certain of guilt, innocence, worthiness, or wickedness. There are points at which any of us would admit that results are more important than processes. Many Frenchmen felt that the problem of Algeria was more important for France to solve than it was for France to preserve normal parliamentary processes. Perhaps the issue of thermonuclear arms control is more vital than any institutional process of politics. But such issues must necessarily be few if a political system is to long survive.

The underlying proposition here is that political societies operate best when the political institutions are accepted by the consensus of the society and when they permit compromise, adjudication, bargaining, and deals. They operate best when sharp breaks in the customary way of doing things are rare and are introduced gradually. As Sir Walter Scott said, "All...good has its ratable proportion of evil. Even an admitted nuisance of ancient standing should not be abated without some caution."[12]

As individuals we have both enthusiasms and objections to various items in the several pieces of legislation passed between 1953 and 1962. But in this we are, so far as we can guess, simply in accord with every member of Congress who voted for the bills.

In particular, it seems to us that the escape clause as it operates cannot restore things to the status quo ante and merely adds an additional measure of uncertainty and instability and that "hope which deferred maketh the heart sick." We would prefer that before trade regulations or negotiations are set, those who are likely to be injured be given a stronger initial opportunity to seek relief, but, once a decision has been in effect for a year or more, action to reverse what is then the prevailing situation should be made more difficult or impossible. The prospect of unpredictable change via the escape clause has a most discouraging effect on business investment in trade expansion.

We have been particularly concerned with the problems of how American leaders learn about the outside world, how they integrate that which they learn with their own immediate concerns, and, finally, what leads them to action. We saw, and this fact makes some people unhappy, that the intelligent and influential men we studied seldom acted on the basis of ideology or conviction alone. In 1954–1955, the liberal trade plea that national interest had to put ahead of self-interest received passive acquiescence from most American businessmen. The majority of them has accepted the doctrine of internationalism. That acceptance was the prerequisite for the long-run success of liberal trade views and for the ultimate decay of protectionism. Immediate action required, however, more than general conviction. Action, to occur, had to be appropriate to a man's specific role. It also usually took place in response to a danger which it was the actor's job to combat. The protectionists understood this principle all through the decade and hard-headedly appealed to people in their business roles on the grounds of competitive threats. The Kennedy leadership in 1962, having also learned this lesson, reversed the liberal strategy. While doing less, perhaps, than the previous administration to build ideological capital for the future through dissemination of liberal trade doctrine, it did more of what counted in the short run, namely, pinpointed organization of those relatively few individuals whose role in life was such that it made sense for them to invest time, effort and good will in the issue. For ordinary citizens, as for congressmen, there are many good things to believe in. What determines actions is not the merits of an issue per se but its relation to the actor's chosen pattern of life. To understand a citizen's action, just as much as a congressman's action, one must look primarily at the man and his whole round of life, not at the issues taken in isolation. In 1962, as contrasted to 1955, the liberal trade leadership understood this principle and mobilized specific and appropriate business interest to respond to the new threat and challenge of the Common Market. Only when the liberal trade organizers learned thus to alert robust motives of perceived interests among people whose job it was to care did they translate vague internationalism into effective expression.

That may not be the way we would like to have seen it, but that is the way it was. The study of politics by American intellectuals has been too much confused by the indiscriminate mixing up of what should be and what is. A more realistic understanding of American politics may help those communicators who are striving for important social goals to work toward them effectively, not futilely. It may, we hope, enable readers who are seeking to improve American political processes to distinguish real dragons from false windmills.

Notes

1. For a handy review, see Hovland, Carl I. "Effects of the mass media on communication," in Lindsey, G. (ed.). *Handbook of social psychology*, second edition. Cambridge, MA: Addison-Wesley, 1954, pp. 1062–1103.
2. In qualification, we note that this proposition may not fully apply to those who have really serious responsibilities to attend to different views, e.g., members of the Ways and Means Committee or of the staffs of the CNTP or Strackbein committee.
3. Strategies more complex than simple advocacy of whatever one wants can be found increasingly discussed in the literature on nonzero sum games and games with communication. Cf. Schelling, Thomas. *The strategy of conflict.* Cambridge, MA: Harvard University Press, 1960; Luce, Duncan; Raiffa, Howard. *Games and decisions.* New York: John Wiley & Sons, 1958.
4. Vincent, C. *Unmarried mothers.* New York: The Free Press, 1961, p. 263.
5. Key, V.O. *Public opinion and American democracy.* New York: Alfred A. Knopf, 1961.
6. Berelson, Bernard. *Voting.* Chicago: University of Chicago Press, 1954.
7. Lippmann, Walter. *Public opinion.* New York: Macmillan and Company, 1922.
8. Lippmann, Walter. *The phantom public.* New York: Macmillan and Company, 1929.
9. Key, V.O. *Public opinion and American democracy*, p. 5.
10. Staley, A. Eugene. *War and the private investor.* Chicago: University of Illinois Press, 1935.
11. For the discussion of the complications of functional analysis, see Davis, Kingsley. "The myth of functional analysis." *American Sociological Review* 24 (December 1959): 757–72.
12. *Guy Mannering*, chapter 6.

7

Trends in Content Analysis Today: A Summary

The previous chapters in this book have each dealt with the use of content analysis in a particular field of knowledge and usually in a particular way. The present chapter is an attempt to report what the men who wrote these chapters said when they confronted each other and each other's problems at the Allerton House conference. It is in short an attempt to seek out the areas of consensus, the common problems, the directions in which workers in the field of content analysis seemed to be moving. But this chapter is not a committee report. It is one man's view of what came out of the conference, and as such it will be stated as the author's exposition of the group's ideas with only occasional references to the conference as such or credits to the members and their individual divergences or individually derived thoughts which the author has freely and gratefully borrowed.

What the Volume Covers

For all the breadth of the topics discussed, their focus has been on one small area of the total range of problems with which content analysis may deal. Table 7.1 illustrates what we have discussed intensively and what we have skirted in discussion or touched on in at most one chapter.

Our interest has been in inference. That need not have been the case. We could have discussed the problem of summarizing vast masses of material by succinct statistical measures. We could have discussed the problem of counting to make descriptive statements about texts more precise. For example, linguists want to know the frequency with which different language forms are used. That is a useful descriptive kind of

From *Trends in Content Analysis* (1959), edited by Ithiel de Sola Pool

TABLE 7.1
Type of Analysis

Uses of Content Analysis	Quantitative, measuring:			Qualitative
	Fre-quencies	Contin-gencies	Inten-sities	
To describe texts	0	0	0	0
To draw inferences from texts as to their antecedents	+	+	+	0
To draw inferences from texts as to their effects	0	0	0	0

*+ = Discussed intensively.
0 = Not discussed intensively.

content analysis, but not one with which we concerned ourselves. Librarians want to know what the flow of books and articles is in each discipline. To do this they analyze the content of each text, classifying it under established headings, and count the frequencies so arising. That, too, is descriptive frequency content analysis and a useful enterprise.

Another type of purely descriptive analysis was discussed extensively at a more recent conference sponsored by the same SSRC Committee on Psychology and Linguistics. That conference on the description and analysis of style brought together literary persons, linguists, and social scientists interested in finding ways to describe the style of a text as such. Its results, which are also due for publication under the title *Aspects of Science in Language*, will in some sense be a companion volume to this one. The present work, however, explores problems of description only as a step toward inference. Our concern has been with inferences from the content of a text to what was going on in the environment in which the text appeared.

These inferences can go two ways. There can be inferences which ask what it was that *led* to a statement appearing, and there can be inferences which ask what was likely to *follow* from the appearance of a statement.

The latter kind of inference we also discussed a little. It may be illustrated by copy testing for example, where one may analyze the characteristics of various texts and then see which ones produce which reactions. The same sort of effect inference is made when one notes different reactions to different advertisements or propaganda pieces, and then searches the texts to find what produced these responses.

Other examples of inferences regarding effects may be found in psychological experiments in which the stimulus material is a text. The texts used for the different conditions of an experiment may be analyzed for inferences about the determinants of the response behavior. Osgood in his chapter pays some attention to what he calls "decoding dependencies," that is, "dependencies of events in listeners and readers...upon the content and structure of messages." But on the whole our emphasis has been on inferences about the sources, not the receivers, of messages.

Thus the uses of content analysis which we did discuss for the most part were those where the inference to be drawn concerns the antecedents of the text itself and conditions of its production. For that kind of research the logic of inference has been most fully analyzed by Alexander George (chap. 1). He was concerned with inferences derived from propaganda issued in World War II and concerning the propagandists' military intentions. But in a strictly analogous way John Garraty was concerned, in chapter 6, with inferences from the statements of a great man in history to his state of tension at the time of writing or speaking. George Mahl, in chapter 3, was concerned with inferences from a patient's speech disturbances to his degree of anxiety. Charles Osgood, in chapter 2, wanted to draw inferences from a man's statements to his underlying evaluations and associations. These are examples of the kinds of inferences from texts to antecedents with which most current content analysis seems to be concerned.

We have now looked along the rows of the table above and we find current content analysis work focused in one of them. Now let us look down the columns. Not only is our focus of attention limited to one use of content analysis, it is also limited to but a few of the types of analysis which could be used to serve that purpose.

Qualitative Analysis

We have not discussed qualitative content analysis in most of the chapters in this volume. True, qualitative methods have been forcefully put forward in the chapter by Alexander George. His conclusion as to the futility of trying to be rigorously numerical in some of the kinds of policy-oriented research with which he was concerned provoked little disagreement among the conferees. But there was a desire to define the areas where his argument applied and the areas where numerical quantification makes sense.

The problem with which George deals is that of explaining the behavior of particular actors in a particular situation. He discusses a kind of detective work. And the best detective, he tells us, is the one with a prepared but open mind ready to spark to any clue which gives the game away, though it occurs but once. George's careful study of intelligence analysis in World War II has fully documented that some such detectives can do very well using "nonfrequency" methods of content analysis. He has also shown that they did much better than their wartime colleagues who tried ad hoc to set up mechanical quantitative procedures for doing the same detective work. Garraty, in similar vein, notes with approval White's procedure in his analysis of Richard Wright's *Black Boy* and Baldwin's in his analysis of Jenny. Each started with an intuitive analysis of a kind that would be familiar to historians or psychiatrists. Certain inferences were successfully made at that stage about the personality and problems of each author. But in each study this preliminary qualitative analysis provided the set of categories to be explored in a more novel and rigorous kind of quantitative content analysis. The latter was then performed and in each of the two cases brought forth truly important insights which the more traditional reading had failed to elicit.[1] It is with this further quantitative step for improving the results of historical research that Garraty was concerned, and each of us was concerned with the analogous problem for his own discipline, the problem of pushing back the frontiers through careful if arduous counting which might add to what we can learn by intelligent intuitive observation. George's point is not in contradiction. He demonstrates why the initial hypothesis-forming phase of a study is essential if one is later to count what is relevant to count, why "nonfrequency" qualitative analysis (to use George's term) also produces some things which a quantitative analysis cannot, why in a practical operation such as intelligence, where time is of the essence and one must choose rather than doing both, an impressionistic analysis is usually preferable to a formal count. However, the logic of the process of inference which George examines leads the scientific researcher to a conclusion different from that of the intelligence operator. It leads him to embrace the rigors and promise of quantitative measurement as a step enabling him to go beyond where he could go otherwise. If, despite the incisive discussion by George of qualitative content analysis for intelligence purposes, we do not put a plus sign in that cell of the table describing our book, it is because nonfrequency analysis was not an area in which the rest of the conferees were working. George's discussion of nonfrequency methods served to make us define the limits of our common problems rather than to pinpoint that as a common one. Most of us were concerned with content analysis for scientific generalization, not for intelligence purposes. And those of us (e.g., Garraty) who were concerned with developing methods applicable to specific situations were seeking exact, quantitative, standardizable ones with which to check and supplement intuitive judgments. Thus we define the area of content analysis in this volume as the counting or measuring of features of a text, and that for purposes of inference.

But the things in a text which can be counted or measured are many and we do not attempt here to discuss them all. The characteristic of the conference was that we discussed measurement of contingencies a great deal. We discussed the measurement of symbol frequencies somewhat less. We discussed the measurement of intensity least of all. Only one paper, Osgood's, deals with that extensively.

Intensity

The desire to measure the intensity of attitudes has been with us from the earliest days of content analysis. One of the first issues explored was the degree of bias in journalistic treatments of partisan issues: which party got more column inches; which got the bigger headlines; which got the better pictures; which got the loaded words. But there are so many ways of slanting a text that measurement of them all has defeated every researcher who has tried it. The usual operational solution has been to settle for the measurement of column inches or some such frequency. There was an underlying assumption that frequency of mention would correlate with intensity of expressed attitude, and so a straightforward frequency count of either inches or symbols, supplemented at most by a positive or negative valence distinction, might provide a useful index of the intensity of feeling. The most common single content analysis categories of past years have been "pro-x," "anti-x," "pro-y," "anti-y," where x and y were opposed sides; and the most common statistic in the results has been proportion of favorable or unfavorable references to x or y.

The assumption that the frequency of statements provides a good index of intensity of attitude is probably reasonable for a large class of cases. By "attitude" here, of course, we mean the attitude expressed in the body of the text, not the covert feelings of the author. Even with this limitation the assumption baldly spelled out sounds absurd, because it is perfectly clear that frequency is only one of a variety of devices by which feeling is expressed. But the experience of more than one analyst who has tried refinements in measuring intensity has been that nothing much is added by other measures than the frequency one. That would suggest that at least in a large class of forms of verbal expression much of the total variance in intensity is accounted for by the one component, frequency.

True, this is simply an allegation or a hypothesis. It is challenged by George and by Mahl, who questions the "assumption that there is an isomorphic relation between behavioral states and quantitative properties of lexical content." The data does not now exist to establish the classes of cases where the assumption is valid, and the classes where it is not, and by how much. We do not want to become victims of our convenient assumption by using it blindly as though it always applied, but it works well enough so that those now working in the field of content analysis have not found it an immediate stumbling block to be removed from the road.

The problem of measurement of intensity is one to which Osgood's chapter addresses itself, particularly in the section on evaluative assertion analysis. The objective of evaluative assertion analysis is to arrive at a measurement of the attitude of the source toward certain attitude objects. It is an attempt to obtain a measure of evaluation, not frequency. The basic data are derived from judges who use a seven-point scale. However, the judgments are made on texts from which all identifying context has been removed, and the resulting evaluations are then used in turn as measures for the final evaluations of each other. This ingenious measure of attitude does not rest upon frequency of appearance, except for the way in which it uses the seven-point scale. It does assume that "an intense connector (± 3) is treated as equivalent to an ordinary assertion (± 1) made three times...." Clearly, it is not easy to measure intensity quite independently of frequency, though evaluative assertion analysis is a start. It is entirely conceivable that similar measures could also be devised for other aspects of intensity besides intensity of evaluation, for example intensity of emphasis, intensity of belief in facts, and so on.

Evaluative assertion analysis is the exception to what we have been saying about the complete dependence of content analysts on the assumption that intensity is simply a function of frequency. The fact that that assumption was generally used was made explicit by several of the conference participants and in several of the papers. For example, in dealing with the problem of the intensity of contingencies between symbols Osgood said: "reflecting the basic psychological principle relating habit strength to frequency of response, the method does indirectly reflect the strength of associations.... The stronger the association between two ideas in the thinking of the source, the more regularly will the occurrence of one be the condition for the occurrence...of the other."

If we are to drop this assumption that frequency will measure intensity, either because the assumption is inadequate or simply to test its adequacy by independent observations, we are led either to the use of judges, as above, or to the use of some linguistic knowledge. Saporta and Sebeok, in their discussion of "marked" and "unmarked" forms, introduce the problem of identifying lexical equivalents which differ only in certain of their connotations, which would include such matters as intensity. The content analyst would like the aid of linguistics in enumerating the lexical and structural forms through which nuances of intensity are conveyed. This is one area where the interests of content analysis and linguistics meet.

Frequency

Counting frequencies was the main activity of content analysts in the 1930s and 1940s. Indeed, for many people that is how content analysis was defined. Berelson's book minus one chapter is almost wholly devoted to such frequency counts. Lasswell's content analyses were frequency counts of symbols; so for the most part were the RADIR studies at the Hoover Institute. The units could vary greatly: there were counts of column inches, of key words, of themes, of literary forms, of types of characters, and so on. But up to ten years ago almost all studies had for their basic logic a comparison of the frequency of certain types of symbolic expression in different segments of text. The comparison might be of texts produced at different times, or by different authors, or in different ideological conditions, or in different states of feeling, or for different purposes; but for each comparison the test was that symbols of type x were significantly more frequent in one body of text than in another.

Such analyses continue to be discussed in this volume,[2] but the striking thing is that somehow a new kind of quantitative analysis had simultaneously occurred to many of the researchers at our conference. We found that we had each in his own way become much more interested in contingencies than in straight frequencies. It was a striking illustration of parallel but independent development in science.

Contingencies

Contingency analysis is a quantitative procedure. It involves count-ing. But the form of the hypothesis and of the critical observations is different from that in a simple frequency analysis. Contingency analy-sis asks not how often a given symbolic form appears in each of several bodies of text, but how often it appears in conjunction with other sym-bolic units.[3] The difference can be expressed both most rigorously and most clearly as the difference between a simple probability statement and a conditional probability statement. Traditional frequency analysis sought to determine the probability that a specified symbol would be drawn in each unit trial as one examined a particular set of texts. Con-tingency analysis seeks to determine the probability that a specified symbol will be drawn, given that other specified symbols are in that or related units.

An early example, perhaps the earliest, is Baldwin's study of the letters of an old woman to which we have already referred.[4] This study, which appeared in 1942, showed the pattern of the woman's associa-tions. It is quite fully described in Garraty's chapter. Ten years later the present author in one of the RADIR studies published a contingency analysis of the contexts in which the word "democracy" occurred, with a view to noting in which periods and countries it appeared along with words signifying representative government, or along with words sig-nifying the common people, or along with words signifying freedom, these being three distinctive strands in democratic ideology. Although the units of analysis, because of their breadth, were not well suited to the purpose of contingency analysis, the contingency method seemed to open up interesting possibilities for analyzing the data. It did in fact show important differences between the Continental mass tradition of democracy and the Anglo-American libertarian tradition. Reporting a straight frequency count of the word "democracy" would under those circumstances have confounded the different ideological traditions.

In the same period, during the years just before our conference, the idea of contingency analysis was independently occurring to a number of us. In 1951 there appeared a report of an interdisciplinary seminar of psychologists and linguists held at Cornell in which two of the present authors, Osgood and Sebeok, participated. Its critique of existing meth-ods of content analysis contained the statement that they "are limited to simple comparisons of frequencies rather than measuring the inter-nal contingencies between categories."[5] Osgood has now devised a set of procedures for measuring such contingencies, and these he describes in chapter 2.

In that chapter he presents three illustrative reports of applications of contingency analysis, one on radio speeches by W. J. Cameron, one on Goebbels' diary, and one on a psychotherapy protocol. He found, for example, that whenever Goebbels talked about factional conflicts among the Nazi elite he was more apt to refer to Hitler than when he talked about other relevant subjects. The Fuhrer came to his mind perhaps in the role of judge and arbiter of Goebbels' conflicts with other leaders. Osgood also found, to cite another example, that the particular psychotherapy patient whose interviews he analyzed talked a good deal about both his mother and heterosexual relations but did not talk about them together. When he talked about one he avoided talking about the other.

Sebeok and Saporta also report in their chapter another current use of contingency methods—on folklore material. They report, for example, a contingency in one culture between the notion of writing and the notion of the devil.

One might add that those of the conference participants who made a strong case for the instrumental model of communication were approaching the same set of problems to the extent that the context which they wished to take into account in assessing meanings was the verbal context provided by the rest of the communication. (Needless to say, this is only one part of the context they wished considered.) Mahl, for example, remarks that "The general classification of silences by all patients at all times in the interview as 'anxious'...would be uninterpretive..." (Silence, of course, is a symbol which can be used in content analysis just as much as any noise which is a symbol. Indeed, the analysis of it as part of grammar goes back to Panini.) But silence is clearly a symbol with different meanings depending on its context. It means different things when it comes from a man who is relaxed than when it comes from one who is tense. Either state may lead him to interrupt his verbal flow, but silence in the context of a large number of broken sentences, errors, and slips is different from silence in their absence. The analyst who wishes to interpret a silence may look to evidence about the state of the author outside the communication, if he has such evidence. But if he has no such evidence, then it is the other symbols in the context of which a symbol occurs that enable him to choose between interpretations. Clearly it is those symbolic contexts that the analyst of contingencies is also examining. The problem of context, thus generally stated, was of interest to all the participants at the conference.

One may speculate as to what were the influences which account for the simultaneous emergence of interest in contingency relations by a number of content analysts previously working independently. Three sources of influence seem fairly clear: the psychological theory of association, the mathematical theory of information, and linguistics.

One of the conference participants commented that the contingency method as used in psychotherapy "is Freud's basic law of association." The subject under discussion when that point was made was the RADIR finding of a contingency in Russian editorials between affect for authority and affect for freedom; the RADIR analyst had interpreted that association as an indication of conflict. The analogy to the procedure of an analyst in psychotherapy is clear. The relevance of the principle of association (in its stimulus response version) to contingency analysis is also discussed in Osgood's chapter. Osgood formulates a principle for the appropriate length of the unit in which to count co-occurrences. The unit, he believes, should be such that associative connections may still be presumed to operate within it. That principle applies, assuming a purpose in which Osgood is indeed interested, that of studying the psychological process of association in the communicator. There was some discussion at the conference of how far this principle would apply where the matter of interest was policy, that is, an attempt to produce a certain effect upon the audience. If, for example, it is the policy of a newspaper to create a certain image of a public official, then the span within which appropriate items might be clustered would be that which might be assumed to affect the association structure of the reader, and that might be a different span from that appropriate to the associational structure of the author. On the other hand, doubt was expressed as to how far policy would be capable of modifying the contingency structure of a text or at least of eliminating contingencies. Osgood suggested that deliberate suppression of a contingency would create a negative contingency. A chance relation might be almost impossible to produce by plan. All these issues are unresolved and remain for future research to explore. However, the discussion of the issue among the participants in the conference makes clear that the idea of contingency analysis was derived by them in part from the analogy of association.

The influence of information theory as formulated by Claude Shannon is equally clear. The publicity which that development gave in academic circles to the method of deciphering verbal codes by means of transitional probabilities of symbols suggested to content analysts solutions to problems that had previously seemed insoluble. That is not to say that contingency analysis is an application of information theory; it is not. It is only an analogous development, sparked by the metaphor of information theory jargon. Still, the genealogy is clear. In *Symbols of Democracy* this author specifically credited Shannon and Weaver as the source of his idea for analysis and justified it as follows: "Words occur in clusters, not at random. A sentence, a paragraph, or an article containing the word 'caste' is more likely to contain the word 'India' than is one containing the word 'reindeer'.... A cryptanalyst can guess from the known words what the unknown words may be. He does this by establishing an actuarial model of the language. The model states the frequencies with which given words appear in association with other given words."

Osgood, who has carried the development of contingency analysis farther than anyone else, also shows the impact of the same set of concepts. He and his colleagues at the University of Illinois, where Shannon's book was published,[6] have worked on the application of information theory to psychology. The Cloze Procedure developed by Wilson Taylor is directly based upon its suggestions. Thus, we have an example of a familiar event in the history of science: a seminal idea in one field sparks an analogous development in another.

The third of the overdetermining influences in the development of contingency analysis was structural linguistics (see chap. 4). The appropriateness of contingency analysis as a method for dealing with texts arises from the very structure of language, the common medium which all content analysts study. Human communication is accomplished by way of a large number of basic units (morphemes) put together in accordance with structural rules.

Recognition of this fact has led structural linguistics to the method of distributional analysis. This may be illustrated by Harris' "Discourse Analysis," published in 1952, which comes very close to being itself a contingency content analysis. "Descriptive linguistics," he says, "which sets out to describe the occurrence of elements in any stretch of speech, ends up by describing it primarily in respect to other elements of the same sentence."[7] Thus if a given morpheme, say "ran," appears in the identical context with another morpheme, say "ate" (e.g., the dog ran; the dog ate), then these are treated as equivalent in linguistic category (clearly not in meaning). These equivalences can in turn lead to secondary equivalences by analogy with the familiar mathematical axiom that things equal to the same thing are equal to each other. By applying such principles beyond the sentence to whole texts, Harris suggested a way of identifying characteristic formal features of a particular writer, or type of literature, or situation of writing. He developed only the method, merely suggesting its usefulness to social science. He said, "It remains to be shown as a matter of empirical fact that such formal correlations do indeed exist, that the discourses of a particular person, social group, style, or subject-matter exhibit not only particular meanings (in their selection of morphemes) but also characteristic formal features."[8] This is a challenge which social scientists have yet to pick up fully. In the chapters comprising the present volume there are several references to the advantages of studying formal features of a person's discourse rather than meanings if one would infer sensitive facts about him, for the former are far less consciously controlled than is his selection of morphemes. (This point is mentioned in almost every chapter.) But the content analyst does not wish to limit himself to the formal features of language alone. He concerns himself both with those and with the meanings selected. As Harris put it, "Any analysis which aimed to find out whether certain words, selected by the investigator, occur in the text or not, would be an investigation of the CONTENT of the text and would be ultimately based on the MEANINGS of the words selected."[9] While Harris excluded that kind of investigation from his own task as a linguist, what he did with regard to the co-occurrence of formal features was so obviously relevant to the problems of the content analyst, and his method so obviously appropriate in some respects to the meaning aspects of language too, that it would have been extraordinary if there had been no impact on content analysis.

As an example of the relevance of "Discourse Analysis" to content analysis let us mention the twelve sample grammatical rules of equivalence which Harris listed. Many forms of content analysis require the reduction of elaborate sentences to a limited number of simple assertions. See, for example, chapter 2 on evaluative assertion analysis, which requires this kind of reduction (e.g., "The unruly prisoner shouted" becomes "the prisoner was unruly" and "the prisoner shouted"). Scores of content analysts have each independently struggled with making a grammar to meet their coding needs with regard to such cases, yet we find that the problem has largely been solved by the structural linguists, and in particular one can turn to Harris' twelve rules designed for the almost identical purpose in discourse analysis.

Linguistics thus suggested to content analysts the way to take account of the structures and contexts in which symbols occur by way of noting the symbolic environments of the symbols of interest. The meaning units which the content analyst counts are themselves not unambiguous. They are multipurpose, and when removed from their contexts are capable of a variety of interpretations. Critics have denigrated frequency analysis for a long time for precisely that reason—it fails to take account of the context and the different things a given symbol may mean. Content analysts have recognized this as a major problem. Taking a cue from linguistics, contingency analysis turns out to be a first step toward incorporating into content analysis some relevant data about the structures with which units are put together....

Representational and Instrumental Communications

There is something important at which the conferees were driving in the distinction between representational and instrumental communication. It crops up in several chapters of the present work. What do we mean by these words? There was undoubtedly some difference of opinion. A rough definition was presented in the introduction[10] and we have noted other definitions in the chapters by George, Osgood, and Mahl. Clearly the terms can refer to at least three different things: a kind of communication, an aspect of a communication, and a model for analysis. Let us illustrate.

Kind of communication. The scream "ouch" in pain is representational communication—it accurately represents the state of its author. A lie is instrumental communication.

Aspect of communication. The single communication "Friends, Romans, countrymen, lend me your ears" had a representational aspect as a demand to be heard (it said what it meant), and an instrumental aspect in its use of terms of identification.

Model For analysis. The counting of the frequency of a name as an index of interest in the person named is analysis according to a representational model—it assumes that the text represents the state of its author. Reading between the lines is analysis according to the instrumental model.

Cutting across these distinctions are some others. The notion that an author is somehow represented by his communication may refer to representation of different levels of the author's complex psyche. The communication may represent his most basic associative processes, or his "true" conscious attitudes, or the overt attitudes which he wishes to communicate.

Cutting across all of these distinctions is another important one. Sometimes above we take "representation" to mean that something in a communication indexes in a stable, recurrent fashion something about the author—what Alexander George would call "direct" content indicators. In that sense the anxiety-revealing speech disturbances which Mahl (who introduced the distinction) analyzes are representations. At other times, however, the term "representational" is taken to refer to "the face validity of the manifest lexical content of a message" (George), or in other words the dictionary meaning of a sentence. In that usage, if we take the symbols present to index anything else than what they say (even if the indexing relation is completely stable), or if for an index we use any aspects of the communication other than the lexical items, we characterize the operation as "instrumental."

All of these somewhat different usages were applied by the conferees in the discussion of a common core of problems. Our task now is to summarize this discussion, and to do so we must obviously choose one set of definitions and stick with it. In the discussion to follow we take as "representational" any content feature which across the body of text with which we are concerned indexes ("directly" in George's terminology) something (anything) about the source. "Instrumental" we take to be that which is manipulated (and thus varied in its relation to the thing being indexed so as to achieve the author's objectives).[11] We have in short accepted the first of the two options in the paragraph just above. The crux of the distinction there lies in how far strategy by the author modifies the indicatorial value of the communications feature we are observing.

Turning back to the three options in the first paragraph of this section, we shall choose to define here not two different kinds of communications but two different aspects of a communication. A man is hot and sweaty; he would like a drink. He wipes his brow and says to his host, "My, it's hot." The representational aspect of the communication is that the man is hot; its instrumental but unspoken purpose is not to convey this fact to the world but to produce the answer "Would you like something to drink?" If it fails to produce the desired result the hot man may vary his strategy and make his communication explicit. He may say "Please give me a drink." That statement is not only instrumental to achieving a certain result; it also represents once more the fact that the speaker is hot and thirsty, for it indicates in a well-established way a fact about the speaker which his strategy did not hide.

The rather complicated statements above about our usage of the terms instrumental and representational may be summarized with some precision if we introduce a formal terminology and set of formal rules. A source may have n states $(s_1, s_2 \ldots s_n)$. The source may independently of these states adopt any one of m manipulative strategies $(m_1, m_2 \ldots m_n)$. The universe may independently be in any one of p states $(u_1, u_2 \ldots u_n)$. Finally the content emitted by the source may be in any one of r states $(c_1, c_2 \ldots c_n)$. The terms representational and instrumental were used to discuss assertions about dependency of states in C on states in S and/or M and/or U.

A representational assertion maps some element c_k into some element s_i. More broadly we may also call an assertion representational if it maps some element c_k into some combination $s_i u_j$. The definition of representational assertions which Mahl uses imposes a further constraint. He calls an assertion representational only if the semantic meaning of an element c_k which maps into an element s_i is the assertion that s_i is a fact.

An instrumental assertion maps some element c_k into some element m_h. A broader definition would call an assertion instrumental if it mapped some element c_k into some combination $m_h u_j$ or (even broader) into some combination $m_h s_i u_j$.

Since we have asserted M to be independent of S, it is clear that any assertion mapping an element c_k into some m_h (an instrumental assertion in the narrow sense) implies the absence of a stable relationship of c_k to any s_i (cf. the example of a mathematical proof in the discussion below).

Obviously, the only complete analysis is one mapping elements c_k into combinations $m_h s_i u_j$. However, we are often lacking in good evidence of which state in M exists. Thus it would often be desirable to find relationships of C (content) and S (source) which are negligibly affected by M (manipulative strategy). That is the justification of seeking to establish representational assertions even about communications which we know to be in many respects consciously manipulated.

Almost every communication has both representational and instrumental aspects. The weight given each may vary. We can set up a scale. A mathematical proof is close to a purely instrumental communication. It is designed to achieve a certain objective, in this case a cognitive one. That objective is controlling. Without making the proof wrong there are but few aspects of it which one can vary to represent one's own peculiar psychic conditions. The state of the speaker is indeed conveyed in some minor ways, but relatively few. On the whole, any two statements of the proof will be much alike regardless of where or when they are given, for the strategies are limited and purpose is controlling. Since the text of the proof is that stable, its relation to the state of the source is highly unstable.

At the other extreme there is obsessional behavior of certain kinds in which the calculated use of communication to achieve a result is less easily discernible than is its quality as conveying the state of the communicator.

This example, however, immediately cries out for qualification. It is perfectly clear that obsessional behavior is not unmotivated. One of Freud's major contributions may be considered to be the application of instrumental interpretations to unconscious processes. The Freudian interpretation of dreams, for example, gives a central position to purpose, designated as wish. The representational symbols are bent to the fulfillment of the wish. So, too, during a psychiatric interview, as Mahl points out, the patient's statements are not interpretable as pure representations of his state, but are rather devices being used to achieve certain objectives, often with regard to the psychiatrist. The patient tries to attract his attention or to get his sympathy and says what will serve these purposes.

So the instrumental aspect appears in all communications, not just in manipulative propaganda of the kind which Alexander George analyzed, though its role in that may be greater. Likewise, a representational element exists and may be sought in the most calculated of instrumental communications. An example of an analysis which uses the representational element in highly manipulated communications is *Movies*, by Wolfenstein and Leites. It is a content analysis designed to identify national myths in one of the most calculated of the mass media. Movies are made for the box office. Every shot is designed to appeal to an imagined audience. It does not represent the aesthetic taste or the emotional states of the authors or directors in any immediate way. Individual idiosyncrasies are ironed out in the collective process of production. Yet in the very process of collectively producing an expression of what the producers conceive to be the fantasy life of their audience, they are representing something about their own image of the culture in which they live. In that lies the creative element in the making of a movie, which emerges despite the influence of box office considerations. There are choices to be made which express the character and environment of the chooser. There is a story to be thought up, pieces to be put together; there is room for associations to float, controlled of course by one's image of the audience's associations. And in this process the fantasies and values of the culture somehow get expressed. There is thus room for analysis of movies, not only in terms of the instrumental calculations which go into them but also as representations of their makers.

Similarly, the fact that a propagandist is given instructions does not eliminate a representational element in his propaganda. A Soviet propagandist, for example, may be told that neutralism in a third country is useful to the Soviets at the moment, and that attacks should be replaced by flattery and encouragement. It is still his problem to decide what constitutes flattery and encouragement, what neutrals will like and respond to. There is thus for him a realm of initiative undetermined by policy, and in that he may reveal some of his images of life.

It may be hard sometimes to know whether an instrumental or a representational assumption gives us a more correct inference as to the reasons for particular symbolic behavior. The contingency noted earlier between symbols of freedom and symbols of authority in *Pravda* editorials was there interpreted as *representing* a conflict within Soviet ideology. It could be taken, however, that symbols of freedom were introduced *instrumentally* to make authoritarian statements more palatable to the readers. There is a third and most likely alternative, namely, that both things were happening at once. But even if we choose to look for representational behavior, we must, as Alexander George has pointed out, be aware of the bounds set by instrumental considerations within which representation of the communicator can operate.

A content analysis which deals with highly instrumental material such as propaganda may work well for a while with certain categories and then break down when the symbolic strategy of the communicator changes. The uses made of given symbols may change in the middle of the count in response to strategy's demands, and entirely new indices may become the important ones for the behavior in which we are interested. Thus in a psychotherapeutic interview the patient's strategy objective may be to get the therapist to talk at a time when the therapist is not so inclined. The patient may try silence, attempting to outwait the therapist. When this does not work he can try telling a funny story to arouse a response. If this does not work he can try being insulting and provocative. The purpose may remain constant as the strategies change. The count of any one symbolic behavior among those chosen for instrumental purposes will be fruitless.

The same thing may be true in the political sphere. A standard pattern of Soviet strategy has been to accuse opponents of exactly that which they intended to do themselves. Stalin used this device extensively and, as Myron Rush[12] as shown in his insightful content analysis of recent Soviet documents, Khrushchev has also used it extensively. For example, Malenkov was accused of being responsible for agricultural policies of which Khrushchev himself was the author. Here is a strategy. Clearly one cannot devise a simple counting procedure in the presence of it. One cannot count everything that Soviet leaders criticize and conclude that really they are for them. That would lead us to conclude that really the Soviet leaders are in favor of capitalism, the United States, production failures, etc. Nor, however, can one count the things that Soviet leaders criticize and assume that those are the things they are against, for from time to time they adopt the strategy of disarming opposition to what they favor by attacking that very thing and blaming it on the enemy of the moment. As Alexander George has argued, the context must be the guide to the strategy being used. Rush's book is an illuminating example of the use of all possible contextual clues for the selection of the appropriate symbols to look for at any given time.

Contingency analysis is a different, more rigorously quantitative way of trying to get at some contextual factors. It of course limits the contexts considered to those in the text. It does, however, permit one to interpret symbol A differently when it appears accompanied by symbol B than when it appears accompanied by symbol C. This is one way to take account of changes in strategy. However he does it, the analyst who is dealing with instrumental texts must take account of the fluctuating strategies of the moment.

While in principle all strategies can fluctuate to meet changing conditions, it is not in practice the case that all strategies do fluctuate within delimited sectors which may be of interest. There are situations within which a uniform set of categories can successfully be applied to a body of texts to make inferences even regarding strategy. But we should remain clearly aware that where that is done we are making a hidden assumption of continuity of strategy. An example would be a study of testimonials in magazine advertisements. Within the institutional context of the American market system it is generally pretty clear that the objective of testimonials is to increase the number of customers buying a product by communicating to them the fact of a positive evaluation of it from someone with whom they identify positively. There is little reason to expect this strategy to change in any normal course of events, although a little imagination can produce hypothetical exceptions, for example using testimonials to change the image of a product so as to avoid government regulatory actions. Normally, however, one can operate in terms of the inference that the appearance of a testimonial represents the desire of a firm to sell more of its product to sectors of the public who could be expected to identify favorably with the kind of person issuing the testimonial. Categories based on these instrumental assumptions could be designed and used in a highly uniform and standardized fashion.

Thus there are situations where even with highly instrumental materials fairly standard categories may enable us to make some inferences as to the intentions of the communicator, but the problem always remains with the analyst to consider whether the assumptions he is using are still valid, or whether instrumental constraints are leading the author to use different symbols at different times for the same purpose and the same symbols at different times for different purposes.

Standardized Categories for Content Analysis

The above considerations lead us directly to another issue on which the conferees did not fully agree. That is the issue of the desirability of finding standardized content analysis categories that could be used by different researchers in different studies to the end that studies would become more comparable and additive. Clearly this is a laudable aspiration and one that has been with content analysts from the beginning. Lasswell popularized the often-copied categories of "pro-self," "pro-other," "anti-self," "anti-other." White's value analysis provides another set of standardized categories. Thompson's motif index is widely used though Sebeok, Saporta, and Armstrong found it unsatisfactory for lack of theoretical basis.

In other fields of social science general tools of a similar kind have proved of great use. The intelligence quotient is such a standardized measure. In studies of the relation of intelligence to some other variable, it is most convenient that there is a standardized measure of at least one of the variables. Garraty noted how useful it would be for historians if relevant "precut" content analysis categories existed.

It is questionable, however, how ready we are to establish standard measures of that sort in content analysis. Such a measure is convenient when a considerable number of researchers are working on the same variable, and when someone succeeds in working out good categories for that variable. It is doubtful that either of those criteria can be met in most areas of content analysis.

Let us take for the moment Osgood's contingency analysis of Mr. Cameron's Ford Hour speeches. It is a study of the structure of an ideology. We may want to ask ourselves what general categories of ideology there are which we want to use in the characterization not only of Mr. Cameron's but of other ideological statements. Certainly a most obvious one is the category of conservative. A number of scholars have conducted studies of ideological texts in terms of conservatism-liberalism. But conservatism is not a single coherent thing; as a category it is a catchall. Intelligence is a catchall, too. As measured it consists of a number of weighted discrete components. Perhaps then we could look at the clusters revealed in the contingency relationships among symbols in the Cameron speeches and come up with a proposed definition of conservatism in terms of contingencies of set symbols. "Perhaps," however, is the word to be underlined. It seems highly dubious that what one would want to call anyone else's conservatism, even if one restricted oneself to contemporary American culture, would be expressed in the same set of symbols and in the same relationships among them. We are probably not yet at the point where we know how to construct a useful content index of conservatism. But here the word to underline is "probably." The way we will know when we can construct a good enough index so that many people will use it is when someone actually develops one.

Until that time there is a good deal to be said for ad hoc categories. Armstrong's classification of objectives in folk stories is such a set of categories. If one asks why the items discovered were grouped under a particular heading to form a category, there is no answer except Armstrong's feeling that they were somehow alike. Another example of that sort of content analysis is Nicholas Vakar's analysis of *Pravda* editorials.[13] What Vakar did was to take the most common nouns from *Pravda* editorials; this gave him a list to compare with the most common nouns in standardized word lists of French, German, English, and pre-Soviet Russian. He then grouped the words in each list to show differences in emphasis on concepts of different types. For example, he found that the pre-Soviet Russian vocabulary and to some extent the French gave "greater emphasis to the expressive aspects of the self" than did the English and German. But such words (feeling, soul, thought, faith, mind) have disappeared from *Pravda*'s main vocabulary. On the other hand, in the *Pravda* vocabulary verbs implying domination or manipulation number eight out of the top twenty and appear elsewhere only in two examples from the German list.

One of the conferees was troubled by this procedure, for, to put it in his words, "If another analyst were to do the same thing, he would come up with a different grouping of words and thus a different set of categories of analysis. That is what makes it hard to accept." One can only agree that that is the fact; two persons looking at the same list of words will choose to group them under different central concepts. They will in short be looking for different things. Not all the conferees, however, agreed that that was bad. To some of us it seemed quite legitimate, in the absence of a prior theory, to make up the theory as one went along, grouping together symbolic elements which seemed in some sense to go together. If one is struck by the predominance of a certain kind of symbolic behavior in a text, it seems an abnegation of one's critical intelligence to refuse to note that behavior as a category because one has not started out realizing its significance or because it has not been identified in other social theories or pieces of social research.

What the analyst who uses ad hoc categories does is to form his hypotheses and validate them out of the same set of data.[14] One can only agree that this is not so good a scientific procedure as getting one's hypotheses first from one set of data or experiences, and then validating them on another. But it is by no means an unknown or totally invalid procedure. There are indeed situations where one has no choice. There may exist only a single set of data. One is then engaged in a kind of detective work. One studies the data, rearranges them, and puts them together in different ways until one finds that hypothesis which explains the puzzling aspects of them. Examples of this kind of procedure are common in natural history. One examines a set of bones to try to reconstruct a prehistoric animal. One may hope to find later another specimen that may confirm or disprove one's reconstruction, but for the moment the validation of the hypothesized reconstruction is in the degree to which it accounts for all the facts in the same set of bones which was used to get the idea.

So, too, the content analyst who has a set of texts which in the fullness of their circumstances are historically unique may be justified in coding them under whatever categories seem best to bring out the significant differences within them. An analysis of the speeches of Mr. Cameron, a unique and unreproducible individual, may well tabulate those symbols which Mr. Cameron himself used regardless of the generality of these categories.

In the Cameron study the list of symbols tabulated in the first place was ad hoc, but the grouping of them into clusters was objectively validated by contingency analysis. That is why the study and the contingency method it represents are such great advances over previous methods. In previous studies the symbols initially counted were determined ad hoc. They would then be grouped into broader classes relevant to interesting hypotheses. These groupings were also ad hoc. Thus one might decide that concern with progress would be indexed by a list of counted terms including progress, advance, modern, old fashioned, forward looking, change, conservatism, and so on. But there was no rigorous standard for inclusion or exclusion. Contingency analysis, while it does not tell us what to look for in the first place (that still requires either intuition or exhaustiveness), does enable us to determine what symbols do in point of fact go together in any given body of text.[15] It therefore begins to open the way toward developing standardized categories by making it feasible to justify and test the relevance of component elements empirically.

There is no single simple answer to the problem of the standardization of content analysis categories. There are gains and losses in standardization. There are times for standardization, there are times for rigorous but unique categories, and there are even times for the free play of the analyst's intuition on what goes with what.

Nevertheless it is clear that for many purposes the development of some kinds of standardized categories is both desirable and sure to come as content analysis progresses. Linguistic uniformities in the medium of communication are likely to provide some of the bases for standardized categories. We noted above, for example, a list of twelve rules of grammatical equivalence developed by Harris. These could become such a set of standard coding rules as they become more widely known by content analysts.

In this conference discussion three areas were identified where attempts at standardized procedures seem likely to be justified soon by reason of both needs and possibilities. These areas in which there was felt to be a possibility of developing standard categories were measuring tensions, valence, and, finally, linguistic categories.

Measuring Tension

It might prove possible to develop a set of categories designed to test whether a speaker or writer—the categories might be different for oral and written communication—is under tension at the moment of communicating. George Mahl's speech disturbance analysis is directed

toward finding such a measure of anxiety in psychotherapeutic interviews, and it does indeed seem that certain forms of hesitation and
speech imperfection do give anxiety away. During World War II there
were attempts made to apply to Hitler's speeches similar analyses of
clues of tensions. Since the conference Charles Osgood has been working on a set of suicide notes which promises interesting results. John
Garraty indicates how valuable a similar measure would be to a historian studying the documents of a past great man. He himself reported
attempts at using such devices as the adjective-verb ratio on letters
written by Theodore Roosevelt, Wilson, and others, at moments when
he knew them to be under tension. He would like to be able to look at
historical documents, at least of the more spontaneous kinds such as
handwritten letters, and be able to say that at that time Wilson, or whoever it might be, was under stress.[16] Alexander George discussed the
usefulness of being able to look at a propaganda document, pick out
some topic, and say of it, "This is something they are really concerned
about." James Jenkins reported an experimental finding that subjects
with high anxiety scores produced unusual word associations and wrote
things with unusual linguistic structures.

Thus the interest exists in a variety of fields, and at least for some
types of material the problem may be soluble. A standardized measure
of tension for materials of a specified kind is conceivable.

Let us consider briefly some of the conditions for the successful
development of a measure of that sort. We noted above that invariant
verbal categories were not likely to be useful where the message was
being instrumentally manipulated. Therefore, in this connection the first
and most important thing we can say is that the measure must be of
things outside the realm of conscious manipulation. No measure of tension based, for example, on explicit statements about being worried is
likely to work, as Mahl points out in his chapter. There are alternative
strategies of rehearsing and denying anxiety, and except with the help
of clues in a rather extensive context it is not possible to say whether
presence or absence of statements of worry attests to its presence or
attests to its absence.

Mahl's speech disturbance measure meets this criterion. Try as they
may, most persons are not able to control verbal slips, sentence breaks,
"ah's," and stutters when they are tense.

Other measures may seek not that which is uncontrollable, but that
which people make no attempt to control. Linguistic categories may
provide examples of that. Our culture attaches little social value to such

things as word order. If we had data on the frequency distribution of the syntactical alternatives in language we might be able to spot mood changes by changes in the choices among them. Generally speaking, if one can find indices in realms which persons do not attempt to control, then standardized measures of the author's state of feeling may prove possible.

Measuring Valence

Similar considerations apply to categories for measuring valence, though with at least one important qualification. For reasons which will prove quite instructive, one is likely to be interested in measuring the explicit judgments expressed in a text, regardless of whether they represent the true feelings of the communicator. (In the case of tension we are normally interested in the source rather than the text.) In short, we may be interested here in making an inference not about the true feelings of the communicator but in measuring the explicit valence in the text he emits. Why that is so we shall examine in some detail in a moment, but before we do so let us consider the interest in and feasibility of valence measures.

Probably the majority of all content analysis studies done to date have used some valence measure. Campaign tracts are characterized as for or against a given side. International propaganda is characterized as friendly or hostile to national entities. Open-ended interview responses are characterized as for or against. The Lasswellian categories of "pro-self," "anti-self," "pro-other," and "anti-other" are widely used. Yet the methods used in most studies for judging valence leave something to be desired by way of rigor. Reliability may turn out to be reasonably good because human beings are so sensitively geared to this dimension of intercourse and because the texts analyzed are often quite blatantly partisan. Yet there are always subtle marginal cases, texts not easily characterized, and biases arising from the context. The problem of validly measuring valence in texts remains an important one.

That is the problem which Osgood attacked with the method he calls evaluative assertion analysis, which is described in chapter 2. It is an extension of interests represented by his work on the semantic differential. Semantic differential data always bring out the evaluative factor as the most important of all. Osgood's evaluative assertion analysis applies this finding about the connotations of words to the analysis of texts. He uses the evaluative leaning of common words to measure attitudes toward objects referred to in a text while hiding from the coder the proper names which would give clues to the context in which the object was named. The method is successful. Thus we now have at least one established standardized measure of valence in communication content independent of the context.

The feasibility and usefulness of such a measure applied to a text regardless of instrumental use may suggest to the reader that some of our earlier comments were overstated. The careful reader may have noted that the above remarks asserted that context-free measurement of symbolic forms which are instrumentally manipulated is apt to be misleading, and that therefore standardization of content measures is most feasible for behaviors below the level of conscious manipulation. Yet now we are pointing to the practicability and value of measuring explicit valences which appear on the face of a text, and nothing is more often manipulated instrumentally than expressions of evaluation. Clearly there is a range of issues here which need clarification, and it is on these issues that much of the discussion among the assembled content analysts focused. We can clarify our conclusions if we make explicit the different purposes we try to serve by content analysis. In trying to lay down rules for use of a tool we must specify what we are trying to do with it. The rules for swinging an ax are different when one is chopping than they are when one is using the back end of it as a hammer.

In table 7.2 we once again list at the left, as we did in table 7.1, the major uses of content analysis: description, inference to antecedents, inferences to effects. This time, however, we match these uses not against kinds of analysis but against kinds of texts, or, more accurately, kinds of textual characteristics to which the analysis can be applied. We distinguish now between those symbolic characteristics which are ma-

TABLE 7.2
Possibility of Standardized Categories

Uses of Content Analysis	Symbolic Characteristics			
	Variable		Invariant	
	Instrumental	Representational	Instrumental	Representational
Description	+	+	+	+
Inferences to Antecedents	0	0	+	+
Inferences to Effects	+	+	+	+

nipulated or varied with circumstances and those which in any particular situation emerge as a kind of automatic reflex. This is substantially but not exactly the distinction between instrumental or purposively controlled communication and representational communication. We noted that there could be within institutional limits instrumental behaviors either so obviously useful for a given purpose (e.g., testimonials) or so dogmatized that their presence justifies a uniform inference. So, too, there can be communication which, though representational in a limited time span, is unstable over a longer one even though not calculated for a purpose. A fad is an example. Different slang expressions express the same mood over relatively short intervals. What our generation would have described as "hot" our children describe as "cool." Thus, variations in usage which require attention to the context and which limit what can be learned by counts of uniform categories arise even in noninstrumental uses of language. Yet for many practical purposes the important variabilities in use of symbols are the instrumental ones, and the invariant patterns are representational.

The question we attempt to answer with table 7.2 is where standardized categories are apt to be effectively used and where they are not. Clearly they can be useful, as we have noted, where the patterns of symbolic use are stable, but they can also be used, even if the material is instrumentally manipulated, where the purpose is purely description. The interesting issues on which the conferees focused arise in the situations represented by the lower left portion of the table, the application of standardized categories to inferences about instrumentally manipulated material.

The proposition implied by the table is that quantitative techniques of content analysis with highly standardized categories are not likely to be useful for inferences about the antecedents of instrumentally manipulated communications but that they might be useful for inferences about responses to them. This is an assertion which is not self-evident; it needs justification. The implicit assumption here is that we are dealing with a mass media system. Content analysis, as all of social science, is so much a part of literate civilization that we are apt to take that assumption for granted and to forget that we are doing so. The assumption is that the act of producing a communication is the act of an individual or of a single and identifiable organized group, while the act of responding to a communication may well be a repeated and scattered act of many different individuals located in many different contexts. One can imagine a reverse situation; then the conclusions in the table would be reversed. An example of this reversal would be a study of American English as perceived and responded to by British travelers in the United States. Here there would be a mass source and individual, easily identified respondents. But in most of our studies it is the other way around. In the usual situation, if we study a text with a view to making an inference about its antecedents, we are studying it in order to learn something about one specific group of persons who can be located in time and place and whose history, prejudices, purposes, and operational code can be identified. Variations in the text can and should be interpreted in terms of their particular strategy.

If on the other hand we look at a text with a view to making inferences about its consequences, we sometimes, in fact often, must think of the words as having a life of their own abstracted from context, for the contexts in which they operate are so varied that we cannot summarize them. Millions of persons may hear the words in as many different contexts. The questions put to ourselves will therefore often have to be about the effects of the text itself as an isolated factor, regardless of the various contexts in which it may occur.

Not everyone who studies communication effects uses this mass media model in which the message received is an anonymous nondescript or rather "multidescript" entity. The psychiatrist, for example, is concerned with a particular person's responses. Even the propaganda analyst who is concerned with mass media may nevertheless find that he has to classify responses by broad categories of situations into which the message comes. Some of the most important findings of modern communications research have been on the ways in which the predispositions of the respondent shape his attention to, perception of, and response to a message.[17] Nevertheless, the multiplicity of ways in which a message is received in a mass media situation means that it makes more sense to describe the message itself as an independent variable than it would if we were concerned with a single receiver and could describe the message as received instead of the message itself.

Clearly the message itself is a separate entity from either its antecedents or its consequences. One could conceivably do a content analysis of messages washed ashore in sealed bottles dropped overboard by unknown persons. Inferences about the antecedents of the messages would be quite free from the helpful warping provided by knowledge of the author. But in real life it seldom makes sense to proceed in that way; one can gain a great deal by taking account of all the instrumental considerations which went into the unique event of composition. The author of mass media materials, however, to some small degree approaches the situation of the sailor dropping the bottle over the side. He does not know who will listen. For the analyst of effects it therefore makes sense to make what inferences he can on the basis of the text alone, regardless of the context of the receipt. It follows that for greater generality our table should really be relabeled. The second row should be labeled "Inferences about identified communicators, whether senders or receivers," and the third row should be labeled "Inferences about unidentifiable communicators."

We were alerted to this set of considerations in the first place by the conclusion that measures of tension could best be made with invariant noninstrumental aspects of communications, while measures of valence seemed useful even where applied to symbols that were instrumentally manipulated. The reason is now clear. The measure of tension is a measure designed to learn something about the specific author of the communication. The measure of valence, among its other uses, is one for the purpose of estimating what is coming into a diverse audience of interest to us. An evaluative assertion analysis of newspaper bias in a campaign, for example, might be for the purpose of learning whether the audience is receiving equivalent stimulus material from the different sides. Its finding might be entirely wrong for any one reader because of his deliberate exercise of selection among reading materials. But we have to wash out that kind of idiosyncrasy if we are trying to generalize about communication to a large and diverse audience.

The general rule is simply that the more one can conveniently learn about the specific language use of the persons of interest, the less sense it makes to rely on standardized categories based on the language itself without interpretation of its private significance to him. On the other hand, the less one is able to say about the specifics of the language use of the persons of interest in the case of interest, the more sense do standardized categories make. There seems to be no issue of principle beyond that.

Valence seems to be something which can be reasonably well judged without reference to the context in which a statement is made. Osgood finds relatively high reliability of coding of masked evaluative material. In that respect expressions of valence seem to be relatively closely geared to the linguistic code in which communication takes place. One of the characteristics of language of which linguists have made a good deal is that there can be agreement on what the code is in the presence of sharp differences in the uses to which it is put. Thus one of the common assertions of linguists is that they do not need a sample from a culture, but only one good informant to tell them about a language. For if a symbol does not communicate to the informant, regardless of whether it is one he would accept or like, then it is not an effective part of the code. In the same way, judgments of valence communicated may have a validity quite apart from the context.

Osgood's evaluative assertion analysis relies upon judges who are users of the linguistic code in which the communication takes place. For the reasons just noted, the judges succeed in making reliable judgments. One wonders whether it is not possible to take a further step and identify the factors which lead the judges to judge as they do. Since in evaluative assertion analysis the judges see only the text and not the context, there must be something in the words themselves which conveys the valence. That which communicates the valence may lie in part in the evaluative loading of particular words; the semantic differential technique can document that. But it must also lie in part in the linguistic structure of the message, for one can presumably make sentences of different intensities by rearranging the same evaluative words. The problem is to identify the different ways within the linguistic code in which evaluation can be expressed. This brings us directly to the central problem in the relation of linguistics and content analysis: how can we relate categories of the language to categories of meaning; what are the different ways in which a single idea can be expressed?

Linguistics and Content Analysis

On the face of it, the relation of linguistics to content analysis should be a close one, but historically it has not been. Both linguists and content analysts analyze texts and are concerned with language patterns, but two differences in their approaches have kept them apart.

Linguists have not been interested in meanings, but only in "the distribution of forms, that is, their privilege of occurrence in relation to other forms..." (chap. 4). Content analysts have not been interested in forms, but only in the meanings which these forms convey.

Linguists historically have not been interested in frequencies. They have tended to consider only whether it was allowable for a given structure to appear, not how often it appeared. Content analysts have been interested only in quantities, not in the difference between that which was not possible of occurrence in the language and that which was possible but occurred in their sample with almost zero frequency.

Both these differences of approach seem likely to be bridged in the near future. The bridges may be built from both directions. Linguistic methods may shed some light on analysis of meanings. Note, for example, the suggestion by Saporta and Sebeok that at least some aspects of the semantic relationship between pairs of related terms could be deduced from distributional data by noting the difference in the distributions within limited texts and in the language as a whole (e.g., capitalism and communism occur in identical linguistic environments in the language as a whole but not in a single author's statements). On the other hand, even if linguistic methods continue to be applied exclusively to formal matters, content analysts can usefully inform themselves of what the available equivalent forms are through which any given meaning can be expressed. The usefulness to content analysts of knowledge of linguistic forms has been put clearly by a psycholinguist, John B. Carroll: "Linguistic and psycholinguistic studies could aid in the formulation of more reliable and valid content analysis categories. Linguistic analysis suggests the possibility of establishing categories based on form classes or substitution groups (for example, the range of ways in which a particular country could be referred to might be described in this way)."[18]

The difference between the nonstatistical approach of the linguist and the statistical approach of the content analyst is already being bridged. Some linguistic scholars, notably B. Mandelbrot, have been working with probability models.[19] The main interest has been on the degree of concentration in the forms used, that is, what proportion of all form usages are provided by any given proportion of the available forms.[20] Most linguists still are satisfied to distinguish roughly between major and minor patterns of the language, but there is a beginning of more quantitative work.

Thus the barriers between linguistics and content analysis seem likely to give way, and it seems probable at least that content analysis methods will be increasingly enriched by knowledge of the findings of linguistic research. Four likely lines of influence suggest themselves. Linguistics is likely to be useful to content analysts (1) by providing a model of a discipline which has successfully treated certain problems of textual analysis; (2) by providing methods for establishing the semantic identity of different forms; (3) by providing methods for stating the relationships between semantic entities in a text; and (4) by suggesting some not otherwise obvious behavioral indicators of the communicator's state at the time of communication.

Linguistics as a Model

We have already noted above that contingency analysis was in part suggested by the notions of distributional linguistic analysis. Linguists observe the environments in which a given form appears. The contingency content analyst in much the same way asks in what semantic environment any given semantic entity appears. It seems probable that the methods used in coping with the former problem may have some suggestive relevance to the latter. Linguistic analysis, for example, treats two forms as identical if they may appear in identical environments. But as Saporta and Sebeok point out, one might treat the probabilities of their appearing in identical environments as in some respects a measure of their meaning. Thus, to use their example, *eye doctor* and *oculist* are closer than *oculist* and *lawyer,* in that there are more meaningful environments in which either of the former pair could appear than in which either of the latter pair could appear.

Establishing the Semantic Identity of Different Forms

Content analysis categories are seldom single morphemes or uniquely defined groups of morphemes. They are usually concepts capable of being expressed in a number of different ways. On the face of it, the counting of verbal expressions to ascertain the extent of or emphasis on certain concepts might be thought to require that we identify the precise verbal forms which convey those concepts. Historically, however, that has seldom been done. Most content analysis procedures use the coder as a judge of what lexical forms convey what meanings of interest. They have relied on the common sense of a coder who was, of course, a user of the language in which the analysis was being done. His common sense enables him to recognize, for example, that the phrases "a man of courage," "a brave man," and "a guy with guts" all mean the same thing.

We noted above Carroll's suggestion that linguistics might provide useful and more objective ways to define categories of equivalent meanings, as for instance the different ways of referring to a country. This author and most of his fellow conferees share this view, but it is not self-evident that there is much to be gained by such linguistic definition of categories. One may wonder how much improvement is to be expected from the substitution of formal linguistic rules of equivalence for common sense in content analysis. With a certain amount of care, reliability can be achieved between coders who are ordinary users of a language. One might argue that the probability of improving upon such human judges is small. Even if that turns out to be true, linguistic analysis can help us to understand what the coder is doing. Even if we do not improve on the "human computer," we want to learn how that computer works when it recognizes quite different forms as equivalent.

Furthermore, it may well be that a better understanding of the alternative forms of expression available for any given meaning will enable us to devise more sensitive and parsimonious content analysis categories for human coders to use. Categories designed by persons lacking sophistication in linguistic forms tend to catch different meanings within the same category and fail to catch the relevant ones. The more refined and rigorous the content analysis the more that is apt to be true. Refinement and rigor come at the expense of the coder's intuitions, as Alexander George emphasized in his chapter. Thus, as content analyses become more refined and rigorous it may well be that analysts need to become linguistically more sophisticated if they are to avoid the dangers of mechanical absurdity. An example of the kind of thing which would be most useful to content analysts, to which we have already referred more than once, is Harris' rules of grammatical equivalence.

Establishing Semantic Relationships

An example of a refinement for which some linguistic analysis would be quite useful comes to mind as we think of the next steps in contingency analysis. To establish a contingency we need a unit of space, and then if we find within that unit both of two symbolic elements we say that we have a contingency. That, however, is a rather simple measure. To note only that two words or two ideas appear in the same paragraph or sentence is not fully indicative of what is communicated. We may want also to know their structural relationship. Mr. Cameron, for example, tends to associate youth and disease. These terms appear in the same speeches. But clearly they are counterposed; they are poles on a single continuum in Cameron's thinking, even though they are not semantically antonyms. On the other hand, it is entirely possible that the antonym of youth, namely, old age, might show up as not part of a contingency with youth and disease precisely because it is an alternative label for the end of the continuum for which Cameron actually uses the label disease. Thus a negative contingency finding might indicate homonyms, one of which was preferred. Osgood, as well as Saporta and Sebeok, note that an empirical contingency can be interpreted in different ways depending on whether the entities related are synonyms, antonyms, or independent of each other.

Clearly it is possible to conceive of a new and more refined kind of contingency analysis which would take account not merely of the co-presence of items, but would code them differently according to whether the linguistic structures relating them showed them to be joined, counterposed, or independent. In such an analysis one would code the symbols Jack and Jill differently in each of the following semantic relationships. Joined: "Jack and Jill went up the hill"; counterposed: "Jack was a boy, Jill was a girl"; independent: successive entries in a telephone book, "Jack Smith, Jill Smith." Such coding of direction and intensity of connectedness was used, it will be recalled, in evaluative assertion analysis.

The value of such combined contingency and structural coding may be brought out by reference to the discussion of the relation of contingency and meaning.

A number of persons, among them Zellig Harris and the present author, have attempted to use intersymbol contingencies or formal distribution as a definition or index of meaning for empirical studies.[21] The assertion is that the meaning of a word may be considered as approximated or explicated by the probability of its appearance given the other words of the context. That this can lead to an oversimple interpretation of meaning has been shown by Saporta and Sebeok in their chapter and by Saporta more fully in a recent article.[22] Let us quote Saporta: "Harris' thesis is perhaps best summarized in his statement that 'if we consider words or morphemes A and B to be more different in meaning than A and C, then we will often find that the distributions of A and B are more different than the distributions of A and C. In other words difference of meaning correlates with difference in distribution.... Although Harris' hypothesis may turn out to be valid, i.e., that there are distributional correlates of meaning difference, some refinement is necessary before the hypothesis can be stated in a testable form."[23] Harris discusses various kinds of pairs of forms "where presumably distributional correlates may be established for differences in meaning."[24] Among these are stylistic alternatives, for example *ain't* and *am not;* synonyms, for example *eye doctor* and *oculist;* pairs from the same grammatical class, for example *oculist* and *lawyer;* and members of two different grammatical classes. The last of these may be defined as never having the same environments. Pairs of the penultimate kind, for example *oculist* and *lawyer,* may differ in meaning corresponding to the amount of difference in their environments.

With regard to these matters Saporta points out several things. For one, opposites tend to share common environments. "Bad and naughty are closer in meaning than bad and good. And yet, the relatively restricted use of naughty might result in its sharing fewer environments with bad than good does."[25] Secondly, members of different grammatical classes, for example *chair* and *sit,* may share more in meaning than pairs from within the same grammatical class. Third, note that two words such as *ser* and *estar* in Spanish may be rather strictly specified for different situations, yet have a single translation (to be) in another language. Finally, the choice of measures of degree of difference in distributions "will in large part determine the degree of correlation."[26]

Thus there are problems in identifying meaning with distribution in the linguists' sense. Some of these same considerations apply to the identification of meaning and contingency, though contingency is a looser concept than distribution, and thus avoids some of the difficulties regarding grammatical class, since forms of different grammatical classes appear freely in the same contingency analysis unit.

If we are to clarify the relation of contingency and meaning, it is perhaps desirable to distinguish three levels of description of lexical practices. The simplest descriptions concern mere contingencies. *Youth* and *disease* are contingent for Mr. Cameron. At the next level we introduce other structural facts. *Youth* and *disease* are contingent but structurally joined by dissociative connectors rather than by associative ones. (Note that that could not necessarily be established simply by the co-contingency of dissociative terms with *youth* and *disease,* if, for example, Cameron always counterposed *youth and vigor* to *disease,* for then there would be many associative "ands" in the unit, too.) At the third level we introduce descriptions of aspects of meaning, *if there are any,* which are not indexed by structural facts at all.

The confusion of these levels in its most extreme form would consist of the assertion, already shown to be wrong, that positive contingency between two words implies similarity in their meaning. A more sophisticated statement asserts that if one described completely the contingencies between any one word and all other words taken not singly but in all possible groupings (the groupings being of course without reference to order), one would have in effect a complete description of the distribution of the word. For the reason noted in the previous paragraph, even that is probably not strictly true, but is an arguable version of the notion that the meaning of a word is the company it keeps. As an abstract proposition it is at least a close approximation. But as a practical matter it is not of much use. It is far more practicable to consider contingency data only for pairs or small groups of words at a time, and to take account of the semantic facts which make the interpretation of identical contingency data on *youth* and *disease, youth* and *old age,* and *old age* and *disease,* for example, all quite different.

In the interesting discussion of these matters by Saporta and Sebeok we are left with a further unanswered but interesting question concerning the relation of the second and third of the above levels of description of lexical facts. Are there semantic facts which cannot be described by distributional facts at all, and how can those semantic facts be objectively described? Can we hypothetically conceive of words having identical distributions and yet different meanings? If so, is there any objective index of the nondistributional element of their meaning? Does the semantic differential technique index such an element, and if so, fully or only in part? Clarification of this order of highly abstract questions about the relationship of linguistic codes and meaning may prove of considerable practical significance for the designing of content analysis categories.

Linguistic Indicators of Behavior

Finally, one of the contributions of linguistics to content analysis is to indicate which characteristics of language use are fixed characteristics of the code and therefore constant between persons and situations, and which characteristics are particular to a speaker or situation and therefore useful as psycholinguistic indices. For example, in a tonal language tone is partly fixed and cannot be used as an index of mood, as freely as it can in English.

Pausal phenomena and speech disturbances (which Mahl described), word order, syllable-word quotients, word-sentence quotients, parts of speech quotients, common words, uncommon words, and many other linguistic phenomena were mentioned as worthy of exploration as psychological indices. The suggestions for indices and their use were numerous and varied. Let us summarize some of the suggestions which came out at the conference.

Newman: It seems to be a natural phenomenon of language to have polar terms [e.g., hot, cold; good, bad; etc.]. That breaks through all the differences you get in linguistic structure between cultures; but the way in which particular concepts are polarized in different cultures varies.

Casagrande and Osgood: Bilinguals under some circumstances revert to constructions which are characteristic of their first language. In a psychiatric interview this may also be revealing of association to childhood. More generally, with respect to age level there are shifting probabilities of different constructions. When a patient is talking spontaneously, those are not something he is likely to control. Does he talk within the patterns of the level to which he is associating?

Saporta: There are also different social levels of a language, formal, standard colloquial, substandard colloquial, etc.; also geographic dialects. What do shifts between these indicate about the state of a speaker?

Osgood: These may also index social relations. Forms of politeness index relationships between people.

Pool: Such choice of language type also indexes the role in which a person conceives of himself or his activity. The fact that we discuss content analysis in academese indicates the class of things to which we conceive of it as belonging. One might find politics belonging to the realm of the ideological or the personal according to the language chosen to discuss it.

Osgood: One might in an experiment have subjects write letters to hypothetical persons having different social roles with respect to the writer.

Saporta: A study has been made of the language that mothers use to children. Mothering language is quite different from normal language.

Casagrande: The use of that would be a clue to emotional states in therapy.

Newman: The width of difference in a subject's spoken and written language might throw light on the control of the individual in assuming roles.

Note that all these suggestions required of the linguists that they study the distinctive features of certain types of language. Some of that sort of work has been done; much remains to be done. The discussion of "marked members" in the chapter by Saporta and Sebeok is a treatment of this problem. The marked elements are equivalent to unmarked elements and sometimes to alternative marked elements except that they convey special connotations. These are not only about the referent, but also about the discourse situation. Thus *he arrived prematurely* for *he came too soon* is a choice of formal language which might index psychological states of the speaker or the social relation in which he is talking. Further linguistic study of such marked forms, particularly statistical linguistic study of their use, would be of utmost help to content analysts.

All of the above comments concern variations in types of discourse within a single language code. Clearly the job of analysis of the available variations and their significance must be done separately for each language. Thus the problems of cross-cultural content analysis are all of the above multiplied by the different language codes involved. Historically a good deal of content analysis research has been cross-cultural.

Most of Lasswell's work and the work of those influenced by him has concerned the parallelisms and divergences of trends in attention to major political symbols in different countries. It has been possible to do that sort of comparative analysis at least within the West because the major political concepts have been shared across linguistic boundaries. Democracy, communism, socialism, parliaments, political parties, peace, war, are the central ideological entities of political discussion in all of Western civilization. Nuances certainly vary, and problems of translation have existed for this kind of analysis, but they were not of such magnitude as to invalidate the procedure (e.g., political issues are much the same in all parts of Switzerland; the definition of the issues is hardly a function of the language in which they are discussed). That is clearly true for as homogeneous a culture area as the West, and is probably, though not certainly, also true for much wider areas. At least in national politics, the major symbolisms of Western ideologies have taken hold fairly extensively all over the world. Miss Martha Jane Smith of New York University recently did a comparative content analysis of Soviet and Chinese communist propaganda to the United States,[27] modeling her technique on the Library of Congress and RADIR studies. There were interesting divergences as well as parallelisms, some probably cultural in explanation and some political. For example, the Chinese put more emphasis on symbols for the people, and imperialism; the Russians did not discuss the Korean War. But none of the divergences would seem to be a product of the fact that the political concepts had been originally framed in different languages. The Chinese have managed to take over the baggage of Marxism-Leninism.

The above comments, however, are impressionistic statements, and open up one more large and important area of psycholinguistic investigation which would be of much use to content analysts. How far do language codes affect the content of the messages conveyable and conveyed in them? That is the question most generally associated with the name of Benjamin Whorf.[28] The discussion which he stimulated has given rise to much of the most interesting recent psycholinguistic research. There is now some fairly strong evidence that the code is not totally without effect at least on such elementary matters as color recall.[29] But the magnitude and scope of influence of the code remains a matter for study and one in which content analysts are bound to have an interest.

All of this suggests that though psycholinguistic indicators will be different in different languages, yet there may be some important cross-language uniformities. There may be some real universals. Perhaps sentence breaks and slips increase with anxiety in every culture and language. Perhaps there are some universal significances to shrill or rumbling sounds. The onomatopoeic quality of sounds can be interpreted with better-than-chance results by nonusers of a language. Aside from any such true universals which may exist, there are also universal categories, the precise indicators of which vary between languages but which can be translated. Newman noted that all languages seem to have polar terms. Osgood's research on the semantic differential suggests that the evaluative dimension is dominant in all. If so, polarity and specifically evaluative polarity could be used cross-culturally in a content analysis study though the indicatorial symbols would be different and differently grouped in each language. Formal language, colloquial language, rude language, mothering language, upperclass language, lower-class language, men's language, women's language, children's language, are probably categories for every language. The linguist, however, must identify the elements in different languages which are equivalent, not semantically, but in serving to identify these varieties of speech. These elements may be very different and not even formally alike. But they help to define universal categories in which the content analyst is interested. The problem is in many ways not unlike that of finding the lexical indicators which in different languages serve to identify the same universal semantic concept. Thus the content analyst interested in cross-cultural research stands to benefit from any progress which linguistics makes on problems of translation. It would seem that the fruitful interchange between content analysis and linguistics is only beginning.

Notes

1. It should not be assumed that qualitative methods are insightful, and quantitative ones merely mechanical methods for checking hypotheses. The relationship is a circular one; each provides new insights on which the other can feed. New insights about a text gained by a quantitative content analysis, once discovered, become obvious and can be used in further intuitive examination of the text. Discovering by quantitative analysis the unsuspected fact that Richard Wright is preoccupied with personal safety, one will then not miss such allusions in an ordinary reading of his works. Indeed, it was suggested at the conference that a good way to train qualitative content analysts was to make them do quantitative analyses, for the rigor of the latter makes them aware of aspects of communication which they might otherwise miss.
2. For a recent example of a frequency content analysis, see Karin Dovring's chapter on land reform as a propaganda theme in Dovring, K. *Land and labor in Europe, 1900–1950*. The Hague: M. Nijhoff, 1956.
3. In Osgood's chapter, in which contingency analysis receives its fullest and best-elaborated statement, he presents it in a pure form which sharply distinguishes it from frequency analysis. Following his procedure one ends up at a certain point with a matrix containing only plusses and minuses representing presence above a critical level (or not) of each symbol in each unit of tabulation. It should be noted, however, that it is quite possible to combine frequency and contingency measurement. We could ask how far the number of occurrences of symbol A departs from the ordinarily expected number if symbol B happens to be present in the environment. Such data would be conveyed if Osgood's Figure 3A or Raw Data Matrix had scale numbers in it instead of just plusses and minuses. Another combination of contingency and frequency data is found in this author's *Symbols of Democracy* (Stanford, CA: Stanford University Press, 1952), in which normal equations are computed for predicting the frequency of one symbol given a certain frequency of certain other symbols in the environment, and then departures of frequency from the expected level are measured.
4. Baldwin, A. L. "Personal structure analysis: A statistical method for investigating the individual personailty." *Journal of Abnormal and Social Psychology* 37(1942), 163–83.
5. Carroll, Agard, Dulany, Newman; Newmark, Osgood, Sebeok, and Solomon, *Interdisciplinary Summer Seminar in Psychology and Linquistics*, p. 27.
6. Shannon, C., Weaver, W. *Mathematical theory of communication*, Urbana, IL: University of Illinois Press, 1949.
7. Harris, Z. "Discourse analysis," *Language*, 28(1952), 1–30, p. 2.
8. Harris, "Discourse analysis," p. 3.
9. Harris, "Discourse analysis," p. 5.
10. "Representational" means that something in the words of the message may have indicatorial validity regardless of circumstances, and it is at the message that the analyst looks. "Instrumental" in a rough way signifies that the important point is not what the message says on the face of it but what it conveys, given context and circumstances.
11. This differs from Mahl's usage since an indicator deviating from manifest lexical content may be quite stable as an indicator. Mahl, in short, selects the second of the options mentioned in the paragraph just above.

12. Rush, M. *The rise of Khrushchev.* Washington, DC: Public Affairs Press, 1958. See also Leites, Bernaut, and Garthoff, "Politburo images of Stalin," for a similar analysis of the speeches on Stalin's seventieth birthday.
13. Vakar, N. "The mass communication index: Some observations on Communist Russian discourse." *Symposium* 10 (1956): 42–59.
14. Alexander George discusses in some detail the relation of hypothesis formation and hypothesis testing. See his *Propaganda analysis.* Evanston, IL: Row, Peterson, 1959.
15. Up to now, in the absence of any means for testing what symbols properly formed a cluster, it has been hard to avoid lumping together things that were different, or counting equivalent categories as separate. One of the problems in content analysis has been that almost any category can be made to seem the most frequent by subdividing the others finely enough. There is no natural standard for fineness of categories. A contingency analysis enables us to set such standards because it provides a measurement of distance between symbols. We can establish a specific distance criterion for a category.
16. Both George and Garraty have published on Wilson, George specifically attempting to elucidate the psychology of the man from the historical records. George, A. L.; George, J. *Woodrow Wilson and Col. House: A personality study.* New York: J. Day Co., 1956, and Garraty, J. A. *Woodrow Wilson: A great life in brief.* New York: Knopf, 1956.
17. See Hovland, C.; Lumsdaine, A.; Sheffield, F. *Experiments on mass communication.* Princeton, NJ: Princeton University Press, 1949; Hovland, C.; Janis, I.; Kelly, H. *Communication and persuasion.* New Haven, CT: Yale University Press, 1953; Berelson, B.; Lazarsfeld, P.; McPhee, W. *Voting.* Chicago: University of Chicago Press, 1954.
18. Carroll, J. B. *The study of language.* Cambridge, MA: Harvard University Press, 1953, p. 120.
19. Mandelbrot, M. "An informational theory of the structure of language based upon the statistical matching of messages and coding," in *Proceedings of a symposium on information theory,* ed. W. Jackson. London: Royal Society, 1950, and "Structure formelle des textes et communication." *Word* 10 (1954): 1–27. See also Herdan, G. *Language as choice and chance.* Groningen: 1956, and the critique of Herdan by M. Halle in *Kratylos* 3 (1958): 20–28.
20. See Whatmough, J. *Language, a modern synthesis.* NY: St. Martin's Press, 1956, chap. 11, and Yule, G.U. *The statistical study of literary vocabulary.* Cambridge, England: The University Press, 1944.
21. Pool, Ithiel de Sola. "Symbols, meanings and social science," in Bryson, L. (ed.) *Symbols and values.* New York: Harper, 1954. Also Harris, "Distributional structure."
22. Sol Saporta. "A note on the relation between meaning and distribution."
23. Saporta. Ibid., p. 22.
24. Ibid.
25. Ibid., p. 23.
26. Ibid., p. 26.
27. Smith, Martha J. "Key symbols in U.S.S.R. and Chinese propaganda to the U.S.A." Ph.D. thesis, New York University, New York, 1958.
28. Carroll, J. B. *Language, thought, and reality: selected writings of Benjamin Lee Whorf.* Cambridge, MA: MIT Press, 1956.
29. Lenneberg, E. H. "Cognition in ethnolinguistics." *Language* 29 (1953): 463–71; Lenneberg. E. H.; Roberts, J.M. *Language of experience.* Bloomington: Indiana University Publications in Anthropology and Linguistics, 1956.

Part II

Societal Impact

Editor's Introduction

"Politics: Who Gets What, When, How"
—Harold Lasswell

Foresight and Hindsight: The Case of the Telephone

To foresee effects of emerging telecommunications technologies, Ithiel Pool began to assemble, step by step, a set of intellectual resources. This selection is a summary of lessons about the validity of methods of forecasting, drawn from the introduction of the telephone. Who foresaw the social impact of the telephone, and by what methods? Were there valid methods that could be applied in other cases?

This retrospective technology assessment was sobering as there were, at the beginning, so few accurate predictions! And yet there were lessons. For example, that the invention of a new technology like the telephone did not alone determine the future: many additional inventions were needed (e.g., bank switching, devices to augment signals over long distances, and the performance of the original invention needed to be improved) to develop the potential and create the pathway for its modern ubiquity. The availability of other individuals who could secure funding and operate businesses played a vital role—i.e., so that market forces could provide a tidal force. And, to build the future, there needed to be visionaries who saw where the creative potential of a new technology could lead and whose vision helped to stimulate other inventions and helped businessmen to secure venture capital.

Communication Technology and Land Use

Several key lessons about the impact of new telecommunications technology emerged from the telephone case and are summarized in this article concerning land use (e.g., the location and size of multisite businesses, effects on urbanization, etc.). Pool found that effects differed in different periods, depending upon the saturation of the new technology (i.e., a critical mass of other people needed to be acquiring a telephone before it made sense to adopt it); other new technologies (e.g., the streetcar, and then the automobile; the construction technologies for skyscrapers); the changing prices of the new services vs. older services (e.g., the cost of office boys to carry messages prior to the telephone); and other factors.[1]

Within social science, Ithiel Pool's view can be categorized as "soft" technological determinism. That is, technology does not compel new technology and lockstep adaptation of the human race as an autonomous force (the "hard" position) with a logic of its own. But it does encourage further inventions, change relative costs, create new possibilities, and make certain futures and pathways *easier* or more attractive, or more likely to be pursued.

Pool's analysis, however, leads to a deeper and more politically relevant conclusion than a well-elaborated "soft" determinism. If you seek to predict the future by the formula of greater x produces greater y, the curious result is that Pool observes effects for y and against y (e.g., urbanization). And, while there is a main effect, the critical discovery is that the type of telecommunications invention represented in the telephone is a technology of *freedom*—that is, the dependent variable is that people are doing, to a greater degree, what they *want* to do because the technology eventually (e.g., at a degree of critical mass, performance, and affordable pricing) provides an increased general capability and more options. This view (also present in his *Technologies of Freedom*) leads to the reconceptualization of the dependent variable that should be the initially specified focus of forecasting (i.e., "free choice"—meaning both freer from constraints and with more capacity) and to the bold predictions of his later work about how freer people and institutions might decide to organize their lives and activities.

The Mass Media and Politics in the Modernization Process

The existence of media gives politicians a vastly increased opportunity for leadership. (p. 223, below)

In this third selection Ithiel Pool reviews the (very different) uses of the mass media in the development plans of communist and noncommunist countries. He suggests a broader framework of eight types of possible impact of the mass media and discusses the convergence of findings, concerning when these effects occur, between American experiments and surveys and these field observations in peasant societies and other cultures: "a happy but rare conjunction of observation with theory in the social sciences" (p. 223, below). The paper then moves beyond content *per se* to begin an analysis of the social and political impacts of such new technologies—for example, in the quotation at the beginning of this section, he notes that any of the mass media give any politicians "a vastly increased opportunity for leadership." (The same type of influence becomes available, in principle, to *anybody* if, using the emerging technologies in the years ahead, they can secure an audience.)

The reader may wish to note, in particular, Pool's brief summary of the use of mass media for education ("distance learning"). At least in the developing world it has proved important to use educational technologies in conjunction with face-to-face relationships with teachers who can use their relationship to engage and sustain motivation. Whether new computer software or interactive video capacities of new technologies can solve this problem remains unanswered.

Four Unnatural Institutions and the Road Ahead

The final selection is a brisk outline of where the analysis is heading. In the background, as he is writing it, Ithiel Pool is also drafting his last (posthumous) book, *Technologies Without Boundaries*, that lays out how different the new technologies will be than in the era of mass communications.

The world has gone through three eras in the past 150 years. From (1) traditional methods of communications in premodern or peasant societies; to (2) one-way mass communications to national audiences; to (3) an emerging era of telecommunications that will be cheap, abundant, high-capacity, interactive, user-controlled, and global and combined with user-controlled computers of rapidly growing capacity. Each of these characteristics represents shifts of resources (and especially control) to the *user*. And, thus, *each* of the new elements contributes to a technology of *freedom* and will probably lead to a far greater reorganization of the world, with a different logic, than was seen for an era of mass market radio and television (and advertising) controlled by only a few institutions.

To put it another way: Pool's argument is that it is wrong to believe that the future of the world will be generated along the same linear trends that popular commentators identified as major effects of earlier communication inventions (e.g., that the telegraph and telephone permitted the management and control of ever-larger bureaucratic organizations). This, Pool argued in the telephone case, was a common error of forecasting: apparently inspired in 1908 by a famous treatise in sociology, popular commentators often have seen new technology, modernization and modernity as one steady progress (i.e., from the *gemeinschaft* of small peasant communities to the *gesellschaft* of impersonal modern societies) and interpreted each new technology as accelerating the story.[2] His argument about "unnatural" institutions seems to imply that people—given freedom—now will seek to restore elements of what was lost (*gemeinschaft*), although there probably will be a wide variation of results as people and institutions, in conjunction with market experiments, explore a range of creative options.

Harold Lasswell's famous framework for the appropriate study of politics ("Who Gets What, When, How?"), quoted at the beginning of this section, also was Ithiel Pool's. It encompassed *all* the processes (not simply the formal actions of governments or activities of politicians) that shaped the bottom lines in people's lives. In this framework, the politics of wired nations are beginning to change deeply, but not as a result of mainstream, liberal, conservative, nationalist, socialist, or self-designated radical political platforms or the categories of analysis and prescription on policy-argument television. New telecommunications technologies will change the "who gets what, when, and how" in the world: the clues for forecasting are provided by a social science analysis that abstracts the critical characteristics that can be initially observed in the impacts of the telephone (the first "wired" invention)—more user-controlled, widely available, low cost, interactive—that made it a technology of freedom. The question of how these potentials can be developed—the barriers, dangers, and policy choices—are the subject of the next section.

Notes

1. The argument that Pool cites, that the telephone was a critical technology to make large urban skyscrapers economically feasible (because the message traffic carried by office boys in densely populated tall skyscrapers would require such space devoted to elevator capacity as to make the skyscraper unfeasible) is intriguing but doubtful. The pneumatic tube offered an alternative for within-building traffic and to deliver messages to a ground floor station for outside delivery. And there were plans underway to connect buildings in parts of Manhattan via an underground network of such tubes.

2. For example, the view of "modern" design and the future that was promoted earlier in the twentieth century and that envisioned homes, buildings, and cities that seemed impersonal, sparse, technological, often with a color palette of white and chrome, decoration with abstract forms, etc.

8

Foresight and Hindsight:
The Case of the Telephone

with Craig Decker, Stephen Lizard, Kay Israel,
Pamela Rubin, and Barry Weinstein

Let us try to go back to the period from 1876 until World War II, to ascertain how people perceived and foresaw the social effects of the telephone. By taking advantage of hindsight in 1976, we can ask which forecasts were good, which went askew, and why.

Forecasters: Good and Bad

Some sensationally good forecasts were made. In 1878, a letter from Alexander Graham Bell in London to the organizers of the new Electronic Telephone Company outlines his thoughts on the orientation of the company; it is such a remarkable letter that we quote it in full in an appendix to this chapter. The letter describes a universal point-to-point service connecting everyone through a central office in each community, to in turn be connected by long-distance lines. Aronson noted in chapter 1 that when the telephone was first invented, it was not obvious that it would be used in that way. Bell briefly considered a path that others were to pursue after he had given up—using the device for broadcasting in a mode like that of the modern radio. The reader can refer to Aronson's interesting analysis of why Bell originally pondered that alternative and why he instead came to a clear perception of the telephone as a conversational rather than broadcasting device. The result was a prevision of the phone system as it exists today, a century later.

From *The Social Impact of the Telephone* (1977) edited by Ithiel de Sola Pool.

The technology that existed then did not permit universal, switched, long-distance service; Bell's description of such a system was a prescient forecast.

The small group of men who created the telephone system did share Bell's vision. Theodore N. Vail and Gardiner Greene Hubbard, in particular, worked to implement "the grand system" they had in their minds—a system in which the monopoly telephone company would provide service in virtually every home and office, linking local systems throughout the nation and the civilized world. They visualized the device as one that everyone could afford and saw it organized as a common carrier eventually surpassing telegraph usage.

Their optimism was not shared by all. In 1879, Sir William Preece, the chief engineer of the British Post Office, testified to a special committee of the House of Commons that the telephone had little future in Britain:

> I fancy the descriptions we get of its use in America are a little exaggerated, though there are conditions in America which necessitate the use of such instruments more than here. Here we have a superabundance of messengers, errand boys and things of that kind.... The absence of servants has compelled Americans to adopt communication systems for domestic purposes. Few have worked at the telephone much more than I have. I have one in my office, but more for show. If I want to send a message—I use a sounder or employ a boy to take it.[1]

In 1878, Theodore Vail, then a young railroad mail superintendent, quit the U.S. Post Office to join the newly organized Bell Telephone Company. "Uncle" Joe Cannon, a young Congressman, expressed surprise and regret that the company had "got a hold of a nice fellow like Vail":

> The Assistant Postmaster General could scarcely believe that a man of Vail's sound judgment, one who holds an honorable and far more responsible position than any man under the Postmaster General, should throw it up for a d—d old Yankee notion (a piece of wire with two Texas steer horns attached to the ends with an arrangement to make the concern bleat like a calf) called a telephone.[2]

Not all the forecasting errors were on the side of stodgy conservatism. There were also wild dreams of the wide blue yonder. General Carty, chief engineer of AT&T since 1907, predicted there would be international telephony one day, and also forecast that it would bring peace on earth:

> Some day we will build up a world telephone system making necessary to all peoples the use of a common language, or common understanding of languages, which will join all the people of the earth into one brotherhood.... When by the aid of science

and philosophy and religion, man has prepared himself to receive a message, we can all believe there will be heard, throughout the earth, a great voice coming out of the ether, which will proclaim, "Peace on earth, good will towards men."[3]

There is a striking contrast in the quality of forecasting and analysis between the small group of initial developers of the telephone and other commentators. Is it because the founders were particularly intelligent men? Perhaps the same mental powers that made them succeed as inventors and entrepreneurs were at work in their forecasts. Or, second, is it because they were living with the subject, eighteen hours a day, year after year? Should we expect the same insight in a congressman's or journalist's quick comments? Third, the telephone pioneers brought together a combination of scientific knowledge and business motivation; Bell was not just a scientist nor Vail only a businessman. They belonged to that remarkable American species of practical technologists, including Morse, Edison, Ford, and Land, who were both inventors and capitalists. They were interested not only in what might be theoretically possible but also in what would sell; the optimism of their speculations was controlled by a profound concern for the balance sheet.[4] Perhaps such concerns are among the crucial ingredients for good technological forecasting.

The activism of the early developers suggests a fourth possible reason for their success as forecasters: they fulfilled their own prophesies. They had the inventions, a vision of how the inventions could be used, and they controlled the businesses that implemented those visions. This theory does not exclude other propositions. The self-fulfilling prophesy of planners can work if, and only if, it accounts for technical and economic realities. Yet the weight we attach to each of the possible reasons for successful prediction and the conditions under which they apply make a great deal of difference to how we would make a technology assessment.

Some Forecasts

We shall offer further speculation about the factors contributing to accurate forecasts, but first we shall examine closely a few predictions, who made them, and how they look in retrospect.

Universal Service

The telephone was an expensive device in its early years; a subscriber paid a flat amount for unlimited service. Furthermore, the combinatorial nature of a network meant that linkage complexity increased faster than the number of nodes. Until fully automated switching, the company's cost of serving each subscriber was greater the larger the number of other subscribers.[5]

With switchboards, the problem was partially solved. Still, as the number of subscribers grew, the operator's job in making the connection grew more than proportionally; a manual switchboard could only be of a certain size. Bell understood this; in *Financial Notes* in 1905, he is quoted as arguing that as the number of people in an exchange increased, the operator's work increased exponentially; hence, the exchanges would eventually all have to be automated:

> In the telephone of the future I look for all this business to be done automatically.... If this can be accomplished, it will do away with the cast army of telephone operators, and so reduce the expense that the poorest man cannot afford to be without this telephone.

One early telephone manager commented that "so far as he could see, all he had to do was get enough subscribers and the company would go broke."[6] Telephone service in large communities was therefore very expensive.[7] In 1896, the fee for service in New York was $20 a month. The average income of a workman in that year was $38.50 a month, a six-room tenement in New York rented for about $10 a month, and a quart of milk sold for 5¢. The first subscribers to the telephone were business offices, not ordinary homes. Residential phones in the AT&T National Telephone Directory of 1896 were almost 30 percent in Chicago, one in six or seven in Boston and Washington, and only about one in twenty in New York and Philadelphia.

Yet Bell's letter of 1878 mentioned connecting "private dwellings, counting houses, shops, manufactures, etc. etc.," in that order; he was not thinking of the phone as just a business device. He talks of "establishing direct connection between any two places in the city," not just a system limited to industrial or affluent neighborhoods. Perhaps it was too early for him to assert categorically, as he did slightly later, that the telephone could even become an instrument for the poor. But the goal of universality, which became one of the watchwords of the Bell System, was there from the beginning.

Though in its first two decades the telephone's growth had largely been in business or among the rich, by 1896 several factors led to a rapid expansion of service. There was the continued acceleration of an ongoing exponential process of growth, and (with the expansion of the initial

Bell patents in 1893) competitors sought to discover and occupy parts of the market not yet served—for example, the fast growing Midwest and rural areas. Perhaps the most critical change, however, was the introduction of message charges. The problem was to reduce the price of phone service for the small user, while still collecting adequate amounts from businesses and larger users.[8] In 1896, the New York phone company abandoned flat rate charges and introduced charges by the message.

Between 1896 and 1899, the number of subscribers doubles; in six years it quadrupled; in ten years it increased eight times. By 1914, there were 10 million phones in the United States, 70 percent of the phones in the world. As Burton Hendrick's October 1914 article in *McClure's Magazine* stated:

> Until that time (1900) the telephone was a luxury—the privilege of a social and commercial aristocracy. About 1900, however, the Bell Company started a campaign, unparalleled in its energy, persistence and success, to democratize this instrument—to make it part of the daily life of every man, woman, and child.

In AT&T's annual report of 1901, President Frederick P. Fish expressed its ethos of growth:

> That the system can be completed and of the greatest utility, it is necessary that as many persons as possible should be connected to it as to be able to talk or be talked to by telephone.... [The user's] advantage as a telephone subscriber is largely measured by the number of persons with whom he may be put in communication.

At the turn of the century the telephone was clearly still a luxury, but the leaders of the industry in the United States foresaw its becoming a mass product, and their forecast was at least partially self-fulfilling: they had planned for growth. In 1912, AT&T published a manual of the urban planning process of telephone systems. It prescribed and explained how to do a "development study" for a city; the result would be a document known as the "Fundamental Plan." Since the average life of materials entering a telephone system was estimated to be fifteen years, the plan was to provide adequate capacity for that period,[9] with a planning goal for an ordinary city of at least one telephone for every eight inhabitants.[10] Typically, ducts were only half filled to allow adequate room for growth.

Among the four hypotheses about why the telephone pioneers' forecasts succeeded, the self-fulfilling prophecy seems most apposite to explaining the success of the forecast of growth. Vail and his colleagues had a dream and they made it happen. It was, as it had to be, a realistic dream or it would have failed. But abroad, where the same technology and equally talented men existed, governments and phone companies were structured differently, they followed a different perspective, and growth was slower.[11] The movement of the telephone system to rapidly become a universal low-cost service was more an entrepreneurial decision than a foregone outcome of social processes.

Long-Distance Service

The original telephones of the 1870s could only operate over a range of about twenty miles. Yet Bell in his 1878 letter had already declared "I believe in the future wires will unite the head offices of the Telephone Company in different cities, and a man in one part of the country may communicate by word of mouth with another in a different place."

Even earlier, long-range communication was assumed by Sir William Thompson (later Lord Kelvin), when judging the technical exhibits at the Philadelphia Exposition in 1876, though most of his report covers which words he had been able to understand and which not, on the primitive device at hand.[12]

Vail also anticipated a far-flung global telephone network and saw that strategic control would lie with the company running the long-line interconnections. "Tell our agents," he wrote to one of his staff in 1879, "that we have a proposition on foot to connect the different cities for personal communication, and in other ways to organize a grand telephone system."[13] Yet he daringly forecast: "We may confidently expect that Mr. Bell will give us the means of making voice and spoken words audible through the electric wire to an ear hundreds of miles distant."

Burlingame described his perception:

> As general manager of the American Bell Telephone Company formed in 1880 (for extension of the telephone outside of New England), Theodore Newton Vail saw with an extraordinary prophetic clarity the development of a nationwide telephone system. This prophecy was expressed in the certificate of incorporation of the American Telephone and Telegraph Company formed in 1885 which certified that "the general route of lines of this association...will connect one or more points in each and every city, town or place in the State of New York with one or more points in each and every other city, town or place in said state, and in each and every other of the United States, and in Canada and Mexico; and each and every other city, town or place in said states and countries, and also by cable and other appropriate means with the rest of the known world.[14]

The first long-distance line was built between Boston and Lowell in 1880 with Vail's encouragement:

> This success cheered Vail on to a master effort. He resolved to build a line from Boston to Providence, and was so stubbornly bent upon doing this that, when the

Bell Company refused to act, he organized a company and built the line (1881). It was a failure at first and went by the name of "Vail's Folly." But one of the experts, by a happy thought, doubled the wire.... At once the Bell Company came over to Vail's point of view, bought this new line, and launched out upon what seemed to be the foolhardy enterprise of stringing a double wire from Boston to New York. This was to be a line deluxe, built of glistening red copper, not iron. Its cost was to be $70,000, which was an enormous sum in those hard-scrabble days. There was much opposition to such extravagance and much ridicule. But when the last coil of wire was stretched into place, and the first "Hello" leaped from Boston to New York, the new line was a success.[15]

By 1892, there were lines from New York to Chicago; by 1911, from New York to Denver; and by 1915, from New York to San Francisco. Experiments with overseas radio telephony took place in 1915, but the first transatlantic commercial service began only in 1927.[16] While long-distance telephony grew rapidly, Bell's and Vail's predictions preceded its reality. There were many technical difficulties, and not everyone anticipated (as did Bell and Vail) that they would be overcome.

Much of the effort to make long-distance telephony work focused on repeaters, devices that rebuilt the deteriorating and fading signals as they passed through long lengths of wire. Berliner developed one. When Vail was out of the company (before 1907), Hayes—the director of the Mechanical Department—decided that the company could most economically abandon its own fundamental research and instead rely on "the collaboration with the students of the Institute of Technology [MIT] and probably of Harvard College." On research concerned with lone lines, however, Hayes made an exception. He employed George A. Campbell, who had been educated at MIT and Harvard, to study the essentially mathematical problem of maintaining transmission constants over long lines of cable. By 1899, Campbell had outlined the nature of discretely loaded electrical lines and had developed the basic theory of the wave filter.

Around 1900, Pupin at Columbia University developed the loading coil which greatly improved the capabilities of long-distance cable. Before 1900, long-distance lines demanded wire about an eighth of an inch thick; the New York-Chicago line consumed 870,000 pounds of copper wire. Underground wires in particular had to be very thick. One fourth of all the capital invested in the telephone system before 1900 had been spent on copper. With the Pupin coil, the diameter of the wire could be cut in half. Then, still later, the vacuum tube and other developments in repeaters made long-distance communication increasingly economical.[17]

Vail wrote in the 1908 annual report (p. 22):

> It took courage to build the first toll line—short as it was—and it took more to build the first long-distance line to Chicago. If in the early days the immediate individual profit of the long-distance toll lines had been considered, it is doubtful if any would have been built.

One obvious speculation as to why the forecast of long-distance communication was so successfully made by Bell and Vail is that the telegraph shaped their thinking; the telephone's invention, after all, had been a by-product of telegraphy. Bell had been employed to create a harmonic telegraph which would carry messages at different pitches simultaneously, and the telegraph's great achievement had been the contraction of distance. It was not surprising, therefore, that when a way was found to make voice travel over wires, a realizable goal seemed to be its transmission over distances. Quite rightly, telephone enthusiasts saw the technical problems as temporary difficulties.[18]

Video

Experiments on transmission of pictures over wires go back long before Bell's telephone.[19] After that invention, many people felt that since a voice could be captured and sent over wires, transmission of pictures was an obvious next step. The difficulties in going from conception to realization were frequently underestimated by nontechnical people. The more naive and less scientifically sophisticated the writer, the more immediate the extrapolation from telephone to television seemed.

Kate Field, a British reporter associated with Bell, projected in 1878 that eventually, "while two persons, hundreds of miles apart, are talking together, they will actually *see* each other!"[20] That belongs in a class of journalistic whimsy along with the *Chicago Journal* suggestion:

> Now that the telephone makes it possible for sounds to be canned the same as beef or milk, missionary sermons can be bottled and sent to the South Sea Islands, ready for the table instead of the missionary himself.[21]

In 1910, Casson made a passing comment in "The Future of the Telephone" to the effect that "there may come in the future an interpreter who will put it before your eyes in the form of a moving-picture."[22] A more serious discussion, *The Future Home Theater*, by S.C. Gilfillan, appeared in 1912.[23] In some respects it is a remarkable forecast, in others a dismaying one:

> There are two mechanical contrivances...each of which bears in itself the power
> to revolutionize entertainment, doing for it what the printing press did for books.
> They are the talking motion picture and the electric vision apparatus with tele-
> phone. Either one will enable millions of people to see and hear the same perfor-
> mance simultaneously...or successively from kinescope and phonographic
> records.... These inventions will become cheap enough to be...in every home....
> You will have the home theater of 1930, oh ye of little faith.

Gilfillan believed that both the "CATV" and over-the-air broadcast form of video would coexist by 1930, and also that there would be a television abundance with libraries of material from which one could choose. He thought great art would drive out bad; he described an evening program of Tchaikovsky, ballet, Shakespeare, education lectures, and a speech by a presidential candidate on "The Management of Monopolies"; he thought the moral tone of the home theater would be excellent. And he pointed out that the difficulties in having all this were not technical but human. Let the reader draw his own conclusions!

In 1938, when the Walker investigation of the telephone industry published its report, television already existed but had not yet reached the general public. The Walker Report projected two ways it could develop:

> Television offers the possibility of a nation-wide visual and auditory communica-
> tion service, and this service might be developed under either two broad methods.
> The first is by the eventual establishment of a series of local television broadcast-
> ing stations similar to the present local radio broadcasting stations...or conceiv-
> able it may develop into some form of wire plant transmission utilizing the present
> basic distributing network of the Bell System, with the addition of coaxial cable
> or carrier techniques now available or likely to be developed out of the Bell
> System's present research on new methods of broad band wire transmission.[24]

The one forecast the report did not make, and which now seems the most plausible, is that over time television would be delivered first one way and then the other. With time unspecified both forecasts may be realized.

Crime

From these forecasts—all of which concerned the telephone system's development—we turn now to forecasts regarding its impact on society. From the first decade of the century, there has been much discussion of the telephone's relationship to crime with diametrically opposite predictions. The telephone is portrayed as both the promoter and the conqueror of crime. A villainous anarchist in a 1902 *Chicago Tribune* short story wires a bomb to a phone to be detonated by his call. But in the happy ending, the bomb is detached seconds before he rings; the police trace his call and catch him.

The telephone is portrayed as part of a process of urbanization with decay of traditional moral values and social controls. The "call girl" was the new form of prostitute; obscene callers took advantage of the replacement of operators by dial phones. The phone company was repeatedly berated by reformers for not policing the uses to which the phone was put. As early as 1907, *Cosmopolitan Magazine* had a muckraking story by Josiah Flynt entitled "The Telegraph and Telephone Companies as Allies of the Criminal Pool-Rooms."[25] Flynt charges:

> Because they are among the country's great "business interests," because the stock in them is owned by eminent respectables in business, and because they can hide behind the impersonality of their corporate existence, they have not been compelled to bear their just share of the terrific burden of guilt. But they have been drawing from five to ten million dollars a year as their "rakeoff" from the pool rooms.... Every one of the estimated four thousand pool rooms throughout the United Stated is equipped with telephones used for gambling purposes and for nothing else.

Flynt charges that 2 percent of the New York Telephone company revenues, or a million dollars a year, was derived from gambling in pool rooms. He rejects the argument that the phone company should not attend to what subscribers say on their lines; the company, he says, knows full well who the criminal users are but simply does not wish to forgo the profits of sin.

Prohibition coincided with the telephone system's years of growth to a national network and total penetration. The bootleggers and the rackets made full use of whatever was available to run their operations; it is hard, however, to take seriously the argument of causality—that somehow there would have been less crime without the telephone.

Side by side with that accusation, one can also find in the 1920s and 1930s the reverse argument. The telephone, it was said, gives the police such an enormous advantage over criminals that law and security will come to prevail in American cities:

> When a girl operator in the exchange hears a cry for help—"Quick!" "The Police!"—she seldom waits to hear the number. She knows it. She is trained to save half seconds. And it is at such moments, if ever, that the users of a telephone can appreciate its insurance value.[26]

There were forecasts that crime would decrease, for the criminal would have little chance of escape once telephones were everywhere and the police could be notified ahead about the fleeing culprit. "Police officials feel that the scarcity of dramatic crimes may be due somewhat to the preventive factor present in modern police communication systems."[27]

In fact, enforcement agencies gradually adopted new communications technologies, but usually only slowly and after their usefulness was well demonstrated. Telegraphy was first used in law enforcement to connect police stations and headquarters, but it was not of great importance until encouraged by the International Association of Chiefs of Police, formed in 1893. Recognition of the need for a complex communication system for crime prevention followed civil service reform and the recognition of police work as a specialized profession.[28]

The problem of communication between the police station and the patrolman on the beat received little attention until the 1880s. Before the telephone, the technology available was that used since 1851 for fire alarms. (Between 1852 and 1881, 106 electric fire alarm systems were installed in American cities.)

> The first electric police-communication system of record was installed in 1867. Between 1867 and 1882 only seven more systems were put in operation.... 56 systems were installed from 1882 to 1891, 76 systems in the decade, and 84...from 1892 to 1902.[29]

A survey in 1902 found that of 148 systems, 125 were telegraphic, 19 telephonic, and 3 mixed. Although police departments had subscribed to telephones ever since the Washington department took fifteen in 1878, they did not deploy them to the beats. In 1886, the *New York Tribune* in an editorial criticized the New York police for not connecting the stations with the central office by telephone as the Brooklyn police had. The *Tribune* remarked that "doubtless the time may come when every patrolman's beat will be furnished with one of these instruments."[30]

The Chicago department had been the first to move in that direction. Between 1880 and 1893, over 1,000 street boxes were installed. The popularity of such systems received a boost in 1889 when a murderer was caught at the railroad station a few hours after all police in the city had been notified of his description by the phone network. Telephone boxes began replacing signal boxes; yet by 1917 there were only 8,094 telephone boxes to 86,759 of the latter in police and fire service. In short, ideas for police use of communications technology were prevalent but their adoption came slowly. One idea which was never adopted, but was discussed by 1910, was that each individual should have a number by which he could be reached telephonically wherever he might be.[31]

Hindsight induces a jaundiced view of the forecasts that saw the telephone defeating crime. Such prognoses, we should note, were not made by developers of the telephone system, nor by law enforcement experts, but rather by journalists and reformers. Yet let us not be too complacent about our hindsight. Why were these forecasts wrong? Even with all the advantages of hindsight, it is hard to say. A priori it seems sensible that an instrument permitting well-organized, dispersed police agents to contact and warn each other about suspects much faster than the suspects could move should make things harder for lawbreakers. Yet crime increased in the same years the telephone became available to the authorities; this tells something about the limits of social forecasting based on assessment of one isolated technology. To understand the anomaly of growing crime in the same period as improved technologies of law enforcement, one must understand such matters as the public's attitude toward minor crime, the judges' behavior in sentencing, the organizational incentives in the legal process, the social structure of migrant and ethnic groups in the society, and the nature and reliability of crime statistics.

We do not understand those matters very well, even with hindsight. The forecast that the telephone would help the police was not wrong; it has helped them. The impact on the amount of crime, however, depended primarily on what people wanted to do.

There is substantial evidence that whatever the net trend in criminal activity, the telephone has added to the citizen's sense of security. Alan Wurtzel's and Colin Turner's study in Chapter 11 on how people were affected by the New York City exchange fire in 1975 supports this. The ability to call for help is an important security, yet the relationship of communications to law enforcement is many-sided and complex.

The telephone became part of the pattern of both crime and law enforcement, affecting both. Criminals and policemen alike came to use the telephone, and it changed the way they did things. There even came to be special telephone crimes and telephone methods of enforcement; tapping is an example of both. Yet it is hard to argue that the level of crime or the overall success or failure of law enforcement had any obvious or single valued relationship with the development of the telephone network.

The Structure of Cities

One of our working hypotheses as we began this study was that the automobile and the telephone—between them—were responsible for the vast growth of American suburbia and exurbia, and for the phenomenon of urban sprawl. There is some truth to that, but there is also truth to the reverse proposition that the telephone made possible the sky-scraper and increased the congestion downtown.

The movement out to residential suburbs began in the decade before the telephone and long before the automobile. As Alan Moyer describes in Chapter 16, the streetcar was the key at the beginning. Today street-cars have vanished, and the automobile and the telephone do help make it possible for metropolitan regions to spread over thousands of square miles. But the impact of the phone today and its net impact seventy years ago are almost reverse. As John J. Carty tells it:

> It may sound ridiculous to say that Bell and his successors were the fathers of mod-ern commercial architecture—of the skyscraper. But wait a minute. Take the Singer Building, the Flatiron, the Broad Exchange, the Trinity, or any of the giant office buildings. How many messages do you suppose go in and out of those buildings every day? Suppose there was no telephone and every message had to be carried by a personal messenger. How much room do you think the necessary elevators would leave for offices? Such structures would be an economic impossibility.[32]

The prehistory of the skyscraper begins with the elevator in the 1850s; the first Otis elevator was installed in a New York City store in 1857, and with adaptation to electric power in the 1880s, it came into general use.[33] "The need to rebuild Chicago after the 1871 fire, rapid growth, and rising land values encouraged experimentation in construction." In 1884, Jenney erected a ten-story building with a steel skeleton as a frame. The Woolworth Building with fifty-seven stories opened in 1913. "By 1929 American cities had 377 skyscrapers of more than twenty stories."[34]

The telephone contributed to that development in several ways. We have already noted that human messengers would have required too many elevators at the core of the building to make it economic. Fur-thermore, telephones were useful in skyscraper construction; phones allowed the superintendent on the ground to keep in touch with the workers on the scaffolding. As the building went up, a line was dropped from the upper gliders to the ground.

As the telephone broke down old business and neighborhoods and made it possible to move to cheaper quarters, the telephone/tall building combination offered an option of moving up instead of out. Before the telephone, businessmen needed to locate close to their business contacts. Every city had a furrier's neighborhood, a hatter's neighborhood, a wool neighborhood, a fishmarket, an egg market, a financial district, a shipper's district, and many others. Businessmen would pay mightily for an office within the few blocks of their trade center; they did business by walking up and down the block and dropping in on the places where they might buy or sell. For lunch or coffee, they might stop by the corner restaurant or tavern where their colleagues congregated.

Once the telephone was available, business could move to cheaper quarters and still keep in touch. A firm could move outward, as many businesses did, or move up to the tenth or twentieth story of one of the new tall buildings. Being up there without a telephone would have put an intolerable burden on communication.

The option of moving out from the core city and the resulting urban sprawl has been much discussed, but most observers have lost sight of the duality of the movement; the skyscraper slowed the spread. It helped keep many people downtown and intensified the downtown congestion. Contemporary observers noted this, but in recent decades we have tended to forget it. Burlingame, for example, said:

> It is evident that the skyscraper and all the vertical congestion of city business centers would have been impossible without the telephone. Whether, in the future, with its new capacities, it will move to destroy the city it helped to build is a question for prophets rather than historians.[35]

Burlingame, before World War II, already sensed that things were changing. The flight from downtown was already perceptible enough to be noted as a qualification to his description of the process of concentration; both processes have taken place at once throughout the era of the telephone. The telephone is a facilitator used by people with opposite purposes; so we saw it with crime, and so it is here, too. It served communication needs despite either the obstacle of congested verticality or the obstacle of distance; the magnitude of the opposed effects may differ from time to time, and with it the net effect. At an early stage the telephone helped dissolve the solid knots of traditional business neighborhoods and helped create the great new downtowns; but at a later stage, it helped disperse those downtowns to new suburban business and shopping centers.

The telephone contributed in some further ways to downtown concentration in the early years—we have forgotten how bad urban mail service was. The interurban mails worked reasonably well, but a letter across town might take a week to arrive. Given the miserable state of intracity communication, the telephone met a genuine need for those who conducted business within the city.[36]

The telephone also contributed to urban concentration in the early days because the company was a supporter of zoning. The reasons were similar to ones motivating cablecasters today. Cablecasters are inclined to string CATV through comfortable middle-class neighborhoods where houses are fairly close together but in which utility lines do not have to go underground; they get their highest rate of penetration at the lowest price that way. Only under the impact of regulation do they cover a city completely.

The situation of early telephone systems was in some ways similar, though in some ways different. The Bell System strongly adheres to universal service as the goal, yet economics also favored first pushing into neighborhoods where there would be most businesses. At the beginning, when telephone systems first graduated from the renting of private lines between a factory and its office into providing a community system on a switchboard, many persons in a particular business or profession tended to be signed up fairly simultaneously. In some of the New England towns, the physicians made up a large proportion of early subscribers. In London, there were few physicians but many solicitors. Eventually the subscribers became more diversified, yet there was still a tendency for customers to be drawn from certain segments of the population until penetration became more or less universal. Telephone companies, therefore, found it in their interest to have stable, well-defined neighborhoods in cities in which they were laying trunks and locating central offices. Shifting and deteriorating neighborhoods were not good for business.

Zoning of a city helped in planning for future services, so the phone companies (along with other utilities) became supporters of the zoning movement.[37] The Department of Commerce's zoning primer of 1923 stated that "expensive public services are maintained at great waste in order to get through the blighted districts to the more distant and fashionable locations." In the initial development of phone service it was economic to avoid blighted neighborhoods. With a bluntness that reflects the times and would be unthinkable today, Smith and Campbell said:

> It should not be taken for granted that this satisfies the requirements unless there is at least one telephone for every eight inhabitants in an average American city, in which practically everyone is white. Where a large portion of the population belongs to the Negro race, or a considerable portion of the population is made up of very poor workers in factories, the requirements will be less. In some cities one telephone to fifteen inhabitants is all that can be expected.[38]

Zoning, along with other efforts at urban planning, became popular around the turn of the century. After the Chicago fire in 1871, building codes were enacted (around 1890) with explicit provisions for fireproofing.[39] Codes dealt with allowable building heights and the location of tall buildings in the city. The idea of a planned city was contained in such books as Robinson's *Town and City* (1901) and Ebenezer Howard's *The Garden City*; zoning actually began in New York in 1916. In the intervening years the phone companies were one of the main sources of information fed into the new urban plans. We have already noted that AT&T urged each local phone company to do a developmental study to arrive at a fundamental plan. To do this they collected large amounts of neighborhood data on the population trends in the city, its businesses, and its neighborhoods; the telephone was used as a device for conducting the research. "The most direct means of approaching citizens on the planning issue was reported in Los Angeles where a battery of phone girls calls everyone in the city to secure reactions, while mailing an explanatory folder."[40]

Part of a telephone development study was a "house count" in which the classes of buildings and their uses were determined.[41] In general, the urban reformers and zoning planners received good cooperation from the phone companies and derived much of their data from phone company research.

On a few points, however, city authorities and telephone interests were sometimes at odds. Zoning was often used to prevent the construction of the tall buildings that were heavy users of telephones. Cities also tried to prevent the growth of suburbs outside their boundaries by prohibiting utilities from extending their services beyond city limits. That, if enforceable, would have been a particularly severe restriction on the telephone system because its whole function required that it be interconnected.[42] Robinson noted in 1901 the connection between telephone communications and family cohesion when a family moves to the suburbs.

Thus we find many relationships between the development of the telephone system and the quality of urban life; strikingly, the relationships change with time and with the level of telephone penetration. The same device at one stage contributed to the growth of the great downtowns and at a later stage to suburban migration. The same device, when it was scarce, served to accentuate the structure of differentiated neighborhoods. When it became a facility available to all, however, it reduced the role of the geographic neighborhood. A technology assessment of the device would be misleading unless it included an assessment of the device available in specified numbers.

The Record of Foresight and Hindsight

We may distinguish between those who made technical or business predictions and those who made predictions about the telephone's social impact. Some men did both (Gilfillan, for example), but a separation according to principle emphasis will be useful.

Technical and Business Forecasters

In our research we have looked at the business predictions of Bell, Vail, Western Electric, Elisha Grey, Edison, Hammond Hayes, chief engineer after 1907, J.E. Otterson, general commercial manager of Western Electric and later president of ERPI, AT&T's motion picture subsidiary, and S.C. Gilfillan, a sociologist and historian of technology.

Bell's excellent predictions about the evolution of the switchboard and central office, automatic switching, the development of long-distance service, underground cables, and universal penetration have already been noted. Vail, too, was remarkably prescient. While Bell made his predictions through either scientific logic or visionary insight, Vail predicted goals to be fulfilled and made his dream of universality happen. While on most issues his sense of strategy was keen, he made some errors, as we judge with benefit of hindsight. When Vail and Carty took over in 1907, they shelved the handset (or French phone) which the company had begun to install. In addition, AT&T moved slowly on the automatic exchange because of its massive investment in manual systems. Independents, such as the Home Telephone Company, and European systems (because they were growing more slowly) could adopt automatic switching more easily and earlier. Finally, Vail underestimated the potential of wireless telegraphy, but Carty convinced him of its importance in 1911. Yet none of these items gainsay his remarkable insight into how to build the business so that it worked.

Western Union and Elisha Grey, on the other hand, demonstrate the drawbacks of preservation on established perspectives. Grey could probably have invented the telephone at least a year before Bell had he realized its commercial value.[43] In 1875 in a letter to his patent lawyer Grey wrote: "Bell seems to be spending all his energies on (the) talking telegraph. While this is very interesting scientifically, it has no commercial value at present, for they can do more business over a line by methods already in use than by that system."[44] In another letter after the Philadelphia Centennial Exposition, he added: "Of course it may, if perfected, have a certain value as a speaking tube.... This is the verdict of a practical telegraph man."[45]

Hounshell points to a number of reasons for Grey's misjudgment: his extensive experience in telegraphy, his association with and his respect for the leaders of the telegraph industry. He committed the fallacy of historical analogy. He and Western Union thought of what the telephone could do to extend the existing telegraph system. Bell was a speech expert who approached the problems of telecommunications from the outside.

Hounshell illustrates the point by the story of one Western Union officer who anticipated the phone's use for transmitting speech between telegraphers. He could not visualize the elimination of the traditional telegrapher.[46]

Daniel Boorstin argues that Thomas Edison committed the same fallacy with the phonograph: he invented it as a repeater because he believed that few people would be able to afford their own telephone. His notion was that offices (such as telegraph offices) would use it to record spoken messages that would be transmitted via phone to a recorder at another office where the addressee could hear it.[47] Partly as a result of this misperception, it took Edison fifteen years to realize the entertainment potential of the phonograph.

Clearly capitalist investors or other market-oriented technical men can forecast badly, too. The combination of technical understanding and appreciation of the market may be a necessary condition for good assessment of a new technology. But capitalist investors fail more often than they succeed. History focuses on successes; failure is treated as a kind of environmental wasteland too dreary to gaze upon. And so innovators who followed the wrong path lost their money and have been forgotten.

Yet the melding of technical and economic considerations has been a key to whatever understanding successes of forecasting have occurred. Where those requisites have been present but foresight has failed, a common and easily identified reason has been a lack of imagination about the range of possible change and perseverance in an established way of doing things.[48]

Forecasts of Social Consequence

The record of social forecasting is far less impressive. To evaluate the forecast record on the telephone's social effects, we have looked at

TABLE 8.1

Relative Concentration on Various Technologies in History of Technology Literature

Reference	Number of References to Different Technologies:*					
	Telephone	**Telegraph**	**Radio**	**Television**	**Railroad**	**Automobile**
I Early Technology (1600–1900):	(9)	(27)	(–)	(–)	(123)	(40)
Kranzburg *Technology in Western-Civilization Vol. 1* (1976) (1600–1900)	7	14	–	–	62	6
Singer, ed. *A History of Technology* (1968) (1850–1900)	2	13	–	–	61	34
II General Technology Histories (Ancient to 1950 +):	(8)	(13)	(17)	(6)	(71)	(56)
Ferguson *Bibliography of the History of Technology* (1968)**	3	6	3	–	33	16
Lilley *Men, Machines, and History* (1965)	4	3	13	5	18	18
Armytage *A Social History of Engineering* (1961)	1	4	1	1	20	22
III American Technology (1700 +):	(77)	(60)	(96)	(47)	(231)	(152)
Boorstin *The Americans: The Democratic Experience* (1973) (1860–1970)	19	10	41	36	64	50
Oliver *History of American Technology* (1956) (1730–1950)	20	24	26	7	85	28
Allen *The Big Change* (1952) (1900–1950)	1	1	3	1	10	15
Burlingame *Engines of Democracy* (1940) (1865–1935)	37	25	26	3	72	59
Grand Totals	94	100	113	53	425	258
Totals II & III only	85	73	113	53	302	218

*Numbers indicate number of pages on which technology is mentioned plus number of different subtopics mentioned in index.

**Numbers for this book refer only to the number of documents on each technology cited in this bibliography.

TABLE 8.2

Relative Concentration on Various Technologies in Social Impact and Trend Literature of 1930s and 1940s*

Reference	Telegraph	Telephone	Radio	Television	Railroad	Automobile	Aviation
Mumford *Technics and Civilization* (1934)	2	4	2	1	7	6	2
Leonard *Tools for Tomorrow*** (1935)	5	5	6	3	3	6	10
Gilfillan "Social Effects of Invention"*** (1937)	1	3	17	19	2	6	15
Ogburn *Machines and Tomorrow's World* (1938)	1	6	7	4	7	19	2
Roger *Technology and Society*** (1941)	1	1	31	4	10	4	6
Ogburn *Technology and the Changing Family* (1955)	–	2	6	10	–	1	1
Totals	10	21	69	41	29	42	36

*Number of paragraphs related to technology except where noted.

**Number of references to technology in index, for these books only.

***From Subcommittee on Technology of the National Resources Committee report, *Technological Trends and National Policy*, Ogburn Chairman, 1939.

writings by journalists, historians, and sociologists. The first conclusion is that they have had very little to say on the subject.

We reviewed the indexes of some histories of technology. The result presented in table 8.1 shows that attention to transportation has been much greater than attention to communication. Among the references to communications, attention to the telephone is salient only in histories of American technology.

Table 8.2 presents a similar analysis of the number of paragraphs devoted to different technologies, mostly from the 1930s. The distribution reflects the bias of social scientists toward the present in contrast to the historians' focus on the past. The technologies the sociologists attended to most were the ones that were relatively new at the period when they wrote: radio, television, automobile, and aviation; the telegraph had receded into the past. But note that the telephone gets less attention than railroads, even though it is younger. Figure 8.1 illustrates the greater focus on transportation than communication, age being held constant.

Quantity, however, is not the key thing; more disturbing is that historians, social scientists, journalists, and current commentators have given us very few significant forecasts or analyses on the telephone's social effects. What few there are tend to add the telephone to a list of forces that are all asserted to work in the same way. Sociological writing of the 1920s and 1930s was heavily shaped by a grand conception (which came to America from Germany about 1908) of the decline of *gemeinschaft* and the rise of *gesellschaft*: the decline of the traditional primary group and the growth of a complex society dominated by impersonal relations. In writing about any technology, the impulse was to make it fit that model. Writers discussed the growth of the city, the breakdown of the family, or some other aspect of this grand historical process, noted how the automobile or some other technical change led to it, and added (as an aside) "along with such other innovations as the telephone, the telegraph, or you-name-it."

Such metatheories without detailed cold-blooded study of the historical facts have obscured the telephone's real history. Its effect has not necessarily been in any single direction, nor in the same direction as other devices such as the mass media, the telegraph, or the automobile.[49] The telephone is a device with subtle and manifold effects which cannot be well guessed a priori. There are, in our society, significant problems of privacy, alienation, crime, and urban environment. In no instance is it clear what the telephone's net effect has been on any of these.

FIGURE 8.1
**Relationship between Date Invented and Attention in the Social Impact
Literature of the Thirties for Transportation and Communication Technology**

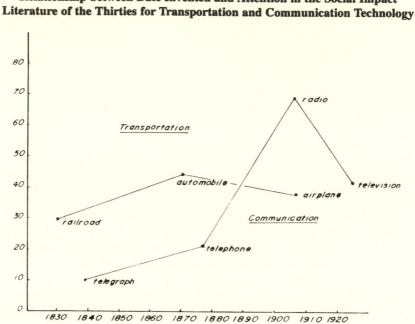

We should not be too harsh about forecasters, however; we have
the benefit of hindsight now, yet it is not much easier to answer the
questions about the past than about the present or future. Postdiction
is almost as hard as prediction; aftcasts almost as hard as forecasts.
What would have happened to American cities if the telephone had
never been invented? Would there, perhaps, have been an enormous
proliferation of teletypewriters to serve some of the same purposes?
If so, would our cities be bigger or smaller than they are today, more
densely settled or more dispersed? It is not much easier to answer the
"what if" questions of history than the "what if" questions about the
future.

Appendix

Kensington, March 25, 1878

To the capitalists of the Electric Telephone Company:

Gentlemen—It has been suggested that at this, our first meeting, I should lay before you a few ideas, concerning the future of the electric telephone, together with any suggestions that occur to me in regard to the best mode of introducing the instrument to the public.

The telephone may be briefly described as an electrical contrivance for reproducing, in distant places, the tones and articulations of a speaker's voice, so that conversation can be carried on by word of mouth between persons in different rooms, in different streets, or in different towns.

The great advantage it possesses over every other form of electrical apparatus consists in the fact that it requires no skill to operate the instrument. All other telegraphic machines produce signals which require to be translated by experts, and such instruments are therefore extremely limited in their application, but the telephone actually speaks, and for this reason it can be utilized for nearly every purpose for which speech is employed.

At the present time we have a perfect network of gas pipes and water pipes throughout our large cities. We have main pipes laid under the streets communicating by side pipes with the various dwellings, enabling the members to draw their supplies of gas and water from a common source.

In a similar manner it is conceivable that cables of telephone wires could be laid under ground, or suspended overhead, communicating by branch wires with private dwellings, counting houses, shops, manufactories, etc., uniting them through the main cable with a central office where the wire could be connected as desired, establishing direct communication between any two places in the city. Such a plan as this, though impracticable at the present moment, will, I firmly believe, be the outcome of the introduction of the telephone to the public. Not only so, but I believe in the future wires will unite the head offices or telephone companies in different cities, and a man in one part of the country may communicate by word of mouth with another in a distant place.

In regard to other present uses for the telephone, the instrument can be supplied so cheaply as to compete on favorable terms with speaking tubes, bells and annunciators, as a means of communication between different parts of the house. This seems to be a very favorable application of the telephone, not only on account of the large number of telephones that would be wanted, but because it would lead eventually to the plan of intercommunication referred to above. I would therefore recommend that special arrangements be made for the introduction of the telephone into hotels and private buildings in place of the speaking tubes and annunciators, at present employed. Telephones sold for this purpose could be stamped or numbered in such a way as to distinguish them from those employed for business purposes, and an agreement could be signed by the purchaser that the telephones should become forfeited to the company if used for other purposes than those specified in the agreement.

It is probable that such a use of the telephone would speedily become popular, and that as the public became accustomed to the telephone in their houses they would recognize the advantage of a system of intercommunication.

In conclusion, I would say that it seems to me that the telephone should immediately be brought prominently before the public, as a means of communication between bankers, merchants, manufacturers, wholesale and retail dealers, dock companies, water companies, police offices, fire stations, newspaper offices, hospitals and public buildings and for use in railway offices, in mines and other operations;

Although there is a great field for the telephone in the immediate present, I believe there is still greater in the future.

By bearing in mind the great object to be ultimately achieved, I believe that the telephone company cannot only secure for itself a business of the most remunerative kind, but also benefit the public in a way that has never been previously attempted.

I am, gentlemen, your obedient servant,

Alexander Graham Bell

Notes

1. Dilts, Marion May. *The telephone in a changing world*. New York: Longman's Green, 1941, p. 11.
2. Ibid., p. 16.
3. Ibid., p. 188ff.
4. Thomas P. Hughes (according to *Science* [November 21, 1975]: 763) notes that Edison was not only a "consummate inventor" but a "complete capitalist." His

notebooks "while devising the nation's first public power system...show on every other page calculations of the system's market potential, the price charged for competing gas illumination, the cost of copper wiring, and other entrepreneurial concerns."

5. That would have been particularly so, as Cherry has noted, without the switchboard. As Arthur Vaughan Abbott calculated in 1894 (Engineering Series, *Bulletin of the University of Wisconsin* 1:4, p. 70), a system for 10,000 subscribers (the approximate number than in New York of Chicago) with a separate line between each pair of subscribers would have taken an underground conduit a yard square, or a pole above ground 1,000 feet high.

6. Dilts, *The telephone in a changing world,* p. 28.

7. In 1904, the AT&T *Annual report* asserted: "As a general principle, it seems perfectly certain that it will always be the case that the larger and more densely populated the community, the higher must be the standard rates for the comprehensive service required for that community. Not only the investment and the cost of operation, but the general difficulty of doing business which can only be overcome by enlarged expenditure, increase in passing from smaller towns and cities to the larger."

8. A further incentive for this change was the growing percentage of AT&T ownership of local phone companies in large cities such as New York. As long as AT&T's revenue was largely from franchise fees for the use of Bell equipment, the company stood to gain from the growth of local companies but not directly from their profitability. As their equity position grew, their direct concern for profitability did, too. Faced with competition from price-cutting independents (some using message rates), it became important to meet the competition at the low end while keeping revenues up. A pricing system that segmented the market maintained earnings. A message charge also served to discourage neighbors' using a telephone and thus increased the likelihood of their getting their own.

9. This figure, which was suggested to local companies for use in the Fundamental Plan, is a rather crude average. More detailed planning in AT&T, of course, used a variety of figures for different types of equipment.

10. Smith, Arthur B.; Campbell, William C. *Automatic telephony.* New York: McGraw Hill, 1915, p. 379.

11. In 1912, Arnold Bennett, in a series of *Harper's Monthly*, gave his impressions of the United States. He begins the fourth (vol. 125 [July 1912], pp. 191–92) commenting: "What strikes and frightens the backward European almost as much as anything in the United States is the efficiency and fearful universality of the telephone. [Just as buildings are pierced everywhere by elevator shafts full of movement so I think of cities as] threaded under pavements and over roofs and between floors and ceilings and between walls, by millions upon millions of live filaments that unite all the privacies of the organism—and destroy them in order to make one immense publicity. I do not mean that Europe had failed to adopt the telephone, nor that in Europe there are no hotels with the dreadful curse of an active telephone in every room. But I do mean that the European telephone is a toy, and a somewhat clumsy one, compared to the seriousness of the American telephone. Many otherwise highly civilized Europeans are as timid in addressing a telephone as they would be in addressing a royal sovereign. The average European middle-class householder still speaks of his telephone, if he has one, in the same falsely casual tone as the corresponding American is liable to speak of his motor car.... Is it possible that you have been in the United States a month without understanding that the United States is primarily nothing but a vast congeries of telephone cabins?"

12. Dilts, *The telephone in a changing world*, p. 4.
13. Casson, Herbert N. "The telephone as it is today." *World's Work* 19 (1910): 12775. Vail understood the strategic advantage of controlling the long lines. From 1881 until 1897 the company issued a national telephone directory, like the national index directory today. Eventually it had to be abandoned for it became too big.
14. Burlingame, Roger. *Engines of democracy*. New York: Charles Scribner, 1940, p. 118ff.
15. Casson, "The telephone as it is today," p. 12776. Casson's tale simplifies slightly in that the Boston to New York was not an instant success. It was initially noisy and had the severe problems of all long-distance lines until adequate repeaters were developed. However, its very existence was a triumph, and quality of service gradually improved.
16. An article in *Current Literature* 50 (May 1911): 504, on "The Immediate Future of the Long-Distance Telephone," reports the laying of an experimental submarine telephone cable between France and England. Conversations between London and the whole European continent are, it says, now possible, and conversations are now possible over up to 1,700 miles of cable. The article looks forward to the time, far in the future, when the whole globe will be linked together.
17. Chapter 15 [from *The social impact of the telephone*] gives the data on the decreasing sensitivity of phone charges to distance.
18. It is worth noting that the same points can be made about Marconi and the history of wireless telegraphy. After Herzian waves were discovered in 1888, a number of scientists recognized that they could be used, as electrical transmissions over wires were already being used, for communications devices. Marconi's important insight, aside from his entrepreneurial ones, was his successfully demonstrated conviction that those waves could go long distances. His great triumph was his transatlantic transmission.
19. Alexander Bain outlines the principles of telegraphic transmission of pictures in a British patent in 1843.
20. Bruce, Robert V. *Bell*. Boston: Little Brown, p. 242.
21. Dilts, *The telephone in a changing world*, p. 22.
22. *World's Work* 20 (May 1910): 12916–17.
23. *The Independent* 73 (October 17, 1912): 886–91.
24. Proposed Report, Telephone Investigation, FCC, USGPO, 1938, pp. 238–39.
25. *Cosmopolitan Magazine* 43 (May 1907): 50–57.
26. Casson, Herbert. "The social value of the telephone." *The Independent* 71 (October 26, 1911): 903. See also Burlingame, *Engine of democracy*, p. 125, and Dilts, *The telephone in a changing world*, pp. 82, 95–96.
27. Dilts, *The telephone in a changing world*, p. 177. She quotes the *Worcester Telegram* on the capture of a gunman: "A bullet killed him, but radio and teletype and telephone had already doomed him" (p. 178).
28. Leonard, V. A. *Police communication systems*. Berkeley: University of California Press, 1938.
29. Ibid., pp. 6–7.
30. Ibid., p. 10.
31. Casson, Herbert. "The future of the telephone." *World's Work* (May 1910): 1908–13.
32. In Mumford, John Kimberly. "This land of opportunity, the nerve center of business." *Harper's Weekly* 52 (August, 1908): 23. The same point was made in the trade journal *Telephony* 4, no. 2 (1902).
33. Glaab, Charles N.; Brown, A. Theodore. *A history of urban America*. New York: Macmillan, 1967. pp. 144–45.

34. Ibid., p. 280.
35. Burlingame. *Engines of democracy*, p. 96.
36. We have noted several times how much worse European phone service was than American. Conversely, the local mail service was often very much better. In many big European cities express letters could be sent rapidly and reliably. There may have been some tradeoff between alternative communication devices for achieving the same goals.
37. Telephone, electric light, gas and trolley companies report that zoning is making it possible for them to eliminate much of their guesswork as to what services they must provide, said John Noland's book *City Planning* shortly after zoning was enacted in New York. Hubbard and Hubbard wrote: "The utility companies as a rule may be counted favorable to zoning. The general attitude of the telephone companies has been expressed in favor of the stability brought about by zoning."
38. Smith and Campbell. *Automatic telephony*, p. 379.
39. In the early years there was considerable concern about telephone wires and safety. The *American Architect and Building News* had a section in each issue on new inventions. It did not note the telephone in 1876, but by 1881 there had been ten references to the telephone in the magazine; four of these concerned safety. There was particular concern about the proliferation of overhead wires.
40. Hubbard, H. V.; Hubbard, T. K. *Your cities today and tomorrow*. Cambridge, MA: Harvard University Press, 1929, p. 93.
41. Smith and Campbell. *Automatic telephony*, p. 379.
42. However, occasionally phone companies took refuge in such restrictions. In *Young vs. Southwestern Telegraph and Telephone Co.* 192 F. 200, 1912, the Arkansas Circuit Court ruled that the phone company was not discriminating when it refused to construct a line beyond city limits.
43. Hounshell, David A. "Elisha Grey and the telephone: On the disadvantages of being an expert." *Technology and Culture* 16, no. 2, p. 159.
44. Ibid., p. 152.
45. Ibid., p. 157.
46. Ibid., p. 145.
47. Boorstin, Daniel. *The Americans: The democratic experience*. New York: Random House, 1973, p. 379.
48. When Vail left the company in 1887, the organization of engineering research fell to Hammond Hayes. Between 1887 and the management reorganization of 1907, the Bell company conducted little fundamental research. Rather, research activities focused upon improvements in apparatus. Sources outside the company contributed the significant breakthroughs in telephone: the automatic exchange system by Strowger in 1889, the loaded coil by Pupin in 1900, and the vacuum tube by De Forest in 1907.
49. Vail's return in 1907 signaled a change in that research philosophy. The obvious frontier was "wireless" communication, made possible by the De Forest patents. Research in that area "would not only react most favorably upon our service where wires are used, but might put us in a position of control with respect to the art of wireless telephony should it turn out to be a factor of importance." (Quoted in Danielson, N. R. *AT&T: The story of industrial conquest*. New York: Vanguard, 1939. pp., 104–5.) The Bell interests rapidly acquired and developed wireless technology and moved on, in Vail's phrase, "to occupy the field" of telephonic research. That is, by 1910 the company was committed to the internal development of both fundamental research and of incremental engineering improvements. Today, the Bell Labs still follow the basic mandate and organi-

zation that followed from Vail's management. See chapters 5 and 8 [*The social impact of the telephone*] for a strong case for the difference between the social effects of the telephone and the mass media.

9

Communications Technology and Land Use

*At the turn of the century, telecommunications had a centripetal
effect on the topography of cities. It encouraged the separation of
offices from factories and the consequent concentration of offices
downtown. Thus telecommunications led to urban concentration.
By the middle of the century, a more flexible and universally available telecommunications technology was used to escape urban
concentration, with both homes and work places moving out of
the city's center and even into exurbia. In that period, the effects
of telecommunications were predominantly centrifugal. In the future, still more malleable communications technology is likely to
give people more choices in how they use it. Until now, each of
the trends and effects noted for communications could be simultaneously noted in transportation. Now, however, in the prospect
of an energy shortage, one of the very likely uses of telecommunications may be to overcome some consequences of high energy
prices. Most particularly, improved telecommunications may be
used to offset the centripetal pressure for achieving energy savings by renewed urban concentration.*

Communications technology, for the last 200 years, has been making operation at a distance increasingly easy. Such a steady trend, one
might presume, should have engendered as one of its consequences a
steady dispersal of population away from crowded city centers. But it
is not so! Why did this trend of better long-distance communication,
which has indeed promoted exurbia and sprawl recently, appear in an
earlier era to have had the reverse effect of encouraging urbanization
around superdense downtowns? And why is it different today?

First published in *The Annals of the American Academy of Political and Social Science* (1980).

When one finds a cause, at one time having one effect and at another time having another, one suspects that an interaction with a third variable is at work. That is the case. We find intriguing interactions among urban topography and three technologies: production, transportation, and communications. Were we examining an earlier era, we would have to add one more variable, security, as a major factor in human agglomeration, but in the modern world the dominant needs served by common settlements rise from economic pursuits. The rise of the modern city came in part from the assemblage of workers near factories and also from division of labor among producers who lived by exchange in markets.

Contributions of the Telephone and Modern Transportation

In the mid-nineteenth century, if one walked up to one of the big, red brick sheds that housed most American factories along the rivers of the Northeast or to one of the similar sheds in Western Europe, one would have found the offices of the company and its president at the front of the same building with the production plant behind. By the 1920s, however, one would have found most corporate headquarters located in Manhattan, or London, or Paris, or sometimes in the downtowns of industrial cities like Pittsburgh, Chicago, Manchester, or Bremen. The factories were not there in the central cities to which the headquarters had moved, but were on the outskirts of the city or in smaller manufacturing towns.[1]

This process of separation of the headquarters office from the plant and the congregation of offices all together is described by Peter Cowen in his book, *The Office*.[2] He notes that in New York "a cluster of central offices...began to accumulate in the late 1880's or early 1890's....In London...the building of offices got under way during the first part of the century."[3] Cowen attributes the character of office activity to three inventions: the telegraph, the typewriter, and the telephone, especially the last two.[4] The company president located himself at the place where most of his most critical communications took place. Before the telephone, he had to be near the production line to give his instructions about the quantities, pace, and process of production. Once the telephone network existed, however, he could convey those authoritative commands to his employees at the plant and could locate himself at the place where the much more uncertain bargaining with customers, bankers, and suppliers took place.

Communications Technology

Before the emergence of telecommunications and power-driven transportation, the limit to the number of people who could assemble in the
city was set by the need for people to go on foot to see each other. J.
Alan Moyer describes Boston in 1850 as a small city with residences,
businesses, and factories intermingled. It was a tightly packed seaport
where people normally walked to their jobs, to stores, and to visit friends
and relatives. Face-to-face communication was dominant; it was a walking city whose densely settled area was within two miles of city hall.[5]

The combination of the streetcar and the telephone allowed this picture to change, with many more people coming to work in the downtown while living further out. Persons who were engaged in routine
production work could be segregated to plants in the remote environs,
but everyone who bargained and engaged in decisions found it important to work in the city.

The early telephones and the vehicles of the day were not habile
enough devices to substitute for one's being located in person at the
center during the day, in easy face-to-face contact with important others. The fidelity of the telephone was poor. It sometimes went out of
order. Penetration was low; as a result, one could not count on being
able to telephone anyone one wanted to reach. The phone provided a
limited link to places where one had arranged for it to be in place; the
streetcar served for a daily commute down and up its radial pattern.
But for diverse important communications, face-to-face contact had to
be available. The limited technologies of the day were neither a substitute for, nor an adequate aid to, personal interaction.

So business first used the new technologies of transportation and
communication to assemble in an enlarged commercial center. While
quantitatively the separation of corporate offices from manufacturing
plants was the most important part of the process of creating a commercial downtown, the same sort of thing was happening in other enterprises besides industry. Before the telephone, doctors, for example,
had to live near their offices to be readily available when needed; typically, in fact, the office was in the doctor's home. The telephone, however, allowed many doctors to separate home and office and to put the
office where it was convenient for the patients to come.[6]

Before the telephone, businessmen, since they had to be in easy
walking distance of their main contacts, located in clusters determined
by occupation. The result was a mosaic city. Every city had a furrier's

neighborhood, a hatter's neighborhood, a wool neighborhood, a fish market, an egg market, a financial district, a shipper's district, and many others. Businessmen would pay mightily for an office within the few blocks where their trade was centered; their way of doing business was to walk up and down the block and drop in to the places from which one might buy or to whom one might sell. For lunch or coffee, one might drop in to the corner restaurant or tavern where one's colleagues congregated.

Once the telephone was available, business could move to cheaper quarters and still keep in touch. A firm could move outward, as many businesses did, or move up to the tenth or twentieth story of one of the new tall buildings. Instead of an urban pattern of a checkerboard of different specialized neighborhoods, the new urban pattern created a large downtown containing a miscellany of commercial and marketing activities that needed to be accessible to a variety of clients and customers.[7]

The development of skyscrapers permitted more and more people to be packed into that downtown. Recognition of how the telephone contributed to a revolution in modern architecture, namely, by the creation of skyscrapers, appears as early as 1902 in an article in *Telephony*.[8] General Carty, the chief engineer of AT&T used the same arguments in 1908:

> It may sound ridiculous to say that Bell and his successors were the fathers of modern commercial architecture—of the skyscraper. But wait a minute. Take the Singer Building, the Flatiron, the Broad Exchange, the Trinity, or any of the giant office buildings. How many messages do you suppose go in and out of those buildings every day? Suppose there was no telephone and every message had to be carried by a personal messenger. How much room do you think the necessary elevators would leave for offices? Such structures would be an economic impossibility.[9]

The prehistory of the skyscraper begins with the elevator in the 1850s; the first Otis elevator was installed in a New York City store in 1857, and with adaptation to electric power in the 1880s, it came into general use.[10] "The need to rebuild Chicago after the 1871 fire, rapid growth, and rising land values encouraged experimentation in construction." In 1884, Jenney erected a ten-story building with a steel skeleton as a frame. The Woolworth Building with fifty-seven stories opened in 1913. "By 1929 American cities had 377 skyscrapers of more than twenty stories."[11]

There were several ways in which the telephone contributed to that development. We have already noted that human messengers would have required too many elevators at the core of the building to make it economic. Furthermore, telephones were useful in skyscraper construction; the superintendent on the ground had to keep in touch with the workers on the scaffolding, and phones were used for that. So in various ways the telephone made the skyscraper practical and thus allowed a burgeoning of city centers.

Another observation from the early days of suburban commuting was that husbands became more willing to leave their wives miles away in bedroom suburbs for the whole day, and grown children were more willing to leave their parents' neighborhood, once they had telephones and could be in instant touch in emergencies. That, too, facilitated the growth of a commuter-laden downtown.

A Reversal of Trends

Side by side with the process of city growth that has just been described, a second trend was getting under way, first in a small way and then massively. That second trend was dispersion from the city to suburbia and exurbia. That movement had started in the decade before the invention of the telephone and long before the automobile; the streetcar initiated the process. Perceptive observers noted the new trend toward decentralization even in the 1890s. Frederic A. C. Perrine, one of the founders of the profession of electrical engineering in America, noted the beginnings of suburbanization in an article about how electricity would reverse the centralizing effects of the steam engine on society. He stressed the impact of the electric streetcar on the city.[12]

Eight years later, H.G. Wells, in his 1902 *Anticipations* of the twentieth century, forecast centrifugal forces on the cities that might lead "to the complete reduction of all our present congestions."[13] A pedestrian city, he said, "is inexorably limited by a radius of about four miles, and a horse-using city may grow out to seven or eight." With street railways the modern city thrust "out arms along every available railway line":

It follows that the available area of a city which can offer a cheap suburban journey of thirty miles an hour is a circle with a radius of thirty miles....But thirty miles is only a very moderate estimate of speed....I think, that the available area...will have a radius of over one hundred miles....Indeed, it is not too much to say...that the vast stretch of country from Washington to Albany will be all of it "available" to the active citizens of New York and Philadelphia.

Wells anticipated "that New York, Philadelphia, and Chicago will probably, and Hankow almost certainly, reach forty millions." The telephone was one factor Wells listed as fostering this development,[14] for he believed that there was no reason "why a telephone call from any point in such a small country as England to any other should cost more than a post-card."[15] Yet Wells, like Jean Gottmann later, emphasized that urban sprawl did not mean uniformity of density.[16] Shopping and entertainment centers would continue to make for downtowns, even as people in some occupations would prefer to move out to the country or work by telephone from home.[17]

A *Scientific American* article of 1914, "Action at a Distance,"[18] has similar themes, but with special stress on the picturephone as likely to make dispersion possible. "It is evident," it starts out, "that something will soon have to be done to check the congestion" of the city. "The fundamental difficulty...seems to be that it is necessary for individuals to come into close proximity to each other if they are to transact business." The article argues that the telephone and picturephone will take care of that.

These anticipations of flight from the city came long before the fact. Even as late as 1940, an evaluation of the telephone's impact on the city stressed its centripetal rather than its centrifugal effect. Roger Burlingame concluded:

> It is evident that the skyscraper and all the vertical congestion of city business centers would have been impossible without the telephone. Whether, in the future, with its new capacities, it will move to destroy the city it helped to build is a question for prophets rather than historians.[19]

He sensed that things were changing. The flight from downtown was perceptible enough for him to note it, but as a qualification to his description of a process of concentration.

Today our attention is focused on the dramatic movement outward and the resulting urban sprawl. We have tended to lose sight of the duality of the movement. The common effect of the telephone, throughout, was to permit a freer choice of residential and work location than in the days of the walking city and the mosaic city. There were two options as neighborhoods broke up, the economics of location changed, and cities grew. One was to move up into the new tall buildings, the other was to move out from the center. Initially, the predominant choice was to take advantage of this new freedom of location to get one's enterprise to the center of the action. Skyscrapers helped make this possible, with millions of daytime workers piled high downtown, it was only possible thanks to the concurrent availability of mass transport and telecommunications.

Later the pendulum swung, and the predominant direction of move-ment was outward. Even some headquarters of corporations moved from Manhattan to Westchester or Connecticut. Small enterprises appeared in the fields around Route 128 or Silicon Valley rather than in lofts in an urban ring between the downtown and the slums, as 1930s socio-logical theory of urban topography would have predicted.

The ring theory of Park's and Burgess's Chicago school of sociolo-gists[20] was essentially American because that model rested on assump-tions of a rapidly growing city, with speculative land values graduated downward from the center, and of heavy taxes proportional to property value. Under those circumstances, one low-rental area in which to put a new and possibly unstable productive plant was in the ring just beyond the downtown, but which was still too far out for high-rise development and in which speculators were holding properties at a loss in the expecta-tion of later appreciation when the downtown spread out. In Europe, with a different fiscal system, a ring of lofts and empty lots at the edge of downtown was not usual. So, in Europe, earlier than in the United States, manufacturing was extensively located in an outer ring, like Paris's red ring of suburbs, but in Europe the ring hugged tightly the city in which the workers lived. Plant location in scattered green sites well beyond the built-up city was a later and also quite American phenomenon.

The new mid-twentieth-century pattern of location was more diverse than that which had preceded it. The typical city that had emerged in the first part of the century had a single hub. A ring theory described it well. What has emerged since the middle of the century is a prolifera-tion of hubs, some of them within the old city but away from the bull's eye, some of them planted beyond the city in green fields, some of them subsidiary downtowns, such as Neuilly or Shinjuku, and some of them specialized single-purpose developments like shoppers' malls or rural industrial parks. The Los Angeles metropolitan area is prototypic of what is likely to develop where there is cheap, good, and universal motor transport and telecommunications. That type of city, as Jean Gottmann emphasizes, is megalopolis and not antipolis.[21] It is not an undifferentiated sprawl of medium-density settlement. It is a highly differentiated geographically dispersed structure of centers and sub-centers with complex interrelations among them.

Homeseekers and businesses adopted such a megalopolitan and in part even exurban location pattern partly because of improvements in telecommunications, and because they had automobiles. The role of the car in making it possible to both live and produce in very scattered locations is obvious. The millions of persons who live in suburbs well beyond the reach of public transportation and without walkable neighborhood shopping streets, who carpool or bus their children to school, go to movies at a drive-in, and drive for shopping to a shopping mall could not exist without cars. And there are also many scattered plants where these people work and to which virtually everyone arrives by car. In the instance of Route 128, the very name of the development is the road which it straddles.

However, good and fast as it might be, transportation by car, with cheap gasoline, would not by itself have permitted such a topography of settlement to emerge. If every message, question, order, instruction, or change of instruction from and to such dispersed homes and plants required that someone jump into a car and drive for twenty to forty-five minutes in order to communicate, no such dispersal of settlement would have taken place. The ability to pick up a telephone and get a message through without moving was just as essential as the car.

The improvements in telecommunications technology between about 1910, when the telephone was mainly found useful in pushing activities into the downtown, and about 1960, when it was more important in allowing activities to migrate out, were not very dramatic, but they were significant.

In the first place, in the United States telephones had become universal over that half century, and with that their use changed. It was all very well in 1910 for the remote office or plant to have a telephone, but its effective use depended on others whom one wanted to reach also having one. To avoid running an errand, to cancel an appointment, or to find out if something or someone was ready to be picked up required a telephone at both ends. One could not assume that a sick worker would telephone in or that a substitute could be telephoned in order to tell him to drive right out. One could not track down a delivery man easily or always expect to be able to reach a customer with a question or information. The universality of telephones made them more valuable to each subscriber.

In the second place, in the early years the quality of telephone service depended heavily on one's location. The gradually growing investment in telecommunication plants was concentrated where users in large numbers could share the cost. Rural subscribers had to be content with party lines and sometimes had to pay for running a line out to their location. Even when a business user was willing to pay for stringing lines to his premises, his rural exchange may not have capacity for added lines. In a rural area, with less redundancy of equipment to fall back on, when a line went out the outage was apt to be more protracted. Also the degradation of the signal with distance was a major problem in the early days and was more severe for scattered customers. That problem was only gradually fully overcome; only young people today fail to react with surprise when a caller from thousands of miles away sounds as though he were calling from next door. Automatic switching was introduced to urban exchanges first, and as direct distance dialing came in, that, too, was in the major commercial exchanges first. So in the early years, one reason for preferring a central location was its superior telecommunications facilities.

Third, the telephone facilities a business subscriber can have on his own premises have improved. Now he is likely to have a fully automated PABX allowing calls to be made without waiting for a switchboard operator, and incoming calls may go directly to his Centrex line, also without operator intervention. Long-distance calls may be made over private lines or WATS lines at a marginal cost that the employee does not have to think about. For an employee who spends much of his day on the telephone, these are important efficiencies.

Fourth and finally, data communication forms much faster and cheaper than telex had become available. For the past decade, in most large companies, employees from many locations have had access to the company's computers either in time-sharing or remote job entry mode. Orders and inventory information can pass to and from terminals.

Everything so far described is now history. We are describing changes in communications technology that were already pervasive enough in the 1960s and 1970s to help explain the numerous decisions made both by business firms and individuals to locate in noncentral and even remote and isolated places. These telecommunications developments were prerequisite to the viability of such new centers as Rosslyn, Bethesda, and McLean near Washington; or Shinjuku, Saitama, and Skuba around Tokyo; as well as to the much more modest sub-subcenters, such as a shopping plaza cut out of green fields or a housing development folded into woodlands.

Now, however, let us consider more advanced telecommunications developments that may become common over the next decades and which may serve to make remote locations even more attractive.

A Look to the Future

One particular development clouds our crystal ball. For the first time in the last two centuries, the trends in transportation do not parallel those in communications. In the late nineteenth century, both the street-car and the telephone provided improved intercourse between selected pairs of points. The convenience this achieved, though considerable, was modest by modern standards, and the topography of both services were rigid. However, as we have already noted, by the mid-twentieth century, universalization of availability of cheap motor transportation and of telecommunications was achieved, as was greater flexibility in the topography of both systems and in their uses. All these developments were common to both communications and transportation.

Now for the first time, the prospect in transportation is of rising prices and consequent restriction of liberal use, while the prospect in communications is of falling prices and abundance. How the balance between concentration and dispersion will work out in this new situation, time alone can tell. Without predicting the net balance, we can, nonetheless, analyze fairly well the direction that will come from communications technology. It is toward more diffusion.

Communications facilities in the past have tended to be organized in a hierarchical geographical structure. At the lowest level were local nodes, perhaps united under regional structures and united under a national one. There can be two, three, or more levels. The American press consists of a simple two-level system in which city newspapers are fed by national news services. American broadcasting is similar, with local stations fed by national networks. The most complex of the networks is the telephone system, sometimes described as the largest machine ever built. Subscriber premises are linked to local exchanges by wire pairs called "the local loop." The local exchanges are connected, ordinarily, by coaxial cable to nearby local exchanges and to a toll exchange on the long-distance network. That toll exchange is connected by microwave, or satellite, or cable to other exchanges and then on down in symmetrical fashion to the subscriber at the other end. Before satellites, the network structure reflected rather closely the volume of traffic, with much bandwidth installed, for example, between New York and Washington, but with little capacity installed on low-traffic routes.

The network of the year 2000 is likely to be quite different. The two technical developments underlying that difference are the coming availability of abundant, low-cost bandwidth from end to end and the low cost of digital switching.

Optical fibers are likely to carry great bandwidth capacity all the way to the customer's home or office allowing him to connect computers, videophones, or almost any communications device directly to the network. Wherever the optical fibers reach—and eventually that may be everywhere—the customer can have top-grade communications services. Also, insofar as the long-distance links are by satellite, the structure of a network with some heavy traffic routes and some thin routes gives way to random access. Every point at which an earth station is placed (within the satellite's beam) is reachable in the same way as every other. There is no difference in cost regardless of the distance traversed, and there is the same quality of service to every point. So the future broad band transmission system will equalize the service to all locations.

Low-cost switching has important effects, too. It is simply one aspect of the revolution in microelectronics. A digital switch is a digital computer that is being used for routing control. With the progress in microelectronics, such computing capability can be embodied on tiny chips all through the network, "Distributed intelligence," as it is called, means that there can be a computer operating a switch—and also for other purposes—in the customer's telephone itself, elsewhere on his premises, on telephone poles outside his building, at any concentrator along the line, in telephone company exchanges, and elsewhere. One configuration which gets entirely away from having exchanges is a packet network. For that kind of service, each terminal had a line to the network to which it is connected by a small interface switch, to the interface at the destination that is recorded on the header. There need be no hierarchy at all among the interface switches.

Another configuration which gets away from the historical hierarchy of exchanges is that of a switched satellite system. In such a system, the customer's telephone has a line to a concentrator and then on to the earth station. From there the signal, along with an address, is transmitted up to the satellite, and there, 22,300 miles above the equator, it is switched to a beam that will reach the particular earth stations to which the receiver is connected.

Even a circuit-switched terrestrial system on a future all-digital network—what is called an "integrated services digital network" (ISDN)—may not have a geographic hierarchy of exchanges. On an ISDN, different functions, like billing, storing of messages when no one is home, and testing the availability of lines, may all be performed by specialized equipment at different places on the network. The distinction between local and long-distance calls may disappear. Some very local calls may never even enter an exchange, being switched at the local concentrator on a pole. Other local calls may be processed for some functions by special equipment hundreds of miles away.

The implication of all these technical facts is that the future telecommunications system is likely to eliminate the disparities in the quality of communications service now found in different locations. Until the energy crisis of 1973, it was a common fantasy in popular literature that advances in communications would engender reruralization. Exhibits at worlds' fairs and articles in popular magazines depicted the home/office of the twenty-first century, set in an idyllic countryside with its resident enclosed in a cocoon of a room, sitting at a console with a video screen, carrying on his business with anyone, to the ends of the earth, by telecommunications. That fantasy in its fullness was always silly, but it captured a small element of reality, namely, that whatever expanded communication facilities the market will offer to customers two or three decades hence can be expected to be available just as well in a rural as in an urban environment. In all locations, be they metropolitan centers or remote hinterlands, the most sophisticated kinds of communications services should be available.

At a price, the customer of such a future communications system can be serviced with pictures of any fidelity he needs, with electronic mail, with word processing, and with voice processing, too. The barrier of price is an important one, but it is a very different kind of barrier from that of the technical impossibility. In the past there were a limited number of things one could do with a telecommunications line. In the early days, one could use it for poor-quality, high-value voice conversations or for telegrams to limited destinations. Later, one could use it to almost anywhere, but still only for relatively standard voice output. For the future, a fairly accurate statement is that one will be able to have at any given terminal whatever quality of video, audio, or text representation one is willing to pay for and will be able to have these at any location without penalty for distance.

Given the rising cost of transportation, it will pay in many situations to substitute investment in sophisticated communications for the expense of travel. How far the energy crunch will lead to geographic reconcentration of activities in urban centers will depend on the cost of communications services good enough to be a satisfactory substitute.[22]

Much of the literature on the tradeoff between telecommunications and travel makes the naive assumption that if people have the means to communicate to a long distance, they will travel less. That is quite untrue. In the first place, traveling and communicating reinforce each other; people travel to see people with whom they have established a communicative relationship, and people communicate with people to whom or

from whom they travel.[23] There is a significant positive correlation between long-distance telephone traffic and travel.

These comments, however, do not contradict what has just been said.
We did not ask previously whether the improvement of communications facilities would in and of itself stop people from traveling. We
asked what people would do in a situation in which an exogenous third
variable, energy prices, forced them to curtail their travel. Under those
circumstances, the geographically dispersed availability of very flexible communications devices could curb what otherwise might be a
strong shift back into concentrated urban centers.

A Closing Observation

The processes described can be generalized in a closing observation
about technological determinism. Usually the physical nature of a technology in its early and primitive form is fairly determinative of its use.
At that primitive stage there is little understanding either of the underlying laws that are embodied in the device or of the technical alternatives. If the technology is to be used at all, it must be used with the
existing hardware. Technological determinism is, therefore, a powerful
force at that early stage.

Later, intellectual understanding of the technology advances, and as
technicians learn how to make the device do what they want it to do,
the degree of technological determinism declines. Social values, goals,
and policies take over, and the technology is shaped to serve them.

In its early days, telecommunications technology had a significant
effect on the character of the modern city, mainly leading to urban concentration. Later, a more flexible telecommunications technology allowed people increasingly to escape urban concentration.

In prospect now is a still more flexible and malleable communications technology that will give people still more choices about how
they will use it. One choice that seems very likely to be frequently
made in the near future is to use telecommunications as a way to resist
the renewed force toward urban concentration that stems from the rising cost of energy.

Notes

1. Cf. Gottmann, Jean; Abler, Ronald; Moyer, J. Alan in *The social impact of the telephone*, Pool, Ithiel de Sola (ed.). Cambridge, MA: MIT Press, 1976.
2. Cowen, Peter. *The Office*. New York: American Elsevier, 1969.

3. Ibid., p. 29.
4. Ibid., p. 30.
5. Pool, *Social impact*, p. 344.
6. "Telephone and the doctor" *Literary Digest* 44 (May 18, 1912): 1037.
7. Cf. Pool, *Social impact*.
8. Carty, John Joseph. "Applications of the modern telephone," *Telephony* 4 (1902): 94–95.
9. Mumford, John Kimberly. "This land of opportunity, the nerve center of business." *Harper's Weekly* 52 (August 1, 1908): 23. The point was first made in the trade journal *Telephony* 4 (1902).
10. Glaab, Charles N.; Brown, A. Theodore. *A history of urban America*. New York: Macmillan, 1967, pp. 144–45.
11. Ibid., p. 80.
12. *Electrical Engineering* 3 (1894): 39.
13. H.G. Wells, *Anticipations*. New York: Harper Bros., 1902, p. 51ff.
14. Ibid., p. 65.
15. Ibid., p. 58.
16. Gottmann, Jean. *Megalopolis*. Cambridge, MA: MIT Press, 1961.
17. Wells, *Anticipations*, p. 66.
18. Suppl. no. 1985 77:39 (Jan. 17, 1914).
19. Roger Burlingame, *Engines of democracy*. New York: Charles Scribner's Sons, 1940, p. 96; cf. also Page, Arthur. "Social aspects of communication development." *Modern communication*. Page, A. (ed.). Boston: Houghton Mifflin, 1932. He notes the relation of the phone to both the skyscraper and suburb, and says it "allows us to congregate where we wish to," p. 20.
20. Cf. Burgess, Ernest W. "The growth of the city" in Park, Robert E., Burgess, Ernest W., McKenzie, Roderick D. (eds.) *The city*. Chicago: University of Chicago Press, 1967. First published in 1925.
21. See his chapter in Pool, *Social impact*.
22. On the possibilities of telecommunications substituting for travel, see Short, John; Williams, Ederyn; Christie, Bruce. *The social psychology of telecommunications*. London: John Wiley & Sons, 1976; Bend, Alex. "Comparing telephone with face-to-face contact," in Pool, *Social impact*; and Hiltz, Starr; Turoff, Murray R. *Network action*. Reading, MA: Addison-Wesley, 1978.
23. Pool, Ithiel de Sola. "The communications/transportation tradeoff," in Altshuler, Alan (ed.). *Current issues in transportation policy*. Lexington, MA: D.C. Health, 1979.

10

The Mass Media and Politics in
the Modernization Process

Introduction

There are four policy issues about the development of mass media which most emerging nations must resolve. As countries pass from the conditions of traditional society to modernity, sometimes they are resolved by deliberation, sometimes by happenstance.

First, and most important, developing nations must decide how much of their scarce resources to invest in mass media. Second, they must decide what roles to assign the public and private sectors respectively. Third, they must decide how much freedom to allow or how much control to impose; how much uniformity to require and how much diversity to permit. Fourth, they must decide at how high a cultural level to pitch the media output.

The communist and noncommunist countries make very different decisions on these matters. The practice in noncommunist countries is for development plans to provide large amounts for the education of children and for the eradication of illiteracy but relatively small amounts for other communications investments. The practice in the communist countries also is to spend heavily for literacy and education but in addition to support expensive programs of exhortation addressed to adults. They invest much in the press, movies, loud speaker systems, etc.

The neglect of mass media development in most of the new noncommunist nations may be documented best by reference to that medium which is most often operated by the government itself, radio. Since in most developing countries it is the medium most effectively available to the planners themselves, what they do with it is a good

From *Communication and Political Development* (1963), edited by L.W. Pye.

index of the importance they really attribute to media development. Egypt has made of radio a major instrument of foreign policy. Most developing countries have done something by way of developing village-oriented radio programs and educational programs, but their efforts are small.

The practice in India is typical of the priorities. There are two radios per 1,000 persons in India. The First Five Year Plan allocated two-tenths of one percent of outlays to developing of broadcasting. It allocated fourteen times as much as that to posts and telegraph. It allocated about sixty times as much to education. But that was only the Plan. Across the board, actual outlays for the five years slipped 15 percent below the Plan, but outlays for broadcasting were allowed to fall short by 45 percent, leaving actual outlays at somewhat over one-tenth of one percent of the total. In the Second Five Year Plan development of broadcasting was given no greater role, being again allowed two-tenths of one percent of outlays. In the Third Plan it is cut down to one- tenth of one percent.

The willingness of countries faced by foreign exchange shortages to ration newsprint or impose severe excise taxes, tariffs, and quotas on radios and TV sets, and even to exclude TV entirely for fiscal reasons, attests to the fact that few noncommunist countries have assigned to the development of the mass media the same significance they have to steel mills, roads, railroads, and dams.

The situation in the communist underdeveloped countries is, of course, quite different. Castro's use of TV, the communist avidity for the Ministry of Information in a coalition regime, the blare of the Chinese omnipresent loud speaker system, and many other examples testify to the great importance attached to the exhortation of adults. The circulation of newspapers in the Soviet Union grew from 2.7 millions in 1913 to 9.4 millions in 1928, to 38.0 millions in 1939, to 44.0 millions in 1954.[1] Frederick Yu gives us comparable figures from China.[2] Capital investment in the production of words is not stinted in communist countries.

It might be argued, though erroneously, that the reason for low public investment in mass media in noncommunist developing countries is that the media are thought to belong properly to the private sphere. It is indeed true that media in the private sphere have developed more rapidly than those in the public sphere. The few commercial radio stations in Asia (e.g., in Goa and the Philippines) have built far larger audiences than the publicly owned stations with which they sometimes compete beyond their borders.

TV on any scale exists in underdeveloped countries only where it has been commercial. Publicly owned TV has been stillborn. TV exists in sixteen underdeveloped countries in the Eastern Hemisphere, with commercial stations in only five of them. No one of these sixteen countries had more than 20,000 sets in 1958, but the two countries with most sets were ones with commercial stations. In Latin America TV has evolved much faster and further; among the fourteen countries there with TV only one bars commercial broadcasting.

Newspapers, which in virtually all noncommunist countries are private, can now be found everywhere, and movies have become a major industry in a number of underdeveloped countries.

But noncommunist developing countries do not limit their governmental efforts in media development in order to gain the efficiencies of private enterprise. They do so rather because they accept the clichés of European socialism about the evils of commercial media; they see government radio and TV as the only proper kind. One might expect governments which hold that view to take up media development seriously, but they seldom do.

A favorable governmental policy is important even for the development of private media. Policy on import of newsprint, development of newsprint sources, placing of legal advertising, telegraph rates, and many other policies may either facilitate or inhibit growth of private media. Thus it can hardly be argued that government need pay little attention to media development because the media are private. There must be other reasons for the policy decision that is usually made to play down investment in mass media. One reason, which we shall shortly consider, is disillusionment with their usefulness. Whatever the reasons, the practice is unmistakable.

Characteristic of noncommunist developing countries is a policy which attaches great importance to literacy and the education of children but little importance to the mass media, and which looks down with some disdain on those more popular mass media which do develop at low cultural levels in the private sphere. Characteristic of communist developing countries, on the other hand, is a policy which attaches enormous importance to hortatory communications through the mass media, and which uses these not only for political control but also as a major stimulus to the carrying through of development plans.

Behind these divergent investment policies lie two different theories of communication as well as two different theories of economic organization. Our objective in this paper is to examine these implicit theories of communication and test them against social science knowledge.

Disillusionment with the Mass Media

The implicit view about the operation of the mass media which we have been describing as widely held by elites in noncommunist nations may be labeled that of disillusionment. The media are conceded a potential function of educating people to support urgent national tasks for development, but they fail at it. The media, so it seems, are ineffective agents of action on behalf of the planners. Agricultural advice broadcast on radio seldom gets followed in practice. Exhortations in the press to change established family or social patterns seem to have no results. People may learn that caste discrimination, or a low-protein diet, or spitting, or dowries are disapproved in the modern world, but they do not change as the planners exhort them to.

But while the Westernizing leaders become disillusioned about the power of the media in their own hands to engender desired actions, they simultaneously believe in the vast powers of the hidden persuaders for evil. It seems that while the media are not effective instruments of constructive action, they have a considerable power to disorient and engender confusion in a society. They produce, for example, a demonstration effect. They engender the revolution of rising expectations. They engender desires for new things about which their readers and viewers learn, but they do not thereby create a willingness to take the actions called for to obtain these good things.

Now what we have just described may seem to be a caricature of a jaundiced view of the role of the mass media in development, but it is more than that. It is indeed a view with a firm foundation in social science research. It is perfectly true that the mass media alone, unlinked to word-of-mouth communication, fail in generating action but do not fail in creating information and desires. We shall document this point later. Here let us simply note that the lukewarm attitude of the governments of most developing countries toward the mass media is a natural concomitant of the weakness of political organization underpinning their regimes. Without an effective political organization at the grass roots to provide word-of-mouth support for the messages the mass media, the latter do not produce desired action results.

From a broader point of view than that of a particular government, other effects of the mass media, such as demonstration effects or raising the level of information may be either good or bad in the long run. But a regime resting on weak political organization can hardly be expected to look with pleasure on forces which introduce shocks to the social fabric while not facilitating control of the short-run action consequences. A regime based on a strong organization of face-to-face leadership can use mass media with great effectiveness as an associated instrument of action. A regime without such organization cannot substitute mass media propaganda for organization. The media do not produce the same results.

Thus the theory of communication that underlies the media investment pattern in most noncommunist developing countries is one which says, first, that the media do not seem to produce major changes in action. (That is true if one considers the media alone.) Secondly, other changes in the short run, such as changes in beliefs and values unaccompanied by appropriate changes in practices, tend to be disruptive. Third, despite the impracticality or dangers of trying to produce changes in the minds of men, it is recognized that such changes are needed for modernization. That is why a seemingly safe investment is made in the very slow-acting medium of education. From the perspective of history we know how disruptive to the old ways education may also be, but the quick-acting media (press, radio, film) act in periods coincident with the span considered in political decision making while education in general does not. For the short run, then, this theory says the mass media are not of great importance, and that is correct if one focuses on the objective of producing action and assumes the media to operate without concomitant political organization.

The Communist Theory of Media Use

The communist theory of mass communication differs at many points from that which we have just outlined. In the first place, and most obviously, it is even more emphatic on the possible negative effects of some messages; oppositional messages are simply banned. Terror assures that only the approved ideas are in the flow to the public, without tolerance of even slight deviations. While this is the most important single difference between communist and free world communication, we do not dwell upon it here since our subject concerns other matters.

The communist theory of mass communication, in the second place, while much concerned with the immediate action consequences of propaganda, is not quite so exclusively focused on them. Although the communist propaganda rulebook requires that the agitator always exhort to specific actions rather than simply advocate attitudes, at the same time communist doctrine recognizes propaganda objectives other than those which action-advocating propaganda may serve. Much more than their opponents, the communists think of using the mass media to produce characterological change. Also they are aware of the possibility of using the mass media as organizational devices, for in communist theory the media are just an adjunct to political organization, not an independent base for political power.

That part of communist theory with which we are here concerned is developed in two pamphlets by Lenin, *What Is to Be Done,* and *Left Wing Communism, An Infantile Disorder.*[3] It has been codified in a number of books by students of Soviet affairs.[4] In *What Is to Be Done* Lenin polemicized in favor of the revolutionists establishing a nationwide legal newspaper inside of tsarist Russia. He conceded the point of his opponents that such a paper under tsarist censorship could not tell the truth as the Marxists saw it, could not agitate effectively, could not, in short, be a spokesman for the views its publishers held. Why then did he want it established, and why did he regard it as of utmost importance? His main reason was that he recognized something which American racketeers have also recognized: that a newspaper distribution system is an excellent nucleus for a political machine. Actually his view was a little bit broader; the whole newspaper apparatus would provide both a function for and a cover for the revolutionary organization on a nationwide basis. There would be reporters who would have to travel around, inform themselves, get themselves in contact with sources of news on legitimate grounds. There would be jobs in distribution for less literate party members. For all of them the existence of something to do in the otherwise stifling environment of a dictatorship, and something which brought them into face-to-face contact with each other in a legal way, would be a major boon to morale. These are the reasons why he wished the newspaper established.

While this approach to the media may in part be explained away as a response to the special situation of maintaining a subversive organization against an inefficient authoritarian regime,[5] it has nevertheless been canonized into general doctrine. The model of media use set in the first decade of this century remains in generalized form the model in communist countries today.

Let us try to codify the operational doctrine briefly.

One: the important thing about a medium is not what it says per se but the social function (a) of its existence as an institution and (b) of the statements in it.

Two: discipline in making the "correct" statement in the media is indeed important—not primarily because of any direct impact of the statements made, but rather as a means to inducing characterological changes in the speakers in the direction of discipline and conformity.

Three: media provide an important activity around which to build organizations. Worker correspondents, discussion groups around key articles, local wall newspapers, etc. involve people deeply in the media.

Four: the media provide an instrument for central direction of organizations dispersed to all corners of a country.[6] The media give the orders of the day to be carried out in face-to-face organization.

Five: words in the media alone do not effectively change people. It takes a combination of the media and direct personal contact to move people to action. It is only through participation in action that deeply held attitudes are changed. By action, however, these can be changed, even down to changing the basic personality of man.

The last point, and to some extent point one, may be clarified by reference to *Left Wing Communism.* In that work Lenin was replying to a group of Marxists who took the view that communists had no business advocating such short-run goals as higher wages, racial equality, and social security. In the first place, the Leftists argued, such goals were unachievable under capitalism, so it was misleading to propagandize for them. Secondly, insofar as the goals were partly achieved, such progress might satisfy the masses; from the communist point of view the worse things got, the better. Lenin rejected both these theses. He conceded that immediate demands were unrealistic, a critic might say demagogic. He too regarded them as unachievable under capitalism. But in that fact he found their tactical merit, for the struggle was everything, the goal nothing. Lenin argued that the communists had to put themselves on the side of what people wanted. There was no danger that success would undercut their revolutionary program, for with unachievable goals disappointment was sure. Finally, and most important, it was in the process of struggle for immediate demands that the masses would be transformed.

That was the old Marxist answer to the challenge: how could socialism turn over factories to obviously lazy, irresponsible, often dissolute people such as one found in fact among many of the workers? The Marxist answer was that capitalism made the workers that way. The experience of expressing autonomy through strikes and revolution would transform their personalities, making new men out of them. In line with that image of the learning experience in the modernization process, Lenin regarded the stimulation of action for immediate objectives as an essential part of all agitational efforts.

Thus it is not some abstract truth-value by which the media are to be judged in communist eyes, but their contribution to action by organized groups of people. The media thus conceived acquire enormous importance to communist regimes. They are an effective organizational device, and, when linked to face-to-face organization, they can be powerful influences on individual action.

Traditional Modes of Communication

In the developing nations Westernized deracinated action-oriented elites without well-organized mass following tend to adopt the first view of the media outlined above, that which we called disillusionment. Certain other elites obviously find the communist approach to mass communication genial. Ever since Sun Yat-sen a surprising number of leaders of developing countries have found the practical political methods of democratic centralism appealing even though they have cared but little about the economics of Communism. Indeed it is its approach to propaganda and politics which has been the most effective part of Bolshevik doctrine in the underdeveloped countries. That is not surprising, for in a few important respects the communist doctrine is closer than is the Western approach to the theory of communication which characterizes traditional societies. It is closer in that it values the social function of a communication above its truth-value. It is closer also in its recognition of the primacy of word of mouth over mass media. It is closer in conceiving of communication as embedded in a process of elaborately organized particularistic relations among persons rather than as a uniform output from the media to a faceless mass.

The similarities that we have just noted between communist and traditional conceptions of communication are not explained by any glib assertions of influence of one on the other, nor by a comforting assertion that the communist approach to communication is backward or primitive. The fact that two of the three theories we have been describing are alike on a number of points is better explained by some peculiar and unique features of the third, or Western theory of communication which set it apart from most human behavior through all time the world over.

To evaluate assertions primarily by a criterion of objective truth is not a natural human way of doing things; it is one of the peculiar features of the Graeco-Roman-Western tradition. This one cultural heritage among the many in human experience has tended to make truth-value the main test of the validity of statements. And truth-value is a rather curious criterion. It is ruthlessly two-valued and dominated by the law of the excluded middle, something which classical Indian logic, for example, never accepted; statements in the latter system would be simultaneously both true and false. The Western criterion of truth-value also assumes that a statement has a validity or lack of it inherent in itself and quite independent of who says it and why. That too is something Brahminical philosophy did not accept; a statement true for a man in one Varna might be false for one in another. The Western criterion of truth assumes further that validity can be tested independently of who does the testing provided certain rituals of procedure are followed. Most cultural traditions do not make these assumptions. For one thing, only in a society with an unusually high degree of mutual trust in interpersonal relationships would people accept statements regardless of source. In most societies facts must be validated by an in-group authority before they can be considered credible. Word of mouth is therefore more trustworthy than written sources. Distrust of those who are not in one's own family, tribe, or caste dominates any objective test of truth in most economically nonexpansive societies.[7]

Furthermore, most of mankind does not regard the truth-value of statements as terribly important. For most of the men who have inhabited the earth the consequences of a statement—for example, whether it will bring the wrath of God upon you, whether it will help you earn a living, whether it will win a loved one—are considerably more important than whether it matches certain abstract rules of transformability into other statements. The Western tradition is unique in the value it has attached to the latter consideration.

So when we say that traditional societies are more concerned with the social function of communication than with its truth-value, we are only saying they are human. Yet their concern with the social function of communications is an important fact.

A statement is valid in a traditional society if it comes from the right oracle. It is not necessarily everyone's right to judge its validity. There are statements within one's own sphere of propriety, and there are those which are outside one's proper role. Daniel Lerner has introduced all of us to the peasant whose reply to the question, what would he do if he were someone else—a foreigner, a radio station manager, a politician, is in effect, "My God! How can you ask me a question like that? I could never be him."[8] The peasant's statement, even in role playing, is considered of no validity. Felix and Marie Keesing document the same point even more extensively in their study of communication behavior in Samoa.[9] There are certain words and certain topics of discussion reference to which is proper only by certain individuals. In Samoa references to those domains in which power is demonstrated by chiefs and talking chiefs is improper for their subordinates. It is not, as in Western dictatorship, that the inferior is obliged to say approved things. It is rather that it is shocking for him to say anything at all in what is not his proper sphere.

The frequent application of social rather than truth-value criteria in traditional societies is further documented by studies of political movements in them. Lucian Pye has shown how to the Malayan communists the primary criterion applied to communist ideology was the power of the leaders. If the communists seemed likely to win, then what the communist leaders said was valid; if they seemed likely to lose, then it was not. It was personal leadership and power which determined the validity of what might be in the mass media.[10]

A study of Cambodia tells us that "information itself is considered sterile by the individual villager until someone of status has interpreted it. The individual does not see it as his role to judge the news."[11]

One might cite examples indefinitely. We could talk about honorifics and the problem of communication in Japan, where it may become hard to express what one has to say until one has gotten around to finding the words appropriate to the person to whom one is talking.

Our concern here, however, is to consider the significance of these matters to the mass media. The mass media represent a peculiar mode of communication in which one does not know to whom one is talking. Broadcasting or writing for the press is like dropping a note in a bottle over the side of a boat. The man who receives it may be king or pauper, relative or stranger, friend or foe.

This is less of a problem in a traditional society, although it is not a problem which is altogether new. All traditional societies have their equivalents of mass media. There is a literature of sagas or folk songs sung to all and sundry. There are assemblages at temples, festivals, or markets where the hawker or priest or actor addresses himself to a motley crowd of persons of all stations. There are proclamations to the multitude. There are ways of calling out to a stranger in the dark. But for all of these there are established conventions. The rules of etiquette prescribe the form of language in which a folk song is sung. The modern media create a host of new situations for which new conventions must be established. How does one answer the phone or talk on radio or write for the newspapers? New conventions will be established, but new conventions are always by definition crude, coarse, and vulgar.

So the mass media in a stratified society inevitably have the problem of vulgarity in a particularly acute way. They can avoid vulgarity by pretending they are addressing their most cultured superiors. This results in media which use only the highest form of the language and which are not understood by the bulk of the population. This happens extensively in Arab countries. It happens often where the media are in the hands of well-educated civil servants aspiring to be intellectuals. The All India Radio, for example, says that its small village audience is its top priority audience, but it also often refuses to use the low Hindi forms which the villagers can understand.

Alternatively, the media may seek out their natural mass audience and alienate themselves from their national elite and its goals. They can do this by turning radical or by turning commercial and sensational or both, for these alternatives are not exclusive. Tawdry apolitical yellow publications or movies may well be produced by a largely leftist press corps. (Private entrepreneurs of sensation may be building part of the political machine Lenin prescribed.) Or it may be that the radical publications themselves provide low-level popular culture, some sort of so-called people's art. It takes either a callous unconcern with the values of one's culture or else an ideology which justifies alternative values to permit intellectuals, bred among the elite or elite aspirants of any society, to produce the kind of more or less debased materials which can communicate to the masses who share only a watered-down version of the culture.

In a traditional face-to-face communication system this problem is not too serious, for there is a high degree of differentiation of communication according to the interpersonal situation involved. The village singers or traveling troupes, though they tell ancient tales, are usually quite skilled at adapting themselves to their audience, often indeed introducing local matters or topical events into the classical frame of their stories. These bards or their equivalents are a kind of bridge between their unsophisticated audience and their own teachers or urban colleagues from whom they learn. Such traditional communicators at the lowest level have at least one foot deeply in their preindustrial society, and they have at best very modest intellectual or cultural attainments. But in the great non-Western cultures they are in turn in contact with a more elevated group of traditional teachers and sages. At each level communication is appropriate to its environment both in literary form and content. Any kind of interpersonal organization, traditional or modern, has such a graded structure of face-to-face communication. Its absence is a problem for a pure mass media communication system.

Granted it is not an insuperable problem. The mass media are also graded, and they divide up a national audience among them by taste and cultural level. But a problem does exist. Some media do have to serve the total society. Where there is but a single local newspaper or radio or TV station, dissatisfaction with it is bound to arise in any differentiated society, and especially so in a dual society such as any developing society is. Even more important is the fact that highly educated or Westernized elites produce the modern media and guide them; such men are often unable or unwilling to address their masses, or they are in conflict when addressing them.

Educating the masses to become like their elite is normally offered as the answer. But that is obviously an illusory solution. Village schools or even new colleges may produce literacy. They do not thereby reduce the circulation of lowbrow, highly popularized media, they increase it.

A recent study in Israel documents an obvious point. It compares the achievement in school of children whose fathers come from culturally advanced countries with children whose fathers come from underdeveloped countries. Although in the same grade-school classes in a heterogeneous community, by the end of the second grade 80 percent of the former could read sentences but less than one third of the latter. Similar results appeared in arithmetic and other tests.[12] The supporting family environment largely determines how much the school communicates. So too with any medium, be it education or a mass medium. What it can accomplish is severely limited, depending upon the functionality of the medium as perceived in the interpersonal environment.

What this signifies is, first, that mass education may be expected to create an audience for only the most popularized and simplified media. Second, media of that kind are the only ones which can serve to induct into modern ways precisely those persons whose familial environment does not push them in the same direction. Education may modernize a child or young man from a household which instills motivation for that goal. It will not effectively modernize the masses. The media, plus associated personal influence on adults, must take over the job at the very low level which schools will achieve.

Media at that low level of popular culture include movies, comics and picture books, and potentially radio and TV. Also particularly effective at this level are the traditional media to which we referred before, and which can be used effectively on behalf of birth control, agricultural conservation, or nationalism. The communists have done a good deal of this, putting out material through traditional storytellers, priests, or players. Some noncommunist movements have done the same. Conservative religious traditional parties, such as provincial movements in India or that of Prince Sihanouk in Cambodia or of the Muslim Teachers in Indonesia, of course rely particularly heavily on a machine built up of bards, or bronzes, or Maulanas. But experiments have been conducted, and quite successfully, in using such channels for modernizing messages too.[13]

These traditional media are particularly effective because they involve an organized machine for word-of-mouth communication. We know that in many traditional societies word-of-mouth is more trusted than the written word, that word-of-mouth everywhere is an essential stimulus to action, that it is more adaptable to the variations in style and manner which are so particularly important in a dual and transitional society; and we might add here that at the early stages of transition, mouths may be more common than newspapers or radios. (Cambodia, for example, has roughly one full-fledged priest for every eighty inhabitants, against one weekly paper in circulation for each 120 inhabitants, one daily in circulation for each 500, and a similar number of radios.)[14]

But it would be a mistake to minimize the equal and often greater importance of the new mass media which contain the new-style popular culture, vapid and lacking in identity as it often may be. There is something universal in the appeal of the film song or soap opera.[15] And there is something significant in their contribution to modernization. In order to understand just what their significance may be, we need to digress here to consider what social science research has shown about the effects of communications on individuals.

The Social Science View of Media Effects

In conjunction with development programs there have been many studies of how to get farmers (and occasionally others) to adopt modern practices. The general finding has been that what occurs when a new practice is adopted is what Katz and Lazarsfeld call the two-step flow of communication.[16] That is to say, the mass media do not lead to adoption directly. They create an awareness of the existence of the new practice, and they provide guidance to innovating leaders. However, actual adoption of a new practice requires either personal persuasion or personal example by a respected opinion leader. Thus the spread of an innovation can be traced from an initiating center, by direct personal contact, out to the periphery.[17] It can also be traced from younger, well-educated, somewhat alienated and relatively cosmopolitan individuals in a community to older, highly entrenched, above-average educated individuals with whom the former are in touch, and then finally to other people in the community who follow the leaders.[18] The adoption of an innovation advocated in the mass media has been shown to depend on interpersonal discussion of it.

The last point has been most dramatically demonstrated in a series of UNESCO sponsored studies of radio listening and TV viewing groups. J.C. Mathur and Paul Neurath, for example, conducted a study of village radio broadcasts in India. In the control situations where these broadcasts were listened to by individuals in usual fashion the radio programs had virtually no effect. Where, however, listening groups were organized and discussions of the programs took place immediately after, the suggestions were often followed.[19] The same thing was found with TV viewing groups in France, and in other places too.[20] Similar results on the role of word-of-mouth communication in clinching media advice have been obtained in marketing studies.[21]

All of these studies add up to the conclusion foreshadowed above: that to stimulate action, mass media exhortations need to be coupled with the organization of face-to-face leadership. Here, however, we must raise the question of whether exhortation to action is indeed the most important use of mass media in the modernizing process. While many studies have examined how to persuade the citizenry to take specific actions, only a few studies have looked at the role of the media in producing transformations in values and personality. Such changes in values and attitudes, it can be argued, are far more important to modernization than are mere changes in actions.

That is perhaps an unusual view, for it is common to assume that changes in men's actions are the really important objective and that changes in attitudes are but a means toward the desired actions. We would argue, however, that it is the other way around. It is, for example, relatively easy to get peasants to plant a particular kind of seed a foot apart instead of six inches apart. This action can be induced by money payments, by terror, by authority, by persuasion, by proving it to be the will of the gods, and by many other means. But the improvement of one such practice does not mean that the peasant has been in any way modernized. A far more significant change would be the development of a scientific attitude toward the adoption of new practices. It is only that kind of internal change in the latent structure of his attitudes that would produce self-sustaining movement toward modernization. Yet the effects of communications in the process of transition has been much studied in relation to specific actions, but only little studied in relation to the much more important matters of values and attitudes.

In this area the most notable contributions have been by Daniel Lerner and David McClelland. They have both put forward the daring thesis that the mass media can have profound characterological effects. Lerner convincingly argues that the media provide their consumers with a capacity to conceive of situations and ways of life quite different from those directly experienced.[22] To have such a capacity for empathy is necessary if a person is to function in a great society. A great society is characteristically one where every business firm must anticipate the wants of unknown clients, every politician those of unknown voters; where planning takes place for a vastly changed future; where the actions of people in quite different cultures may affect one daily. If, as Lerner argues, the media provide the means for empathically entering the roles that affect a man in a great society, then the characterological contribution of the media to modernization is indeed significant.

McClelland's thesis has less face plausibility but is documented persuasively. It is that certain types of media content may help to raise achievement motivation and help to develop a consensus supporting it, and that such high achievement motivation is in turn a major necessary condition for development.[23] If McClelland's results, based in part on studies of children's literature, are even partly confirmed, they too are vitally important to any theory of development.

Now the interest of the Lerner and McClelland theses for our present paper is that neither of these depends upon a two-step flow of communication. Neither of them is predicated upon opinion leaders or political organizations paralleling the media. They are concerned with effects which the media have directly.

This suggests that the conclusion that the effectiveness of the media in the process of modernization depends upon their being linked to a well-developed organization of face-to-face influence is too simple. It is not wrong, but it is partial. It is true for certain of the potential effects of the mass media but not for others. And so we stop here to set up a typology of what the effects of the mass media are.

These effects are of two main kinds: effects upon the individuals exposed to them, and institutional effects arising from the very existence of a mass media system.

Among the direct and immediate effects which exposure to the media may have upon the individuals are changes in: (1) attention; (2) saliency; (3) information; (4) skills; (5) tastes; (6) images (7) attitudes; (8) actions. Changes in any one of these may in turn change each of the others: changes in one's actions may change one's attitudes just as changes in one's attitudes may change one's actions; changes in the information one has may change one's distribution of attention, or changes in what one attends to may change one's information. Yet it is possible analytically to distinguish these changes and to consider the differences in the conditions for each kind of change.

Various experimental and survey results suggest that the mass media operate very directly upon attention, information, tastes, and images. Election studies, for example, show that the campaign in the mass media does little to change attitudes in the short run, but does a great deal to focus attention on one topic or another.[24] It also affects the saliency of different issues. Television studies have shown that TV has relatively little direct effect on major attitudes, but it does develop tastes (good or bad) and provides much image material to stock the mind of the viewer.[25] Harold Isaacs' studies of image formation also support the notion that these scratches on the mind can be picked up casually from the most diverse sources, including literature, movies, etc.[26] The effect which media have on images is also the effect on which Lerner built his theory; empathic capacity is the ability to imagine a situation. And such effects are indeed ones which the media have directly.

Changes in skills and attitudes are less apt to be brought about by the mass media operating alone. Here the best we can say is that sometimes they are but often they are not. Often face-to-face relations with a human being toward whom the learner has considerable cathexis is essential for producing changes in those variables. We can, for example, classify attitudes as being of greater or lesser rigidity and saliency. Lightly held attitudes may readily be molded by mass media alone, but not deeply entrenched ones. The experimental literature on the framing of survey research questions is probably as good evidence on this point as any. Responses to low-saliency questions are shifted readily by question wording, new information, or almost anything. Other attitudes stand up under any media barrage. Psychotherapy shows that to change deeply rooted attitudes requires the development of an intense relationship with a reference person. So too the literature on teaching, that is, the imparting of skills, demonstrates that while many skills can be learned from reading, or TV, or movies, the learning of difficult matter requires a level of motivation that is engendered only in a relationship with an important reference person who demands the effort.

Finally, we return to actions, changes in which, as we have already noted, are almost always checked with reference persons before an individual embarks upon them.

Changes of all of these variables are important in the process of development. But they enter the process in different ways. For example, a conclusion stated much earlier in this paper holds, we now see, for some of these kinds of change only. Changes in actions and in some skills and attitudes will not be effectively produced by mass media alone; rather, the effectiveness of the mass media in influencing them will be a direct function of the effectiveness of political organization to which the mass media are an adjunct.

On the other hand, certain of these changes toward modernization will occur as the mass media develop, whether or not strong political organization exists. Note what these changes are. They are changes in attention, tastes, information, images. That is exactly the revolution of rising expectations! General findings of social psychology based largely upon American experiments and surveys have led us to exactly the same results as area students have formulated from experience with the politics of development: a happy but rare conjunction of observation with theory in the social sciences.

The Media as Institutions

What functions can the mass media perform in the process of political development? We have just noted that there are certain kinds of impact on their audiences which they easily produce, and certain others which they can produce only in conjunction with political organization. We remarked above that in addition there is another class of effects which mass media have (a class of effects well noted by Lenin): namely, effects by virtue of the existence of the media as institutions in the society.

For example, the existence of media gives politicians a vastly increased opportunity for leadership. As happened also in the West, the growth of plebiscitarian politics goes hand in hand with the growth of the press. The press enables the politician to act on a national scale. It puts into the headlines all over the country topics which are otherwise no part of the experience of the citizens in each separate locality. It transforms these topics into issues. It enables the political leader to give the word of the day simultaneously to the whole country on something which the press has made salient for all of it. It makes national parties possible because some issues are the same throughout the country. And a modern media system with wire services does this better than a set of struggling local print shops putting out papers.

The press also gives the politicians a recognized national code of procedures by which to confirm status. A highly segmented society is apt to suffer from lack of consensus not only on matters of substance but even on the facts of what has been decided. Anything which establishes a public record of policy decisions, of assignments of prestige (by column inches or anything else), and of responsibilities can be useful. Of course a party press in which the different papers give very different pictures of the world does not achieve this purpose. But under many circumstances a press consensus enables everyone (including the party leader himself) to know, for example, who is the party leader.

A mass media system permits the unification of a nation in many nonpolitical ways similar to those we have just been describing. The existence of daily price quotations facilitates the establishment of a national market. Media encourage a national art and literature by holding up products against each other. The media broaden the relevant reference groups in discussions. The same kinds of processes of national organization through the media take place in social life, in cultural life, in economic life, and in party politics.

The media also serve as educators for and employers of a new kind of politician, one who is issue oriented and ideologically oriented rather than oriented to personal identifications, The media provide some of the few jobs in mobile professions in many underdeveloped countries. Those are miserably paid and grossly exploited professions, but they are ones not tied rigidly to either traditional statuses or castes nor to a Western style educational system. The media thus provide a niche where political men of a new kind can ensconce themselves. They provide a base from which such men can operate in attacking the old elites. The media often provide a livelihood for such politicians while they wait for the opportunities of politics or while they engage in the day-to-day work of political organization. The media create some of the few chances for men who are not notables to become politicians by vocation in poverty-stricken countries.

Conclusions

Neither these points about how the media can give rise to a political class and to political activity nor the earlier points about how the media generate rising expectations make rapid mass media development seem a happy prospect to leaders attempting to hold together a fragile balance in barely viable states about to explode. But in this field as in others the processes of change are not going to be stopped. The media can be a far more potent instrument of development than has yet been recognized in almost any noncommunist developing nation or by American development planners. But for their potential to be effectively used, their development must also be linked to effective grassroots political organization.

Notes

1. 1913–1939 figures from Inkeles, Alex. *Public opinion in Soviet Russia.* Cambridge, MA: Harvard University Press, 1951, p. 144; 1954 figures from UNESCO, *Basic facts and figures.* Paris: UNESCO, 1956.
2. See chapter 16 of this volume [Pye, L.W. (ed.). *Communication and political development.*]
3. Lenin, V. I.. "What is to be done." In *Collected works*, vol. IV. New York: International Publishers, 1929, pp. 89–258; *Left wing communism, an infantile disorder.* New York: International Publishers, 1940.
4. See, especially, Selznick, Philip. *The organizational weapon.* New York: McGraw Hill, 1952 for a discussion of the relation of the media to organization; Bauer, Raymond A. *The new man in Soviet society.* Cambridge, MA: Harvard University Press, 1952 for Soviet views on the possibilities of producing characterological changes; and Leites, Nathan. *A study of Bolshevism.* Glencoe, IL: The Free Press, 1953, for a general codification of communist doctrines of political tactics.
5. Lenin's approach to media use may also be regarded as a generalization of the materialist conception of history, which minimizes the importance of the ideas expressed and exaggerates the importance of institutions.
6. Note that the most important magazine in Russia is probably *The Agitators Notebook,* a journal which gives the two million oral agitators their guidelines for the next few weeks of meetings.
7. Keesing, Felix; Keesing, Marie. *Elite communications in Samoa.* Stanford, CA: Stanford University Press, 1956; cf. also Blair, Thomas. "Social structure and information exposure in rural Brazil." *Rural Sociology* 25 (March 1960): 65–75.
8. Lerner, Daniel. *The passing of traditional society.* Glencoe, IL: The Free Press, 1958.
9. Keesing, F and M. *Elite communications in Samoa.*
10. Cf. Pye, Lucian., *Guerrilla Communism in Malaya.* Princeton, NJ: Princeton University Press, 1956; Gude, Edward W. "Buddhism and the political process in Cambodia," manuscript, 1961, p. 15.
11. Edward W. Gude, "Buddhism," p. 14.
12. Smilansky, Sarah. "Evaluation of early education." In Smilanky, M.; Adar, L. (eds.) *Educational studies and documents* 42 (*Evaluating educational achievements.* Paris: UNESCO, 1961, p. 9.

13. Cf. Damle, Y. B. "A note on Harikatha," in *Bulletin of the Deccan College* XVII (Poona) for a discussion of the role of such traditional sources in dissemination of ideas about caste. For descriptions of this kind of communication, see Milton Singer, *Traditional India: Structure and change*. Philadelphia, PA: The American Folklore Society, 1959.

14. Edward W. Gude, "Buddhism."

15. For a description of comics, popular songs, radio, soap operas, movies, and magazine stories in a non-Western culture, see Hidetoshi Karo. *Japanese popular culture*. Tokyo: Charles E. Turtle Co., 1959.

16. Katz, Elihu; Lazarsfeld, Paul F. *Personal influence*. Glencoe, IL: The Free Press, 1955. For a review of the literature see Katz, E. "The two step flow of communication." *Public Opinion Quarterly* 21 (1957): 61–78.

17. Cf. Hagerstrand, Torsten. *On Monte Carlo simulation of diffusion*, mimeographed.

18. Cf. Coleman, James; Katz, Elihu; Menzel, Herbert. *Medical innovation: A diffusion study*. Indianapolis, IN: Bobbs-Merrill, 1966. *The adoption of new products*. Ann Arbor, MI: Foundation for Research on Human Behavior, 1959. Rogers, Everett M. "Categorizing the adopters of agricultural practices." *Rural Sociology* 8 (1943): 15–24. Rogers, E. M. and Beal, G. M. "The importance of personal influence in the adoption of technological changes." *Social Forces* 36, no. 4 (1958). Ryan, Bryce, Gross, N. C., *Research Bulletin No. 372: The acceptance and diffusion of hybrid seed corn in two Iowa communities*. Ames: Iowa Agricultural Experiment Station, 1950). Wilkening, E. A. "Informal leaders and innovators in farm practices." *Rural Sociology* 17, no. 3, (1952): 272–75. Lionberger, H. F. "Community prestige in the choice of sources of farm information." *Public Opinion Quarterly* 23 (1959): 110–18.

19. Mathur, J. C.; Neurath, Paul. *An Indian experiment in farm radio forums*. Paris: UNESCO, 1959.

20. Cassirer, Henry. *Television teaching today*. Paris: UNESCO, 1960. Cf. also UNESCO series on Press, Film, and Radio in the World Today: Nicol, J.; Shea, A.; Simmins, G. J. P. Canada's Farm Radio Forum, 1954; Dumazedier, J. *Television and rural adult education*, 1956; Anon., *Rural television in Japan*, 1960.

21. Katz and Lazarsfeld, *Personal influence*.

22. Lerner, *The passing of traditional society*.

23. McClelland, David. *The achieving society*. Princeton, NJ: Van Nostrand, 1961.

24. Lazarsfeld, Paul F.; Berelson, Bernard; Gaudet, Hazel. *The people's choice*. New York: Columbia University Press, 1948. Berelson, Bernard; Lazarsfeld, Paul F.; McPhee, William. *Voting*. Chicago: University of Chicago Press, 1954.

25. Himmelweit, Hilda, Oppenheim, A. Vince, P. et al. *Television and the child*. London: Oxford University Press, 1958. Schramm, Wilbur; Lyle, Jack; Parker, Edwin. *Television in the lives of our children*. Stanford, CA: Stanford University Press, 1961.

26. Isaacs, Harold R. *Scratches on our minds*. New York: John Day, 1958.

11

Four Unnatural Institutions
and the Road Ahead

Since the time of Bodin, and certainly since Condorcet's "Esquisse d'un tableau historique des progres de l'esprit humain," men have generally assumed that there is a pattern to human history such that the future will differ from the past. That is a novel thought. Through most of the millennia of human history fundamental change was so slow that men's natural assumption was that their world would not differ greatly from that of their great-grandfathers or that of their great-grandsons'. There were of, course, changes like famines, wars, floods, and epidemics, but they followed no epochal laws or patterns. History could be conceived as "one damn thing after another." Chronicles of these events there might be, but an epic of man with a plot of intrinsic evolution (and not just some magical creation) could only be conceived when individuals could perceive systematic change taking place within the time frame of their own comprehended experience.

The Jewish and Christian myths were among the earliest perceptions of a plan to history. The plot involved creation, sin, and the fall of man, a long struggle of penance, and an ultimate messianic resurrection. History, "the unrolled scroll of prophecy," made sense as such a divine plan. Indeed, when in the eighteenth century, the idea of progress was secularized by Condorcet and others, it may have been freed from some of its mythological baggage, but it still had a transcendental character that cried out for explanation.

The Darwinian process of selection was one way to account for a trend of infinite perfectibility. Any notion of history more complicated than such unidirectional progress—"a cyclic poem written by time upon the memories of a man" as Shelley called it —was harder to explain

From *The Human Use of Human Ideas* (1983), edited by Shuhei Aida.

except by a divine plan. The nineteenth-century notion of scientific laws of history in which "nature" determined the character of society at different stages, misperceived science, and merely substituted the word "nature" for the word "God." Though such sacro-scientific theories may now fail to satisfy us intellectually, they continue, in an era when men recognize the fact of change, to appeal to a profound desire to know where we are going. We are haunted by the question of whither!

The Darwinian explanation of progress makes much sense. It implies that what exists today in the most advanced societies meets some human needs, for it was selected by an evolutionary process. Those human institutions that have evolved over millennia of change may be ones that help the species to survive. But it would be a profound misunderstanding of evolutionary ideas to assume that the process of natural selection necessarily makes life better in all respects for each individual in the species (after all, some species such as bees and ants thrive by their total subordination of individuals). The pleasure principle may play an important role in mediating the process of selection, but that fact does not guarantee that the conditions of life that get selected for survival are the same as those in which we as individuals would find our greatest happiness.

Indeed, it would be very surprising if the features of contemporary society, so alien from the natural environment of our species, were not also to a considerable degree distasteful to the human organism. After all, for almost all of the span of man's existence on earth, people lived in tiny tightly knit primary communities, met perhaps fifty other persons in a lifetime, and talked but little, and that little, mostly in the context of familiar emotional ties where few words were needed. It would be strange, indeed, if organisms that had lived in such a milieu for a couple of hundred thousand years would be entirely at home living in cities of millions, interacting socially not with fifty people, but with two orders of magnitude as many, and spending all but a few minutes a day in their lives in enclosed boxes called buildings.

The society in which we live today is characterized by four quite unnatural major institutions (among others). These are:

- the nation state
- bureaucracies
- cities
- and a class structure in which manual labor is performed by an underclass and mental labor by an elite.

These four institutions all grew up together in the past 500 years. Each had its antecedents. Cities existed in the ancient world, long before modern manufacturing and commerce made the city the habitat of the majority of the population. There were city-states and empires long before the world was partitioned into (now 130) sovereign nation-states. There were mandarins and samurai before there were white collar bureaucrats. There were classes and there was class exploitation, but the members of ruling classes in the past often based their power on personal prowess in combat or on physical possession of land and goods, rather than on moving pieces of paper.

The above four institutions of contemporary society are all well adapted to each other and also well adapted to a communication system using printed mass media. The size of a typical nation state is such that print media can be economically distributed around it in a day, or at most several. A few of the largest nation states are so large that newspapers are based in many separate cities, but more often the national press is the capital's press, published in the major city and circulated daily around the whole country. The unifying language in its canonical form is taught in the schools which are also the source of literacy. The state organization functions through the forms of bureaucracy, built (as Max Weber and other have pointed out) on the written document. Thus those who write, rule, and organize the manual labor of the large number of others who make and move things. Industrial and bureaucratic activities are centered in great cities (and indeed create such cities). In those cities the densely conglomerated population can be well addressed via movies, TV, and the press, produced by an intelligentsia but enjoyed by all.

As Aristotle recognized, the optimal size of the city-state was set by the ability of people to gather together to transact business. One could likewise argue that the optimal size of the nation-state was set by the limits to which printed matter in the vulgate language could be rapidly transported and delivered.

Radio and electronic communication have begun to change that situation. Starting with telegraphy in the nineteenth century it became possible to transmit the printed word instantaneously over vast distances. However, that was very expensive. It was so expensive that the early newspapers limited their telegraphed text to a short column of cryptic bulletins, leaving the more expository treatment to wait for the mails. But with the coming of radio the cost of addressing millions of people scattered over large areas dropped drastically. The natural perimeter of communication ballooned outward.

In the United States public policy sought to create a broadcasting system modeled on the newspaper system with local broadcasting stations in every town. "Localism" was the basic philosophy of the legislation. It worked, however, only to a limited degree. While no licenses were given for stations with power enough to blanket the country, networking was used by the broadcasters to turn the local stations for many hours a day into mere retransmission points. The vast reach of broadcasting could not be totally denied.

In the 1930s short-wave broadcasting made radio a global phenomenon. For the first time frontiers became totally permeable. No customs officer could stop subversive material any more. In Stalin's Russia less than 2 percent of the population had access to short wave; today the majority do. That fact has been a powerful force for change.

Nonetheless, international broadcasting, international telephony, and other forms of transborder electronic communication are still small in scale compared to the communication within nations. We still live in an era of preponderantly national communication systems. So if we look only at the present world, nationalism seems to be as strong or stronger than ever. We are struck by the extent to which the four institutions that we have mentioned as characterizing the modern world— the nation-state, bureaucracies, cities, and the segregation of manual and mental labor—are well adapted to each other, and also well adapted to the main media of communication of the nineteenth and first part of the twentieth centuries. They are, however, ill adapted to a number of new developments in the world's economy and particularly to its communication systems.

We have no crystal ball, but there are a number of trends well under way, of sufficient magnitude that it would indeed be astonishing if they did not continue into the future. Among these we may mention four: the development of a global economy with transactions having externalities that are felt across borders; rapid and efficient transport of persons and things; electronic communication; and intelligent machines. These trends are fundamentally at odds with the institutions that we have mentioned as characterizing the modern world till now.

There is little reason to doubt the power, or the persistence, or the revolutionary character of these new trends. Trade has existed as a global phenomenon for hundreds of years, but the oil crisis of 1973 was the first time in history that the economy of the whole world was instantly and simultaneously impacted by single set of transactions; before that the crises or transformation that occurred in one place sent ripples or waves spreading sometimes to the ends of the earth. But the oil crisis was not a wave phenomenon; it was a single crisis everywhere.

The fact is explained by the low cost of modern oil shipment. Before modern means of transportation the cost of bulk goods would double in a hundred miles from their origin. Today the shipping costs of wheat or oil almost vanish in the interregional differences in their costs of production. The same sort of thing is happening to human travel. Recently, despite the fall of the dollar and America's continental remoteness, one in ten U.S. citizens vacationed abroad. In this era of the Concorde, Jules Verne's *Around the World in 80 Days* brings a smile of amusement.

The changes in electronic communication are even more revolutionary. Electronic transmissions, as we have already noted, are no respecters of boundaries. Yet up to now economics has kept international telephony and short-wave broadcasting as secondary features of the global communication system, but that will not be true for much longer. Three technical changes will result in distance becoming a negligible factor in the cost of communication. The most obvious reason for distance insensitivity of communications costs is the use of satellites. When messages travel to and from a satellite on the geostationary orbit at 36,000 kilometers above the equator, it makes no difference how far apart, within the beam, the point of origin and destination may be.

However, the cost of terrestrial transmission is also becoming more and more insensitive to distance. With broadband digital transmissions, whether over microwaves, through light conductors, or cables, the cost of additional kilometers falls to relatively trivial levels. Finally digital switching and store and forward devices make message processing within a network a complex activity in which distance covered is a minor factor in the cost. In a modern packet network packets travel by random routes, so that on an international network one piece of a message may have traveled through several countries, another piece through several others, and few pieces by the most direct route.

The result of all these technological advances is that global interactions in business, government, science and culture will no longer be merely possible, but also so cheap as to become the usual way of conducting affairs. In that sort of world the nation-state will no longer be able to effectively control communication flows across its borders and therefore no longer be in command of problem solving activities within it.

Increasingly, the important problems in life can only be handled on an international basis. Among the problems that nation-states cannot solve individually are pollution, ocean resources, space resources, and spectral resources. For example, efficient use of the geostationary orbit has to be transnational, for there are, apparently, large economies of scale. The inappropriateness of national allotment of the geostationary orbit was illustrated by the obsolete political outcome of the 1977 World Administrative Radio Conference at which a plan was adopted giving each nation a spot on the orbit and five frequencies in the 12–14 GHz band for direct broadcasting. The fact of the matter is that there is no conceivable way of avoiding massive congestion on the orbit if each nation puts its own small satellite up there for all the different uses for which fixed satellites will serve.

The only sensible solution is one in which nations share large platforms with a variety of antennas and also switching facilities aboard them. Already a dozen nations are turning to Intelsat to provide domestic satellite communications, while only a few are seriously planning their own national satellites for telecommunications.

The problem of interference between separate facilities will become increasingly acute as high powered beams come to be used to send and receive messages directly from rooftop antennas rather than through each nation's terrestrial communications monopoly. A commercial service of that sort is about to be launched in the United States by Satellite Business Systems. By law, the SBS connections can only be located in the United States, but technically reception is possible anywhere within the beam regardless of boundaries. Satellite interconnections of the future can (and if efficiency is a criterion will) in many instances completely bypass national communications systems as they go from sender to satellite and directly to the receiver.

So the nation-state will decreasingly be an effective unit of planning and action in the world that is being created by electronic communication of messages and money, as well as by efficient transport and intelligent machines. Nations will increasingly find that they can no longer effectively control the operations of commerce or the cultural life of their people, as such activities come to be carried on in whatever location is most hospitable, at the will and for the service of people everywhere. Banks (or whatever intermediary financial institutions succeed what we now call banks), will offer their services to anyone who can pick up a telephone anywhere. Journalism, research, and information activities will be conducted globally on distributed computers and distributed data bases. The physical facilities will be located wherever the local authorities are hospitable.

Let me not overstate the case. Local government and community planning did not disappear with the passing of the city-state. So governance over large natural regions like nations will not disappear either; but as those matters that sovereign nations can handle by themselves become fewer and fewer, the absolutism of contemporary notions of nationalism and sovereignty will seem increasingly obsolete, and the power of national governments will begin to decline.

Just as trends in communication threaten to erode the power of the nation state, so too they threaten the institution of bureaucracy. Centralized bureaucracy operates by the hoarding and control of information and of its dissemination. In a bureaucracy there are channels that must be followed. A communication system based upon electronic abundance undercuts such a system of restricted channels. The physical capability will exist for anyone anywhere to communicate and share information with anyone else anywhere else.

The process of breaking communication hierarchies began with the telephone. If one looks at early journalistic treatments of the telephone one finds concern that a woman picking up the phone may find herself talking to a strange man. In some of those articles there is advice to subscribers to have their servants answer the phone to avoid finding oneself talking to social inferiors. An early article in praise of the phone notes how a magnate in Wall Street can talk to the foreman in the bowels of a mine that he owns in Pennsylvania bypassing the layers between them. When President Kennedy took office he caused shivers to go through the bureaucracy by his habit of phoning assistant secretaries and deputy assistant secretaries that he knew from before, instead of phoning their bosses at the cabinet level. In the American government today most serious business is carried on by telephone across hierarchical lines, violating all the classic descriptions from Max Weber and others about how bureaucracies work by passing pieces of paper up and down the chain of command. Only in American foreign posts does the old description still hold. Numerous technicians have pointed out to the State Department that modern telecommunications makes it possible to give each foreign service officer abroad a terminal at his desk which would permit him to communicate at will with any terminal back in Washington or elsewhere in a foreign post. The gains in efficiency would be enormous over the present reliance on airmail for most things and on telex or telephone through a bottleneck, for priority messages. But the suggestion is always rejected; the foreign service is clinging hard to the notion that the ambassador is head of the country team and everything must pass through him. It will not be long, however, before this fiction dies and every member of the team finds himself able to talk to anyone back home in the executive branch, or for that matter in the legislative branch or in the press. Is it any surprise that this prospect provokes alarm?

The statement that anyone will talk to *anyone* else anywhere should not be confused with the statement that anyone will be able to communication with *everyone* everywhere. Time imposes limits; there are only twenty-four hours in the day. The telephone removed the physical limit on who could talk to whom, but conventions regarding acquaintanceship, appropriateness, and importance evolved and checked phoning beyond certain limits. In the domestic U.S. bureaucracy, phoning cuts across organizational lines, but officials know the limits as to whom to call. However, the choices of interactions, even if limited, are not constrained by the principles that have been applied in the past. New conventions emerge.

The phone has been with us for 100 years and yet bureaucracy is as rampant as ever. What reason is there to believe that communication technology, for all its flexibility, will reduce bureaucracy in the future. The point is that up to now written communication has retained the same canonical form that it had in the nineteenth century. A document is a considered and fixed representation of an idea. It places a responsibility on its author. To avoid such crystallization one may use the telephone, but in the end, in a bureaucracy, a document must be produced.

Computers and electronic mail, however, give to documents the same flexibility which a phone conversation had. A memo entered into a word processor can be edited at will by anyone who receives it at his terminal. It can thus have any number of infinitely varied forms none of which need necessarily have precedence over any other. There may never be a printed version which is authoritative. The document may remain a retrievable set of bits in memory, edited and restructured and copied into other memories at will. The implications for copyright, for the organization of science and learning, and for bureaucracy are enormous.

In the ancient world versification was introduced to give some fixity of form to oral sagas that would otherwise have varied infinitely. The notion of sacred scripts was also introduced to preserve texts; any deviation in copying them was deemed a sin. With the coming of printing, secular prose acquired a fixity that it did not have before. In the days of manuscripts, lawbooks, for example, existed in the royal court and perhaps in a handful of copies in major centers. Local magistrates had to interpret the sense of the law from memory. With the coming of printed law books, every court could have the letter of the law at hand. Hundreds or thousands of copies of the canonical text came off the same press in indistinguishable form.

Now we are moving into an era in which text is displayed on a CRT in its fugitive form, and even printout is produced in single copies on demand from the dynamic store of an electronic memory.

If we believe that electronic communication is promoting the atrophy of nation-states and the atrophy of bureaucracies, can we believe that despite that there will be a world of great cities. One might imagine a new Hanseatic League tied together by verbal and material commerce, but that seems unlikely. Co-location of people (i.e., cities) loses much of its importance if remote communication is easy. We can anticipate that interaction with people at a distance and interaction with those closer at hand will become of much more nearly equal efficiency. Work done by machines, rather than by human hands, will be easily controlled from a distance.

The pattern of densely populated cities with sparse agricultural areas between them is already giving way to complex megalopolitan regions. Cities, before the invention of telephones, streetcars and automobiles, were walking cities. One had to be able to go from one end to the other on foot. To reduce the duration of long walks different activities concentrated in small neighborhoods. A city was a checkerboard of single-activity neighborhoods, still signaled, in old cities, by names such as Market Street or Ironmonger's Lane.

With the coming of public transport, cities spread, and with the coming of the telephone, entrepreneurs moved their business to cheaper locations, and also nearer to their customers, without losing contact with their suppliers, bankers and labor pool. In the first part of the twentieth century the downtown became a center of offices and department stores, while production moved to the outskirts. To meet the demand for office blocks, skyscrapers were put in the heart of the downtown. Without the telephone, as well as the elevator and steel-frame, these tall buildings would not have been possible. In 1902 someone figured out that if businesses had to continue using errand boys instead of phones in skyscrapers, the traffic would have required an elevator well of such size as to make such tall buildings uneconomic.

So a dual process was taking place of urban concentration along with spread of both industry and residence to suburban periphery. Instead of cities we now have in regions like Bos-Wash or the Ruhr a network of population concentrations extending over hundreds of miles. There is every reason to expect this process to continue with an ever more complex division of labor among centers of population density.

Urban concentrations will not end any more than will nations of bureaucracies, but they will be transformed perhaps beyond recognition. Population projections for the year 2000 tend to show that virtually all the growth of the world's population will be in urbanized areas. The rural population of the world may perhaps remain fairly constant, and so there are likely to be then, as there are now, vast areas of forest, desert, fields and wilderness. But the urbanized areas may be less distinguishable into finite cities, and very likely there will be vast areas of exurbia in which people will seek an urban way of life in a rural atmosphere. Abundant communication may make that possible. Cities and exurbia each have their attractions, but the balance between them is profoundly changed by telecommunications and the changed structure of work.

The structure of work has already changed in the most advanced societies to the point where the majority of the working population are workers with brain rather than with hand. The documentation of that remarkable trend is found in the work of Mark Porat on the United States. His study is now being replicated under OECD auspices in various other countries. In 1900, according to Porat's figures, 13 percent of the U.S. labor force were in information occupations as against 27 percent in industry. By 1950 31 percent of the labor force were in the information sector, by 1960 42 percent, and by 1970 46 percent.

That is a revolution! Stop and think for a minute about those figures. In a quarter of a century, the proportion of the labor force moving paper or other information media instead of things has gone from one fourth to one half of the total labor force.

That extraordinary rate of growth in the information sector will not continue. The large number of white collar workers makes it now economically attractive to develop labor-saving devices for intellectual activity, in the same way that in the last century when production required large masses of manual workers, it paid to invent labor-saving devices. Just as large numbers of persons, including many who are no longer manual workers, use machines, to do things which used to require manual labor (e.g., a washing machine or a car), so in the future we may expect large numbers of people to use thinking machines, though not necessarily to be themselves employed as white collar workers. What occupations can we expect to grow in a society in which the agricultural sector in the U.S. has declined to 4 percent of the labor force (a figure incidentally for a very productive agricultural country), and in which the industrial working class may be expected to decline to a similarly tiny number as automata take over assembly lines, and in which clerical work too begins to be automated by computers and so comes to require a sharply reduced part of the labor force? The jobs that will remain to be done by human beings are those that require a specifically human kind of interaction. These are service jobs such as those performed by a waiter, or nurse, or counselor, or teacher. Such person to person services are likely to absorb an increasing portion of the labor force. We now know how to build machines to automate the more routine intellectual as well as manual functions, but we do not know how to automate the experience of a human relationship.

If what we have anticipated as a consequence of electronic communication is even for the most part correct, we are at the edge of a vast transformation of society. We seem to be moving towards a society in which nation states will lose much of their power, in which bureaucracy gives way in part to more equalitarian and distributed modes of decision making, in which cities are replaced by megalopolitan regions, and in which only a small minority of the population remains engaged in the classic forms of productive toil that have been the lot of most of mankind until now.

These prospects of drastic change have very little in common with most political platforms that advocate drastic change. Most movements that are self-described as radical are highly urbanistic, or nationalistic, or oriented to obsolete class structures, or to central bureaucratic planning. The changes that we can see on the horizon are much more drastic than that. They are changes that arise out of the very nature of electronic communications technologies. They reflect the ease with which communication can operate over global distances, and the abundance of bandwidth that can now be made available to all, without producing any exhaustion of the earth's resources. They reflect the ability of digital communications to operate under the control of thinking machines. They reflect the ability of intelligent machines to handle degrees of complexity far beyond anything conceivable with non-electronic devices, and at the speed of light. These technological facts have profound social and political consequences. People who think about social change in traditional political terms cannot begin to imagine the changes that lie ahead. Conventional reformers cast their programs in terms of national policies, or in terms of laws and central planning. But in the end, what will shape the future is a creative potential that inheres in the new technologies of electronic communication and machine intelligence.

Part III

Technology, Policy, and Freedom

Editor's Introduction

As the world passes from an era defined by the technology of mass communications, the emerging inventions in telecommunications technology will have different social and political effects because they have different characteristics. The new telecommunication technologies will be technologies of freedom (i.e., freedom from constraints, and providing greater capability) because they will be low cost, abundant, high-capacity, interactive, user-controlled and available on a global scale, and combined with user-controlled computers of rapidly growing capacity. The trends in this new technology which underlie Ithiel Pool's analysis will be visible to the reader in the rapid growth of the global Internet and related technologies in telecommunications and computing. An example, however, may help for purposes of discussion.

On my desk is an announcement from Yale Medical School discussing a new, second series of global briefings, an Internet research colloquium, that is connecting to desktop PCs of educators, public health professionals, students—and anybody else who is interested—in 140+ countries.[1] Their (user-initiated and user-controlled) global television channel is rudimentary (audio + slides is what the available public domain technology permits to most users) but it is obvious that the technology will continue to improve quickly. And, for practical purposes (once the lectures are prepared and digitized), the Internet brings the best and latest ideas, and interaction with leading researchers, to a global audience without charge.[2]

For most of world history, this would have seemed almost inconceivable. Virtually free, global, user-initiated and user-controlled television channels? Across national boundaries, without a licence and without asking for permission? And building common frameworks for international cooperation to solve urgent global problems, with many of the people in the loop who could make this happen?

The Medical School initiative is not a challenge to the power of governments. Indeed, it is a benefit. The first global seminar in the Yale series was given by Dr. Ruth Berkelman from the U.S. government's Center for Disease Control. She was able, so to speak, to address the troops (3,500+ leaders in international public health) worldwide and begin to explain new leadership in U.S. policy: the technology accomplished purposes that writing an article alone could not have achieved and saved her months of jet travel. Similarly, in a later session the senior official of the World Health Organization who coordinated emergency response to an Ebola outbreak in Zaire linked in from Geneva and did admirable service to his agency by conveying—whatever an earlier image of WHO had been—an impression of a remarkably competent, knowledgeable, and committed leader. And several weeks later, when a "mad cow disease" outbreak occurred in Great Britain, senior scientists came to New Haven, briefed their colleagues worldwide, and conducted a serious technical discussion about the outbreak, their assessment of dangers and uncertainties, and the rationale for the government's policy. The technology helped to organize informed support.

The announcement from Yale also suggests that there is a degree of technological determinism (however soft or hard it might be) in the enthusiasm of engineers to push the envelope:

> A lot of new components will be added to this series of EIINet seminars: an EIINet Forum (for a discussion of the various issues related to the topic of the week), videoconferencing of some of the seminars (we could provide a "bridge" for those interested in receiving the seminars live), RealAudio with multi-user streaming capabilities (this would eliminate the need to download the whole Audio file before listening to it), simultaneous multimedia presentations of the seminars (so that the slide show is seen in sync with the audio file, eliminating the need to "click for the next slide" at the lecturer's prompt).

With this touchstone, let us turn to the selections in this final section.

Tracking the Flow of Information

To analyze global communication systems in the same way that economists analyze economic systems (i.e., the reader will recall that this was Ithiel Pool's intention, expressed in the first selection of this volume) there needs to be a set of basic indicators of trends. This article, from *Science*, is the first report from Pool's project to get an initial set of good measures, and it is the first rigorous assessment of trends toward a global information society. There are many remaining steps and several issues that need to be addressed in counting word-equivalents, as Pool recognizes (e.g., how many words *is* a picture worth?); however it is the trend of each media type, rather than the formulae that seek to see them as potential substitutes for one another, that is of the greatest interest.

The Public and the Polity

During the late 1960s Ithiel Pool edited a summary volume to assess what the new scientific revolution in political science, that began at the University of Chicago, was contributing to our understanding of the classic questions of political science. (Among his arguments is the assertion that most of traditional political philosophy has been disagreements about empirical questions: even on this score, he did not see recycling arguments among ideologues as especially productive.)

For purposes of this volume, the key lesson that Pool asserts is that the traditional zero-sum argument about the power of government vs. individual freedom is mispecified, at least for democracies or other regimes that are capable of adjustment, adjudications of claims on the basis of shared rules, and so on. A freer nation, or world, need not be more chaotic, or rebellious or dangerous if quite specific conditions are met. A less prominent and limited government can be a more effective and stable government if men, in their freedom, build a strong civil society of other institutions and working relationships. Thus (for example) a growing informal global network of public health professionals (like the Yale network), can enhance the capacity of government officials when they are seeking to achieve goals that have legitimacy and wide assent.

Citizen Feedback in Political Philosophy

This essay, written as cable televison was becoming more widely available, asks what feedback and accountability systems will improve government performance? In the era of mass media, the feedback that is presented by news stories, criticism, and scandal on the front page of mass circulation newspapers or on television serves a prominent (and perhaps vital) role. Pool's paper raises the question of whether new interactive communication technologies can be adapted to improve feedback, accountability, and performance without being captured and manipulated by office-holders.

International Communication and Integrated Planning

This brief address is a forthright expression of a lesson that Ithiel Pool drew from his studies of forecasting. He argues that it is premature—because nobody knows enough, during periods of fast technological change—to do government planning. There are too many empirical unknowns, including the stream of future inventions that need to be known, even for philosopher kings (a test which, as he had concluded in Bauer, Pool, and Dexter, it is rare to see being met by elected officials.) *Thinking* should be integrated, but the wisest role of governments is to facilitate the experimentation and competition of the market.

Technology and Confusion:
The Satellite Broadcast Controversy in the U.N.

In the 1970s, the growth of communication satellites, and the specter of direct satellite broadcasting across national boundaries without the consent of the government of the populace, ignited stark fears (especially, anti-U.S. fears) at the United Nations. The editor of *Foreign Affairs* invited Ithiel Pool, as a senior member of the Council on Foreign Relations with competence in this field, to publish his views. When William Bundy saw the article, he quickly withdrew the invitation and the article is published here for the first time. The reader will recognize a sharpness to Pool's judgments that normally received a more diplomatic expression in his work.

I have included this article because, while Pool was right about the technical ignorance of the U.N. system twenty years ago, the world, now, *is* on the verge of hundreds of LEO (low earth orbit) satellites, and new stationary-orbit satellites, that will broadcast across national boundaries, directly to individuals. Whether similar global political passions are about to be re-ignited, or whether the companies and governments involved have altered their views and fears after twenty years, remains to be seen.

From Gutenberg to Electronics:
Implications for the First Amendment

Policies for Freedom

These final selections go together. Jointly, they reflect an effort to rethink the justifications for legal doctrines and the role of government regulation of communication technologies. And to build coalitions that could act strategically to anticipate battles and remove roadblocks that might slow the growth of the new technologies of freedom.

Pool's fundamental argument is that three logically inconsistent legal regimes govern communications technology: (a) the traditional laws governing free speech and press, which provide the greatest opportunities for freedom (e.g., no laws that restrict, no prior restraint; etc.); (b) the law of common carriers (e.g., postal systems, telephones) where there has been economic regulation, limited rights to monitor (e.g., wiretap) and content restrictions (e.g., what cannot be sent through the mails); (c) the recent law of mass communication systems (e.g., radio, television) with substantial government licensing and oversight review of operators; content restrictions (e.g., fairness doctrines, monitoring for violence and pornography); and other controls.

The danger is this: the new electronic/digital technologies will shift these different technologies toward a common form. Thus, individual discussions and the flow of news will be carried over computer networks and telephone lines to mass audiences. Which legal regime will apply? Pool began to write about these issues, in the late 1970s, to alert partisans of freedom that the role of government regulation needed to be reconsidered, else traditional freedoms would be lost by applications of the more restrictive legal doctrines of (c) mass communications to all forms of communications.

The argument in *Technologies of Freedom* also goes another step. It assesses the justifications for maintaining the restrictions of common carrier (e.g., telephone) and mass communications technology in light of the new inventions. The earlier justification for government regulation, Pool argued, was bandwidth scarcity—for example, you could only have three broadcast television channels in an urban area; or the economics of the telephone made it feasible to string only one set of copper wires to every home. However, Pool argued, new technologies would progressively make all forms of communications available, in abundance, at low cost. Thus, all of the nation's (and world's) telecommunication systems could (and should) be deregulated. The argument has been remarkably persuasive, and the confidence with which governments have adopted it has been strengthened by the far-sighted interpretation of their self-interests, by large telecommunication companies in the U.S. and other countries, who see enormous profitability from bringing new communications technologies to people worldwide.

Freedom and Forecasting

Against this background, I think a final comment is helpful about predictions: The forecast of greater freedom leaves unanswered the next

question, "What will people *do* with greater freedom?" Is there guidance, implicit in Pool's writings, beyond the changes in the four unnatural institutions he identified in the earlier selection?

Advocates of new technologies—and even the public, in public opinion polls—often anticipate high-minded results. (Radio would bring
opera and symphonies to the masses. The Internet will allow high school
students across the country to access the transcripts of presidential press
conferences, download weather reports from Kenya, and browse the
Library of Congress...) But freedom offers no guarantee except choice:
it is always possible that the new electronic technologies also will find
ready viewers for a media circus of superficiality, dizzying overstimu-
lation and sensationalism, image, misdirected priorities or produce—
depending upon who is drawn to use the new technologies—newly
retribalized, readily monitored, totalitarian societies.

In one respect, it may be possible for social science to estimate the
effects of greater communication capability and freedom by a cross-
sectional analysis, following Ithiel Pool's lead of looking at the current differences between the most regulated and least regulated current
technologies.

In this perspective, American broadcast television has been an "unnatural" institution. A limitation of three broadcast channels in each
urban area led competitors to align themselves into three national networks (ABC, NBC, and CBS), each seeking maximum profit in a national market and producing inoffensive and generally benign,
common-denominator entertainment and news analogous to the competition of mass market fast food restaurants (Wendy's, Hardee's,
McDonald's), located near one another with menus that resemble one
another. (Also, the actors were subject to government regulatory review and the loss of licenses in the event of sharp public complaint.)
The new medium, with its national revenue bases, also shaped a more
homogeneous national culture and cognitive maps (national evening
news programs) and the dialect of American English on broadcast television was standardized by selecting Salt Lake City.

By this comparative analysis, the content of television should begin
to resemble the wider variation (and lower mean) of the print media.
Public interest programming (a necessity for licensing) probably will
drop. There will be television analogs to the *National Inquirer*. Competitive pressures will increase the number of low-budget (and, in part,
low-quality) shows and a greater degree of sensationalism and "info-
tainment." Depth reporting of news and public affairs will tend to dis-

appear on mass-market networks. And other results probably will differ from wholly idealistic expectations, a point that was made candidly by Larry Ellison (founder of Oracle), one of the multibillionaires of the new computer and telecommunications industry who will be testing what a national or global public, free of government regulation, might pay for. He was asked, in a recent interview, about emerging strategies and plans, including such interactive "killer applications" as video (e.g., movies) on demand; home shopping channels; video games; direct-response advertising; and gambling:

> [Gambling] is going to be huge. We are a bunch of sinners, as Pat Robertson might say. He will be able to come on and tell us about our sinning, and when we get tired of that we can go back to gambling. I don't think people are anxious to introduce this service right up front. I think we are all trying to be socially responsible and try to get the health care and education applications up before we get the pornography and gambling up.[3]

In addition, there can be thousands of new, inexpensive channels (hundreds of thirty frames per second commercial quality, and an almost unlimited number of simpler do-it-yourself-with-whoever-is-interested national or global Internet channels like the Yale project) that, like small circulation journals, can serve niche (rather than mass) markets. These, in turn, could help to organize and empower anybody, from global medical networks to political groups that were previously unorganized, marginalized, and ignored in mass markets. (We already have seen this phenomenon underway: as new technology made possible the expanded capacity of cable television, the television evangelists of the political right emerged, with organized political followings and cash incomes provided by the new technology.)

Thus, a homogenized, cosmopolitan, and tolerant culture is not an inevitable and sole consequence of new telecommunications technology. It will depend upon what people want. Soon, if people decide they really do not like one another or the homogenizing option of the mass communication culture, they can begin to retribalize and live within separate and fragmented realities and neighborhoods surrounded by electronic walls. Black channels, Jewish channels, Hispanic channels, Chinese-American channels, youth channels (MTV), regional channels, etc. The new tribes may have an electronic (rather than geographic) organization and some may broadcast hatred over a now-free-of-regulation Internet at anybody who will listen. Political power may become more readily available to charismatic, demagogic personalities skilled in the use of television, now with ready access to channels unconstrained by licensing review.

On the other hand, since we are reasoning by analogy with the freedom to publish, I think it is fair to judge that freedom of the press, despite the wide and sometimes offensive range, has been consistent with stable democratic governments.

I think Ithiel Pool is right that there is a freer world in the making (by causal pathways different than voting for liberals, conservatives, socialists, or self-described radicals), a freer world with the extraordinary potential to be a better world, for more people, than any we have seen. Yet there are no guarantees that social science can offer. Except the observation, in the spirit of "soft" determinism, that good people with constructive purposes need to step forward, with financial support, to develop the creative potentials of the new technologies.

Notes

1. The URL is http://info.med.yale.edu/EIINet. The subject concerns emerging infectious diseases, a problem that has both scientific and organizational challenges. Until recently, medical researchers believed that antibiotics were a permanent achievement. Now, it is clear that Darwin was right and, to the virus world, the human race is meat. There is steady mutation and adaptation and, as in the case of AIDS, breakouts of new combinations that modern travel patterns disperse globally. There is credit due to many people associated with this pilot project, including Joshua Lederberg and a global scientific planning group that he helped to organize, Drs. Robert Ryder and Michael Merson, and Ms. Lindsey Holaday. And an early source of inspiration in Ithiel Pool's work concerning the potential contribution of satellite technology to the creative process in international agricultural research (Pool, Freedman, and Warren, 1976).
2. That is, the marginal cost is effectively zero and there are no charges by Yale. There are unwarranted (monopoly) charges by communication carriers in underdeveloped countries, and a great deal of work ahead to deal with this problem and assure full and affordable access, especially outside of capital cities in underdeveloped countries.
3. Interview with Larry Ellison, *Broadcasting and Cable* 124, no. 3 (January 17, 1994): 84, 86, 132.

12

Tracking the Flow of Information

By using words transmitted and words attended to as common denominators, novel indexes were constructed of growth trends in seventeen major communications media from 1960 to 1977. There have been extraordinary rates of growth in the transmission of electronic communications, but much lower rates of growth in the material that people actually consume, representing the phenomenon often labeled information overload. Growth in print media has sharply decelerated, and a close relationship is found between the cheapness of a medium and its rate of growth.

Identification of social indicators that track changes in the human condition have been prerequisite to much of the progress of the social sciences. Early economics focused extensively on foreign trade because of the data that existed in the form of customs records. More recently, cost-of-living and unemployment indexes have played a large role in policy analyses. Now indexes of cultural and political trends are increasingly being used. Among those that have had a major impact are Scholastic Aptitude Test scores and polls rating the president. In these instances, the existence of a usable time-series measurement has stimulated research and analysis seeking to explain the observed results.

In this article, some findings from new indexes intended to measure trends in the development of an information society are presented as well as some explanations for what has been found. The trend in modern industrial societies to move toward becoming information societies is most commonly measured by the balance between white- and blue-collar employment.[1] A Department of Commerce study[2] shows the information sector rising from about 1/20 of the work force in 1870 to

First published in *Science* (1983).

about a third in 1950 and about half of all employees today. A study by the Organization for Economic Cooperation and Development[3] of nine industrialized countries shows parallel trends in all of them. In Japan the information sector grew from 18 percent of the work force in 1960 to 30 percent in 1975, and in the United Kingdom, it grew from 27 percent in 1951 to 36 percent in 1971.

While white-collar employment is a useful index of information activity, additional insights can be obtained from measures that more directly describe the flow of information itself rather than an important but loose correlate of it. The volume of words flowing through such media as broadcasting, publishing, the mails, and telecommunications might be such an index and might reveal some of the fine structure of what is generally called the information explosion. Such a measure, developed from a "census of communication flows," is discussed below.

Among the major findings from this census are that while there had indeed been a rapid increase in the information being made available to the public, the offering of informational material is growing far faster than what is being absorbed. (The way in which that distinction has been made is described below under methods of measurement.) Although the largest flow of words in modern society is through the mass media, the rate of growth is now fastest in media that provide information to individuals, that is, point-to-point media. The growth in both mass and point-to-point media has been greatest in the electronic ones. Print media are becoming increasingly expensive per word delivered while electronic media are becoming cheaper, and costs seem to predict well what is used. The implications of this finding for the continued health of various media are considerable.

By compiling data on trends in the circulation and in the use of seventeen public media of communication, we found that from 1960 to 1977, words made available to Americans (over the age of ten) through these media grew at the rate of 8.9 percent per year, or more than double the 3.7 percent growth rate for the gross domestic product in constant dollars. However, the words actually attended to from those media grew at just 2.9 percent per year. Per capita consumption of words from those media (allowing for population growth) grew at but 1.2 percent per year.

The modesty of that growth in consumption of information, despite the presence of large growth in the information available, is often described as information overload. More and more material exists, but limitations on time and energy are a controlling barrier to people's consumption of words. Given any particular employment and lifestyle, there is a limited potential for expansion of attention to media as a whole. Much of the small growth that is found can be accounted for by the shift in population from blue to white collar employment and lifestyle and the associated rise of educational levels.

For those who are producing information, this difference between trends in supply and consumption means that each item of information produced faces a more competitive market and a smaller audience on the average. People see or hear a decreasing proportion of the total information that is available to them.

The data compiled for our study cover the years 1960 through 1977. The data are incomplete after 1977 since it takes years for some statistics to be published. In the period of observation, much of the growth in the flow of information was due to the growth in broadcasting. In 1960, an estimated 58 percent of the words that Americans actually heard or read through the measured media came to them by television or radio; by 1977, the figure was 69 percent. But toward the end of that period the situation was changing: point-to-point media were growing faster than broadcasting. Some data available up to 1980 show that trend to be in most respects continuing, though cable systems are giving a new spurt to television.

Methods of Measurement

The methodology for making our estimates was first developed at the Ministry of Post and Telecommunications in Japan by Tomita and his co-workers.[4] Our study in the United States was done in association with a revised Japanese study, conducted jointly by Tokyo University and the Japanese Research Institute of Telecommunications and Economics.[5]

The key decision was to translate all flows of information into the unit of words. This requires ascertainment of the typical word rate for such activities as telephone conversations or the reading of mail, books, and magazines. However, a distinction was made between words supplied and words consumed. Our definition of a word supplied is that it is available at the premises of a person so that all he or she would have to do to hear or read it would be to choose to do so, requiring at most the turning of a switch or opening to a particular page. Thus the number of words supplied by television would grow not only if broadcasters said more words, but also if the number of receivable stations increased (for example, by cable television importing additional signals) so that the listener had more alternatives at hand, or if second television sets came into the home so that different members of the family could choose different stations at once. The data from which the supply time series were calculated were thus primarily data on the activity of information industries; these do not take into account the behavior of the audience.

Words consumed are those that the members of the population actually heard or read. The basic data from which such estimates are derived are behavioral surveys such as time-budget studies. Such data are generally collected by broadcasters in their audience studies but are much less generally available for other communications activities. Television ratings tell us how many people watched TV at a particular hour. Occasional sociological time-budget studies tell us how many minutes a day people spent in reading and other activities, but such data are sparse. For person-to-person media such as telephone calls, first-class letters, or telegrams, words supplied and words consumed probably do not differ greatly; there are no good data on the percentage of inattention. Therefore, no distinctions were made between how many words were spoken or written in such media and how many the receiver heard or read. But for mass media the difference is large and important. The number of words in a book that is brought home is not necessarily the number read. The two different time series have to be distinguished.

In fact, distinctions can be made on four levels. First, there is the act of authoring; each word in a newly composed statement would be counted once if we were measuring that. Second, there is the act of publishing. In a count of words published, the same words would be counted twice if they were published twice, as in different newspapers or different reprints, but the count would not include the number of exemplars that reached individuals. A third level is what we have called words supplied, for which not only is the number of times a word has been published counted, but also the number of individuals to whom it has been made available is counted. And the fourth level is words consumed—namely, how many words individuals choose to absorb. Our study deals only with words supplied and consumed.

If these data turn out to be useful then no doubt many of our estimates will have to be revised as new, fuller, and better-adapted raw time-series and behavioral measures become available. These first results share many of the infirmities of any work with index numbers, particularly new and unexercised ones. The measures are derived by secondary analysis of data collected for other purposes, and not always consistently. Thus audience measures for TV ratings and for newspapers, each collected by the industry, are not necessarily fully compatible. Nor are all data reported annually, so that interpolations and extrapolations had to be used.

In general, with use of these data, as of any index number, more credence should be given to trend changes than to comparison of different situations. Many decisions go into the construction of any index number, and these apply differently in different situations. Thus comparisons of the unemployment indexes of different countries or even of different population segments in a country (for example, students, old persons, and middle-aged persons) is likely to be less valid than comparisons of the unemployment index in one situation as it changes over time. Unemployment means different things in different systems. So, too, a spoken word is not exactly the same thing as a written one, and the records kept on the circulation of newspapers, which are thrown away at the end of the day, are not exactly comparable to any records kept on books, many of which are passed along informally. Yet a standard operational definition can provide a basis for stable comparisons over time.

We were able to compile data in the United States on seventeen different mass or point-to-point media (table 12.1). The most important omissions are conversations and internal memoranda. These were omitted because usable time-series data were not available. In general, in corporate offices, more than 90 percent of the documents that circulate are distributed within organizations and do not go outside into the mails.[6] Thus, the so-far-omitted informal means of communication are important flows that must be examined further.

Growth Trends: Mass versus Point-to-Point Media

The use of any medium, as of any commodity, is a function of its cost. In figure 12.1, an arrow for each medium that we examined tracks a trend from 1960 to 1977. On the horizontal axis is plotted the cost of transmitting 1,000 words to a single potential audience member in constant dollars, and on the vertical axis is plotted the number of words so supplied. Broadcasting, measured in this way, is extraordinarily cheap.[7] For one cent, a thousand words are made receivable by radios belonging to families encompassing more than a thousand individuals, which is understandable in the light of the fact that a radio transmission is potentially receivable in an area inhabited by hundreds of thousands or millions of persons. Broadcast words are cheap enough to be given away free which they are. At the other extreme, a telegram costs about ten cents a word, which accounts for its low and vanishing use.

TABLE 12.1
Media in the United States for which Censuses of
Communications Flows were Tabulated, 1960–1977

Mass Media	Point-to-point media
Radio	First-class mail
TV	Telephone
Cable TV originated	Telex
Records and tapes	Telegrams
Movies	Mailgrams
Classroom education	Facsimilie
Newspapers	Data communication
Magazines	
Books	
Direct mail	

In the upper left quadrant of figure 12.1, at costs below a penny a thousand words supplied, are the mass media. In the lower right quadrant are the point-to-point media. People are willing to spend one or two orders of magnitude more to communicate with the specific individuals with whom they wish to interact than they are to put out or receive messages "to whom it may concern."

Data communication represents an especially interesting case, particularly if one projects the curve, which has in fact continued, up to the present. The growth in computer networks and the fact that they are used as messaging facilities has undercut telegraphy and even its more efficient form, Telex. The volume of domestic Telex use grew at a rate of 18 percent per year from 1960 to 1970 and then declined at 14 percent per year through 1977; international Telex has continued to grow, for it reaches many subscribers abroad, but in the United States computer networks are replacing it. Computer networking is for the first time bringing the costs of a point-to-point medium, data communication, down to the range of costs characteristic of mass media.

That fact helps us to understand certain developments in communications which are currently the subject of much popular speculation. Information retrieval from data bases (or its popular version, videotex) is perceived as a revolutionary challenge to ordinary publishing, and indeed it may be that. Computer data processing and digital communication seem likely to allow information to be provided in response to individual inquiries at costs competitive with mass production of infor-

FIGURE 12.1
Trends in Volume and Costs of Communication for 17 Media, 1960–1977
(Plotted on Log by Log Scales)

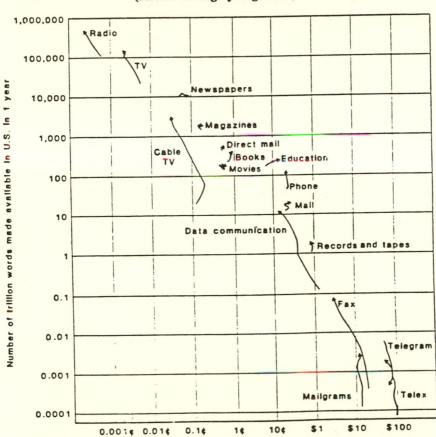

mation products. If the functional relation represented by the rather tight diagonal corridor on the graph in figure 12.1 continues to hold, that suggests approximately what volume of data communication is likely to occur at such costs.

The rapid growth of data communication (27 percent per year) and the continued growth of telephony (just below 6 percent per year) has produced a continuing growth of point-to-point media with the rate of growth rising for these media as a whole from the general level of 5.5 percent for the entire period since 1960, to a rate of 7 percent in the last three years of the time series.

In the 1960s, and one would assume the 1950s too, the dominant trend was toward a society in which a relatively few sources of mass media material—particularly broadcast entertainment—were occupying an unprecedented portion of the national attention. The preeminent force in shaping that trend was the growth of television. In the 1970s a reversal began that in two ways led to less massive domination of the flow of communication by a few mass media. First some fragmentation of the mass audience was taking place because of an increase in the number of channels (for example, by cable systems and added broadcast stations); second, the growth of individually addressable point-to-point media became more marked. The growth rate of television was 11 percent in words supplied and 4 percent in words consumed for the entire study period 1960–1977 but was 7.5 percent in supply and 3 percent in consumption from 1972 to 1977. In the years from 1972 to 1977, the aggregate rate of growth for mass media words consumed was 2 percent per year, and in words supplied only 5 percent per year, while the rate of growth in point-to-point media was 6 percent per year.

Aggregate figures are subject to domination by a few media since there are order-of-magnitude differences between media in the sizes of their flows. Still the generalization about the mid-1970s slowdown in the rate of growth of mass media words supplied holds up individually for radio, television, records and tapes, education, newspaper, and magazines. It does not hold for movies, which were recovering from their post-television slump, books, direct mail, or of course, cable television.[8] The generalization about the sustained growth of the point-to-point media holds for data communications, telephones, facsimile, and Mailgrams but not for first-class mail, telegrams and Telex.

Closely related to these changes in both the mass media and point-to-point media is the striking trend from print to electronic media (figure 12.2). The supply of words in print grew but slowly from 1960 for a decade and then entered a plateau or even slight decline. At the same time the flow in electronic media was growing rapidly.

There is widespread impression that there has been a decline in reading in America. Television is usually blamed, but the evidence is somewhat more complicated. A number of studies in several countries[9] show a significant drop in reading when television is first introduced and

FIGURE 12.2
Growth Trends of Print and Electronic Media, 1960–1977

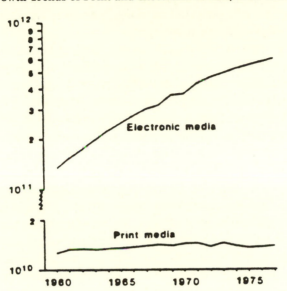

then a gradual recovery, though not necessarily to pre-television levels. Our data do not cover the period of the first introduction of television. In the period that we observed, the aggregate of words supplied in print grew steadily until about 1968 after which there is no uniform trend. The growth for the whole period was half a percent per year, but for the years after 1968 it was zero. This change in the later years holds for magazines and first-class mail as well as for newspapers, which are the dominant medium in the group; it does not hold for direct mail or books.

For the purpose of evaluating reading by the public, the relatively reliable figure on words supplied is far less relevant than the figure on words consumed, for which we are dependent on scarce sociological time-budget studies. Our data support the impression of a decline in reading from printed media, though how far this would hold up if reading from screens or reading at work were included is an open question. Consumption habits are much more stable than the supply of information material. For the most transient material (for example, weather reports) there is perhaps some shift away from use of newspapers, magazines, and books toward obtaining such material from radio and television, while there may be continuing use of print to obtain less evanescent material. Our data on this are too weak, however, to reach a confident conclusion. Insofar as our consumption data are reliable, they indicate that the per capita volume of words taken in by reading of print as a whole seems to be declining. Both in 1960 and 1977 we have an estimate of 1.5 trillion words a day read from print media in the United States. But in that period the population was growing, and per capita the number of words read per day from the tabulated media seems to have declined from an average of 11,000 to 8,500 words for adults.

The shift from printed media to electronic communications can be observed in both the mass and point-to-point media. If we compare radio and television on the one hand, with newspapers, magazines, and books on the other, we find that in 1960 67 percent of the words consumed from those five media came from the two electronic ones; that rose to 79 percent by 1977. If we compare use of telephone and first-class mail among the point-to-point media, we find that the postal service was the source of 22 percent of the words from these two media in 1960 but only 14 percent in 1977.

Many factors enter into how choices are made among media. One factor is gratification. Some people enjoy spending many more hours watching television than reading. Another obvious factor is the adaptability of a medium to particular functions; a letter serves for sending a bill, a telephone call for an urgent reminder. Communications researchers have studied extensively such topics as the relative effectiveness of different media for changing a vote, for making a purchase, or adopting health practices. One factor that has received little attention is cost. There is a good reason for that neglect. How, in the absence of a common denominator, can the cost of a magazine and a movie be compared or the cost of a facsimile and a classroom presentation?

A Common Denominator

It was to address the issue of costs, among others, that we adopted a common denominator, the word, although it is not the relevant common denominator for all purposes. If one is interested in producing a particular effect, such as persuading someone to buy a product or to adopt family planning, one does not care how many words are used in different media; the common denominator one cares about is sales or births. Without any illusions about having established a universal common denominator, it is worth considering how far cost per word enters into some of the differences in trends among media. Indeed there turn out to be striking variations in cost trends, most notably between electronic and print media.

Between 1960 and 1977, there was a marked decline in the cost of supplying words through the aggregate of all the media that we measured, but an increase in the cost per word actually consumed. This is not a matter of inflation; we used constant 1972 dollars for the comparison. Setting the number of words supplied per dollar in 1960 at 100, we find that productivity of each dollar spent in supplying words rose to 180 by 1977, while the productivity of each dollar spent, evaluated by whether the words achieved attention, fell to seventy. In short, the technology for putting out information greatly improved through electronics, and as a result much more material was put out. Indeed much more was spent in total in putting information out even though the cost per word went down. However, with the audience only modestly changing its attention, the net input of words to the audience that was achieved by the greater output of words, coupled with the greater expenditure, showed diminishing returns.

A few media showed a pattern of rising costs per word supplied (figure 12.1), and for each of these there were consequences, including restricted growth or in some instances even decline. Education showed the most striking increase in cost. Education is defined in our study as words in the classroom and is estimated by contact hours, students present, and rate of word passage in a classroom situation. We used the words consumed per dollar in 1960 as the base and set that at 100; the index in 1977 had fallen to 46. This index is obviously not a measure of quality of education; it could even be considered the inverse, for smaller classes cause the index to fall. But it is an index that has some relevance to the concerns that exist in American society about the efficiency of educational expenditure.

In all the print media the productivity of expended dollars in achieving consumption of words has declines but most notably in newspapers and the postal service. With 1960 as the base year and the productivity index (words per dollar) set at 100 for each medium, the index in 1977 for newspapers is 62 and for first-class mail is 76. (For magazines, direct mail, and books the 1977 figures are 93, 90, and 84, respectively.) These figures reflect the rising costs of paper beyond the general level of inflation and the rising costs of labor intensive delivery systems. Indeed, when these media are excluded, we find that for most media the cost of achieving consumption of words of information has remained fairly constant. For all media together, excluding education and newspapers, the index of productivity of expenditures in producing consumption of printed material was 101 in 1977.

It is in the electronic media that dramatic declines in cost have offset the increased costs in print media and education. For point-to-point media as a whole, the index of productivity of expenditures in producing a flow of words was 105 in 1977 compared with 100 in 1960. (Recall that for the point-to-point media the distinction between words supplied and words consumed is not made.) That figure includes first-class mail that showed a declining index. If we look only at the media used for telegraphic record transmission (telegrams, Telex, Mailgrams, facsimile, and computer networks), though some have been displacing others, the advances in the electronics have moved the aggregate index of words supplied or consumed per dollar from 100 in 1960 to 1,425 in 1977.

Concluding Remarks

The shift in the eighteenth and nineteenth centuries from a largely agricultural to a largely industrial society was of profound historical significance; the shift is now taking place from a largely industrial society to one in which most effort goes into, and most value is produced by, information-processing activities may be of equal importance. Experience of the social sciences is that prerequisite to the effective analysis of such macro sociological phenomena is the construction and collection of measures of the processes taking place. The efforts to conduct communications flow censuses in Japan[10] and the United States are initial attempts to create such indicators of the flow of information material.[11] Collection of viable social indicators, however, generally requires sustained effort by social institutions. A great deal of refinement of design and expensive data collection goes into any maintained and useful social indicator.

The initial communications flow censuses have used publicly available time series that were constructed for purposes quite different from those to which they were put in the census. The calculation of words supplied by a medium generally starts with a standard series of circulation or program production figures and applies factors to the basic data relating to secondary distribution or receivers available in households.

To the availability figures thus derived, one then applies estimates of the number of words per issue or per minute. In calculating consumption of words, one starts with time-usage data on people's reading, listening, or viewing habits and applies factors derived from studies of talking or reading rates. Few of these figures are very reliable. However, constant errors will have less impact on conclusions about time series than on conclusions about absolute values, since most of the series used are collected in the same way year after year.

Trends that have created the widespread feeling of information overload are supported by these series. So too is the fragmentation of the audience. Mid-twentieth-century sociological generalizations about the growth of a mass society are contradicted by the data that show recent trends toward the use of more diversified and point-to-point media. Also shown by the data is the shift from Gutenbergian to electronic media. The significance of that trend may be reflected in new styles of use of information media, including interactive retrieval, long-distance communication, and intelligent processing of records.[12]

Notes

1. See Machlup, Fritz. *The production and distribution of knowledge in the United States*. Princeton, NJ: Princeton University Press, 1962; see also Porat et al. (2) and Organization for Economic Cooperation and Development (3). While the most commonly used index of the growth of the information society is the structure of employment, the goal of such economic analyses is not just to measure the trends, but also to use national income accounts to explain the causes of these trends (see Jonscher, C. in *Information economics and policy*. North Holland, Amsterdam, in press).

2. Porat, M. U. et al. *The information economy*. Washington, DC: OT Special Publication 77–12, Department of Commerce, 1977.

3. Organization for Economic Cooperation and Development. *Information activities, electronics and telecommunications technologies: Impact on employment, growth and trade*. Paris: OECD, 1981.

4. Tomita, T. *Telecommunications Journal* 42 (1975): 339; *Information census flow*. Tokyo: Ministry of Posts and Telecommunications, 1975.

5. Pool, I.; Inose, H.; Takasake, N.; Hurwitz, R. *Communications flows: A census in the United States and Japan*. Tokyo: University of Tokyo Press, 1984.

6. Since we compiled our original data, we have gained access to some significant new data on paper flow in offices with the cooperation of the Xerox Corporation and are extending our data.

7. Programming costs are not included in the data in figure 12.1 or elsewhere, nor do we include the investments consumers must make to receive communications, such as the cost of a television set. All costs mentioned are costs of causing a message to be transmitted to its receivers.

8. Our definition of cable television was limited to material that was not relayed from the standard broadcast stations, the transmissions from which continued to

be evaluated in the TV series, regardless of whether picked up over the air or from a cable system. In the period since 1977, the added stations and programs provided by cable systems have resulted in an increase in television viewing time by cable subscribers.

9. Himmelweit, H.; Oppenheim, A. N.; Vine, P. *Television and the child.* London: Oxford University Press, 1958, pp. 335–36; Schramm, W.; Lyle, J.; Parker, E. *Television in the lives of our children.* Stanford, CA: Stanford University Press, 1961, p. 15; Robinson, J.P. in *Television and social behavior,* vol. 4. Washington, DC: Government Printing Office, 1974, pp. 410–28; Lyle, J.; Hoffman, H. R. ibid., p. 135; Vuuren, D. P. van in *Proceedings of the 4th international conference on experimental research in tv instruction,* Newfoundland: St. John's, 1981, p. 10; Furu, T. *The function of television for children and adolescents.* Tokyo: Sophia University Press, 1971.

10. See note 4, above.

11. See note 5, above.

12. I thank R. Hurwitz for assistance on this article. The U.S. study was done at the Research Program on Communications Policy at MIT with the aid of a grant from the John and Mary Markle Foundation.

13

The Public and the Polity

Introduction to the Problem

About two hundred years ago two books appeared which between them raised the major issues that have dominated political thought for the two centuries since. These were Rousseau's *Social Contract* (1762) and Adam Smith's *Wealth of Nations* (1776).

These two books in very different ways addressed themselves to a common and distinctly modern problem, namely, *how the mass of men in a participant society can obtain what they individually desire without thereby tearing society apart.*

The central problem of sixteenth- and seventeenth-century political theory had been how a commonwealth could exist at all, given the savage nature of human beings and the conflicts of interest, desires, and religious faiths that divide them.[1] Eighteenth-century political thought, the product of a slightly less turbulent era, asked not so much how a commonwealth could exist at all, but how it could exist and still allow individual citizens their just desires. Eighteenth-century writers sought to optimize on two values—in Rousseau's words, "what is prescribed by interest" of the citizen and "what right sanctions" as just.[2] This dilemma of freedom and order has been a central topic of political theory ever since. Ingenious writers have invented various theories to reconcile individual choice with social values.

In this chapter I wish to hold some of these theories, notably those of the schools of Rousseau and Adam Smith, up to the test of the findings of contemporary empirical political studies. How do these theories stand up against the facts that contemporary social researchers have so painstakingly assembled?

From *Contemporary Political Science* (1967).

Can Political Theories be Tested by Empirical Studies?

The results produced by empirical research are relevant materials against which to test classical political theories. The interesting issues in normative political theory are in the end generally empirical ones. Only rarely do arguments over policy turn on irreducible conflicts of value. More often they are arguments about the facts of situations to which the values are applied. Most men agree in valuing freedom and also equality, and order and also progress. Political theorists are not in much conflict about the merit of such values.

There does exist, however, one interesting problem in political theory which is strictly normative. That is the problem of evaluating mixes of desiderata. Such incommensurable values as freedom, equality, stability, and progress may all be good, but how shall one choose among different combinations of them?

Let us digress for a moment into this central problem of normative political theory. It may be called the "utility problem," or in still more modern terminology, the "dynamic-programming problem." We behavioral social scientists generally pride ourselves on the progress of empirical political research while judging political theory to be in a sad state. Actually, however, it is far from clear that empirical research has discovered any new facts, but on this strictly normative problem of program packages more progress has been made in the past half century than in all the previous 2,000 years of political theory put together. If that is so, then it is a political theory rather than empirical political science that is being revolutionized in our time—even if most political theorists do not know it.

The work that has contributed to our newly acquired ability to talk sensibly about complex mixes of values is general located in the mathematical theory of choice as developed by von Neumann, Arrow, Simon, Kantorovich, Dantzig, and others.[3] These writers have for the first time made it possible to talk rigorous sense about how to have as much as possible of several good things that cannot be traded off fully against each other.

I am willing to make the rash assertion that this is almost the only interesting strictly normative problem in contemporary political theory.

This fundamental problem of value mixes aside, for the rest, when men differ in their policy conclusions it is usually because of differing empirical judgments about how a chosen package of values may be achieved.

Is There a Conflict between the Goals of Democracy and Stability?

Among the mixes of political objectives most often sought are popular democracy on the one hand and wise governance on the other. Long before eighteenth-century political writers posed the issue between freedom and order sharply, Aristotle had sought to describe how a polity could successfully merge elements of democracy and oligarchy. Most authors who have dealt with this subject, like Aristotle, Rousseau, Madison, and Tocqueville, have believed that stability was more easily achieved under authoritarian rule and that popular participation had a propensity to degenerate into anarchy. Most of them sought to discover means by which a community could be both stable and free, regarding this as a goal difficult of attainment.

The political science classics differ in their precise solution to the dilemma, but they are pretty well agreed on the statement of the problem. They are largely agreed that full political participation incurs grave dangers for the polity. They believe that the serious engagement of the entire public in political life is likely to be destructive of order. Here is an important proposition in traditional political theory. Does modern social research sustain this assumption?

Whatever the classical theorists may have said, and whatever social research may tell us, and we shall return to that later, we should note that popular American political thought does not accept the postulate that popular government and wise government are hard to reconcile. On the contrary, the lay ideology of our society values political participation unqualifiedly. Most people in contemporary America believe that the more of it, the better the government will be. The popular American assumption is that popular government is good government and that the source of political evil is usually special-interest influence.

Thus an intellectual issue exists. The corpus of political theory writings proclaim a dilemma between democracy and stability. The American lay tradition does not concede the disruptive character of popular participation in government. What do contemporary empirical political scientists have to say to us on this issue, if anything?

The outstanding modern essay on this subject is Berelson's concluding chapter to *Voting*[4] in which he maintains that a measure of public apathy is a condition without which a democratic polity would be torn apart in a bitter struggle, but is that a conclusion on which empirical research is agreed? Does the multimillion-dollar effort of social science over the past four decades enable us to choose between the postulate of popular American doctrine that sees citizen political participation as an unmitigated good and the postulate of classical political theory that sees citizen political participation (whatever its virtues) as a risky process in which self-seeking is likely to be destructive of public welfare?

Thirty years of survey research and other field studies have unquestionably given us a quite unprecedented knowledge of what our public is really like. We know, as no classical author ever did, just how much or how little participant, or alienated, or hostile, or passionate, or class conscious, or politically involved our common men are. We know as Aristotle, for example did not, just how much or how little difference there is in native intelligence and acquired political information between males and females, between people of good family and poor, between nation and nation. We know that on many of these points the classics were in error. But has anything that we have learned in the past thirty years of intensive empirical study of contemporary societies put into question the classic conclusion that public participation threatens public order?

Ironically, two sets of empirical studies seem to lead us to opposite conclusions. Studies of political development, on the whole, seem to support the classical view that political participation and public order are hard to reconcile, whereas most studies of American politics would lead us to the conclusion that the classics were fighting windmills and that a participant society is more stable than an oligarchic one.

What is the testimony of the developing world? In the Congo, in Vietnam, in the Dominican Republic, it is clear that order depends on somehow compelling newly mobilized strata to return to a measure of passivity and defeatism from which they have recently been aroused by the process of modernization. At least temporarily, the maintenance of order requires a lowering of newly acquired aspirations and levels of political activity. The so-called "revolution of rising expectations" creates turmoil as new citizens demand things which the society is unable to supply. Movements which express demands that cannot be satisfied do threaten the cohesion of those commonwealths.

In our society, too, the civil rights movement likewise demonstrates that the demand for citizen rights is often in conflict with the value of order. The issue of militancy and compromise is always irreconcilably present in that movement. There are those who would stir up people to ask for freedom now regardless of consequences and those who would go slowly to preserve the body politic.

But except for such occasional reminders that we too have the classic dilemma of democracy and order, the important thing about the United States is that it has indeed resolved this dilemma to a very significant degree. We have a system that does well enough on both of these values to make us much less aware of the significance on this dilemma than were our eighteenth-century forebears.

Because of its success as a popular government, the American political system is an excellent test case by which to measure the notions of traditional political theory about the dilemmas of democracy. We have a system that does well enough on both the value of participation and that of order so that it provides a good measure of the relevance of the theoretical solutions offered in the classics. Do empirical studies of what actually happens in American politics show any correspondence to the various suggestions offered by classical political theory as to the conditions under which these opposed values might be reconciled? If the United States offers an opportunity to test theories about how order and political participation can be reconciled, at the same time the empirical studies of the developing areas, where the conflict of these values is acute, provide good material by which to test the genuineness of the dilemma.

Political Participation and Political Stability: A Review of the Literature

What is it that the classics have said about how to reconcile democracy and order? Time permits us to review only a few of the main proposals. Three key elements have time and again appeared in the writings about good or bad forms of democracy. These are:

1. A large middle class
2. Civic virtue
3. Freedom from intermediary organizations between the citizen and the state

Writer after writer has claimed that, if citizen participation is to be reconciled with orderly government, one, or two, or three of these prerequisites must be present.

In this section we shall review what some past writers have said about these three elements and their role in making orderly democracy possible. Then we shall return in the subsequent section to an examination of the findings of empirical political science about democracy and order.

The Classical Formulations

There is a ritual in American political science curricula that passes for the study of political theory. That ritual is the memorization of the names of a score or so of great political theorists and some ten or a dozen sentences of summary of what each of them wrote. The reader who has suffered through this ritual may be reluctant to forgive our doing something like it again. Still, it is worthwhile to recapitulate what has been said in some of the classic writings on the problem of political participation and political stability. The classics are a major source of our present conceptions of what the problem is. We shall, therefore, beg the reader's indulgence as we succinctly recapitulate the comments of at least three main writers on the problem of participation and order, namely Aristotle, Rousseau, and Smith.

Aristotle (in the fourth book of the *Politics* which he explicitly labeled as being concerned with the empirical issue of what is practically feasible in the real world) addressed himself to the problem of how to set up a polity that would have both a measure of equalitarian justice for the masses and a measure of wisdom arising from orderly leadership. It was a constitutional form that could simultaneously embody elements of oligarchy and democracy. Among his empirical conclusions about how to achieve this mix of values were the findings that (1) a large middle class; (2) procedures embodying the rule of law; (3) attitudes on the part of the political actors that valued the common good rather than their own advantage; and (4) the use of mixed modes of selection for office that gave effective representation to the different interests within society conduce to such a stable but free society. Not much of interest was added to Aristotle's formulation until Rousseau.

Rousseau was responding in the *Social Contract* to a challenge posed by Hobbes. Hobbes had presented a disturbing thesis about how society would have to act to optimize on a single value, namely, internal order. Rousseau sought political practices that would simultaneously permit both freedom for the citizen and a well-ordered society—that would avoid both anarchy and tyranny. He found the solution in the consent of the governed. To be free in a stable, organized community, the members of the public, so Rousseau argued, must consent to the organized community which exercises control over them. If they consent to being compelled by the society, then they are free. But Rousseau recognized that consent to the mere existence of a sovereign community, though the most essential consent of all, is a pretty minimal freedom. For a more extensive freedom within an orderly community there must be extensive deliberation and consent by the citizens to the manifold laws that control them. The more extensive the citizen's participation and consent, the greater his freedom. Consent to all laws, however, will arise only if the citizen places higher than his individual preference regarding any particular law, his desire that the general will of the citizen-body should prevail. Only if each citizen is that sort of virtuous citizen, desiring that the general will shall rule even over his special interests, is he going to be free when the state infringes his special interests. When that eventuality of infringement of self-interest occurs, only he who has preferred the common good to his own is free in the sense of having willed that which was done.

The Rousseauian answer, then, is that only in total submission to the community will all find themselves free. None will rule them then, except that community to which they in their civic virtue have consented. All are equal in their submission to their community.

To assure that equality, intermediate organizations between the citizen and that state should be avoided. Such institutions as the corporation, the interest group, and the political party all tend to increase the chance of some special interest prevailing, rather than the general will.

Civic virtue in the citizen-body (meaning identification with the community) and the elimination of special-interest organizations are, then, among the main conditions that according to Rousseau will permit a state to be stable though the citizens feel free in it. A charismatic leader, a lawgiver, may help bring the citizens to this desirable resolution. Other empirical conditions for achieving this difficult set of desiderata, such as size of state, are also discussed by Rousseau.

The Rousseauian view that for a stable commonwealth citizens would have to subordinate their special interests to a virtuous concern for the general interest was challenged within fifteen years by Adam Smith's ingenious thesis that the seeking of individual advantage could promote rather than destroy the wealth of nations. Smith concurred with Rousseau, however, in considering the elimination of organized interest groupings to be an essential condition for this desirable outcome. Both of them argued that, in an atomized society in which factional coalitions were prevented and in which each individual citizen acted by himself in accordance with an appropriate rule of behavior, the common good would emerge despite the diversity of human aspirations. The difference between Rousseau and Smith was in the behavioral rule required of citizens if socially desirable outcomes were to follow. The

Rousseauian rule was that each citizen must subordinate himself. He must altruistically will that which he believes all citizens would will if they acted in that same way. The Smithian rule was that each citizen should seek his own advantage. Smith thus rejected the centrality of at least one of the three usual postulated requirements for order with freedom, namely, civic virtue, while he continued to accept one, namely, absence of intermediary organizations.

Let us not oversimplify the statement of Smith's view. Smith wrote two books of which only one is widely read. Before *The Wealth of Nations*, he wrote *The Theory of Moral Sentiments*. The basis of moral sentiments, he argued, is sympathy. It is that which makes possible such solitary groupings as the family. However, secondary groupings such as the nation, he believed, cannot rely upon being the beneficiaries of such virtuous altruistic motives.

In effect Smith dismissed the Rousseauian rule of behavior for achieving social welfare as unrealistic and impractical, at least for use in large, impersonal institutions. Yet such institutions clearly do sometimes serve the common good. Smith's contribution was to clarify how it could happen that (in Mandeville's words which inspired Smith's inquiry) private vices could lead to public benefits.

From a contemporary point of view, both the Smithian view and the Rousseauian view of how to reconcile individual freedom with stable government seems sociologically deficient on at least one point. Neither recognizes a significant role in producing stable government for classes, castes, estates, tribes, factions, movements, guilds, pressure groups, parties, or associations. In quite different ways, both theories have been used as justifications by ideologies committed to the destruction of such feudal or pluralistic intermediary organizations subordinate to the state. The laissez-faire version of this opposition to coalitions and cartels is sufficiently familiar to need no elaboration here.

The Rousseauian view also led to a political ideology in which there was only the individual and the state, but with the state being an all-absorbing total one.[5] Rousseauian liberals when they wrote constitutions in nineteenth-century Latin America, for example, included bills of rights that, although they resembled American federal and state bills of rights on most points, differed on one. Where an American bill of rights would proclaim freedom of association, some Latin American nineteenth-century constitutions contain a clause against estates or associations.[6] The fascist and communist total states were the extreme version of the doctrine that subordinate groupings with special wills in conflict with the general will of the state must be destroyed. The line of influence from Rousseau through Hegel, the French revolutionary extremist sects, and Marx to Lenin, Mussolini, and Hitler is unmistakable.[7] Marx carried the Rousseauian dialectic to its logical limit. He contended that the destruction of all forms of segmentation within the society, be it classes, division of labor, competition, city and country, brain and brawn, or ruler and ruled, would give the individual freedom via total absorption of him within the homogeneous commune.[8]

Thus in both the Smithian and the Rousseauian version of the theory of the individual and the state, the public as a complex system of linked institutions and relationships disappears. In different ways, both versions argued that political participation could be reconciled with political stability only by smashing all such special relationships and allowing only isolated individuals to interact with each other.

The Sociological Writers

In the nineteenth and twentieth centuries a more realistic view of the public emerges in what may be called the "sociological writers," of whom the pioneer is Alexis de Tocqueville and the most important other representatives are M. Ostrogorski and Max Weber.[9] These writers recognized the positive contribution that intermediary organizations could make. They no longer argued that the way to have a stable society, despite citizen participation, was to atomize the citizen-body into a mass of anomic individuals.

All three of these sociological writers were preoccupied with the same central problem that we have been following through from Rousseau on, namely, how a participant or democratic society could nonetheless be orderly and reasonable. All three of them were acutely conscious of this dilemma, because all three were torn in their personal political views between a nostalgic attachment to the supposedly coherent structure of the *ancien régime* in which gentry provided the natural leadership for society and a recognition of the morality and inevitability of equalitarian mass participation in politics. All three therefore addressed themselves to the question of how a society could be democratic and still not become victim of revolutionary turmoil and mass tyranny.

The analytic method of all three was also similar. They each proceeded in the empirical fashion that has become characteristic of contemporary political science, that is, by careful case studies followed by speculative generalization.

Tocqueville chose his case studies well. France provided his examples of the *ancien régime* on the one hand and of the potential for a Rousseauian mass society after the Revolution on the other. The United States provided his example of the way in which "democracy" (a term he used as a synonym for "equality") could be combined with individual freedom and good government.

His look at the empirical facts led Tocqueville in one important respect to turn the classic view on its head. The facts seemed to indicate that a mass society, far from being an anarchic one, was likely to be an oppressively conformist one. In agreement with Aristotle, Rousseau, *The Federalist Papers*, and other classics, he saw the danger of anarchy as inherent in the conflict of organized special interests. But in disagreement with his precursors, he saw the process of democratization as a process that destroyed such special-interest groupings and created a monopolistic Rousseauian general will. Freedom, not order, was the value whose destruction he feared under democracy.

Tocqueville argued, in opposition to Rousseau, that it was precisely the strength of intermediary organization in America, such as churches, independent courts, local governments, voluntary associations, etc., which made it possible to have a participant or democratic society and for it still to be a free one.

Perhaps we can make the subtleties of these intellectual developments clearer by a somewhat schematic formulation of the different viewpoints we have summarized. We are examining what different writers have said about the relations among four elements:

- Political participation
- Political conformism or oppression
- Intermediary or factional organization
- Political stability or instability

The classic position was that

Mass Political Participation
leads to
Intermediary Organization
leads to
Instability

The classic solution was to cut the first causal link, and by avoiding intermediary organizations, to retain political participation with stability.

Tocqueville's position was that:

Mass Political Participation   *Intermediary Organization*

leads to   leads to

Political Conformism ← — — —→ *Instability*

Balance

Note that Tocqueville did not accept the view that democratic political participation leads to intermediary or factional organization. Rather, he thought of intermediary organizations as being essentially aristocratic, as characteristic of the *ancien régime*, and also as opposed to the spirit of democracy. In this latter view he was both original and probably wrong. To justify this view, he had to misperceive American reality in a very significant respect. He had to see intermediary organizations in the United States as somehow an independent counterweight to America's democratic tendencies, not as an outgrowth of them. In America intermediary organizations have always been thought of as natural by-products of citizen self-expression, not as embodiments of historic privilege. There were no feudal estates to be combatted in the name of freedom. Rather, to Americans the central authority has always appeared as the specter of the potential oppressor.

The Federalist Papers illustrate the American perspective on these matters.[10] "Faction" was Madison's term for what we have been calling "intermediary organizations." Like Hobbes and Rousseau, he saw the latter as a source of chaos, conflict, and anarchy. But (in opposition to Rousseau) the suppression of such faction was considered by him as a violation of the citizens' freedom and thus an evil equal to that of faction.

The schematic presentation of Madison's view would be the classic one:

Political Participation

leads to

Faction=Intermediary Organization

leads to

Instability

But he rejected the proposal of cutting the first causal link as an oppressive solution.

Thus the American tradition has seen interest organization and freedom of association as an expression of participant citizenship, not as a limitation upon it.

Tocqueville observed the extent of association activity in the American political process and observed that it did not tear the society apart. In America, as Tocqueville presented it, the disruptive effect of intermediary organization was acceptable, even desirable, because it neatly balanced an opposite tendency of democracy, namely Rousseauian centralization and the despotism of the majority. Tocqueville believed the basic American trend to be toward leveling, toward uniformity, and toward conformism, moderated fortunately by the existence of intermediary organizations, which contributed a spice of differentiation and autonomy to an otherwise dully conformist base. Tocqueville missed entirely the possibility that the formation of subordinate groupings might be the very basis of the democratization of American society rather than a fortunate counterweight to the democratic trend.

Note that in the two volumes of Tocqueville's otherwise magnificent work the Bill of Rights is never once mentioned. There is a long chapter on the Constitution.[11] For all it says, the first ten amendments might not exist. Could it be that Tocqueville made such an elementary error as to have read an unamended copy of the Constitution? It seems unlikely. It is true that in the 1830s the Bill of Rights was still a relatively unimportant portion of the Constitution. It was only after the Civil War that the Fourteenth Amendment plus court decisions extended both the effects and the range of application of what were originally redundant statements on the limits of the powers of the Congress. Nonetheless these clauses were a portion of the Constitution and their adoption was a significant indicator of the spirit of American democracy. Tocqueville's failure to note even their existence is most plausibly explained as a case of selective perception. The emphasis in the Bill of Rights on the autonomy of the individual and on the freedom of spontaneous subordinate groupings to act did not fit his image of the homogenizing tendency of democracy, and so he never mentioned it.

Ostrogorski and Weber carried the sociological insight that intermediary organizations had a positive role to play one step further than did Tocqueville. In their writings, the basic thesis of Hobbes, Rousseau, Adam Smith et al. about the basically disruptive character of subordinate organizations in society is finally rejected. The classic view that as the turbulent lower classes enter political life the pursuit of special interests leads to anarchy gives way in these twentieth-century writers to a much more subtle perception of what actually happens in the political process. What Ostrogorski and Weber observed is that mass organization, far from tearing society apart, provides a cement that binds the newly participant masses to the society in which they live. In direct contradiction to the classical view, the sociological studies concluded that democratization was impossible except through the development of parties, political machines, interest groups, and other intermediary organizations.

The sociologists pointed out that traditional predemocratic society had provided the individual with affiliations and with leadership, determined by the ascribed status into which he was born. Without a substitute for those affiliations, the individual, they concluded, is helpless and lost as he confronts in the state a remote, impersonal entity which he cannot understand and with which he can identify only as an abject subject. For men to belong to the commonwealth in any meaningful sense, they must belong to elements of it that are closer to them, more understandable by them, more amenable to their influence than is the central executive power.

Partisan professional politicians who organize parties and pressure groups are, therefore, if they act responsibly, the key individuals who make possible the stable functioning of a mass society. That is the high calling of the vocation of politics, as Weber called it. Intermediary organizations led by such politicians with a "calling" serve more as a web that binds the individual partisan to his society than as a divisor that tears the society apart in conflict.

The Contribution of Behavioral Research

We have now reviewed some political theories; the time has come to test them against the results of recent research. We have reviewed what a few classic writers have said about the political conflicts which mass desires engender. We have also reviewed the newer sociological theories that attribute a stabilizing rather than a disruptive role to intermediary organizations. Let us now consider what, if anything, empirical research has added.

The sociological insight that factional organization forms the basis of loyalty to the larger unit has permeated modern political science. Following on the heels of Weber and Ostrogorski with ever more detailed case studies and ever more complex and precise methods of observation, innumerable studies have elaborated on the role of groups in the political process.

What has this detailed research gained us? What refinements have been made by contemporary research on the broad sweep of historically based empirical generalizations provided by Weber in *Politics as a Vocation?*

Basically, what Weber wrote in 1918 still stands as the best formulation of our present understanding of political leadership and political mass organization. There are, however, a number of points which a new Weber, if one were to come along, would have to deal with slightly differently if he were to synthesize equally brilliantly our present understanding of the participation of the public in the political process.

1. In the first place, in the past twenty years we have recovered and broadened some of the insights of Adam Smith. Our understanding of the processes of bargaining and competition not only in the economic field but also in the political field has been greatly advanced by what in shorthand can be labeled "game theory" and "bargaining theory." The classical Smithian demonstration of the fact that competition could result in mutual advantage applies to a special case, that of perfect competition. It is the situation in which there are no coalitions or intermediary organizations but simply individual bargainers. It is an unrealistic situation even in economics, but in politics it is so unrealistic as to have been of little interest.

Modern bargaining theory has broken loose from the narrow constraint of the assumption of perfect competition. Recent work has made possible much more general analysis of the conditions under which stable solutions to conflict exist.[12] It has demonstrated the existence of stable Pareto optima in some types of coalition situations more broadly relevant than perfect competition. It has, on the other hand, identified other types of bargaining situations, such as that of the prisoners' dilemma, in which there is no obvious stable solution.[13] It has identified some key variables that determine whether there is a stable outcome to a conflict—such variables as the presence of focal points, communication restraints, time perspective, and so on. These determine whether or not partial conflicts of interest will serve to divide a society or will actually weld it closer together. The work of Schelling above all and also of Rapoport, Iklé, Shapley, Shubik, Kahn, Homans, and others has made it impossible any longer for a sophisticated political scientist to think of conflict as a simple additive evil, the more of which there is, the more unstable is the society.[14] On the contrary, we have learned to analyze the structures in which conflicts occur so as to assess whether the conflicts decrease or actually increase the stability and unity of a society. Conflict can do either.

2. A second topic on which our understanding has advanced thanks to the research of the past three decades is that of the relationship of the leader and the public. Weber's concept of the charismatic leader or Rousseau's of the lawgiver was one that was empirically illustratable by them but was rather unexplained and unexplainable in the pre-Freudian literature. Rousseau, Weber, and others noted how a leader can be the node around which a plural of people can be organized into a public. In Rousseau's rather anomic society, in which no groupings of citizens were to exist, the lawgiver, a great leader, might help the people to find the general will. Rousseau's totalitarian disciples all seized upon this notion, developing the cult of the individual as a substitute for genuine political organization. Weber worried about the potential power of demagogues and addressed himself to the problem of how to create responsible political leadership. However, the question of what binds the public to such leaders is something that has been well analyzed only since Lasswell, Erikson, and others took the insights of Freud and applied them to politics.[15] Today it is a cliché to call a political leader a father figure—so fast has the unthinkable become banal. Today it is quite normal for political scientists studying the civil rights movement, or *caudillismo*, or the absence of responsible leadership in Vietnam, to collect data on such matters as father-son relations in the family.[16] We are not surprised if a researcher finds that the prevalence of the authoritarian father, or the absent father, or the weak father sets a pattern for adult political behavior. Such an explanation will still engender controversy, but it is one that can no longer be laughed out of court.

The classic theories noted that a leader could help meld a diverse and conflictful society into a working unity. More recent studies help us to understand how.

3. Also thanks to the psychologists, our understanding of the processes of citizen decision making and of persuasion have improved greatly. Specifically, we have learned that small face-to-face groups play a part in political socialization and political action which nations or other large communities can never play. We have learned that there are respects in which the "general will" cannot replace cathexis to the small group.

According to the classical model of political decision making, the rational citizen considers the various alternatives, decides which he believes in, and acts accordingly. (In the Smithian model he considers which alternative best serves his interest; in the Rousseauian model, which conforms to the general will. But even if the rule is different, still the citizen reaches a conviction by evaluating alternatives against a clear rule of judgment and then acts accordingly.)

The behavioral study of citizen action has demonstrated that the relation of conviction to action is far less intimate. The influences that produce conviction do not necessarily change actions, and the influences that change actions do not necessarily involve change of conviction. Leadership by a great charismatic figure, for example, is apt to have more influence in providing a behavioral model for the citizen-body than in producing conversion of their beliefs.[17] For example, the change from Eisenhower to Kennedy as a national leader produced great changes in the national posture toward political life. The slogan "let us begin" symbolized the new spirit. But there were very few major changes in the policies on which the nation was to begin. Even fewer of these changes involved persuading the citizens to change their minds about their beliefs or ideologies.

That familiar example illustrates part of a process of citizen action that has been documented in detail in numerous social science case studies. Studies of voting, of troop surrender, of strikes and riots, of adoption of agricultural innovations, and of voluntary-association activity have all shown a similar process of mobilization of citizens into action.[18] Propaganda, public information, and news all serve to select *attitudes* for saliency from among those attitudes that are already well established, but *action* on them depends crucially on personal leadership by respected reference individuals. The most effective of these reference persons so crucial in controlling action are the members of small, close-knit, face-to-face groups.

Primary groups are also influential in producing the conversions in beliefs that do occasionally take place among adult citizens. Such groups are, however, much more effective in socializing those whose convictions have not yet been formed, such as the young, and they are important in an irreplaceable way in channeling social action by their members.

Any theory of political participation would be archaic if it failed to take into account what we now know about the role that group processes play in political action. Contemporary political theory stresses the importance of groups. Mere awareness of their importance is, however, something less than a political theory.

One can easily debunk the literature of group theory in political science by saying that it simply asserts the importance of groups over and over again.[19] That criticism has some validity. Many case studies describe pressure-group activities with no conclusion drawn other than that people participate in groups. But the study of group-influence processes has taught us more about groups than that. The study of group processes has enabled us to understand the process of identification through which groups acquire their hold.[20] It has enabled us to identify the part of the political process (particularly mobilization for action) in which cathexis with a person or group plays the greatest part. These specific insights about group processes reinforce the conclusion which we discussed at some length above, namely, that the only way in which people can be bound loyally to a large society is by identifications with small subgroups within it.

To the extent that this conclusion is so, a stable commonwealth is promoted by the existence of loyal intermediary groups within it. His majesty's loyal opposition is a factor for stability, not instability. The expression of its dissident views is far less important a fact about its political role than that it guides people as to how dissent should be expressed and binds them into playing the game by those rules. An anomic society which does not foster control by subgroups over the members of the society is headed for turmoil much more surely than one which encourages pluralistic loyalties to various intermediary organizations.

4. Another area in the theory of democracy that we understand somewhat better than before, thanks to empirical research, is that of political alienation and politicization. We have learned a great deal about the conditions for a participant society. We could still profitably understand it a lot better than we do. Alienation has been the subject of highly opinionated essayistic writing and also of a modest amount of hard-headed behavioral research. Politicization has been studied mainly in biographical studies of political leaders for whom politics has become a way of life.

Indeed, in regard to the ordinary citizen, we have studied political alienation somewhat more than we have studied politization,[21] although a number of studies have been made of the meaning of politics to ordinary men, notably Lasswell's *World Politics and Personal Insecurity*, Lane's *Political Life*, Smith, Bruner, and White's *Opinions and Personality*, and the currently popular studies in the field of political socialization.[22] Nevertheless, most of what we have learned about civic culture we have learned by studying people who are less trustful of the polity, less participant in it, less interested in politics, and less confident of their power to change things than we think they ought to be. They are certainly less politicized in these ways than a Rousseauian model citizen would be. We have looked at Turkish, Malayan, Indian,

Mexican, Venezuelan, and other peasants and why they do not feel that they can shape their future by political activity.[23] We have looked at Boston voters, negro voters, and working-class voters with an eye to examining their discouragement with the political process.[24] We have examined depolarization in totalitarian countries and the stratagems by which people avoid both the lies and the risks of politics there.[25] We are only beginning to look at the culture or psychology of exceptionally politicized groups. We should look more at why some peasants, for example, the Viet Cong, come to feel that they can get advantages by politics; why some ethnic groups, for example, the Malays in Malaysia or the Irish in Boston, see politics as a most promising channel of mobility; why many voters around the world find a politically organized society more attractive than one that works out its problems by private initiatives.

It is easier, unfortunately, to catalog the work that has been done on the subject of alienation and politicization than to summarize the relevant conclusions. One thing that research has pretty well documented is the erroneousness of the widespread belief that industrial mass society makes men feel increasingly inefficacious and alienated. According to that dubious view, men in the small communities that characterized preindustrial rural life felt more able to cope with and more at one with their community than do urban men today. That is another Rousseauian notion that seems to fall before the evidence of case studies. Almond and Verba, Lerner, and others have made it hard to accept that fantasy and have demonstrated that, if anything, the facts are the other way around.[26] A participant civic culture comes in with modernity.

The participant citizen, it should be stressed, devotes only a very limited portion of his total time and a measured amount of his emotional energy to politics. He is not the politician by vocation. No society could stand the strain of having more than a small minority among it living *for* politics or could afford the cost of having more than a small minority living *from* politics. A politicized citizenry is interested in political news and enjoys it, but political news is not of enough saliency to call for changing the course of the citizen's professional or private life. A politically involved citizenry is one that has confidence that political processes can produce desired outcomes, but desired outcomes of a fairly impersonal and unimmediate sort. Whereas at one extreme alienated citizens do not expect *any* desirable outcome from politics, and whereas at the other extreme politicians expect payoffs of personal significance to their own lives and careers from politics, politicized citizens in the middle expect results that may make the total environment of life better, but they do not expect any clearly identifiable immediate benefit to themselves. The politically involved citizen is not like a politician any more than he is like an alienated citizen.

It is, therefore, necessary to understand the process of popular politicization in somewhat different terms than we understand the process of the choosing of politics as a way of life.[27] The politically involved citizen is not someone who like a politician chooses the political arena as a grand stage on which to act out in large his emotional conflicts. Psychological factors do play a large part, but in ways that differ in important respects from their operation on politicians.

What do we know about citizen politicization?

We know that a vested (even if indefinite) interest in the results of the political process (or in Lipset's phrase, "the relevance of government policies to the individual") increases politization.[28] Government employees, recipients of subsidies or licenses, and people whose jobs depend on public policies are more active politically than the general run of citizens.

Such citizen vested interest in politics comes in two forms. There are persons who know that they might gain or lose according to the outputs of the political process, for example, according to what laws get passed or what appropriations are made. There are others whose vested interest is in the respect and prestige which political action itself confers, independent of the outcome. Officers of civic groups have a vested interest in politics just as much as do persons at the public till; interest by citizens in politics often pays off for them in status.

We know also that persons who feel that they can be effective in politics are more likely to become involved in it.[29] The acceptance of the possibility of progress has been one of the chief ideological supports of the spread of political participation in the modern world. Until the late eighteenth century, most men throughout history have assumed that their lives would be much like their fathers', and their sons' lives much like theirs. There might be change as fortunate seasons and famines rotated or as war and peace alternated, but these changes would be random or cyclical, not progressive. They might help some and hurt others, but they would not change the general character of man's life. Only in the last two centuries have any significant number of men accepted the notion that man's life on earth can become what he chooses to make it.[30] Political participation becomes a much more hopeful thing if one believes in progress.

The propensity to political participation also varies among personality types, but in ways that are not yet well understood. We know the characteristics of persons with high need for power, as scored in the Murray need system. We know, for example, that, in contrast to high achievers, these are people with great faith in luck and magic. But the evidence is not clear as to how far or in what situations politics at the citizen level attracts those with high need for power as against high need for affiliation.[31]

We know that political participation is a product of stimulation in early life. Children from political families remain political. Political socialization takes place early.

Knowledge about the political world stimulates interest in politics. One of the greatest factors for making modern societies participant has been the spread of mass media which inform the citizen about public affairs. The growth of the press and of political life have gone hand in hand. The media have made it possible for people to imagine themselves in the shoes of high decision makers and have thus enabled millions to answer the question, "What would I do if I were president?" This question is an unthinkable one to many traditional men.[32] It is the most conventional of casual conversational subjects for men who have been immersed in the modern news media.

For a citizen to enjoy the game of discussing things that are the business of the ruler, acting as if he himself were the ruler, a certain kind of identification with the ruler is required. Such identification is promoted in various ways. Providing an object for such identification is a king's main job. For a society to be politicized, there must be someone, be he only monarch or also ruler, whose daily life, personal passions, pleasures, and pains are all exhibited to the public by the mass media. That exhibition permits the public to live his life as part of their own.

Another condition that promotes identification by a citizen with his government is the presence among his rulers of people in some respects like himself. The respected ruler may be an ego ideal rather than *just* ego, but to be an ego ideal he must still in some sense be ego. Classical theorists, with the notable exception of Aristotle, have usually misdescribed the democratic decision process either as one where policies conform to the public's views or as one where the leaders are those persons whom the public most respects. At least equally important in democratic practice is the public desire that the rulers should be people of their own kind—people like themselves. Where the long ballot prevails, the dominant decision rule for an unaffiliated voter is to vote for any candidate about whom he knows something that suggests that the candidate is like the voter himself, for example, in ethnic origin, class origin, geographic origin, etc.[33] A government by people like oneself is a government one can trust to share one's approaches, attitudes, and viewpoints even on issues as yet unknown. It is also a government one might be able to approach in a moment of need. Thus one of the most striking features of democratization, wherever it has taken place, has been the emergence of plebeian politicians, of machine bosses with a common-man air, of noncosmopolitan nationalist leaders who dress and talk in the style of their soil. These demagogues, as Weber understood, are an essential link between the masses and their government.

It is, of course, a subjective matter who it is that appears to be like oneself. A sharply divided society without mobility is apt to define peers rigidly. They may be limited to members of one's own class or race. In a highly mobile society, on the other hand, it may be more possible for citizens to feel represented by whoever it may be who has achieved power.

Another thing we know is that politization is reduced if political participation is unpleasant or dangerous. People whose friends or relatives have views at odds with their own tend to withdraw from politics rather than argue and be looked down on. Wives become less interested in politics when they disagree with their husbands. People under cross pressure attend to political news less than those who are firmly decided on where they stand.[34] Service personnel, a merchant, or anyone with something to sell is apt to become neutral rather than offend any potential client. A Vietnamese peasant would rather be a "little man" than invite the ire of a punitive Viet Cong terror squad. Subjects of a dictatorship usually become apolitical; every totalitarian regime, while trying to mobilize the citizenry for passionate political involvement, has actually in the end depolitized them because it makes the penalties for political error greater than the rewards for political participation. The Red Guards in China today may demand of the citizens that they parade and write *tatzepao*, but their net effect on ordinary men is to make home and silence more appealing. Conversely, tolerance of diversity encourages political participation.

Among other factors that favor political participation are some that have already been discussed earlier in this chapter, namely, a propensity to broad and somewhat abstract group identifications, the existence of intermediary organizations, and a high level of trust and probity in the polity. These factors we earlier discussed insofar as they bear upon how a democratically participant commonwealth may also be stable. But they come up in that context only because they are among the conditions for having a participant society at all. We were concerned before with their consequences. Here we mention the same topics in cataloging conditions that we know lead to participation.

A propensity to a certain level of indirection in dealing with problems characterizes political men. There are many ways of solving problems and seeking advantage besides politics. Politics is a rather indirect path to one's goals. If a student sees few good job prospects waiting for him after university, or if a local person sees foreign occupiers getting the best jobs, there are many possible things to do about it. He can work harder, or migrate, or change professions, or put himself at the service of the privileged few, or turn to the solace of religion, or turn to banditry. It is not obvious that the thing to do is to join a movement aimed at changing the constitution or laws. Only a person partially inhibited from direct attack upon the source of his frustrations and therefore inclined to act upon them in the sublimated form of semiabstract symbols will turn to politics as a solution to those frustrations.[35]

Persons inclined to that degree of symbolization and indirection attach themselves to at least moderately broad symbols of identification such as their nation, their class, their ethnic group, or their party. They may be contrasted to the types of persons who define their ingroup as exclusively their family or clique and thus destroy the operation of responsible politics. They may also be contrasted to persons who seek so to act that nothing human is alien and their brothers are all mankind. The political person has enemies; politics for him is largely his fight against his enemies, but he also identifies with groups broad enough to be meaningful in the arena of national struggle.

These considerations lead us back to the topic of intermediary organizations and to the question raised in the debate between the classic and sociological theorists of whether those help or hurt in the creation of a great community. They define a bit more sharply than we have up to now the role of intermediary organizations in the political process. Except when aggressive nationalism mobilizes citizens for struggles against other nations, political identifications are bound to be less than all embracing within the commonwealth. Political identifications do, however, achieve a scope sufficient to make loyalty, devotion, and cooperation possible with persons who are only secondary contacts, persons who are not members of one's family. Creating that kind of attachment, that kind of trust, that kind of limited altruism within the political public, is the great accomplishment of democratic politics.

We pride ourselves in this country on our propensity to community organization, at our proliferation of voluntary associations and of welfare organizations, as we should pride ourselves too on our lobbies and pressure groups. All of these can exist only in an atmosphere of trust within such groups and respect for the rules of the game within which these groups function. These are virtues that may seem petty by the standards that Rousseau laid down, requiring the virtuous citizen to give himself totally to the whole community. They may seem petty by the standards of absolute moralists on the edges of politics who claim an equal love for all humanity. But politics, when it is used to force men to the impossible demands of an absolute ethic does not, as Weber pointed out, create a humane society. It creates a humane society when it civilizes, traps, and channels into constructive directions some of man's more partial, hostile, and self-serving impulses.

Insurgency and Stability: Two Paths of Participation

The empirical study of politics in America thus seems to have rebutted the classical theorists' fears of the dire consequences of special interests and intermediary associations. It seems, on the contrary, that far from threatening the stability of a polity, democratic politics with its vested interests, conflicts of interests, partial loyalties, and moderate politization can, under some circumstances, provide the most stable of governments. It can create conditions where ordinary human beings develop strong attachments to the commonwealth and high levels of practical trust among themselves.

That such stability is not the only possible outcome of political participation is apparent, however, as soon as we look at the developing nations. All around the world there are movements of men whose fathers were silent subjects in non participant colonial societies, who are taking to the politics of murder, terror, and revolution as ways to gain the good things of modern life. In the Sierra Madre, in the Andes, in the rubber plantations of Malaya, in the rice paddies of Indonesia, in the caves of Yunan, and in the highlands of Vietnam, men convinced that theirs is the wave of the future have waged political warfare on their fellow countrymen, hoping thereby to gain the benefits of modern technology, medicine and science.[36]

Why is it that participant politics can in one place so fully refute the classical fear of the turbulence of the masses and in another place so fully confirm it?

The answers are not far to seek and have in recent years been increasingly spelled out in studies of political development. One way of summarizing what this new literature has told us is to assert that those revolutionary movements in the new nations are trying to achieve political participation in societies where many of the conditions of participation, listed in the preceding section of this chapter, are missing. They are seeking to achieve participation in the shaping of their nation's political destiny under conditions in which mobility is limited, where the wealth available seems like a fixed pie, where there is no clear prospect of steady progress toward a better life, where mutual trust outside the family hardly exists, where the average citizen feels thoroughly inefficacious, and where the degree of abstraction from and sublimation of personal goals into relatively broad political identifications is rather low.

The typical revolutionary movement is an attempt at a great leap forward in a society in which the prerequisites for its objectives do not yet exist. It is an attempt by a small band of restless men to claim the right to shape the future, a right that a truly participant society gives in a limited degree to everyone.

One of the things that turbulent, politically underdeveloped societies lack is a broad consensus on loyalty to the commonwealth as a whole and to the rules of the game in it. That is indeed an essential requirement for a stable participant society. It is one of the key characteristics of a well-developed political culture. Bodin, Hobbes, and Rousseau were quite right in maintaining that without a firm concession of supremacy to the sovereign, stability is impossible. The sovereign enforces the rules within which competitive games may be played. Loyalty to such rules makes competition a stable, limited relationship. Without such loyalty to the rules, competition would become nasty, brutish, and unpredictable.

It has always been clear to all radical adherents of laissez faire except for the anarchists that at least a night-watchman state that enforces contracts is indispensable. Defenders of freedom and individuality have, with few exceptions, recognized that a certain minimum consensus on the organization of the social order, a certain minimum restriction on individualization, is essential for a free polity to survive.[37] Thus the classical defenders of freedom have recognized that the possibility of diversity within society depends upon the existence of a consensus in support of the commonwealth and in support of the legitimacy of its authorities against all attacks upon them. On that point empirical social research and classical political theory are in full accord.

However, what seems clear in the light of our contemporary socio-logical perspective, but did not seem clear to the classical writers, is that such respect for the commonwealth will be granted only by men who see the commonwealth ready to respect and promote within itself the aspirations and loyalties of its component parts. The Viet Cong guerrilla is a man who does not believe that his village's special inter-ests can be expressed within the political system of the government. The Venezuelan student terrorist is a man who does not believe that the special concerns of the progressive intelligentsia can be expressed within the political system of his country. The prospect of participation by special interests within the public is the condition for the public's at-tachment to the overall sovereignty of the commonwealth. Once that attachment exists, then, as Adam Smith first tried to show, and as con-temporary social science has shown further, it becomes possible to de-sign a system in which conflict is the condition of stability.

Notes

1. Bodin, Hobbes, the Monarchomacs, and the Politiques all identified the sover-eign (to use Bodin's word) as the key instrument for keeping life from being anarchic war of all against all.
2. Also note the Federalists' concern for avoiding the twin dangers of anarchy and tyranny, Adam Smith's balancing of moral sentiments and self-interest, or Tocqueville's slightly later search for democracy with liberty.
3. See von Neumann, John and Morgenstern, Oskar. *Theory of games and eco-nomic behavior.* Princeton, NJ: Princeton University Press, 1944; Arrow, Ken-neth J. *Social choice and individual value.* New York: John Wiley & Sons, Inc., 1951; Simon, Herbert A. *Models of man.* New York: John Wiley & Sons, Inc., 1957; Dantzig, George B. *Linear programming & extensions.* Princeton, NJ: Princeton University Press, 1963; Kantorovich, L.V. *The best use of economic resources.* Cambridge, MA: Harvard University Press, 1965.
4. See Berelson, Bernard R. et al., *Voting: A study of opinion formation in a presi-dential campaign.* Chicago: The University of Chicago Press, 1954.
5. Cf. Hegel, Georg W. F. *The philosophy of right.* Knox, T. M. (ed.), Fairlawn, NJ: Oxford University Press, 1942; Karl Popper, *The open society and its enemies.* London: Rutledge & Kegan Paul, Ltd., 1945. The consequences of Rousseauian thought would seem to justify Eulau's view (in chapter 3 [in *Contemporary po-litical science*]) that Rousseau simply denied the existence of the problem of representation. He certainly abolished the problem; it is not clear that he did not analyze it fairly deeply while so doing.
6. See Constitution of Argentina, 1853, Art. 22; Constitution of Paraguay, 1870, Art. 31; Constitution of Bolivia, 1871, Arts. 19, 32; Constitution of Colombia, 1886, Art. 47; Constitution of Costa Rica, 1871, Art. 34.
7. See Popper, *The open society;* also Rosenberg, Arthur. *Democracy and social-ism.* New York: Alfred A. Knopf, Inc., 1939.
8. Marx, Karl. *The German ideology* (1845-1846). New York: International Pub-lishers Company, Inc., 1960; also *The communist manifesto* (1848).

9. Tocqueville, Alexis de. *Democracy in America* (I, 1835, II, 1840), revised F. Bowen; Harry Reeve. New York: Alfred A. Knopf, Inc., 1960; Gilbert, Stuart. *The old regime and the French revolution* (1856). Garden City, NY: Doubleday & Company, Inc., 1955; Ostrogorski, Moisei. *Democracy and the organization of political parties* (1902). Garden City, NY: Anchor Books, Doubleday & Company, Inc., 1964; Weber, Max. *Politics as a vocation* (1919). Philadelphia, PA: Fortress Press, 1965. Cf. also Barker, Ernest. *Political thought in England from Herbert Spencer to the present day*. London: Williams & Norgate, 1915; Follett, M. P. *The new state,* New York: Longman's Green, 1918; Figgis, J. N. *Churches in the modern state.* London: Longman's Green, 1914.

10. Cf. especially no. X.

11. Tocqueville, *Democracy in America* I, chap. 8.

12. Von Neumann and Morgenstern, *Theory of games*; Luce, Duncan, and Raiffa, Howard, *Games and decisions*. New York: John Wiley & Sons, Inc., 1958; Schelling, Thomas C. *The strategy of conflict*. Cambridge, MA: Harvard University Press, 1960; Riker, William H. *The theory of political coalitions*. New Haven, CT: Yale University Press, 1962; Iklé, Fred C. *How nations negotiate*. New York: Harper & Row, Publishers, Inc., 1964.

13. Luce and Raiffa, *Games and decisions*, p. 95ff.; Rapoport, Anatol. *Fights, games and debates*. Ann Arbor: The University of Michigan Press, 1960.

14. Schelling, *Strategy of conflict*; Rapoport, *Fights, games and debate*; Iklé, *How nations negotiate*; Shapely, L. S.; Shubik, M. "A method for evaluating the distribution of power in the committee system," *American Political Science Review* 48 (1954): 787–92; Kahn, H. *On thermonuclear war*, 2nd ed. Princeton, NJ: Princeton University Press, 1961; Homans, G.C. *Social behavior: Its elementary forms*. New York: Harcourt, Brace and World, Inc., 1964. Karl Deutsch's chapter in this volume does not necessarily contradict the view being presented here, but perhaps offsets any implication that might be read into this chapter that conflict is no problem.

15. Lasswell, Harold D. *Psychopathology and politics* (1934), second edition. New York: The Viking Press, Inc., 1962, and *World politics and personal insecurity* (1930). New York: The Free Press, 1965; Erikson, Erik, H. *Childhood and society*. New York: W.W. Norton and Company, Inc., 1950.

16. Moynihan, Daniel P. "The negro family: Case for national action," U.S. Department of Labor, Office of Policy Planning & Research, March 1965; Slote, Walter. "Case analysis of a revolutionary," in Bonilla, Frank; Silva Michelena, José (eds.). *A strategy for research on social policy*. Cambridge, MA: The MIT Press, 1967.

17. Kris, Ernest; Leites, Nathan. "Trends in Twentieth Century Propaganda," in *Psychoanalysis and social sciences*. New York: International Universities Press, Inc., 1947, pp. 393–409.

18. Berelson, *Voting*; Lazarsfeld, Paul F. et al., *The people's choice*. New York: Columbia University Press, 1948; Shils, Edward A.; Janowitz, Morris. "Cohesion and disintegration in the Wehrmacht in World War II," *Public Opinion Quarterly* 12 (1948): 300–15; Mintz, Alexander. "Nonadaptive group behavior," *The Journal of Abnormal and Social Psychology* 46 (1951): 150–59; Lee, A. M.; Humphrey, N. D. *Race riot*. New York: Holt, Rinehart and Winston, Inc., 1943; Lipset, S. M. et al. *Union democracy*. New York: The Free Press, 1956, pp. 176–200; Rogers, Everett M. *Diffusion of Innovations*. New York: The Free Press, 1962; Katz, Elihu; Lazarsfeld, Paul. *Personal influence*. New York: The Free Press, 1955; Lippitt, Ronald et al. *The dynamics of planned change*. New York: Harcourt, Brace & World, Inc., 1958; Schein, E.; Bennis, W. *Personal and organizational change through group methods*. New York: John Wiley & Sons, Inc.,

1965; Hero, Alfred O. "Voluntary organizations in world affairs communication," *Studies in Citizen Participation in International Relations* 5, World Peace Foundation, 1959.

19. Lowi, Theodore J., "American business, public policy, case studies and political theory," *World Politics* 41 (July, 1964): 677–715.

20. Freud, Sigmund. *Group psychology and the analysis of the ego.* London: The International Psychoanalytical Press, 1922; Lasswell, H. *World politics and personal insecurity*; Redl, Fritz. "Group emotions and leadership," *Psychiatry* 5 (November, 1952), pp. 571–96; Grodzins, Morton. *The loyal and the disloyal.* Chicago: The University of Chicago Press, 1956.

21. Levin, Murray. *The alienated voter.* New York: Holt, Rinehart and Winston, Inc., 1960; Morris Rosenberg. "Some determinants of political apathy," *The Public Opinion Quarterly* 43 (Winter, 1954); Almond, Gabriel; Verba, Sidney. *The civic culture.* Princeton, NJ: Princeton University Press, 1963.

22. Lasswell, H. *World politics and personal insecurity*; Lane, Robert E. *Political life.* New York: The Free Press, 1961; Smith, M. Brewster et al., *Opinions and personality.* New York: John Wiley & Sons, Inc., 1956; Cf. also Lipset, Seymour M. *Political man.* Garden City, NY: Doubleday & Company, Inc., 1963; Hyman, Herbert H. *Political socialization.* New York: The Free Press, 1959; *The Annals of the American Academy of Political and Social Science* col. 361 (September, 1965). Note also the Civic Training series published by the University of Chicago Press in the 1920s and 1930s; for example, Samuel N. Harper, *Civic training in Soviet Russia*, 1929; John M. Gaus, *Great Britain: A study of civic loyalty*, 1929.

23. Frey, Frederick. "Surveying peasant attitudes in Turkey," *Public Opinion Quarterly* 27 (Fall, 1963): 335–55; Rural Development Research Project, Reports no. 3, *The mass media and rural development in Turkey*, and no. 4, *Regional variations in rural Turkey.* Cambridge, MA: Center for International Studies, MIT, 1966; Lerner, Daniel. *The passing of traditional society.* New York: The Free Press, 1958; Pye, Lucian. *Guerrilla communism in Malaya.* Princeton, NJ: Princeton University Press, 1956; Carstairs, M. G. *The twice born.* Bloomington: Indiana University Press, 1958; Dube, Shyanna G. *Indian village.* Ithaca, NY: Cornell University Press, 1955; Lewis, Oscar. *Life in a Mexican village.* Urbana: The University of Illinois Press, 1963; Mathiason, John R., "The Venezuelan campesino," in Bonilla and Michelena, *A strategy for research on social policy*; Almond and Verba, *The civic culture.*

24. Levin, *The alienated voter*; Lipset, *Political man*; Kornhauser, William. *The politics of mass society.* New York: The Free Press, 1961; Milbrath, Lester. *Political participation.* Chicago: Rand McNally & Company, 1965; Glanty, Oscar. "The negro voter in northern industrial cities." *Western Political Quarterly* 8 (September, 1960).

25. Inkeles, Alex; Bauer, Raymond. *The Soviet citizen.* Cambridge, MA: Harvard University Press, 1961, p. 322ff.; Cantril, Hadley. *Soviet leaders and mastery over man.* New Brunswick, NJ: Rutgers University Press, 1960, especially chapts. 5 and 6; Mihajlov, Mihajlo. *Moscow summer.* New York: Farrar, Straus & Cudahy, Inc., 1965; Johnson, Priscilla; Labedz, Leopold (eds.). *Khrushchev and the arts.* Cambridge, MA: The MIT Press, 1965, especially the introduction; Zoshchenko, Mikhail. *Nervous people and other satires.* Gordon, Maria and McLean, Hugh (trans.). New York: Random House, Inc., 1963.

26. See Almond and Verba, *The civic culture*; Lerner, *The passing of traditional society.*

27. See Lane, *Political life*; Almond and Verba, *The civic culture.*

28. Lipset, *Political man*, p. 185.

29. See Almond and Verba, *The civic culture*, chap. 9; Rosenberg, "Political apathy."

30. Pye, *Guerilla communism*; Condorcet, Marquis de. *Esquisse d'un tableau des progres de l'esprit humain.*(1795); John B. Bury, *The idea of progress*. London, Macmillan, 1920.

31. McClelland, David. *The achieving society*. Princeton, NJ: D. Van Nostrand Company, Inc., 1961; McConaughy, John B. "Certain personality factors of state legislators in South Carolina." *American Political Science Review* 44 (December, 1950): 897–903; March, James. "The power of power" in Easton, David (ed.) *Varieties of political theory*. Englewood Cliffs, NJ: Prentice-Hall, Inc., 1966.

32. Lerner, *The passing of traditional society*; See also Speier, Hans. "The historical development of public opinion" in *Social order and the risks of war: Papers on political sociology*. New York, 1952. In Samoa ordinary men feel it improper even to use the words that refer to political power. Cf. Keesing, Felix; Keesing, Marie. *Elite communications in Somoa*. Stanford, CA: Stanford University Press, 1955.

33. Pool, Ithiel de Sola. "Voters' information on candidates in primaries." *PROD* 1 (September 1957): 15–18. In his chapter in this book Professor Eulau discusses theories of representation. The theories he cites, such as Burke's, all neglect the identification aspect of representation. Among the writers he cites, only Aristotle, whom Eulau does not credit with a theory of representation, deals with the value of the ruler being like the ruled.

34. Berelson et al., *Voting*, pp. 97, 337.

35. Lasswell, *Psychopathology and politics; also World politics and personal insecurity*.

36. Pye, *Guerrilla communism*.

37. Cf. Lowe, Adolph. *The price of liberty*. London: The Hogarth Press, Ltd., 1937); Simons, Henry C. *Economic policy for a free society*. Chicago: The University of Chicago Press, 1948.

14

Citizen Feedback in Political Philosophy

Electronic devices for citizen feedback may be new, but the philosophical issues posed are old. New gadgets may make possible instantaneous polling or national town meetings, but the question has been with us since Plato of where, when, and which citizens should be heard.

It is easy to debunk the more naive notions of how to use electronics in politics. One science fiction fantasy has the public engaged in a national town meeting on cable TV with various issues being debated and then decided by an instant push-button vote. War could be declared on Monday, canceled on Tuesday, and declared again on Wednesday, depending not only on which demagogue was most effective but also on who happened to be home and was not tired of politics from last night's session. If full-time congressmen with substantial staffs cannot keep up with the details of a thousand bills and thousands of pages of appropriations, even though they do most of their work in specialized committees, it is clear that part-time citizens cannot do the job.

But that is putting up a straw man. No one who has given the matter even a few minutes' thought proposes such a scheme. More modest approximations to the national town meeting are either schemes providing for occasional referenda on major issues or purely advisory polls. These may be useful devices, but these, too, have their problems.

Referenda may be useful in a democracy, but California's experience illustrates what happens when referenda are too frequent and too easy to put on the ballot. Year after year appealing crackpot notions go on the ballot, debated not in full text but by bumper stickers and billboards whose total context is often no more or no less than "yes on 9" or "no on 14." Changing the polling place for such referenda from a precinct firehouse to a button in the living room is probably a step

From *Talking Back: Citizen Feedback and Cable Technology* (1973).

away from giving the vote which the citizen casts that singular importance that might lead him to take adequate time for thought. It is hard to
see what is gained by voting from the home, other than keeping the
citizen dry if it rains.

As for opinion polling, the accuracy of a poll depends above all on
drawing a truly representative sample. The votes of those self-selected
citizens who choose to watch a political program and then choose to
push a response button tells us little about how the rest of the public
feels.

Push-button voting in Congress is an equally dubious idea. During
the time taken for a roll call vote, Congressmen are scurrying back to
the chamber from whatever they have been doing, getting themselves
informed as to what the vote is about, what its parliamentary consequences will be, and how those informed fellow members whose general views they share intend to vote.

In short, casual push-button voting has little to recommend it.

But if we stopped at this point we would miss the truly profound
significance of the new technology of electronic citizen feedback.
There are better things to do with it than encouraging ill-considered
votes and unreliable polls. What the future may hold is only carica-
tured by such proposals.

To put things in perspective, let us consider five issues that a political theorist might raise about any system of political representation or
political participation, including the new electronic ones.

First, there is the issue of whether the prime justification for encouraging citizen participation is the psychic satisfaction that it gives to the
participating citizen or the achievement of better governmental performance. In a forthcoming paper, Charles Murray raises that issue in regard to rural development programs in Thailand. The community
development literature, Murray points out, contains many pleas for increasing the degree of participation in the planning and development of
projects for rural communities. But the justification (when any is adduced) is most often in the form of evidence that if people are given
some voice they will feel more committed to the projects, feel better
about them, and have better morale. But whether participation will produce more miles of irrigation ditch, more latrines—or less—is a question generally left unanswered. Murray meets this issue directly. He
shows by careful statistical analysis that at least in Thai villages local
participation pays off in results but to a degree that differs with the
dependency of the content of the particular project on the knowing of

local facts about which the villagers are more expert than the outside advisors.

In the early 1950s the same issues were raised regarding task group organization. A classic study by Lippett and White[1] found that democratic groups had higher morale than authoritarian ones but did not find that they produced more. So too, Bavelas,[2] in experiments on message transmission in groups with different structures, found that diffuse equalitarian structures produced better morale than did centralized authoritarian ones, but they did not generally do more work.

These results raise a fundamental value issue about the purpose of government. How does one weigh the trade-off between the public welfare that arises from being treated with respect and equality and that which arises from delivered outputs?

Closely related is the issue between two criteria for political action: civic involvement in the polity versus a felicific calculus of individual benefits. Two hundred years ago, within fifteen years of each other, two men wrote the classic treatises on either side of that issue. Jean-Jacques Rousseau in the *Social Contract* argued that in a world of conflict the only way that men could be free without tearing society apart was if each assumed as his own desire that the general will of the society should prevail. Only when each citizen civic mindedly and freely subordinated his personal interests to the good of the whole would each be free in that act of subordination. From this Rousseauian paradox stemmed the concepts of freedom as being a willing subordination to society, held by Hegel, Marx, and the totalitarians.

But Rousseau was not unanswered. His contemporary Adam Smith also wrote of order in a world of conflict. The theory of laissez faire developed in the *Wealth of Nations* was a demonstration that there are circumstances in which each may freely strive for his individual advantage and the outcome nonetheless may be order and public benefit. Economists, from Adam Smith on, sought to define ever more precisely the circumstances and conditions in which mutual self-seeking would have stable and beneficial or unstable and harmful outcomes.

One of these conditions for a stable society clearly is, as Rousseau, too, recognized, that the competitors each personally value the rules of the game and value the society that enjoins obedience to those rules. Business competitors have to believe in enforcement of contracts, respect for property, and honest bargaining, or competition becomes mayhem. Football players have to love the game and respect the referee, or it will no longer be football.

Thus there is no polar opposition between the role of the participating citizen as fighting for his own interest and his role as a duty-bound participant in a civic effort. Society requires a complex pattern of these two elements. When, how, and in what relation these elements must appear for society to be both stable and free is a complex matter at the heart of political theory. An example of that complexity is the issue of whether the fostering of vigorous citizen feedback will produce commitment to the polity or active pursuit of self-interest, or both, or neither.

Depending upon how one feels about the goals of government as being some organic general welfare on the one hand, or payoffs to the individual citizen on the other, one may view the potential contribution of new information technologies as being primarily to the leader or primarily to the led. This is the third issue to which I turn.

Over-the-air television has given the president the capability of talking directly to the American people in one type of giant town meeting. In all communities personal leadership is one dominant fact of politics. Very few families, or clubs, or offices, make decisions by equalitarian discussion among all concerned. Whether we like it or not, the empirical fact is that in such environments personal loyalty of the led to leaders gives legitimacy to a process in which a few individuals actually dominate decision making.

Mass society tends to weaken the bonds of personal attachment between leader and led. The power holder is more often an unloved, unknown person. The boss in the factory or the administrator in a university, the union boss or the high public official—all are chronic targets of disaffection.

For heads of nations, radio and television have provided some means to partially restore a personal tie between the leader and his followers. Franklin D. Roosevelt did it in the United States when he introduced the fireside chat. Adolf Hitler at the same time, but in a very different way, used radio to establish his direct relationship with the German people. Television renews this bond even better. Richard Nixon, hardly one of the most charismatic of politicians, has nevertheless increasingly chosen to talk directly to the American people on all major occasions and to hold fewer and fewer press conferences for the reporters. And it has worked well for him.

Thus the electronic national town meeting may work far better for the leader than for the led. The gadgets that enable one person to communicate to many are far easier to use and make effective than those that enable millions of scattered individuals to somehow answer back.

And while it is popular these days to deplore political "manipulation" and "elitism," an objective treatment of the issues has to point to both sides of the coin. The very existence of a stable, happy society depends upon the population forming a positive cathexis to a leader who represents their aspirations and values. This, Freud argues in *Group Psychology and the Analysis of the Ego* is the crux of the formation of any group. So, too, Rousseau argued that the great lawmaker, a respected national hero, might be necessary to help individuals to find the general will. A Washington, Lincoln, Roosevelt, or Churchill becomes a symbol of faith around whom the nation can cohere.

However, the argument for electronic citizen feedback is that technology can reverse this process and help the citizens make their leaders listen to them. Is that possible, or is it inevitable that in the electronic forum the citizens, even if they push feedback buttons, are really responding to leaders made more effective by the same electronic devices?

A fourth fundamental issue concerns the time dimension in deliberation and decision making. Democratic principles require that the public have the government they want—but over what time period: every minute, every day, every four years? The system of checks and balances about which every American schoolchild learns is in large part a system for slowing up decision until everyone has had a chance to be heard and until second thoughts have had a chance to jell. Bills go through committees, two houses, and then to the president and sometimes cycle back again.

Finally, one may ask whether the function of the democratic political process is the airing of all views so that they can be considered fully by whoever reaches decisions, or whether democracy means the actual making of decisions by majority rule. The latter is the more common view, but there is a strong case for the former.

In point of fact, the U.S. Congress devotes a very large part of its efforts to investigations, to hearings, and to resolutions that do not have the force of law. In the great debate on Vietnam, for example, there has hardly ever been a major vote on a decision. The appropriation bills for it are passed without much problem. The great dramas have been on resolutions such as that on the Gulf of Tonkin or on setting withdrawal policy, or in investigations of atrocities, refugee care, defoliation, official secrecy, and responsibility for the decisions made.

A critic might denigrate that congressional behavior, alleging that a process that avoids decision making is a charade to fool the public while changing nothing. But a very good case can be made to the effect that political debate in the Congress, as in election campaigns, is properly a process of airing issues rather than one of reaching decisions. Very few policy decisions are all-or-none matters. Most are necessarily incremental and concern degree and direction of some continuing activity. Research on budgets has shown, for example, that the best predictor of next year's budget is this year's budget. At most there is a change of a few percentage points here or there. Thus, for example, if the Congress of the United States were to decide this year that highway construction is despoiling the countryside and that public transport is what is needed, it could not make that decision promptly. Some roads are already under construction. Others need feeders to be useful at all. For such reasons alone a decision now would make only small changes in the next budget. Furthermore, suppose that in a radical mood all road construction were stopped and railway construction started; the next election might bring in a Congress with opposite views. Probably any policy on either side would be better than the scattered incomplete starts that would exist if each Congress thought that it should legislate de novo, in spite of the prospect of another Congress reversing its decisions. Road construction versus public transport is not an all-or-none issue. It is a matter of how much to spend on each of them and where. On such matters of detail the general public has no clear view. Each individual wants some roads built and others not. Majority voting can only indicate the general direction of movement.

Thus, the case can be made that the important thing about the democratic process is that it allows the venting of all considerations. It allows issues to be formulated and coalitions to form around them. The actual decisions are reached in many ways: by passing general laws, by executive decisions, by changing the responsible officials, by bargains and deals, by judgments in the law courts, by letting events take their course, or by some combination of these. But in a participant society all of the modes of decision are under the pressure of full and free comment by those who would like to affect the process.

What has all this got to do with electronic feedback?

Perhaps if we keep these issues in mind we may visualize uses of interactive cable television in politics as more plausible than a town meeting on a national scale. There is no reason to believe that an interactive terminal in every home will make ordinary men replace private concerns with civic ones as their priority activity or make them regard the "vibes" of politics as "their thing" in preference to having efficient delivery of services. Nor is there any reason to believe that just because the communication is electronic, political leaders will or should listen passively to instructions from the cable rather than use the same communications devices to exercise leadership. It is nonetheless true that the new communications technologies can be used to make democracy work better. Let us consider how. One may well ask why it makes any difference that the complaint box is electronic. One could write a science fiction story about a society on another planet that had expensive electronic devices for recording complaints and in which an inventor came along and created a new device consisting of a cheap wafer-like object called paper and a short marking stick costing about 29¢ called a pen, and a system called the mails whereby for eight cents one could have a complaint delivered to the responsible person in a permanent record form called a letter. What a vast step forward in participatory democracy that would be.

In fact, letters *are* important, but even though we use them we are dissatisfied with how that system works. What the parable tells us is that no mechanical device will by its mere existence solve the problem of making bureaucracies responsive. It tells us that it is not enough that a device for registering complaints exists. One must consider how it is used and how its use can be made attractive to the public. So for the electronic complaint box one must ask how that technology can be used to do things a little better than we now do them with the mails and the telephone.

The mails are cheap but do not give that instant feedback that modern psychology has shown to be so valuable as reinforcement of any behavior. Also, writing letters requires, for a good half of the population, skills in which they are deficient; therefore the process is discouraging. The telephone call does give instant feedback and does not call on writing skill, but it leaves no permanent record for the bureaucracy to act upon. Also, it is often hard to find the proper place to which to address one's call. And it is a little more frightening to say nasty things to a live person than to a blank piece of paper. In short, each present available medium has its limitations.

New technology can be designed to overcome these problems. One can design an electronic complaint box to avoid that frustrating aspect of phoning, not knowing how to get the right person at the other end of the line. One may not know who he is, or, if one does know, he may not be easily reachable. One can design an electronic complaint box to avoid the frustration of letters that, although they may ultimately be bucked to the right person (or at least the trusting citizen believes they have been), still provoke no feedback, perhaps for weeks, that anything is happening.

An oral message can be recorded on a tape to provide a permanent record on which someone has to act. There can be immediate human or machine acknowledgment of receipt. A continuous computer record could be kept of where the complaint is in the processing path, and periodically a message could be printed out on the home console as to where it has moved and how it is being handled. That mode of handling of spontaneous citizen-generated complaints might be sufficiently more effective than what exists today to encourage a considerable increase in citizen activity in registering their dissatisfactions with the authorities.

For sensitive issues that generate much complaint, CATV could be used in another way at the initiative of the authorities. A public official could schedule citizen feedback sessions not unlike the appearances of candidates. For example, every week at a certain hour the school superintendent could get on the cable for dialogue with the public. Visible on the screen, he could answer questions phoned in. That can be done today on over-the-air radio or TV for high-priority matters. What cable adds is enough channels to make that worthwhile if only fifty concerned parents choose to watch and question.

Such a system would be undermined and its use discouraged if only the same few self-selected busybodies tuned in every week. A canny superintendent would focus each program at a different school or grade and would notify at least a number of people in the special population that he wanted to reach, thus assuring himself meaningful participants in his telemeeting.

Better communication technologies that create more efficient, more extensive, and more intensive interaction between public figures and their constituents may reduce the sense of alienation by making the public figures better able both to respond to their constituents and to influence them. There is no electronic difference between these two processes. They are both enhanced by efficient two-way communication. The specter of electronic manipulation is simply the other side of the coin of the hope of electronic democracy.

Closer interaction between citizen and official is not necessarily either a good or a bad thing. There is no healthy politics without leadership any more than there is manipulation without it. He who is disturbed at this thought should read once more the classic essay on this subject, Max Weber's *Politics as a Vocation.* Weber in 1919 wrote presciently about the specter of totalitarianism looming then on the horizon. That was the direction organized mass movements could and did go in Europe between the wars. Weber's prescription against that trend was better mass political leadership. He knew that the dangers inherent in mass mobilization could not be met by having less of it but only by affecting its character. The narrow path between mobilization of the people by demagogic populist hysterias (whether of left or right) on the one hand and the political silence of bureaucratic reaction on the other can be trod only by popular movements led subtly by politicians morally committed to liberal values.

This is an overly simple summary of a very profound and complex essay, but for our purposes it will do. The point here is that there is no distinction between the electronics that make demagogy easier and those that make responsible politics easier. It is the men who use them that make the difference. Modern society needs better modes of communication between the people and those in power. It needs to lessen the citizen's sense of alienation, his sense of powerlessness and isolation. To do so it must provide communications that are faster, more individualized, and more responsive than are the mass media today. Electronic, computer-controlled, broadband, two-way facilities can make such communications possible. But whether the outcome of that new technology will be the "dark night" of ideological manipulation or the responsible politics of liberal discourse depends not on the technology but on men.

Let us then, in closing, look at the new communications technology from a committedly liberal point of view. Let us ask ourselves how the increased communication capabilities can be used in ways that promote open discourse and pluralism in society.

The first thing to note is that increased citizen feedback via electronic consultation may well make it harder, not easier, to make high-level decisions. It may well increase the cost of the political process. The decisions that get made with wide public consultation may conceivably be better ones, but one cannot avoid the fact that bringing everyone into the discussion is a costly, time-consuming process that often generates stalemates. Consider civil rights, for example. It was a widely recognized conclusion of social scientists working on civil rights in the 1950s that the way to integrate places of work, restaurants, parks, or swimming pools was just to do it without discussing it at all. If not discussed, the physical presence of blacks tended to be taken for granted as natural, but once the issue was raised, polarization, dispute, and deadlock followed.

On the other hand, it is also true that to move the race relations struggle beyond the winning of small battles required the forcing into national consciousness of the moral issue in the negro's status in America.

This example illustrates one conclusion that needs to be underlined. Citizen feedback in large communities like a nation is primarily useful as an educative process that serves to bring issues into the public consciousness and to get them defined. It is likely to make the reaching of decisions on the matters on which it operates more costly, more time consuming, and more difficult, but at the same time it makes for deeper commitment and understanding when the decision is made. What follows is that highly politicized national decisions must be small in number. A nation can debate seriously perhaps half a dozen issues at a time, but not more.

It follows that if electronic citizen feedback is, as it can well be, an instrument for increasing the politicization of the populace, then the scope of high-level decisions on which it is brought to bear must be severely restricted. A national or other large community that tried to politicize everything would tear itself apart in endless conflict.

Worse still, the problem is not that attempts at total citizen participation lead to chaos. Worse than that, movement and reforms that proclaim as their goal the securing of massive direct democracy end up producing the contrary. So-called people's revolutions become totalitarian. The dictatorship of the proletariat becomes the dictatorship of the Party. The supposed voice of the *Volk* is really the voice of the Führer. It cannot be otherwise, for with or without electronic devices, the citizen body has neither the time nor capacity to handle everything in public affairs at once. If a pretense is made at comprehensive direct democracy, then the participant populace must be organized into a disciplined structure for anything at all to get done. The demand for total citizen participation is thus invariably in reality a demand for authoritarian citizen organization.

A liberal democratic policy, then, must be predicated upon the fact that there is a price for increased citizen involvement and participation. If the price is not to be less freedom and more authoritarianism, then the price must be a reduction in the scope of political action. Direct citizen participation is clearly desirable and possible, and the newer communications technologies make it more possible, but only for a tolerable portion of the citizens' time, over well-organized topics, and with due process—otherwise it becomes a pretense.

The restrictions on citizen action in a liberal democracy are many. The Bill of Rights restricts political action that is at the expense of the freedom of other individuals. Other rights, such as privacy, also restrict political actions by one set of citizens against another. Some topics, such as religion in the United States, are barred as topics of public policy. Nonetheless, democracy certainly implies a very wide latitude of subject matter for proposals, complaints, and issues that a citizen may inject into the political arena. Liberal democracy requires, however, that the issue once raised be subject to a procedure that allows time and opportunity for rebuttal from those who care to rebut; it further requires notice to those who might be affected before action is taken and also protects the citizen body from being subject to the constant harassment by political controversy that is of significance to only a few.

In this respect, as in others, the hallmark of liberalism is concern for procedures. It is a concern that whatever is done be done in accordance with established rules designed to assure fairness. So, too, must it be with electronic feedback. A communications system that allowed any self-designated group to inject itself at any time into organized decision processes is a violation of the freedom of those who do not choose to be vigilant and politicized all the time. Specifically, the notion that every city council meeting and school board meeting or congressional hearing should be on the air with electronic feedback influencing its processes is an absurdity whose consequences would be the opposite of the intent of those who propose such processes. Just as today there are scheduled occasions for citizen participation with limited agendas (which we call election campaigns, public hearings, and demonstrations), so, too, with electronic feedback. The more intense and real the involvement that electronic feedback creates for the citizen in public affairs, the more crucial it is to limit the scope of its operation and what is affected. If citizens are brought, by effective personal participation, to the point of caring very deeply about political outcomes, then there had better not be too many important political decisions, for every time one is made there are losers as well as winners.

It is a fact of politics that the more active citizens are more partisan and care more.[3] The young McCarthy-McGovern activists, for example, repeatedly tell us that if they do not win this next time around, their "generation" (or, more accurately, those among them who share their views) will be turned off on the political process because society does not choose to listen. They have identified a very genuine dilemma. The more politicized a minority like themselves becomes, and the more vital the sphere of politics, the more disillusioned they will be at society's failure to accept their version of the truth. Thus the price for having a politically active citizenry in a free society is a sufficient devaluation of political decisions so that losing is not intolerable to the losers.

To understand how this may be, let us introduce a distinction that students of small group behavior and organization have found useful, namely, the distinction among democratic, authoritarian, and laissez-faire structures.[4] Both democratic and authoritarian groups reach collective decisions as to what the group as a whole will do, though by very different means, one by consensus and one by elite fiat. On the other hand, laissez-faire, or individualistic, organization lets each person go his way. That is neither democratic, nor undemocratic; it is on a different dimension.

A liberal society deemphasizes political decisions in that way. It reduces as far as possible the areas where there must be consensus. It does so in various ways. It does so in part by delegating as many decisions as possible to small subunits, for example, state and local governments and corporations (which are also chartered public bodies). These subordinate units may each act differently, thus avoiding the trauma of all-or-none political decision. A politicized population living in such a pluralist system was the Jeffersonian ideal. It is in contrast to the Rousseauian version of the democratic ideal (with its totalitarian implications) that requires a collective decision by all for the good of all.

The newer technologies of communication promise to be favorable to pluralism. In contrast to today's mass media, the new technologies work best in providing means for linking small specialized populations and in providing feedback from them. There are few ways other than a gross opinion poll in which electronic feedback mechanisms can create interaction on the scale of millions or hundreds of thousands of persons. Those feedback devices are likely to work best on the scale of tens or hundreds or low thousands. Such technologies as graphic display of cumulated audience reactions or storing, forwarding, abstracting, and retrieving of questions and comments from the participants can make seminar-type procedures possible for what are now lecture-size audiences. The economics of teleconferencing makes feasible interactions among mini-audiences scattered over a distance at savings in both cost and effort over travel. At the same time CATV is inherently a neighborhood device, at least in its current stage of development as less than a fully switched system and is therefore favorable to community organization.

Perhaps, then, the most important way to think about citizen feedback in the CATV era is not as a device that the president or the Congress will find easy to use, nor as a device that will give citizens much more voice in those top-level decisions, but rather as a device that will promote grass-roots interactions among citizens with special interests.

Is this a good thing or a bad thing? Like all trade-offs, it is some of each. It makes meaningful and intensive citizen participation possible— far more possible than it can be at the national level, except sporadically. But on the other hand, a devolution of the focus of politics to the local and interest- group level may make this already inchoate nation even harder to unify and govern than it is now.

We are now in the realm of prediction. How the conflicting forces will balance out is uncertain. What it will mean to American society is that each citizen can participate more effectively in his own community and perhaps feel that he is heard more than he is today, and that at the same time the resulting special-interest groups will become more powerful and better organized.

Perhaps it is not so much a matter of prediction, but more a matter of planning. Perhaps if we understand these processes and the trade-offs involved, we can create feedback devices and practices that will both let people feel more efficacious in their own groups and also somehow strengthen our national consensus. Whether we can do that I do not know, but understanding what is at stake is the first step toward trying to achieve both those seemingly antithetical goals.

Notes

1. Lippitt, Roland; White, Ralph K. "The social climate of children's groups," in Barker, Roger G. et al. (eds.) *Child behavior and development.* New York: McGraw Hill, 1943.
2. Bavelas, Alex. "Communication patterns in task oriented groups" in Lerner, Daniel; Lasswell, Harold D. *The policy sciences.* Stanford, CA: Stanford University Press, 1951.
3. Berelson, Bernard; Lazarsfeld, Paul; McPhee, William. *Voting.* Chicago: University of Chicago Press, 1954, pp. 246ff.
4. See Lewin, Kurt in *Human nature and enduring peace,* 3rd Yearbook, Society for the Psychological Study of Social Issues. Murphy, Gardner (ed.). Boston: Houghton Mifflin, 1945, p. 303ff; and Mead, Margaret. *Cooperation and competition among primitive people.* New York: McGraw-Hill, 1937.

15

Communication and Integrated Planning

Integrated planning, a holistic approach and several other fash-
ionable catchwords belie much of the current trend in trying to
find similarities in dissimilar components in a single process.
While there are obvious benefits in trying to see the world as an
entity, Ithiel de Sola Pool looks at integrated planning from the
other side of the fence and suggests that there are also advan-
tages to a more diversified approach.

When our Canadian hosts invited me to give the talk here today on
integrated communications planning, my reaction was to tell them that
I was the wrong person to give that talk because I did not believe in
integrated planning. It is almost implicit when one uses golden words
like "integrated" that one is talking about a good thing. So if one sets
up a session with a title like "integrated planning" one generally assumes that that is a desirable goal and that the subject of discussion
will be why the world needs it and how to achieve it.

Well, our hosts had fair warning and the opportunity to accept my
declination. But either out of gentlemanly sportsmanship or out of a
desire to have a controversial session our hosts kindly persisted and
said they really wanted me to talk and say whatever I pleased. So here
I am.

Now why on earth would anyone be troubled by the slogan of integrated communications planning? The simple answer is that there are
real advantages to pluralism. There are advantages to multiple initiatives. There are advantages to allowing specialists to do their specialized things. There are advantages to the clash of competing efforts.
There are, of course, limits and a need for a shared framework. Our

First published in *Media Asia* (1981).

purpose today is to define what the needed framework consists of. It is not necessarily true that the present state of the world errs on the side of an inadequately comprehensive and integrated framework. Perhaps in some instances there is too strong a framework already.

To clarify my argument I should like to talk about three examples:

* standards
* satellite orbit & frequency allotments
* the relation of the ITU to UNESCO and the rest of the U.N.

Standards

Standards are essential to effective communication. A radio transmitter and its receivers have to be built to common modulations. Motion picture film has to be a standard width to fit in cameras. Indeed, the alphabet is a standard and so is language. I am here assuming we all agree on the interpretation of the letters s, t, a, n, d, a, r, d and of the word "standards," or else I would not be communicating with you.

The ITU [International Telecommunications Union] has two important standard-setting organizations, the CCIR dealing with radio and the CCITT dealing with telecommunications. Now no one would suggest that these organizations—which do standardize telegraphic codes—should go into competition with the Academie Francaise or *Webster's Dictionary* in standardizing the language we speak and write. That would be a reduction ad absurdum, far from the intention of any advocate of integrated planning. But just where do we draw the line?

Even if we limit ourselves to standards within the present domains of CCITT and CCIR, there are real drawbacks to adopting standards along with their essential uses. Every standard is a brake on innovation. An inventor may think of a better way of doing something, but if his invention fails to conform to existing standards, it will have a hard time getting adopted.

Fortunately, therefore, it is usually quite hard to get a standard adopted. Each country or each manufacturer has an interest in having their special wrinkle placed on the technology. So usually before the CCITT or CCIR can reach agreement on a standard. that standard has already become a de facto standard, frequently because a preeminent firm such as IBM or Kodak, or dominant agencies such as PTT, have settled on it and made most customers assume that particular practice.

There are only a very few instances of the formal adoption of a standard in advance of its widespread implementation. X-25 is perhaps the

star example. It was clear to the industry that if incompatible com-
puter-packet networks were built side by side or in different countries,
much of the value of such networks would be lost since they would be
expensive to interconnect. So a standard, namely X-25, was adopted,
following closely, it is true, the practice of the main existent networks,
and strongly protested by a few advocates of new approaches. This was
done before packet nets had come to be widely used. Most users and
administrations are happy to follow that common standard allowing
interconnection.

A strong case can be made for the wisdom of X-25, but networks, a
major purpose of which is to provide universal interconnection, are
precisely the application for which such a case can best be made. Let us
compare it with the troublesome case of videotapes and videodiscs. We
users have all suffered from, and been annoyed by, the incompatibili-
ties of equipment of different makes. But, we would not in the end be
better off if some planners had been able in advance of late technical
developments and of market experience to impose a single method of
recording. That would have killed development.

There is no easy answer to the question of when it is wise to freeze a
standard. There are great advantages to having standards, but there are
also advantages to going through the painful process of trial, competition and error. There is certainly no way in which planners, however
wise they may be, can effectively replace the present process.

That process is one in which technical specialists reach agreement
only when national and industrial interests that they represent reach a
compromise that all see as in their interests. There has to be consensus
because they have no sanction behind their decision beyond the shared
realisation that standards are necessary and should be supported.

That is far from a problem-free system, but it is unlikely that across
the board the job would be done better by more general authorities
less familiar with the technical details, and by abandoning the imper-
fect process of market experimentation. The present unintegrated and
consensual standards-setting process has much to be said for it in
most situations.

Orbit Planning

My second example is orbit planning. In 1977, the direct satellite
broadcasting WARC adopted a plan for 12–14 GHz use. Within the
next year it began to appear that the plan rested on erroneous technical

assumptions. With the passage of time that seems more and more probable. The 1977 image of the satellite future saw the geostationary orbit being populated by modestly sized satellites, mostly each belonging to some nation, and spaced a degree or two or more apart. Each satellite would serve its country by an uplink and downlink at different frequencies in a beam roughly corresponding to the perimeter of the country. Given that image, it made some sense to worry about orbit crowding and the fairness of the allocation of spots and frequencies.

In the three years since 1977, there has been much discussion, first, of giant space platforms and, more recently, of satellite clusters. A giant space platform would be an antenna farm in the sky. A platform large enough to carry all the needed antennas would be placed in one location over a continent. There are advantages to this. Switching can take place on board the space platform, so a message or program sent up from one location can be switched to another antenna beamed down to another location. Implicit in this is the use of spectrum-saving techniques in which very narrow beams play an important part. Large beams overlap extensively, requiring each to have a separate frequency. But look at the pattern in figure 15.1. Four frequencies repeated over and over in little beams will cover any area without interference. That is but one of several frequency-reuse techniques that can be implemented on the large sophisticated equipment carried on a space platform.

However, space platforms have one important disadvantage. While their enormous cost is shared, still the large investment is in an inflexible design. A decade or two later one may have to put up a new, more modern platform, but in the meantime a lot of things are immutable. Reaching agreement on periodic big investments will be hard.

That difficulty is extensively overcome by space clusters which, instead of being bolted together, have separate satellites positioned in a cluster. Each is a few hundred meters or a kilometer or so from the next. Instead of antennas being connected by wires for switching, they are interconnected by very low-powered, very narrowly focused microwaves. That way interference problems are minimized in the cluster. New satellites can be put up in the cluster when needed or taken down, one at a time at any time. In other respects the cluster operates like a platform.

Such clusters (or platforms too, for that matter) require international cooperation and planning, much more cooperation in fact than either the present system or the 1977 plan, but the scheme of cooperation is very different from that of the 1977 plan.

FIGURE 15.1
Reuse of Four Beams

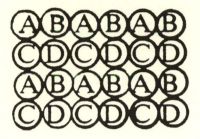

Clusters or platforms minimize the problem of orbit and frequency assignment, which is what the 1977 plan is all about. At the extreme, one could conceive of all the antennas on the geostationary orbit being at three locations, serving one third of the globe each.

A cluster or platform system solves the problems of orbit and frequency scarcity far better than anything else yet proposed, but to operate it would require something like Intelsat.

What is proposed is an elaborate engineering project requiring standardized switching, and agreement also on all sorts of other protocols. One could maintain the formality of national ownership of various pieces of the system such as antennas or satellites, just as at present, cable operators maintain the fiction of national ownership half way across the ocean. But just like a cable, it really has to operate as one system.

I don't want to suggest that this is the final satellite system that technologists will devise. New developments will undoubtedly make what I have just said obsolete, just as the 1977 scheme is now obsolete.

We can draw some lessons about planning from all of this, nonetheless. Planning is undoubtedly necessary, but its results are almost always wrong. It tends to freeze obsolete systems into use. Given these weaknesses of planning, good planning generally defers decisions as long as possible. It keeps options open as long as possible. The decisions that do have to be made should be as narrow as possible.

Of course, the words "as possible" in the above conclusions are weasel words that camouflage inevitability of differences of opinion on specifics. One person will feel that the time has come when a planning decision is inescapable. Another will disagree. There is no way to eliminate such differences. We are discussing principles. And I am arguing that the goal of integrated planning is wrong. The right principle is planning only when necessary.

ITU and UNESCO

Let me turn to my third and last example: ITU and UNESCO. Integrated planning would imply that these two very different organisations should coordinate more closely. That would be a disaster.

One of the things that has made ITU the success that it has been is its refusal to become involved in issues of content. The ITU is an engineering organisation. One would have to be incredibly naive not to recognize that hidden in much of the technical debate are the political interests and ideologies of the member countries. But to abandon the convention that political concerns must be hidden inside of technical arguments would vastly reduce the effectiveness of the organisation. Its podium would become the scene of propaganda debates. These explicit confrontations would reduce rather than increase the chance of agreement.

May I indulge in one more reductio ad absurdum. Do we want the ITU to try (like a McBride Commission) to tell the world's print press what sorts of things it should publish? Of course not!

But that is not such a reductio ad absurdum. The technology of the print press and of electronic publishing is rapidly merging. News may be delivered by teletext, videotex, computer terminals, facsimile as well as from printing presses. So can advertisements. ITU will in any case have to deal with frequencies and with technical standards that these "newspapers" of the future require. If ITU allows itself to consider content along with technical requirements, what I called a reductio ad absurdum could end up being reality.

So let us keep our planners each working in their own specialized and narrow domains. Let us confine their bureaucratic imperialism rather than encouraging it by telling them to recognize the full implications of what they are doing and to plan in an integrated way.

Indeed it is true that everything affects everything. It is particularly true for communications. Communications occurs in every aspect of life. Nothing is done without communicating. The slogan "integrated communications planning" is a plea for communications specialists to claim a concern for education and health, race relations, and world peace.

In arguing against the wisdom of encouraging communications planners' claim to more power, I am not asserting that this unity of reality is untrue. On the contrary, I am asserting it is true. Communications really is everything. For scholars, for thinkers, for analysts, for organisations like the IIC, the implication is that they should draw their nets widely. They need to look at communications in an integrated way. For those with power, however, and that includes official planners, the implications are the reverse.

The whole history of freedom consists of efforts to confine authorities to their strictly restricted domains. Bills of rights and constitutions have denied to power holders their plea that power over one domain may be used to control some other. Religious authorities often wish to extend their moral concerns to the regulation of business and politics, while political authorities consider that their responsibility for the national interest gives them the right to require religious conformity. Walls against that kind of integrated view have been built in all free societies; but these are walls only on the exercise of authority. No one denies that religion, politics, and business have implications for each other.

Reality is truly one whole. Those of us who describe reality, but forgo the right to plan what others do, need not avoid looking at the truth of integration as it is. The IIC [International Institute of Communications, the sponsor of the 1980 meeting for which this paper was prepared—LE], to use our organisation as an example, should be concerned about communications and health, communications and education, communications and racial equality, communications and development, communications and world peace. From such integrative perspectives we may judge and criticize what communications planners are doing. But let us not engage in the fantasy that if we can get some all-wise philosopher kings to plan communications in all its complexity, they will rule us better. Communications planners are in the first place not philosopher kings, and, furthermore, in a good society—contrary to what Socrates thought—even philosopher kings should have their authority narrowly confined.

16

Technology and Confusion: The Satellite Broadcast Controversy in the U.N.

On November 9, 1972, by 102 to 1, the U.N. General Assembly referred a Soviet draft convention on television broadcasting from satellites for consideration by its Committee on the Peaceful Uses of Outer Space. The minority of one was the U.S. The issue itself was unimportant, but we may well wonder what produced that outcome.

One cause was the changed character of the U.N. In the heyday of its democratic idealism, in 1948, the U.N. General Assembly adopted the Universal Declaration of Human Rights, of which Article 19 said:

> Everyone has the right to freedom of...expression; this right includes freedom...to seek, receive, and impart information and ideas through any media and regardless of frontiers.

By the 1970s a new majority of states thought less of individual rights than of the wishes of governments. In 1972 UNESCO, an organization originally created to promote free cultural exchange, adopted a Declaration of Guiding Principles on the Use of Space Broadcasting which contained such injunctions as:

II.   2. Satellite broadcasts shall be essentially apolitical.

VI.   2. Every country has the right to decide on the content of the educational programmes broadcast by satellite to its people.

IX.   1. It is necessary that States...reach or promote prior agreements concerning direct satellite broadcasting to the population of countries other than the country of origin...
      2. With respect to commercial advertising, its transmission shall be subject to specific agreement between the originating and receiving countries.

For *Foreign Affairs* (1975), unpublished.

That passed 55 to 7 with the U.S. in the minority.

That same year at the U.N., the Soviet Union, not satisfied with an unenforceable UNESCO declaration, introduced its draft convention on direct satellite broadcasting. Two years later, the debate continues, though moderated somewhat by some increased sophistication on both sides.

The new atmosphere in the U.N. is not the whole explanation of those one-sided votes and certainly not the explanation of any recent steps back from polarization. The story of the direct satellite broadcast controversy is also the story of how difficult it is for political bodies to understand technical complexity. To a large extent the debate has been about imaginary technological dangers unrelated to reality.

To laymen or science fiction enthusiasts, satellite broadcasting may be a prospect without limit. From the time of the first Sputnik, writers have foreshadowed the day when TV pictures beamed from space could bring education and cultural exchange into TV sets in every village, desert, island, and city of the world. "With the help of a large Sputnik," said Soviet Prof. S. Katayev in December, 1957, "Moscow television programs could easily be relayed not alone to any point in the Soviet Union, but also far beyond its borders." (In those days, when the Soviets dominated outer space, they did not yet argue that such outer space activities might become a dangerous intrusion.) Arthur Clarke, in an oft-quoted remark, talked of the technical means to "drag the whole planet out of ignorance" and Sulwyn Lewis in a UNESCO pamphlet said, "Dramatic could be the satellites' contribution to world education, because of the great superiority of their television relay over the ordinary direct transmission between ground stations.... With a single satellite, one-third of the earth's surface can be reached." The U.S. information effort, too, sought every occasion to magnify the achievements of the American space effort. It became hard to doubt that if the Americans could put a man on the moon they could put a picture on a TV set anywhere on earth.

The technical realities are distinctly more complex. Satellite broadcasting is not all of one piece and not everything is equally feasible. There are at least five distinctions that anyone discussing the question should understand.

1. First and most important is the distinction between broadcasting from a satellite *direct* to the viewer's TV set vs. *redistribution,* that is, transmission from the satellite to a ground station which then retransmits to the home set.

There is actually a finer graduation. At one end is the present system of redistribution satellites which transmit to great regional dish antennas in ground stations costing hundreds of thousands or millions of dollars. Such expensive sophisticated equipment on the ground requires less power and less focused beaming capability in space. Alternatively, at substantial cost for larger and more advanced satellites one can have smaller ground stations, down eventually to so-called community antennas. There is debate about their likely costs, but whether they cost $1,000 or $10,000 they are too expensive to put in every peasant hut or even in every American home as an adjunct to a $150 TV set, but not too expensive to put one in each village, or in each school, or CATV system head-end, or even on an apartment house. That is still not direct broadcasting and it still gives local authorities in undemocratic countries power to control what will be transmitted from the antenna and thus what individuals receive.

The next step, that to direct broadcasting to the home, requires a still more sophisticated satellite and a still cheaper antenna and adapter. Again the possible price is arguable with claims as far apart as $40 to $500 or most likely $200—$300. That is called direct broadcasting to augmented receivers. The last step, not within the realm of realistic possibility in this era, is direct broadcasting to unaugmented receivers.

For the United States a satellite regional redistribution system for TV would cost between 50 and 100 million dollars, a system broadcasting to say 10,000 community receivers might cost about 200 million dollars, a direct broadcast system to augmented receivers well over 10 billion dollars. Clearly the third alternative is not going to be chosen.

2. The wavebands used for broadcasting must be distinguished. The spectrum is a scarce resource, and TV uses large chunks of it. (One can put about 1,000 telephone circuits in the bandwidth required for one TV transmission.) Various segments of the spectrum are allocated by ITU agreements and by national policies to different purposes. Not all frequency bands are equally desirable for all purposes.

The TV sets in any given country are built to receive certain assigned wavelengths. To broadcast from a satellite to a country one would either (a) have to find an unused TV broadcast wavelength, which is unlikely; (b) broadcast illegally using an otherwise assigned band, interfering with local broadcasts; or (c) broadcast in a novel region of the spectrum in which there is unused space, and distribute or sell adapters to the public to attach to their sets to make that wavelength receivable.

ITU rules require prior coordination if the frequency to be used will have a harmful effect on radiocommunication services in a receiving country. Thus even without further agreements restricting the contents of satellite broadcasts, it is already the case that legal direct satellite broadcasting requires coordination between sender and receiver about the frequencies to be used.

3. An important distinction is between intended broadcasting and spillover. There is no feasible way to prevent some Canadians from being in the range of U.S. television, nor some Israelis in the range of Jordanian, nor some Estonians in the range of Finnish; and similar border spillover will occur with satellite broadcasting too. Borders do not follow the orderly curves of radiation limits. In the U.N., as in the ITU, those countries that wish to control satellite broadcasting have gradually come to recognize this fact and now generally address their proposals to controlling *intended* transmission from one country to another, for example, a TV Free Europe, not spillover from a country's legal domestic use of its assigned wavelengths.

4. There are orbiting satellites and satellites in geostationary orbit 22,300 miles above the equator. In that location a satellite orbits at the same speed as the earth rotates, thus staying always above the same point on earth. Only such satellites are practicable for direct broadcasting. There are a limited number of equatorial "parking spaces" for them; some of those locations are technically better than others. There will be a growing need for international cooperation in the assignment and use of those "parking spaces" and thus a strong motivation by all countries to use them in ways that will not invite cold war games of jamming and interference with a valuable and fragile asset.

5. A final, and very important distinction is between *cooperative* and *unwanted* direct satellite broadcasting. With cooperation between the receiving and sending countries (which may, of course, be the same country) direct satellite broadcasting to augmented receivers will clearly be technically possible in the near future. It may be economically absurd in most places, but in some places it will even make sense. For example, even if it costs $500 a set to provide TV reception to Eskimos in Alaska or to remote Indonesian islanders, it might be worth doing if the programs carry schooling to the children there. In general, satellite transmission to community antennas or to augmented individual sets makes social and economic sense where the population is sparse and where terrestrial broadcasting facilities do not yet exist. Under those circumstances one can by use of satellites avoid the investment required

to install terrestrial microwave relays and local transmitters. Satellite transmission can at one sweep cover a wide area indiscriminately, something which terrestrial transmission cannot do. On the other hand, to double or quadruple the cost of every set makes no sense whatever in densely populated areas with millions of sets, particularly if the terrestrial broadcasting facilities are already in place.

We can, therefore, conceive of direct satellite broadcasting being introduced to a few remote locations in the next decade, but only by a carefully developed plan in which the transmitting and receiving authorities cooperate to assure compatibility both of equipment and spectrum allocation. That is a *cooperative* effort. *Unwanted* broadcasting is another matter. It is hard to find a persuasive scenario by which a transmitting country could, against the wishes of the receiving country, broadcast to homes on any significant scale.

Unwanted direct TV broadcasting from satellites is thus probably a nonissue. It is not going to happen in any period that one can foresee. And yet it has become an intense psychological concern for many countries in the U.N. Why?

Among those who are alarmed by direct broadcast satellites (DBS), two important causes of concern emerge: technical unsophistication and the reality of concentration of power in space activities.

1. Evaluating technical facts: An endemic problem in policymaking is that those who must make decisions are in no position to judge the technical facts. Be it regarding energy, arms control, or communications policy, those who make the decisions and those who have the facts neither understand nor trust each other.

In this age of scientific marvels, laymen find technicians particularly noncredible when they denigrate their own capability. The magicmaker when he says he cannot perform as desired is suspect of protecting a covert interest. The physician who says he knows no cure is suspect of lazy evasion. The scientist who says pollution levels cannot be brought down far enough is suspect of serving industrial profiteers. In the DBS debate a widespread reaction to those who minimize the prospects of DBS has been one of suspicious disbelief. The argument begins "if you can put a man on the moon, then..." And to detailed explanations of technical problems, the laymen's reply is that these problems may vanish with scientific breakthroughs.

The technical limitations on the prospects of DBS are only vaguely sensed by the diplomats who have to deal with the issue. The United States sends large delegations to meetings of the Committee on the

Peaceful Uses of Outer Space and to its Working Group on Direct Broad-cast Satellites; among them are technically qualified people. The Ca-nadians have good technical back-up in Ottawa. From most of the other countries the representatives are international lawyers or members of the permanent U.N. delegation, and rarely do they have an independent judgment on technical issues.

So one reason why the DBS panic has reached such intensity in nor-mally sober circles has been the sense of uncomprehended magic with which it, as all satellite activities, is viewed. And the magic is not in neutral hands. It is the monopoly of one space power, the U.S.

2. Concentration of power: Until April, 1974, the United States was the only power that had been able to put a satellite into geostationary orbit. Canada has a domestic communication satellite, Anik, up two years before the U.S., but it is a Hughes satellite launched by NASA. The Soviet Union puts men in space, and has the Orbita communica-tion satellite system in daily practical use, but until April, 1974, it had not achieved synchronous orbit. Clearly, however, the U.S. monopoly will not last. Nonetheless for other countries it offers little satisfaction that someday soon two superpowers will each be able to offer them communication services for hire.

Given its monopoly position, the United States has been more than normally sensitive to the nationalist pride of other nations. The United States could have put a satellite up and treated the world as customers. The U.S. need never have accepted Intelsat, a genuinely international organization with a flexible voting arrangement that gradually reduces U.S. power. So too, ERTS, the earth resources satellite program, pro-vides all its information to any country that asks. But the subject of our concern is not whether the U.S. has been virtuous; it is how others feel. That is more affected by the imbalance of power than by how well the monopolist behaves.

Fear of technological magic and fear of a superpower's influence are the reasons for worldwide concern about direct satellite broadcast-ing. The pattern differs from country to country. Let us consider the U.S. position and that of three groups of countries: The Soviet bloc; the developing countries; Canada, Sweden, and France.

1. The U.S. position: The American goal has been to maximize ulti-mate opportunities for satellite usage. This has led to procrastination regarding DBS regulation. Rules that seem reasonable now may well turn out to burden developments that are now unforeseen. Until abuses of satellite broadcasting appear, the United States government has seen no reason to act against them.

Furthermore, the American position is predicated upon the belief that the free flow of information across borders is a good, not an evil. In any case, under our Constitution, it is not for the government to act as censor.

Thus the American position has been to make satellites, outer space, and information flows via them accessible to all on the freest possible terms. We have acted to make NASA launch capabilities, ERTS resource mapping capabilities and Intelsat communication capabilities available to all.

In the last year, however, the United States has been forced by its isolation to move from opposing any regulatory agreement to favoring adoption by the U.N. of general principles about the conduct of satellite broadcasting, but principles that support free flow of information, not its restriction. Behind the new international consensus that some statement of principles should be adopted there remains continued divergence as to what that statement should be. American opposition to any restrictive or binding instrument remains firm.

2. The Soviet position: One Soviet motive for presenting a convention on DBS was undoubtedly to seize a target of opportunity where the votes were against the U.S.

A more specific Soviet motive may be to create a precedent against short-wave broadcasting. The Soviet draft convention and also their more recent statement of principles is worded to refer exclusively to "direct television broadcasting with the help of artificial earth satellites." By keeping the DBS issue cleanly focused on TV, and not simultaneously reaffirming their long-held view that short-wave political broadcasting is a violation of international law, the Soviets can count on support, much of which would only be jeopardized by a broader attack on cross-border broadcasting, a practice in which most nations (the Soviets included) engage. However, Soviet arguments, both in the U.N. and in publications, are based on broad principles of sovereignty, not on special problems of TV. Scattered throughout their speeches are occasional acerbic references to short wave broadcasts described, for example, as "centres of misinformation the prototypes of which may be Radio Liberty, Radio Free Europe, the Voice of Israel, and some others sowing misinformation and slander."

The basic principle of the proposed convention and of the Soviet statement of principles is that of prior consent: No country should be broadcast into unless it agrees to it in advance. The theoretical basis for requiring such consent is the doctrine of sovereignty. If once accepted in the DBS context, the notion that sovereignty implies prior consent to broadcasts would apply equally to short-wave radio.

There is, in addition, a third possible Soviet motive for concern about DBS. Only about three-quarters of the Soviet population live in areas with adequate TV reception: in those areas, penetration is essentially complete, with over 40 million sets in the public's hands. There is increasing evidence, however, that the unreached portions of the USSR population are not going to be reached soon by any announced extension of microwave and ground relay stations. The growth in numbers of TV sets has for the first time slackened, a normal saturation phenomenon. A number of Soviet publications have referred to coverage of remote Siberian areas by direct satellite transmission. In short, there are indications that the Soviets may have a plan for creating a DBS system of their own for their remote sparsely settled areas. Perhaps, if they have such a plan, they are concerned that once the dish antennas are installed there, and once the augmented receivers are in place, the United States would seize the opportunity to broadcast to them. Thus Soviet motives for seeking to regulate direct broadcasting include a generalized fear of American efforts at penetration, on the model of Radio Free Europe and Radio Liberty.

3. The Third World position: What the developing countries fear is what has come to be called cultural imperialism. Broadcast satellites, they often believe, will impose an American commercial and alien culture upon them. The basic document for the First Arab Conference on Space Communication (Amman, September 23—26, 1972) asks:

Are we...—the developing countries—threatened to become the scapegoat of such space propaganda machinery which is controlled by the major states?

The ministers of education of the Andean states in Latin America rejected in 1970 a U.S. originated proposal for an educational satellite—the Cavisat project. A resolution said:

Unilateral management of transmissions by satellite, either by state or by nongovernmental entities, can easily be misused to disturb the habits, the standards of values and cultures of the receiving countries.

In the 1972 debates of the First Committee of the General Assembly on the Soviet draft convention, the theme of cultural imperialism surfaced often.

Diaz-Casaneuva (Chile): A great Power...employing subterfuge and fallacy and appealing to a false conception of what is known as "freedom of information" seeks to consolidate its domination over the passive masses of the dependent or underdeveloped nations. (1867, pp. 47–51)

We are justified in wondering what it might mean to the people of Latin America to be bombarded by imperialist monopolies through direct television broadcasting, by means of artificial earth satellites, freed of all and any control and without any thought given to international law. (1867, p. 56)

Pohl (El Salvador): Under the impact of these new technical resources the underdeveloped nations might suffer a crisis of historical and cultural identity...they would be left with nothing of their own and would be following blindly in the footsteps of the developed countries. (1862, p. 7)

Azzout (Algeria): Television broadcasting by satellites raises the question of the preservation of the cultural heritage of peoples and the originality of our national cultures...

The USSR may, on occasion, initiate action, but unless it appeals to third-world fears it does not have the votes. Indeed some delegations have supported the Soviet initiative more as a barrier to Communist propaganda than American. Such are the shadows in the nightmare world that DBS has conjured up.

4. The positions of Canada, Sweden, and France: Fears are not limited to third world countries. Sweden, Canada, and France have been leading promoters of restrictions on satellite broadcasts. They too view with alarm the prospect of American commercial TV competing with their public broadcasting. For Canada the concern is realistic, though unrelated to satellites. It is cable television that is competing with the Canadian broadcasting companies. One-third of Canadian television homes are already served by CATV or about 40 percent of those in locations where cable is available. Eight out of ten Canadian TV viewers (including those on the border who can receive U.S. stations over the air) can and often do watch the U.S. commercial networks. Nationalists resent this. The president of the CBC has called cable a "brutal technological revolution."

It is ironical that satellites have become an object of debate about results that are due not to them, but to other technologies, such as transportable videotapes and CATV. Democratic Canada does not claim, as do many countries, the right to censor what its citizens choose to receive. In large numbers they do choose to watch material to which social policy objects. It would be politically unacceptable in democratic Canada to ban such materials; but satellite broadcasting, as a mere symbol on the horizon, with no clientele because it does not yet exist, is an ideal object for raising the issue of cultural dominance by the colossus to the South. The issue is thus raised without confronting the thorny implication of depriving anyone of their chosen programs.

Small culture areas, like Sweden's, are particularly vulnerable to cultural intrusion. TV, transmitted several hours a day, 365 days a year, is a voracious consumer of expensive production. No small country or linguistic area can produce enough good programming to fill that time. The solution is to import. Imports constitute one-third of CBC's programming and of Sweden's and about half of Latin America's, but only 1 percent of U.S. network broadcasts and 5 percent of central Soviet broadcasts.[55] While U.S. dominance in program exports is declining, American productions are by far the largest number bought. That fact bothers cultured, idealistic, didactic public servants of the sort who control many of the European public broadcasting monopolies. Such welfare-oriented Swedes, for example, do not find it attractive to offer the world's airwaves to American violent commercial TV. Nor are they, as neutralists, inclined to recognize that cross-border broadcasting by Radio Free Europe or Radio Liberty has been a liberalizing and enlightening influence in the communist world. For them, that concedes too much to the cold war.

Furthermore, Swedish representatives have found that by championing the case of the less developed nations against cultural imperialism, they have gained credit with the third world, something that neutral Sweden values.

But Sweden and Canada have not advocated the flatly restrictive position proposed by the Russians in their draft convention. The Soviet draft convention would require prior consent by the receiving country before TV could be legally transmitted from a satellite (Article V). It would also require specific consent to advertising (Article III), ban war propaganda, violence, pornography, and various other kinds of undesirable content (Articles IV and VI), and require that broadcasting be done only by organizations under government control (Article VII). Article IX states, "Any State party to this convention may employ the means at its disposal to counteract illegal television broadcasting of which it is the object, not only in its own territory but also in outer space and other areas beyond the limits of the national jurisdiction of any State." This last Article would seem to allow not only jamming but also destroying an offending satellite.

The Swedish-Canadian position seeks, rather, international agreement on a set of broad principles, not an enforceable convention. One of these principles would be prior consent. The main Swedish-Canadian goal, however, is to promote regional groupings of countries that would cooperate in developing satellite broadcasting in their regions.

France has taken a more restrictive position, resembling that of the Soviets and the Latin Americans. The French would adopt rules banning the broadcasting of "propaganda for war or which violates human dignity," "ads without prior consent of the receiving State," or "tendentious information." They would impose on news broadcasters "an obligation to reveal the sources of all information broadcast." The French motive may include protection of French cultural leadership in Francophone developing countries.

Other advanced democracies have increasingly moved towards positions of the Canadian-Swedish type. Australia, for instance, which had been one of America's few supporters in defense of the free flow of information, swung under its new Labor government to the principle of prior consent.

So, by 1973, the United States found itself essentially alone. To meet this isolation, the American representatives at the Fifth Working Group session in Geneva in March 1974 finally suggested the adoption of a draft set of principles on direct satellite broadcasting. Unlike the earlier Soviet and French proposals, these would have no binding power, and unlike the Canadian and Swedish proposals, the principles proposed do not include prior consent. This American move was well received. The Japanese (who are experimenting with community antenna-type reception) and the British were favorable. But the central issue of prior consent vs. free flow of information remains. The issue has now been referred from the Working Group to the Legal Subcommittee of the Committee on Peaceful Uses of Outer Space where presumably over many months or years, and perhaps unsuccessfully, an attempt will be made to hammer out a document.

Alternatives for American policy: What difference does America's isolation on this issue of satellite broadcasting make and what are the American options?

It can be argued that the matter makes almost no difference. The Committee on the Peaceful Uses of Outer Space and its subcommittees and working groups have a tradition of proceeding by consensus. They never vote. The General Assembly could, nonetheless, adopt a resolution, but it would have no binding force. Even a convention would mean little if the prime space power declined to sign it.

Furthermore, as we have already seen, unwanted direct satellite broadcasting is a symbolic, not a real, issue. For all the intensity of the fears that are expressed today, for all the posturing about it in international debates, it will not occur in the relevant future. Ten years hence the

U.N. committees may still be seeking consensus on things that no one has seen and which have never happened. Hopefully, with time the discussions would grow more realistic, focusing on technologies that actually emerge, such as cooperative satellite broadcasting, occasionally direct, but more often to community antennas.

Yet, for the U.S. to disregard the genuine, if misaimed, concerns about cultural imperialism that DBS stirs may be shortsighted. Important precedents and principles are being laid down in the debate about DBS even if in the end it proves to be a fantasy. Direct satellite broadcasting is but one instance of a phenomenon of increasing frequency: a new technology with impacts that leap national frontiers. Pollution, ocean resources, and energy share this trait with satellite broadcasting. Exaggerated insistence on sovereignty makes all these problems hard to handle.

Furthermore, the precedents set on DBS affect the free flow of information in a variety of ways. Acceptance by the U.S. of the principle of prior consent would be untenable and presumably unconstitutional. The American government would, if it accepted that rule, be bound to prevent persons in the United States from transmitting messages via satellite that other countries chose not to accept. Our government would be in the position, not only of enforcing our own laws against libel, sedition, unfair balance, and copyright violation, that is, laws that conform to our First Amendment, but also the laws and policies of the receiving country. That is not a posture that the United States government can assume.

The Soviet and some other delegations have recognized that the prior consent rule, which they advocate, is incompatible with the American practice of leaving the content of what is broadcast in the private domain, not subject to control by the government. To avoid such devolution of responsibility they propose to affix responsibility on governments for whatever is broadcast. That too is clearly incompatible with the U.S. conception of freedom of the press. While the First Amendment may carry no weight for them, there is a broader conception of freedom to which the United Nations is historically committed. That is the tradition enshrined in the Universal Declaration of Human Rights and in the UNESCO idea of the free flow of information. For a U.N. body to endorse governmental control over what individuals in one country say to individuals in another via satellite or via any other means, would be a substantial reversal of that tradition. In the years since World War II, the ever widening channels of international communication have been a major instrument both for modernization and for liberalization in authoritarian lands. Short-wave broadcasting, used by virtually every major nation, has been the main source of understanding of what was going on abroad for dissidents in countries as disparate as the Soviet Union and South Africa. Sociological studies have found foreign broadcasts, scientific and cultural exchange and foreign trade to be major contributors to modernizing attitudes and practices in developing countries. UNESCO has promoted intellectual contact. It has tried to reduce the burden of customs duties and similar restrictions on books and other products of culture. The U.N. has provided a way for complainants in dependent territories to get their message out to the world.

Thus, quite aside from what kind of document the U.S. as one country could sign, there is a strong case to be made under the established traditions of the community of nations for the undesirability of a precedent for burdening the flow of messages between peoples with governmental controls.

Nonetheless, there are certain kinds of regulations that stem inexorably from the peculiar nature of electronic media. From the beginning of broadcasting it has been recognized that the scarcity of spectrum and the problem of interference make some rules necessary that are not needed for print. The ITU emerged as a rare example of an international organization that operates in a technical regulatory domain. For satellite broadcasting, as for other broadcasting, international agreements, noninterference, sharing of resources, and respect by others for each nation's use of its air are essential for orderly use of the scarce spectral resource.

Indeed, in the satellite broadcasting era that becomes truer than ever. The nations of the world recognized in the international Convention on the Peaceful Uses of Outer Space that the playing of tactical games with each other's satellites and with satellite communications would only deprive each other and the world of valuable assets. So far the nations of the world have behaved well in outer space. There is every reason to believe that agreements at the technical level can continue to be reached in the U.N. and ITU by nations mutually interested in avoiding being provocative to each other in their use of satellites. Technical agreements are easier to reach than agreements about the content of the messages transmitted. Often the same goals of amicable communication can be reached by technical cooperation, as well as, or better than, by substantive regulation of content.

Agreements on technical cooperation offer the best prospect for avoidance of confrontation that would follow from the legalistic and unrealistic pursuit of prior consent. Since for technical reasons direct broadcasting of TV programs seems unlikely without cooperation by receiving countries, it seems reasonable for the family of nations to affirm the general principle that cooperation is the optimal way to implement satellite broadcasting. That kind of affirmative stance in contrast to negative legalistic prohibitions corresponds to the U.S. desire to encourage satellite usage. However, such a stance becomes persuasive only insofar as its advocates are ready to take concrete actions to provide satellite communication capacity for shared uses. The design of the system, and the organization and funding of it determine far more than do verbal generalities whether the satellite broadcast system will serve the educational and developmental needs of LDCs and the communication needs of the U.N., or whether these social uses for satellites will be disregarded in fact.

An example of a matter on which technical cooperation can serve better than restrictions on content is meeting the legitimate resentment by less developed countries of the one-sidedness of the flow of communications in the contemporary world. It is already true without satellites that most of the world's news services are based in the U.S., Europe, and the Soviet Union, that 40 percent of translations of books are from English and another 35 percent from French, German, and Russian, that the largest single group of TV program exports are from the U.S., and so on for most media.

Restrictions on nonexistent direct satellite broadcasting or adoption of rules for prior consent will not improve the balance. Such rules will not create any new flow of information either among the LDCs or from them to the rest of the world.

On the other hand, if attention is given to it, satellites services can be designed to serve the needs of the LDCs. Small, cheap local ground stations and the development of satellites appropriate to them can provide communication to and from villages far sooner and more cheaply than could be done by way terrestrial microwave relays or cables. Such a system of satellite broadcasting designed for community antennas rather than for either large regional ground stations or augmented individual receivers is the kind that has been discussed for education in India, Brazil, Indonesia, Africa, the Andean countries, and Alaska. An experiment is currently starting in India.

Hardware alone, even if designed to meet the communication needs of the LDCs, will not assure that the communication flow is two way. To help redress the balance requires organized political and social arrangements to encourage broadcasting originating outside the leading powers. One possibility is for the U.N. itself to have a transponder. The U.N. could provide a world news and TV channel designed to pick up the story of the developing world from all over and to relay it, in many languages, to the nations of the world. This would be a new and different international source of programming to help balance the ones presently available.

American delegations have, on many occasions, indicated a receptiveness to plans for handling satellites in ways that would enhance their value to the using countries. However, without a strong constituency in the U.S. to push any particular action, those expressions have remained but invitations to proposals by the rest of the world. To place all the responsibility for designing practical uses for satellite broadcasting on countries without scientific and technical experience in space communications is unrealistic. The United States needs to actively promote plans that will put satellite communications at the service of shared international, cultural, and informational goals. Through satellites modern information and library services can be made available at low cost to the poorer lands. Satellites can provide low cost two-way exchanges for education and entertainment. The active pursuit of such mutually advantageous activities to the point at which satellite communications have become familiar, useful services, not an ill-understood cloud on the horizon, is the most effective remedy for misperceptions of DBS.

17

From Gutenberg to Electronics: Implications for the First Amendment

Free speech and free press enjoy more judicial protection today then ever before. The right of protesters to picket, of advocates to parade, and of journalists even to libel public figures are sedulously protected by the Supreme Court. Not since before the Civil War have antidemocratic movements had so few members and so little influence. And yet, perhaps, some day, looking backwards, we may see this era as one in which the First Amendment was undermined. The problem stems from a failure of the law to reflect how electronics is taking over the technology of communication.

Except for conversation, any communication requires some technical infrastructure: sheets for paraders; paints for artists; paper, presses, and postal service for publishers; spectrum for broadcasters; transmission circuits, switchboards, and terminals for telephone and telegraph. Some infrastructure elements are dispersed, disaggregated, easy for each communicator to own and operate for himself—a copying machine, for example. Other elements are by nature a single system for a whole society—a telephone network for example.

We may in our minds picture polar types of infrastructure: at one end private facilities lending themselves to free speech by being distributed to many owners, each to use as he sees fit, and at the other end collective goods compatible with free speech only if users have access to the monopoly, unrestricted and uncontrolled. Real-world communications systems are mixtures. Publishers own their printing presses which under the First Amendment they use as they will but their product they distribute through the postal monopoly.

Historically, free speech gained or declined with the strategic dominance of dispersed or centralized structures. A monopoly service or

First published in *The Key Reporter* (1978).

rationed resource can be a weapon for social control, or conversely, diffusion of a communication device could promote individual expression. Printing, for example, was the seed of modern free speech and press; thousands of publishers could each publish independently. Electronic networks are different; it remains to be seen how a communications system embedded in them will be conducive to free speech or to controls.

The First Amendment was originally defined in conflicts about printing. American law takes account of a long British history of rules requiring licenses to publish, of taxes on publications, of criminal libel suits against critics of the government and also a history of protest against such censorial procedures by the mentors of American politics.

European authorities reacted to the printing press by enacting controls and censorship over the explosion of troublesome literature. (The Church's *Index Expurgatorius* was a sixteenth-century device, not a medieval one.) The British government at first allowed only members of a recognized guild to print, and only in the already established plants in the city of London and in Oxford and Cambridge. An act of 1643 requiring licenses for printing was protested in Milton's free-speech classic, the *Areopagetica*. American law adopted Milton's view of licensing publications as anathema; it is what the courts call "prior restraint" on speech, which is not allowed under the First Amendment.

Special taxes on the press, such as those levied in England for 150 years after the Licensing Act expired in 1693, have been overturned by the Supreme Court. Taxes on newsprint, on ads, and on newspapers themselves were used to raise the costs of a press that the government found obnoxious. The colonists protested just such a tax in 1765 in the stamp tax riots. So the American constitution as interpreted by the Supreme Court bars taxes on the press that do not apply equally to any business.

Throughout the eighteenth-century, journalists who attacked public officials might be prosecuted for committing "seditious libel." The printer Zenger, for example, in 1735 was accused of libelling Governor Cosby of New York. An obstreperous colonial jury acquitted him. The U.S. Supreme Court has now carried that libertarian position to the point of ordinarily denying public figures the right to sue for libel. So in the domain of print the First Amendment largely means what it says, that Congress can "make no law abridging freedom of speech, or of the press." But we have in this country a trifurcated communications system. Besides the domain of print, and of other means of communication that existed in the days of the nation's founding, such as the pulpit or the public meeting, there is also the domain of broadcast media. They live under a very different legal regime from print. The courts have justified that difference by a supposed scarcity of radio spectrum. Nature, the courts argue, precluded for broadcasting the freedom of access to spectrum that exists to the printing press. So broadcasters, selected by the government for merit (in its eyes), are assigned spectrum to use fairly and for community service (as publicly defined). The principles of common carriage and of the First Amendment have been applied to broadcasting in only atrophied form.

The third domain of communications is that of common carriers: the telephone, the telegraph, and the postal system. To them a third set of policies has been applied. In the process, electronic communication has lost the constitutional protections of no prior restraint, no licenses, no special taxes, no regulations, and no laws.

Every broadcaster must be licensed, a requirement begun in 1912, almost a decade before broadcasting, when radio was used mainly for maritime communication. Interference was bothering the Navy; to control it, licenses were required for radio transmitters. In America receivers (which cause no interference) were not licensed, but now satellite receivers are. Cable television, though it causes no over-the-air interference, is also licensed and regulated. The FCC controls which broadcast stations a cablecaster may, and must, carry. Until the courts blew the whistle, the rules even barred a pay channel from performing movies that were more than three or less than ten years old. Telephone bills are taxed. A computer network that offers communication services must be licensed, and will be only if it satisfies the government that it serves "the public necessity, interest, and convenience," including showing that the system will pay. Right now the FCC is engaged in a "computer enquiry." The Communications Act of 1934 requires it to license and regulate communications common carriers, but says nothing about computing. The FCC, therefore, is seeking a formula that will distinguish between a computer network used for computing (which is none of its concern) and one used for communication (which it is obliged to regulate). The problem is that they are indistinguishable. Computer code traveling from one terminal through computers to another is both computed and communicated whether the message is an airline reservation, or a mathematical sum, or a news story. Still, the FCC seeks a way to leave computing unregulated while licensing and controlling communications. The irony is that the Constitution has it the other way around. Congress's power stops at communication.

The mystery is how the clear intent of the Constitution, so well and strictly enforced in the domain of print, has been so neglected in the electronic revolution. Partly it is because the new communications devices started out not being seen as media of expression. An example was the very first electronic medium, the telegraph.

In court cases concerning telegraphy, the First Amendment is almost undetectable. The principles applied were those of commerce and railroads, not those of the printed word. The early telegraphs carried so few words at such high costs that people thought of them not as extensions of the self, but rather as business machines. British figures for 1854 show half of all messages related to the stock exchange and 31 percent more were commercial; the press disappeared in the 6 percent "others." But press traffic grew fast; by 1880 in the U.S. it was 11 percent of the business, a figure achieved in Britain in 1912. So the perception of the telegraph as a business machine with little in common with culture, learning or politics was even then a misperception. Yet it prevailed, and so the law applied to telegraphy was not that of the press, but that of the railroads.

As the railroads spread across the land, the doctrine of common carrier law evolved as a means to hold them to the public interest and prevent them from using their monopoly position to discriminate to their own advantage. As common carriers, they were required to serve all equally, at the same rates for the same service.

The new telegraph network had so much in common with the railroad network that the application of common carrier law seemed natural. Both networks were primarily instruments of commerce; both required the exercise of eminent domain to spread across private lands; both had monopolies over particular routes; both could discriminate if allowed to. So in 1886 Congress included in the Post Roads Act some remarkable privileges for telegraph companies, such as the right to run their lines freely along public roads and across pubic lands and to cut trees there for poles, but on condition that they operate like common carriers. The courts, too, saw the telegraphs as "instruments of commerce," required like other common carriers to provide service without discrimination.

That common carrier concept was certainly in the public interest, but what was missing from that purely commercial view was recognition that the telegraph was also an instrument of speech and press. For about the first decade of the telegraph that was an understandable misperception for neither the press nor the telegraph companies were sure that they were made for each other. They eyed each other with interest and jockeyed for position.

Even before the Washington-New York line was finished on June 7, 1846, newspapers had started experimenting with the telegraph. On May 12 of that year the *New York Tribune* started the first column of telegraph bulletins. They were as brief and condensed as possible because the cost was so high, sometimes a nickel a word, occasionally as low as two cents a word. Papers tried, as regular and important customers, to negotiate press rates, as low as 1/2 or 1/3 of normal. Individual newspapers, however, could not afford much telegraphic news. If the press was to use the new facility it would have to do so cooperatively; that led to the concept of a wire service: A.P. in 1848 and Reuters in 1851.

Telegraph companies, however, tried to become news services themselves. They sought to be not only carriers, but like broadcasters today, news publishers too. In the United States in the 1840s telegraph companies were offering news services to papers for $5 to $10 a week. Their bright young telegraphers located in every community doubled as reporters.

One telegraph company, the New York-Boston line, declined to carry the A.P.'s traffic. That sort of discrimination would have been important under any circumstances, but it was particularly important then (before the transatlantic cable) because ships from Europe with the news reached the Northeast before they reached New York—usually Halifax first. With access to the Boston-New York leg denied, A.P. would always lose the race to deliver European news. A.P.'s reply was aggressive and successful; they built a parallel telegraph line.

The same sort of battle was fought in Europe, and again won by the newspapers. The provincial newspapers to a large extent bought their news from the telegraph companies. Several of these British companies refused to carry stories from correspondents of single papers.

The discontent of the British press with dependence on telegraph companies led to nationalization of telegraphy in 1869. The Association of Proprietors of Daily Provincial Newspapers attacked the "despotic and arbitrary management" of the telegraph companies, and announced that they were forming their own cooperative press service. Parliament investigated, and in the end turned the domestic telegraphs over to the Post Office with the injunction that the Post Office have no part in collecting news.

However silent the courts, free press issues were there aplenty in telegraphy. For example, Western Union and A.P. later made an exclusive contract giving A.P. stories priority on the lines and freezing out competing press services and telegraph companies. These abuses, however, had been defined as commercial acts, and the government's response was commercial common carrier regulation.

Nonetheless, wherever means of communication are inherently central systems, the common carrier principle of equal treatment of all has given major protection to free speech. Still, such a regime is very different from that of widely diffused printing presses regarding which Congress may make "no law"; it is a regime with dangers. The temptation to use the central system for political control is there; so is the impulse to spread the monopoly over activities that might otherwise be diffused.

The history of the postal system illuminates the process. That history is a drama in three acts. In act 1, a monopoly is created for reasons of expanding, rather than controlling speech. In act 2 we see temptation to use the resulting power, until in act 3 the Supreme Court, as hero, rescues the Constitution.

Before the British Post Office began in the seventeenth century, the Crown farmed out patents for carrying its correspondence. To make these franchises attractive, those who won them were allowed to sell service to the public too, and no one else was allowed to compete. That scheme for cheap official communication established the postal monopoly.

To make ends meet, postmasters needed still other sources of revenue; publishing news was a natural one. Their post office distributed the paper, and was also a center to which news came, a matter of importance in an era before reporters had wire services. Also the postmaster was a political favorite; the government would let him publish.

It takes little imagination to guess, and guess rightly, that postmaster-publishers used their postal powers to discriminate against competing papers. A postmaster might not charge himself for carrying his own papers, and so began free or subsidized newspaper delivery, like today's second-class postage rates.

Getting the news was harder for a citizen in the eighteenth and early nineteenth centuries than it is today. The need was expressed by John Calhoun: "Let us conquer space," he wrote, "It is thus that a citizen of the West will read the news of Boston still moist from the press. The mail and the press are the nerves of the body politic." A main justification for having a federal postal system was to aid the dissemination of news. In 1832 90 percent of the bulk of the mails consisted of newspapers, though they provided only one-ninth of the revenue.

Postage for newspapers, under the first Post Office Act, was one cent each and every publisher was allowed to send a copy of his paper free to each other newspaper in the country—thus providing at public expense a primitive equivalent of a news service. From 1845 to 1847, local newspaper delivery was free within thirty miles. In 1851 free delivery was again voted, this time within the county of publication. When in the 1870s free mailing ended, very low second-class mailing rates continued.

Such federal help was crucial to the growth of the press, but such carrots, just as much as sticks, entailed visible dangers of government power. In 1792 Congress established monopoly in carriage of mail. In words of 1825, it forbade commercial transport of letters, packages, or other mailable matter "between places, from one to the other of which mail is regularly conveyed." The purpose was to shield government revenue from the impact of competition. But a carrier with a monopoly has a potential grip on what people can communicate.

In 1836 the Senate discussed the matter. President Jackson asked Congress to ban antislavery propaganda from the mails, but the Senate refused, concluding that Congress had no such power. Said Senator Calhoun,

> If it be admitted that Congress has the right to discriminate...what papers shall or shall not be transmitted by the mail, [it] would subject the freedom of the press, on all subjects, political, moral, and religious, completely to its will and pleasure.

In 1877, in *ex parte Jackson* (96 U.S. 727), however, the Supreme Court rejected Calhoun's argument; Congress it said, could decide what was mailable. A lottery operator named Jackson had been jailed for mailing tickets. Justice Field held that Congress could decide that lotteries were immoral and not to be sustained by postal service. But what of the danger of censorship? He resolved that dilemma by arguing that whatever materials the Post Office would not carry, citizens were free to deliver in any other way.

American views of postal monopoly have swung between the positions of Calhoun and Field; sometimes monopoly has been justified on the ground that it did not imply control of contents, and sometimes control of content has been justified on the ground that alternative channels existed.

From this confusion of doctrine, precedents resulted during the Victorian reform era both supporting monopoly and also control of what could be mailed. Moralism and meliorism were in the air. Proponents of all sorts of good causes, like temperance, labor, and women's suffrage were seeking to set wrongs right.

The use of the postal system for reform began in 1865 with the Comstock Act, named after the vice crusader. It barred obscene matter from unsealed mails and scurrilous epithets and devices from post cards. In 1868 and 1872 Congress barred illegal or fraudulent lotteries from the mails. Until then, the Post Office had been acting, in effect, as an accomplice in the violation of state laws. Four years later Congress banned all lotteries from the mails regardless of their legal status in a state. By 1888 the ban on obscenity had been extended to the contents of sealed mail. In 1890 came the most flagrant confrontation to freedom of the press; newspapers with lottery ads were banned from the mail.

At President Theodore Roosevelt's urging, the attorney general interpreted the seditious content of an anarchist journal as "indecent" and in 1911 Congress amended the law to define indecency to include "matters of character tending to incite arson, murder, or assassination."

In 1912 prize fight films were barred from the mails. In the 1930s enforcement of registration of securities by the SEC was facilitated by making it illegal to use the mails for selling unregistered securities.

By the time of World War II, the Post Office had acquired a manifold role in the control of communication. But at that point the court stepped back from the situation that it had created by accepting both a postal monopoly and the right of the federal government to determine what is mailable. The turning point was the case of Hannegan v. *Esquire* in 1945. Justices Brandeis and Holmes in a pair of earlier dissents, which are now the law, took exception to the view that citizens had any alternative to the postal service. In Hannegan v. *Esquire,* the Supreme Court embraced their doctrine. Postmaster Hannegan had tried to deny second class mailing privileges to *Esquire* on the grounds that that then somewhat raunchy magazine was not serving the public interest, the purpose for which Congress had granted low rates to periodicals. That, the court said, was not a matter for the postmaster general to determine. The postal system remains an essentially neutral highway on which all sorts of views may travel at will.

What we now begin to see is a new electronic superhighway on which all sorts of communication can travel. Newspapers and services already sell information not only on paper, but also through electronic systems like the *New York Times'* data bank. Library information is on-line in computerized retrieval systems. Printing is done by computer composition; reporters file their stories via electronic networks to their paper's computer, where it is edited, sent to composing machines to be printed, and also sent by facsimile to remote printing plants, and sent on-line to instant users. Electronic message systems are burgeoning. Politicians will have to learn to campaign with cassettes, CATV, and teleconferences, as well as by broadcasting. Education uses this highway too. Yet the electronic media of expression are tightly regulated as to who may provide what service to whom, which suggests a disturbing question: if virtually all communications become electronic, will the legal norm that governs them be the civil liberties tradition of the print media or the regulated tradition of the electronic media? As publishing becomes an electronic activity, will the producers of text find themselves under the same regulations that govern electronic communications? Inadvertently, a few decades hence, publishing may have ceased to be a realm free of government regulation. Publishers may end up like broadcasters today, with one eye constantly on government agencies.

18

Policies for Freedom

As computers become the printing presses of the twenty-first century, ink marks on paper will continue to be read, and broadcasts to be watched, but other new major media will evolve from what are now but the toys of computer hackers. Videodisks, integrated memories, and data bases will serve functions that books and libraries now serve, while information retrieval systems will serve for what magazines and newspapers do now. Networks of satellites, optical fibers, and radio waves will serve the functions of the present-day postal system. Speech will not be free if these are not also free.

The danger is not of an electronic nightmare, but of human error. It is not computers but policy that threatens freedom. The censorship that followed the printing press was not entailed in Gutenberg's process; it was a reaction to it. The regulation of electronic communication is likewise not entailed in its technology but is a reaction to it. Computers, telephones, radio, and satellites are technologies of freedom, as much as was the printing press.

Trends in Communications Technology

The technologies used for self-expression, human intercourse, and recording of knowledge are in unprecedented flux. A panoply of electronic devices puts at everyone's hand capacities far beyond anything that the printing press could offer. Machines that think, that bring great libraries into anybody's study, that allow discourse among persons a half-world apart, are expanders of human culture. They allow people to do anything that could be done with the communications tools of the past, and many more things too.

From *Technologies of Freedom* (1983).

The first trend to note is that the networks that serve the public are becoming digital and broadband. Today, the only broadband signal received by the ordinary household is its television picture. It is sometimes questioned whether there are any other uses for which an end-to-end broadband digital network available to every household and workplace will be demanded. Such a network would allow two-way transmission of high-definition pictures and text in whole volumes at a time, along with voice, videotex, and other low-speed services, but why should that be wanted? There are, indeed, good reasons. High-definition pictures are not just fun. As manual mail service gets less reliable and more expensive, the sending of magazines, catalogues, videotapes, and videodisks electronically rather than physically will become an attractive option. Nor is text delivered in whole volumes at a time just a luxury. Text a page or so at a time, even if it comes faster than one can read, is satisfactory for electronic mail or for retrieving pages one knows one wants, but it does not do for browsing. To use a terminal the way one uses a bookshelf or filing cabinet, one must be able to thumb randomly through thousands of pages. And when computers talk to computers, even though the size of the files they flip back and forth may be modest, a second is too long for them to wait; their bursty traffic requires large bandwidth for short periods. Millions of offices and homes may have computers and want bandwidth enough for them. So if people at home or work want high-definition moving pictures, if they desire two-way video for teleconferencing or teleshopping, if they wish to browse in libraries rather than just reading predefined pages, and if they compute, then the demand for end-to-end broadband networks will exist.

To serve the public, there will be networks on networks on networks. Separate nations will have separate networks, as they do now, but these will interconnect. Within nations, the satellite carriers, microwave carriers, and local carriers may be—and in the United States almost certainly will be—in the hands of separate organizations, but again they will interconnect. So even the basic physical network will be a network of networks. And on top of these physical networks will be a pyramid of service networks. Through them will be published or delivered to the public a variety of things: movies, money, education, news, meetings, scientific data, manuscripts, petitions, and editorials.

Another trend to note is toward increasing sophistication of the equipment on the user's own premises. Since the output and input of networks may be either printed on paper, shown on a screen, or declaimed in sound, the equipment needed on the customers' premises will be costly. Although the costs of computer logic, memory, and long-distance communication are falling, the uses that people want to make of them are expanding even faster. A $4,000 microcomputer can today do things that would have required a million-dollar computer a few years ago, when few would have predicted that millions of ordinary people would spend $4,000 for that home gadget. In the future, many millions of households will similarly desire large-size high-definition screens, cameras to originate video, and large memory devices to retain libraries of information for work and pleasure.

American industry is speculating that the percentage of disposable income spent on information activities will grow. Companies are positioning themselves to be in that industry. Banks like American Express and manufacturers like Westinghouse are investing in cablecasting; companies like Boeing are selling time-sharing services; and storekeepers like Sears Roebuck are experimenting with videodisk catalogues. Investors see the biggest dollar growth not in transmission or its hardware but in software and the equipment located on the customer's premises. This conclusion is what led AT&T to accept divestiture of its local phone companies in exchange for the freedom to sell information services and equipment to final customers. The science fiction version of the information work station of 2001 with beeps and sirens, flashing lights and video screens, may be fantasy, but the point is right: that is where expense will lie.

Paradoxically, big customers and decentralization will both gain from the development of more elaborate terminal equipment. However splendid may be the homeowner's equipment, it will be only a humble version of what will exist in plants and offices. Companies with information service and carrier billings in the millions will invest in their own networks, leased circuits, compression devices, and other marvelous gadgets designed to help them operate efficiently or cut costs. Depending on the structure of the vendors' and carriers' tariffs, different alternatives will pay off. One trade-off will be between buying communications capacity so as to improve management control and buying local processing power so as to cut communication costs. Trends between such centralizing and decentralizing alternatives may zigzag as technological and tariff changes affect relative prices, but the costs of computing equipment used to store data locally, to compress it, and to process it will probably fall farther and faster than the costs of transmission.

This trend favors decentralization. More and more will be done at the distributed nodes of networks to economize on transmission. That dispersion will be pushed farthest by big users, for they have the resources and technical capability to do so. When in large enterprises the competence and autonomy of scattered nodes are thus strengthened and their subservience to a center is thus lessened, the result, paradoxically, may be decentralization.

Another obvious trend is that with the new technologies, the world is shrinking. To talk or send messages across the world is coming to cost little more than communicating in one's own region. The charge for a call from New York to Los Angeles is now little more than for a call from New York to Albany. Both involve identical costs for the local loops and switches, for setting up the call, and for billing. The variable cost of extra microwave links is a minor item. With satellites, distance becomes almost totally unimportant. Patterns of human interaction will, as a result, change. There will be less cost constraint to do business, consult, debate, and socialize within one's own region only. There will be more freedom to do so with anyone anywhere with whom one finds affinity.

This development, along with the development of multiple technologies of communication and of cheap microprocessors, will foster a trend toward pluralistic and competitive communication systems. With hundred-channel cable systems, videocassettes, videodisks, ISDNs, and network links to thousands of on-line information services, there should be a diversity of voices far beyond anything known today. Telephone monopolies are being broken up. Before computers, phone administrations forbade connecting any "foreign attachment" to their network; today in the United States, Japan, Great Britain, and elsewhere, customers are being allowed to buy terminals at will and to attach them. Before microwave and satellite transmission, phone administrations had a monopoly in stringing wires from city to city, but these new nonwire transmission media are often managed by different enterprises. In the United States such competition already prevails in long-distance service, and local exchange service will not long remain completely monopolistic. Digital termination service, cellular radio, and cables carrying voice and data will all compete with the local phone company.

There is no reason to assume that the communications network of the future will be a single large organization with a central brain. It may be so, but it need not be. Having a hierarchical structure governed by a central brain is only one way to organize complex systems. A human being is organized that way; so is a nation-state. But the capitalist economy is not, nor is the complex system of scientific knowledge, nor is the ecological system of the biosphere. For an uncentralized system to function, there must be some established ways of interconnecting the parts other than by command; the interconnections may be managed by conventions, habits, or Darwinian processes. Capitalist property rights are enforced by laws; language is enforced by custom; creatures in the biosphere do not survive if they cannot metabolize other species.

An uncentralized set of communications systems can function as a single system only if traffic on each network can move through interfaces onto the other networks. The critical requirements are three: the right to interconnect, conformity to technical standards that make interfacing possible, and a directory system.

The variety and autonomy of networks for special groups and services may grow rather than decline, though most of them will interconnect with each other. Some of these networks will and others will not have their own central brains. The different kinds of communication—video, voice, and text; informational and emotive; public and personal—are likely to require differently designed networks, even if interconnected.

Digital technology promotes the trend toward distributed processing throughout the system and against a central brain. It is easier to convert one system of 0,1 pulses into another such system than it is to interface the analog memoryless communications systems of the past. A directory search in the absence of a single universal list is more likely to succeed if it uses intelligent digital devices that scan associative data structures at nanosecond speeds and that communicate with all nodes at the speed of light than if it is bound by the slower circuit switching of the past.

Perhaps the most remarkable trend to note is one whereby the artificial intelligence of computers will increasingly create and read many of the messages on the networks of the future. These computer-composed messages sent from computer to computer may mostly never be seen by a person at all. In an electronic funds transfer, only a few bits are needed to say debit an account by $27.50. Most of the traffic involves checking and rechecking to see whether the signature is authentic, whether money is available, and what balance is left.

The future of communications will be radically different from its past because of such artificial intelligence. If media become "demassified" to serve individual wants, it will not be by throwing upon lazy readers the arduous task of searching vast information bases, but by programming computers heuristically to give particular readers more of what they chose last time. Computer-aided instructional programs similarly assess students' past performance before providing the instruction they need. The lines between publication and conversation vanish in this sort of system. Socrates' concern that writing would warp the flow of intelligence can at last be set to rest. Writing can become dialogue.

Such are some technical features of the communications system that is emerging. Technology will not be to blame if Americans fail to encompass this system within the political tradition of free speech. On the contrary, electronic technology is conducive to freedom. The degree of diversity and plenitude of access that mature electronic technology allows far exceeds what is enjoyed today. Computerized information networks of the twenty-first century need not be any less free for all to use without let or hindrance than was the printing press. Only political errors might make them so.

Communications Policy

In most countries the constitution sets the framework for communications policy. America's basic communications policies are found in three clauses. Article 1, Section 8, gives Congress the power to establish post offices and post roads. The next clause gives Congress the power "To promote the Progress of Science and useful Arts, by securing for limited Times to Authors and Inventors the exclusive Right to their respective Writings and Discoveries." And the very first amendment prohibits Congress from passing any law abridging freedom of speech or of the press. This package of provisions provided publishers with the support they needed but barred the government from interfering with their free expression.

In the comparatively simple American society of the eighteenth century, when the media depended largely on the slowly changing technology of the printing press and when government consisted of the relatively spare mechanisms of the courts, Congress, and a tiny executive branch, communications policy issues were few. They arose most often from the ability of the government to use its fiscal powers both for and against the press. The American people did not oppose the government's use of its fiscal powers to support the press. The authorities did so through the postal system, official advertising, and sinecure appointments. The idea that government should stand at arm's length from the press developed later; the earliest federal policy was to foster the media. The other possibility that government might employ its coercive powers against the press was prohibited by the First Amendment.

As Congress, the executive branch, and the courts dealt with innovations in communications technologies and, during the two centuries following adoption of the First Amendment, sought to formulate policies appropriate to them, the Amendment's original principles were severely compromised. The three main decades of such change occurred at intervals a half-century apart. In the 1870s Congress and the courts extensively restructured postal policies, imposing censorious restrictions. Also in that decade, and shortly before it, the system of common carrier regulation of telegraphy evolved. Fifty years later, in the 1920s, radio broadcasting began. For that medium Congress required that broadcasters be chosen and licensed by the state. Then half a century later, in the 1970s, computer networks, satellites, and cable systems came into extensive use. Some of the regulatory responses to them seem quite unconstitutional.

Both the 1870s and the 1920s were decades of ambivalence about civil liberties. In the 1870s a rising reform movement about both morals and economics challenged the prevailing philosophy of laissez faire. Movements for temperance, prudery, voter registration, and labor protection clashed with ideas of minimal governance. Reformers pressed for acceptance of the regulation of mail as an instrument of censorship. The 1920s saw the Palmer raids, on the one hand, and the Brandeis-Holmes dissents and decisions, on the other. The sensitivity of the Supreme Court to the First Amendment, starting in the 1920s and particularly after World War II, led it to blow the whistle and stem the trend toward postal censorship.

It was in the 1920s, however, that communications policy in the United States most seriously lost its way. Without adequate thought, a structure was introduced for radio which had neither the libertarian features of the common carrier system nor those of the free market. The assumption of the new system was that spectrum was extremely limited and had to be allotted to chosen users. In Europe the chosen user was generally the government itself; in America it was private licensees. Since only a few would be privileged to broadcast, government felt it must influence the character of what they broadcast. The broadcasting organizations, unlike common carriers, selected and produced programs, but unlike print publishers, who also select what appears, there was no free entry for challengers. So government stepped in to regulate the radio forum and shape the broadcasters' choices.

By this process of evolution there came to be three main communications structures in the United States: the print model, free of regulation in general; the common carrier model, with government assuring nondiscriminatory access for all; and the broadcasting model, with government-licensed private owners as the publishers. The choice between them is likely to be a key policy issue in the coming decades. A convergence of modes is upsetting what was for a while a neatly trifurcated system. Each of the three models was used in its particular industries and for different types of communications. As long as this was the case, the practices in some industries might be less true to the First Amendment than the practices in others, but it did not much affect those media that remained in the domain of the First Amendment. What happened in one industry did not matter greatly for what happened in another.

If this situation were a stable one, there would not be much cause for worry, for if the nation retained a free printed press through which all viewpoints could be expressed, it would not lose its freedom even if broadcasting were totally government controlled. Having print as an island of freedom might be assurance enough against total conformity to authority. But the situation is not stable.

Very rapidly all the media are becoming electronic. Previously the print media were affected, but not themselves transformed, by the electronic media. The electronic media grew and enlarged their field of action but left the older media fundamentally what they had been before. This is no longer the case. With electronic publishing, the practices of the electronic media become practices of the print media too. No longer can one view electronic communications as a circumscribed special case whose monopolistic and regulated elements do not matter very much, because the larger realm of freedom of expression still encompasses all of print. Telecommunications policy is becoming communications policy as all communications come to use electronic forms of transmission.

Soon the courts will have to decide, for vast areas that have so far been quite free of regulation, which of the three traditions of communications practice they will apply. The facts that will face the courts will be a universally interconnected electronic communication system based on a variety of linkable electronic carriers, using radio, cable, microwave, optical fiber, and satellites, and delivering to every home and office a vast variety of different kinds of mail, print, sound, and video, through an electronic network of networks. The question is whether that system will be governed as are the regulated electronic media now, or whether there is some way of retaining the free press tradition of the First Amendment in that brave new world.

Resource Constraints

Historically, some media operate by different rules under the First Amendment from those applied to publications in print because of the existence of scarcities in the resources used in producing them. Abundance and scarcity of resources are the two ends of a continuum. At one end, communication is entirely unconstrained by resources; in the middle are situations in which there is constraint, but everyone can nonetheless have some ration of the means to communicate; and at the other end the constraints are such that only a privileged few can own those means.

Conversation illustrates the optimal situation in which communication is totally without resource constraints; the only limit is one's desire. There is also sidewalk enough in most places that anyone can picket a building without excluding others from passing by, though not when hundreds want to picket in the same place at once. In practice there is no resource bar to forming a congregation to worship together, as witnessed by storefront churches and congregations that meet in members' homes. Similarly anyone can send a petition or write a letter of protest. The property required to carry out these acts is trivial.

Even in such domains, where normally anyone can communicate at will without noticeably reducing the opportunities for others, there are exceptional situations in which one person's wants do constrain others. Conversation may be abundant, but conversation with a particular partner is an imposition on that person. Assemblage as a congregation can be almost costless if in a member's home, but building a large church on a desirable lot is not. In each of these situations the cliché formula is that people have the right to do as they wish, so long as they do not interfere with the rights of others. But communication in such situations involves so few resource constraints that no special institutions are set up to deal with them.

The situation is more complex when the resources for communication, while not unlimited, are available enough that by reasonable sacrifice and effort a person can get hold of some. In this situation allocation by the institutions of property and the market becomes a useful norm. An example is the printed magazine. Even the poor, by scrimping and cooperating, can produce periodicals, and some of them do. There are church bulletins for modest congregations, labor and protest papers, adolescent club and school papers. There are thousands of little magazines with stories and poems by unknown amateurs. To convert a publication into a success requires talent, capital, and energy; if the talent and energy are there, the capital may even be borrowed.

In such situations of moderate scarcity, however, not all people can have whatever means of communication they want. The means are rationed. The system of rationing may or may not be equitable or just. There are an infinity of ways to partition a scarce resource. The method may be strictly egalitarian, as that which requires all legal candidates to be offered the same amount of air time under the same terms during an election campaign. The method may be meritocratic, as that which gives free education to those who score high in exams. The method may recognize privilege, as that which allows a descendant to inherit a communications medium or a seat in the House of Lords. The method may recognize cultural values, as that which occurs when a foundation makes grants to museums or symphonies. The method may reward skill and motivation, as that which allows communications institutions to earn profits that depend on their efficiency.

Each of these criteria for allocation has its value, and actual public policy represents different mixes of them. Equality may have both rhetorical appeal and a great deal of merit. Yet few people would opt for totally equal access to scarce means of communication, quite independent of considerations of talent, motivation, or social value in their use.

Property rights in the means of communication are a major method of allocation, but different property schemes produce different allocations. In some property schemes, if people who have radio frequencies do not use them, their right lapses and the frequencies revert to the allocating agency. This is like the small print which reads, "This ticket is nontransferable." In a market scheme, however, the owners may, within the limits of the law, pass on their resource to someone else as a gift or as part of a deal. A market scheme is predicated on a lack of faith in administered wisdom; it treats whatever allocations exist as a starting point only. It assumes that the distributed wisdom among the property holders is greater than that of a central planner.

The law creating a market defines the mix of deals that may be made and specifies some as illegal. A person moving may sell a house, but perhaps under zoning laws it may not be turned into a tavern. A shipowner with a radio license may sell a ship, including the radio facilities, but may not turn the ship's frequency to broadcasting. A cablecaster may sell a system to someone else but, under American rules, may not sell it to the owner of a television station in the same town.

Property is, in summary, simply a recognized partition of a resource that is somewhat scarce. A market is a device for distributing the use of that property. It measures the value people attach to different uses; it allows for shifts in the uses; and it depoliticizes decisions by decentralizing them. But a market is not a single device; it is a class of devices, and public policy defines the market structure.

Where some resource is either very scarce or not easily divisible, ordinary markets function badly. Spectrum, given the way it is now administered, is scarce enough that every small group cannot have its own television station. A telephone system is indivisible in that what is needed is a universal system. In such cases of monopoly or partial monopoly of the means of communication there are problems for free societies. It was for such situations that the common carrier approach was developed in the nineteenth and early twentieth centuries. Common carriers are obligated to offer their resources to all of the public equally. In the American constitutional system this is an exceptional fallback solution. The basic American tradition of the First Amendment is either the free-for-all of free speech or the competitive market of the early press.

Since scarcity and indivisibility of resources compel a departure from the print model, it is important to estimate what major scarcities and indivisibilities will appear in the evolving electronic media. Despite the profusion of means of communication that are coming out of the technology of the late twentieth century, a number of truly scarce or indivisible elements will remain in the communications system. Despite the cliché of broadcast regulation that frequencies are exceptionally scarce, spectrum is not one of them. If spectrum were allotted by sale in a market, the prices would not be prohibitive, for there are now numerous alternatives, such as data compression or transmission by coaxial cables or optical fibers, which would become economic in the presence of relatively low costs for air rights. Spectrum is only of medium scarcity.

The orbit for satellites is today what spectrum was in 1927, something that at first glance seems inherently and physically scarce. If the technology of orbit usage remained that of the 1970s, orbital slots in the Western Hemisphere would have run out by about the time this book got published, and in many other places shortly thereafter. However, techniques for orbit and spectrum saving are multiplying. The real problem is spectrum, not real estate on the orbit. There is abundant space for the satellites themselves. The difficulty is to find frequencies for communicating to and from the satellites without causing radio interference. Polarization, spot beams, time-division multiplexing, on-board switching, and direct satellite-to-satellite microwave or laser links are among the techniques that help. These require agreement to use technically efficient methods, which may not be the cheapest ones. The orbit problem turns out to be a special case of the familiar spectrum problem. To keep prices down requires agreement on and compliance with efficient standards and protocols. But at a price, as much of the resource as is wanted is likely to be available.

Though neither spectrum nor orbital slots are too scarce to be handled by normal market mechanisms, there are other more severe elements of monopoly in the system. One is the need that basic communications networks be universal in reach. If anyone is to be able to send a message or talk to anyone else, there must be universal connectivity, directory information, agreed standards, and a legal right to interconnect.

Another element of communications systems that makes for central control is the need to traverse or utilize the public's property. The social costs of not granting the right of eminent domain for transmission routes are very high. Also streets have to be dug to lay cables. These requirements affect many people who are not direct participants in the arrangements.

Finally, there are areas of natural monopoly where the larger the firm, the more efficient its operation, so in the end the smaller competitors are driven out of business. This has been the case for American newspapers. They depend heavily on advertising by merchants. Where there is more than one paper in a town, merchants find it more efficient to advertise in the larger one, and the smaller ones wilt. The situation was similar when there was more than one phone company in a city; customers joined the larger system because there were more people whom they could then call. Customers would also pick the larger cable system if more than one served a neighborhood. The larger system that shared the fixed plant costs among more subscribers could charge less, and with more revenue it could offer more or better programs.

In communications, economies of scale are found especially in wire or cable transmission plant. The large investment in conduits reaching everywhere dominates the equation. There is no such strong economy of scale either in over-the-air transmission or ordinarily in programming or enhanced services. Where economies of scale and therefore natural monopolies do exist, some form of common carriage access is appropriate. It exists in phone service. Common carriage in some form may well come for cable as well.

Although there are elements of natural monopoly in both newspaper and electronic carrier markets, common carrier procedures have been applied in one and not the other. A newspaper may be the only one in its town, yet still it enjoys all the privileges of the ordinarily competitive printed media. Under the First Amendment, as interpreted in the Tornillo case, it cannot be forced to yield access to anyone. The issue of whether, as a monopoly, it should be so compelled is not a trivial one. Barron's argument in Tornillo was not dismissible lightly, but the court did reject it and continued to give newspaper owners full autonomy of editorial decision.

The fact that the newspapers have maintained such freedom from a requirement that normally goes with monopoly distinguishes them from cablecasters, who are ordinarily required by their franchises to provide some access. Historical complexities, not simple logic, account for this paradox. In both cases, but especially for newspapers, the scope of the monopoly is incomplete. At least as important is the fact that newspapers, reared in the tradition of a free press, have behaved so as to discourage the issue from arising. Newspapers, as they moved into the status of monopolies, had the wisdom to defuse hostility by acting in many respects like a common carrier. Aware of their vulnerability, they voluntarily created something of an access system for themselves. Unlike their nineteenth-century ancestors, they see themselves as providing a forum for the whole community. They not only run columnists of opposite tendency and open their local news pages willingly to community groups, but also encourage letters to the editor. Most important of all, they accept advertising for pay from anyone. Only rarely does a newspaper refuse an ad on grounds of disagreement. If newspapers were as opinionated as they used to be in the days when they were competitive, public opinion would have long since acted against their unregulated monopoly.

Furthermore, newspapers are far from having a complete monopoly. Newspaper publishers, like cablecasters, argue that they are not a monopoly in an appropriately defined market. Even if there is only one newspaper in a town, there are many ways in which opinions get distributed in print. A handbill or periodical of opinion competes with a newspaper in the marketplace of ideas. News magazines and suburban papers also compete.

The Tornillo decision is not likely to be reconsidered. Newspapers are facing growing competition. Electronic information services and specialized national newspapers will erode still further their local monopoly. If such monopolies have not constrained open discussion in print up to now, they are even less likely to do so in the future.

Cablecasters claim that their situation is no different from that of the press, so they deserve exactly the same treatment. They argue that they too will maintain an open forum. Perhaps fifteen years hence one will be able to say that the cable industry saw the writing on the wall and behaved in a statesmanlike manner. Maybe it too will have voluntarily made channels available to all, even leasing channels to competitors. Maybe by then the newly emerging technology of a broadband ISDN on the telephone network will also have made it no longer sensible to talk of cable monopoly. But there is reason to doubt such expectations. The technical solution may come slowly, and the forecast of statesmanship is hardly supported by present behavior. Newspapermen come from a tradition of political combativeness and First Amendment principle; cablecasters come from the tradition of show business. Newspapers are an unregulated industry proud of their independence from the state; cable is a regulated franchised business. To look to the cable industry for such sensitivity to First Amendment considerations as to prevent the access issue from becoming intense is probably unrealistic.

There are economic reasons why radical surgery to separate carrier from content in cablecasting would not work in America. There is not now, nor will there be in the near future, the volume of carrier business needed for private cable businesses to expand in this way. But given the temptation for a cable monopoly to stifle uses that do not interest it, and given the self-serving positions against requirements for channel leasing that the industry has taken; there is good reason for city governments, when franchising a cable monopoly, to require that at least leased access on a nondiscriminatory basis be provided. There are ways in which this can be done without destroying the economics of the systems. Nor does a leasing requirement in a franchise deny cablecasters their First Amendment rights.

Cable monopolies, owing to the physical problems of traversing the city's terrain, exist by grace of government franchise. Local newspapers are natural economic monopolies. This is a difference of a kind the courts have recognized. The distinction can be stated in terms of resource constraint. Local newspaper monopolies arise from choices that consumers and suppliers make in the market, not from the existence of constraints that are so severe as to prevent the effective making of such market choices. Nonetheless, until the electronic media shake the present newspaper structure and bring readers into easy contact with competing news sources, local press monopolies will remain common. The paradox will continue of a monopolized print medium enjoying the freedom of the print tradition, while common carrier and regulated practices continue for electronic media, some of which operate under severe resource constraints and should therefore be obliged to provide access, and others of which do not.

The precise structure of common carrier regulation as embodied in the FCC's common carrier rules and the 1934 Communications Act is quite properly being questioned as burdensome. But the core of the common carrier concept, namely that a vendor with monopoly advantage in the market must provide access to customers without discrimination, remains often applicable to basic electronic carriers, as it was in the past to the mails.

The Policy Debate about Monopoly

Fear of monopoly has been at the core of most current communications policy debates and of most proposals to depart from the First Amendment tradition. "Monopoly" was the word used in 1927 by those attacking AT&T's attempt to set up a broadcasting common carrier. It is the word now being used by postal and telecommunications administrations in defense of their exclusive right to carry messages among the public. It is the word used to justify special restraints on AT&T.

Monopoly implies a single entity, but what is generally discussed is rather a matter of degree. A company of sufficient size to affect the market in which it operates is said in popular discourse to have some monopoly power. The television networks are frequently called monopolies, though there are three of them. The word "oligopoly" exists, but not in lay discussions. Furthermore, it describes only one of the ways in which partial monopoly power may exist. The very small publisher of a neighborhood shopping throwaway is most often a monopolist in the neighborhood but is in fierce competition for advertising with the city daily newspaper and thus has very little market power.

Market power is not identical with social or political power over communications, though they are closely related. The monopoly situations that are of concern for liberty are those where some resource needed to communicate is scarce enough that whoever owns it has considerable power over others who seek to use it. The economist's analysis focuses rather on power over other suppliers who compete in the market. A political analysis focuses instead on who gets to use the airwaves of a station that is licensed or who can send messages when a carrier controls the practical means for delivering them.

In rhetoric, the United States government favors diversity of voices and seeks to break up communications monopolies. The reality, however, is more ambiguous. Few monopolies exist from economic factors alone, and fewer still survive by private coercion alone. Mafiosos are not that strong. The force that preserves most monopoly privilege is the law. Some monopolies rest on patents, others on copyright, still others on franchises or licenses, some on property rights in unique locations, and many on regulatory policies that protect vested interests against assault. Most monopolies exist by grace of the police and the courts. From a social point of view some are desirable, others undesirable; but most would vanish in the absence of enforcement.

Antitrust policy, and thus most current debate over communications policy, has focused on the market-produced monopolies, for the monopolies that the government establishes by patents, copyrights, franchises, and laws are exceptions to the antitrust laws and so are perfectly legal. The government does not challenge them. When American government does grant a monopoly, its attitude is sometimes ambivalent. Monopoly grants are often designed to give a privilege and at the same time to limit it. Both copyrights and patents, for example, are for finite terms, require disclosure, and may not be used to keep a product off the market. They are monopolies intended in the end to promote rather than restrict access.

While the intent of regulation is often to provide some modest protection for the weak, the ultimate outcome is often more protection for the strong. American broadcasting regulation follows a policy of localism, that is, protecting local stations so a few superstations do not dominate the national air. This policy protects an oligopoly of broadcasters in every city. It gives them advantages not only in their own community but also against still bigger would-be national monopolists. Often regulation is thus used to give smaller companies some monopoly protection against larger ones. For decades neither AT&T nor Western Union were allowed to go into international telegraphy; it was reserved for four international record carriers which, it was believed, would be crushed if the domestic communication giants were allowed into the intercontinental business. For satellites too the policy of "open skies," by excluding AT&T, assured business in the formative years to a group of oligopolists.

The legal crutch that preserves weak companies is exculpated in the name of competition. If the crutch were removed, it is said, one more company would disappear, leaving fewer and larger contenders in control of the field. Thus in a normal communications environment there are little monopolies and big ones; each argues for the essentiality of its privilege, and each enjoys at most only a bit of monopoly.

Regulation, whatever its motives, tends to create these islands of segregated activity. Some firms are protected from others. Also, it is easier to control an activity when it is not mixed in with ones that are unregulated. A mix of competition and monopoly creates the possibility of cross-subsidization. Profits from a sheltered activity may be used to cut prices in competitive fields. The primary goal of antitrust policy in telecommunications has been to ensure that no one entity is simultaneously in both the naturally monopolistic portions of the phone business and in competitive markets.

At the same time, the goal of deregulation has been to free companies from the bonds of regulatory convenience and allow them to experiment in the market with the efficiencies of new technologies and joint products. In the United States this unleashing has been enjoyed by AT&T, but only AT&T without local operating companies. It has not been done for the postal service, nor is it likely to be done for such a tax-supported enterprise, though the same result may be achieved through private express carriers.

The postal system has an office in every neighborhood and delivery to every door. Historically, this made it seem a natural organization for also handling small parcels, which it now handles everywhere. It also appeared a natural organization for delivering telegrams. In countries where they are still delivered, this is done through the post office or else at enormous loss. Post offices also serve as convenient government field offices. In many countries a poor person's bank, plus the sale of money orders and sometimes insurance, is handled through the post office. The advantage of sharing joint costs among many functions of a distribution plant was perceived even at the birth of postal service, when monarchs got cheap mail service for themselves by allowing the recipients of their postal patent to carry the public's letters for a fee. Daily, to-the-door delivery could conceivably be made less of a fiscal burden if milk, eggs, newspapers, and mail were all handled together. It would be good economic policy for a postal service to get into other businesses in competition with haulers, telecommunications companies, banks, and dairies. Similarly telephone companies, which have a virtually universal billing system and a network for moving funds, may become billing services and, following that, credit organizations and financial intermediaries, or what are ordinarily called banks. By the same token banks may become communications carriers. Certainly computer and aerospace companies may find that they have the skills and facilities to offer transmission services. IBM, Comsat, and Aetna Life Insurance formed Satellite Business Systems to link computers and other business facilities.

Present American deregulatory policy encourages such competition. Any company can get into the game, except ones with a substantial monopoly position that could be used for anticompetitive practices. The popular cry now is to let the market determine which alternative vendors with their different joint costs, organization, and skills can efficiently provide each service. Increasingly, the government is allowing AT&T, Western Union, the international record carriers, the specialized common carriers, and the satellite companies onto each other's turf, and also for that matter banks, computer companies, railroads, and any company at all.

At least as important as ideology in causing communications deregulation has been technological change. The use of coaxial cable and of ever higher frequencies has eroded spectrum shortage. The introduction of microwave transmission in the 1930s eliminated the problem of right of way. Microwave frequencies, though not unlimited, were abundant enough to allow a substantial number of competing carriers. Satellite communication has reinforced this trend, for nothing prevents there being several competing satellite transmission organizations.

Deregulation, however, is a pragmatic policy. The argument made against regulations has been that they are inefficient and unnecessary, not improper. It holds that with converging technologies, the removal of controls will produce competition. Where this does not turn out to be the case, the deregulators are ready to step back in and regulate. But in the arena of speech and press we need also to consider other guidelines that have been left in the outfield in recent policy controversies—ones that recognize the preferred position of freedom of discourse.

Guidelines for Freedom

Difficult problems of press freedom, as well as of economics, arise at the intersections of regulatory models. When resource constraints are small and circumstances neatly fit the historical pattern of publishing or when resource constraints are severe and circumstances fit the historical situation of a common carrier, then norms exist. The difficulties arise in situations that have elements of each. This was the problem in deciding about the broadcasting system in the 1920s; it is also a problem in the regulation of electronic networks today.

Regulators find it convenient to segregate activities and to keep each organization on its own turf. Much of regulatory law consists of specifications as to who may engage in what activities. Frequency allocations are made for particular uses; CBers or amateurs may not broadcast entertainment; public broadcast stations may not carry ads. In the United States, AT&T and Western Union have been largely partitioned, with AT&T kept out of telex and telegraph traffic and Western Union kept out of voice. Deregulation loosens such restrictions and allows companies to move onto each other's turf. But some segmentation persists.

A price is paid for this rigid delimitation of turf, not only in efficiency and innovation but also in freedom of speech. The notion that government may specify which communications entity is allowed to participate in particular parts of the information industry's vertical flow is hard to reconcile with the First Amendment. To research and write, to print or orate, to publish and distribute, is everyone's right. If government licensing of reporters, publishers, or printing presses is anathema, then so also should be the licensing of broadcasters and telecommunications carriers.

Yet the repeated argument has been made, which may be right or wrong in particular cases, that some degree of natural monopoly prevails in particular parts of the communications field. Whether because there were thought to be only eighty-nine broadcasting frequencies, or because having more than one company digging up the streets was intolerable, or because the carrier that reached most persons was the one most worth joining, it seemed likely that a dominant organization would gain control of a communications resource that other citizens also needed. Under these circumstances the best solution seemed to be to define a monopoly's turf narrowly and to require those who had the monopoly to serve all comers without discrimination.

Since the institutions in such strategic positions are usually basic carriers of physical signals, one way to narrow their domain is to separate the carrier from content-related activities. But there are problems in doing this, in terms both of undercutting the economics of the business and, in America, of bending the Constitution. The unfortunate compromise that has often followed is to license and regulate the monopoly.

Such limited franchises have a way of being extended beyond their original rationale. Enfranchised monopolies that at one time are thought simply to reflect in an orderly fashion the natural realities of the market, and are indeed intended to restrict monopoly, get converted into matters of right. Stations and carriers that are licensed simply to ensure good service by carefully selected organizations when monopoly seems inevitable come to see themselves, and to be seen, as having a vested right in their franchise. Regulatory powers assumed by the government to cope with monopoly also acquire a life of their own.

This faces the communications field with a dilemma. Not all parts of the communications system fit well under the preferred print model. Bottlenecks do exist where there are severe resource constraints. And the regulations that in those situations seem to be required have an insidious bent. They acquire legitimacy; they outlive their need; they tend to spread. The camel's nose is under the tent.

Yet when there is severe scarcity, there is an unavoidable need to regulate access. Caught in the tension between the tradition of freedom and the need for some controls, the communications system then tends to become a mix of uncontrolled and common carrier elements—of anarchy, of property, and of enfranchised services. A set of principles must be understood if communications in the electronic era are to hold as fully as possible to the terms of the First Amendment. The technology does not make this hard. Confusion about principles may.

The first principle is that the First Amendment applies fully to all media. It applies to the function of communication, not just to the media that existed in the eighteenth century. It applies to the electronic media as much as to the print ones.

Second, anyone may publish at will. The core of the First Amendment is that government may not prohibit anyone from publishing. There may be no licensing, no scrutiny of who may produce or sell publications or information in any form.

Third, enforcement of the law must be after the fact, not by prior restraint. In the history of communications law this principle has been fundamental. Libel, obscenity, and eavesdropping are punishable, but prior review is anathema. In the electronic media this has not been so, but it should be. Traffic controls may be needed in cases where only one communicator can function at a particular place at a particular time, such as street meetings or use of radio frequencies, but this limited authority over time and place is not the same as power to choose or refuse to issue a license.

Fourth, regulation is a last recourse. In a free society, the burden of proof is for the least possible regulation of communication. If possible, treat a communications situation as free for all rather than as subject to property claims and a market. If resource constraints make this impossible, treat the situation as a free market rather than as a common carrier. But if resources for communication are truly monopolistic, use common carrier regulation rather than direct regulation or public ownership. Common carriage is a default solution when all must share a resource in order to speak or publish.

Under common law in the nineteenth century, vendors could not be made common carriers against their will. If they offered a service to the general public, it had to be without discrimination, but if they chose to serve a limited clientele, that was their right. This philosophy applies well to publishing. One would not require the Roman Catholic *Pilot* to carry ads for birth control or a trade union magazine to carry ads against the closed shop. But these cases assume that diverse magazines exist. A dilemma arises when there is a monopoly medium, as when a monopoly newspaper in a town refuses ads to one party and carries them for another.

In the world of electronic communications some but not all of the basic physical carriers, and only those, seem likely to continue to have significant monopoly power. It is hard to imagine a value-added network having the dominance in a community that a local newspaper has today. Even now the communications monopolies that exist without privileged enforcement by the state are rare. Even basic physical conduits become monopolies precisely because they cannot exist without public favors. They need permissions that only the state can grant. These favors, be they franchises to dig up the city streets or spectrum to transmit through the air, may properly be given to those who choose to serve as common carriers. This is not a new idea. In 1866 telegraph companies were given the right to string wires at will along post roads and across public lands, but only if they became common carriers. Where monopoly exists by public favor, public access is a reasonable condition.

Fifth, interconnection among common carriers may be required. The basic principle of common carriage, namely that all must be served without discrimination, implies that carriers accept interconnection from each other. This principle, established in the days of the telegraph, is incorporated in the 1982 AT&T consent decree. All long-distance carriers have a right to connect to all local phone companies. That is the 1980s outgrowth of the 1968 Carterphone decision which required AT&T to interconnect with an independent radio-telephone service. Universal interconnection implies both adherence to technical standards, without which interconnection can be difficult, and a firm recognition of the right to interconnect.

Carriers may sometimes raise valid objections to interconnection. Some will wish to use novel technologies that are incompatible with generally accepted standards, claiming that they are thereby advancing the state of the art. Also, when they handle highly sensitive traffic, such as funds transfers or intracompany data, they may not wish to be common carriers and bear the risks of having outsiders on their system. Such arguments are often valid, though they may also be used to lock a group of customers out of using the carrier.

An argument in favor of general interconnectivity is that it facilitates market entry by new or small carriers. It also makes universal service easier. It may even be useful for national security, since a highly redundant system is less likely to be brought down. In short, there are conflicting considerations that must be balanced. As a policy, the requirement of interconnection is a reasonable part of a common carriage system.

Sixth, recipients of privilege may be subject to disclosure. The enforcement of nondiscrimination depends critically on information. Without control of accounting methods, regulatory commissions are lost in a swamp. I once asked the head of the Common Carrier Bureau of the FCC what he would ask for if he could rub Aladdin's lamp. "Revelatory books" was his reply.

Yet American lawmakers, who have imposed far more oppressive and dubious kinds of regulation, such as exit, entry, and tariff controls, have never pushed the mild requirement for visibility. Apart from requiring accounts, legislators have been highly considerate of proprietary information. A firm that enjoys the monopoly privileges which lead to being a common carrier should perhaps forgo, like government, some privileges of privacy. Unbundled rates for cable leasing, for example, help reveal who is being charged for what. Disclosure is not a new idea. Patents and copyrights are privileges won only by making their object public. The same principle might well apply to action under franchises too.

Seventh, privileges may have time limits. Patents and copyrights are for finite periods, and then the right expires. Radio and television licenses and cable franchises, though also for fixed periods, are typically renewable. Some monopoly privileges that broadcasters and cablecasters have in their licenses could expire after a fixed period. This is a way to favor infant industries but limit their privileges when they become giants.

Eighth, the government and common carriers should be blind to circuit use. What the facility is used for is not their concern. There may be some broad categories of use. Emergency communications often have priority. Special press rates for telegraph have been permitted, though their legality in the United States has been questioned. But in general, control of the conduit may not become a means for controlling content. What customers transmit on the carrier is no affair of the carrier.

Ninth, bottlenecks should not be used to extend control. Rules on undeliverable mail have been used to control obscene content. Cablecasting, in which there is no spectrum shortage, has been regulated by the FCC as ancillary to broadcasting. Telegraph companies have sought to control news services, and cable franchisees have sought to control the programs on the cable. Under the First Amendment, no government imposition on a carrier should pass muster if it is motivated by concerns beyond common carriage, any more than the carrier should be allowed to use its service to control its customers.

Tenth, and finally, for electronic publishing, copyright enforcement must be adapted to the technology. This exceptional control on communication is specifically allowed by the Constitution as a means of aiding dissemination, not restricting it. Copyright is temporary and requires publication. It was designed for the specific technology of the printing press. It is in its present form ill adapted to the new technologies. The objective of copyright is beyond dispute. Intellectual effort needs compensation. Without it, effort will wither. But to apply a print scheme of compensation to the fluid dialogue of interactive electronic publishing will not succeed. Given modern technologies, there is no conceivable way that individual copies can be effectively protected from reproduction when they are already either on a sheet of paper or in a computer's memory. The task is to design new forms of market organization that will provide compensation and at the same time reflect the character of the new technology.

The question boils down to what users at a computer terminal will pay for. For one thing, they will pay for a continuing relationship, as they will continue to need maintenance. It may be easy to pirate a single program or some facts from a data base by copying from a friend of a friend of a friend who once bought it. But to get help in adapting it or to get add-on versions or current data, one might pay a fee as a tender for future relations. The magazine subscription model is closer to the kind of charging system that will work for electronic publishing than is the one-time book purchase with a royalty included.

A workable copyright system is never enacted by law alone. Rather it evolves as a social system, which may be bolstered by law. The book and music royalty systems that now exist are very different from each other, reflecting the different structures of the industries. What the law does is to put sanctions behind what the parties already consider right. So too with electronic publishing on computer networks, a normative system must grow out of actual patterns of work. The law may then lend support to those norms.

If language were as fluid as the facts it represents, one would talk in the electronic era of serviceright, not copyright. But as language is used, old words are kept regardless of their derivation, and their meanings are changed. In the seventeenth century reproducing a text by printing was a complex operation that could be monitored. Once the text was printed on paper, however, it required no further servicing, and no one could keep track of it as it passed from reader to reader. In the electronic era copying may become trivially easy at the work stations people use. But both the hardware and the software in which the text is embodied require updating and maintenance. In ways that cannot yet be precisely identified, the bottleneck for effective monitoring and charging is migrating from reproduction to the continuing service function.

Not only in copyright but in all other issues of communications policy, the courts and legislatures will have to respond to a new and puzzling technology. The experience of how the American courts have dealt with new nonprint media over the past hundred years is cause for alarm. Forty years ago Zechariah Chafee noted how differently the courts treated the print media from newer ones: "Newspapers, books, pamphlets, and large meetings were for many centuries the only means of public discussion, so that the need for their protection has long been generally realized. On the other hand, when additional methods for spreading facts and ideas were introduced or greatly improved by modern inventions, writers and judges had not got into the habit of being solicitous about guarding their freedom. And so we have tolerated censorship of the mails, the importation of foreign books, the stage, the motion picture, and the radio." With the still newer electronic media the problem is compounded. A long series of precedents, each based on the last and treating clumsy new technologies in their early forms as specialized business machines, has led to a scholastic set of distinctions that no longer correspond to reality. As new technologies have acquired the functions of the press, they have not acquired the rights of the press. On print, no special excise taxes may be applied; yet every month people pay a special tax on their telephone bill, which would seem hardly different in principle from the old English taxes on newspapers. On print, the court continues to exercise special vigilance for the preferred position of the First Amendment; but other considerations of regulatory convenience and policy are given a preferred position in the common carrier and electronic domains.

Since the lines between publishing, broadcasting, and the telephone network are now being broken, the question arises as to which of these three models will dominate public policy regarding the new media. There is bound to be debate, with sharp divisions between conflicting interests. Will public interest regulation, such as the FCC applies, begin to extend over the conduct of the print media as they increasingly use regulated electronic means of dissemination? Or will concern for the traditional notion of a free press lead to finding ways to free the broadcast media and carriers from the regulation and content-related requirements under which they now operate?

Electronic media, as they are coming to be, are dispersed in use and abundant in supply. They allow for more knowledge, easier access, and freer speech than were ever enjoyed before. They fit the free practices of print. The characteristics of media shape what is done with them, so one might anticipate that these technologies of freedom will overwhelm all attempts to control them. Technology, however, shapes the structure of the battle, but not every outcome. While the printing press was without doubt the foundation of modern democracy, the response to the flood of publishing that it brought forth has been censorship as often as press freedom. In some times and places the even more capacious new media will open wider the floodgates for discourse, but in other times and places, in fear of that flood, attempts will be made to shut the gates.

The easy access, low cost, and distributed intelligence of modern means of communication are a prime reason for hope. The democratic impulse to regulate evils, as Tocqueville warned, is ironically a reason for worry. Lack of technical grasp by policy makers and their propensity to solve problems of conflict, privacy, intellectual property, and monopoly by accustomed bureaucratic routines are the main reasons for concern. But as long as the First Amendment stands, backed by courts which take it seriously, the loss of liberty is not foreordained. The commitment of American culture to pluralism and individual rights is reason for optimism, as is the pliancy and profusion of electronic technology.

Bibliography of the Works
of Ithiel de Sola Pool

Pool, Ithiel de Sola. *The symbols of electoral programs in France.* Master of Arts Thesis, Department of Political Science, University of Chicago. Typescript. Thesis T24732. 1939.

Leites, Nathan C.; Pool, Ithiel de Sola. "On content analysis." Paper prepared at the Experimental Division for the Study of War Time Communications (Harold D. Lasswell, chief). Document No. 26. 1 September 1942. Typescript.

Pool, Ithiel de Sola. *Communist propaganda in reaction to frustration.* Experimental Division for the Study of Wartime Communications Document No. 27. Washington, DC: Library of Congress, 1942.

Pool, Ithiel de Sola; Leites, Nathan. "Interaction: The response of Communist propaganda to frustration." In *Language of politics: studies in quantitative semantics,* edited by Lasswell, Harold D.; Leites, Nathan. New York: George W. Stewart, 1949. (Reprinted: Cambridge MA: MIT Press, 1968 [c1949]. pp. 334–81.)

Pool, Ithiel de Sola. "Who gets power and why." Review of Harold D. Lasswell, *Power and personality,* Dinko Tomasic, *Personality and culture in Eastern European politics,* Bertram Schaffner, *Father land,* Lyman Bryson, Louis Finkelstein, R. M. MacIver (eds.), *Conflicts of power in modern culture. World Politics* 2, no. 1 (October 1949): 120–34.

Pool, Ithiel de Sola. "Democracy in a world of tensions." In *Democracy in a world of tensions,* edited by McKeon, Richard; Rokkan, Stein, pp. 328–53. Chicago: University of Chicago Press, 1951.

Lerner, Daniel, with the collaboration of Ithiel de Sola Pool and George K. Schueller. *The Nazi elite.* Stanford, CA: Stanford University Press, 1951.

Pool, Ithiel de Sola, with the collaboration of Harold D. Lasswell [and others]. *Symbols of internationalism.* Hoover Institute Studies Series C, No. 3. Stanford, CA: Stanford University Press, 1951.

Lasswell, Harold D.; Pool, Ithiel de Sola. *The comparative study of symbols.* Hoover Institution Studies v. 87. Stanford, CA: Stanford University Press, 1952.

Pool, Ithiel de Sola; Schueller, George. "The constitution of the state." In *Fundamentals of political science,* edited by Flechtheim, Ossip K., pp. 201–45. New York: Ronald Press, 1952.

North, Robert C. with the collaboration of Ithiel de Sola Pool. *Kuomintang and Chinese communist elites*. Hoover Institute Studies. Series B: Elite studies, no 8. Stanford, CA: Stanford University Press, 1952.

Pool, Ithiel de Sola; Lasswell, Harold D.; Lerner, Daniel L. *The "prestige papers": A survey of their editorials*. Stanford, CA: Stanford University Press, 1952. Reprinted in *The prestige press: A comparative study of political symbols*. MIT studies in comparative politics series. Cambridge, MA: MIT Press, 1970.

Pool, Ithiel de Sola. "The state: Its elements and attributes." In *Fundamentals of political science*, edited by Flechtheim, Ossip K., pp. 111–72. New York: Ronald Press, 1952.

Pool, Ithiel de Sola, with the collaboration of Harold D. Lasswell [et al]. *Symbols of democracy*. Hoover Institute Studies. Series C, Symbols; no. 4. Stanford, CA: Stanford University Press, 1952. Reprinted: Westport, CT: Greenwood Press, 1981.

Pool, Ithiel de Sola. *The economic conditions of political freedom*. Ph.D. Dissertation (Volume W1593). The University of Chicago, 1953.

Pool, Ithiel de Sola. "Symbols, meanings, and social science." Paper from the Thirteenth Symposium of the Conference on Science, Philosophy and Religion in Their Relation to the Democratic Way of Life. In *Symbols and values: An initial study*, edited by Bryson, Lyman; Finkelstein, Louis; MacIver, R. M.; McKeon, Richard, pp. 349–60. New York: Harper and Brothers, 1954.

Speier, Hans; Bruner, Jerome; Carroll, Wallace; Lasswell, Harold D.; Lazarsfeld, Paul; Shils, Edward; Pool, Ithiel de Sola . "A plan of research in international communication." Condensation of the Planning Committee Report, Center for International Studies, Massachusetts Institute of Technology. *World Politics* 6, no. 3 (April 1954): 358–77.

Pool, Ithiel de Sola, with the collaboration of George K. Schueller [et.al.] *Satellite generals: A study of military elites in the Soviet sphere*. Hoover Institute Studies. Series B: Elites; no. 5. Stanford, CA: Stanford University Press, 1955. Reprinted: Westport, CT: Greenwood Press, 1975.

Pool, Ithiel de Sola; Keller, Suzanne; Bauer, Raymond A. "The influence of foreign travel on political attitudes of American businessmen." *Public Opinion Quarterly* 20, no. 1 (Spring 1956): 161–75. Reprinted as PS-229 in the Bobbs-Merrill Reprint Series in the Social Sciences.

Pool, Ithiel de Sola, guest editor. *Studies in political communication*. Series: *Public Opinion Quarterly* 20, no. 1 (Spring 1956). Princeton, NJ: Princeton University Press, 1956.

Pool, Ithiel de Sola. "Variety and repetition in political language" in Heinz Eulau, Samuel J. Eldersveld, and Morris Janowitz (eds.) *Political Behavior*. Glencoe, IL: The Free Press, 1956.

Pool, Ithiel de Sola. "A critique of the 20th anniversary issue." *Public Opinion Quarterly* 21, no. 1 (Spring 1957): 190–98.

Pool, Ithiel de Sola. "Orientation of Fulbrighters going to India." Memorandum to IEES, ditto, 1957.

Pool, Ithiel de Sola. "Public opinion and elections." *NEA Journal* 46, no. 6 (September 1957): 380–83.

Pool, Ithiel de Sola. "Voters' information on candidates in primaries." *Political Research: Organization and Design* 1, no. 1 (September 1957): 15–18.

Pool, Ithiel de Sola. *Indian images of America.* Typescript, 1958.

Pool, Ithiel de Sola; Prasad, Kali. "Indian student images of foreign people." *Public Opinion Quarterly* 22, no. 3 (Fall 1958): 292–304.

Pool, Ithiel de Sola. "What American travelers learn." *Antioch Review* 18 (Winter 1958): 431–46.

Pool, Ithiel de Sola. "Foreword." In *Japanese popular culture* by Hidetoshi Kato, 9–13. Rutland, VT: Charles Tuttle, 1959.

Pool, Ithiel de Sola; Shulman, Irwin. "Newsmen's fantasies, audiences and newswriting." *Public Opinion Quarterly* 23, no. 2 (Summer 1959): 145–58.

Pool, Ithiel de Sola, ed. *Trends in content analysis; papers.* Urbana: University of Illinois Press, 1959.

Pool, Ithiel de Sola. "Trends in content analysis today: A summary." Chapter 7 In *Trends in content analysis; papers,* edited by Pool, Ithiel de Sola, pp. 189–233. Urbana: University of Illinois Press, 1959.

Pool, Ithiel de Sola. "TV as a new dimension in politics." In *American voting behavior,* edited by Burdick, Eugene; Brodbeck, Arthur I., pp. 236–61. Glencoe, IL: The Free Press, 1959.

Bauer, Raymond A.; Pool, Ithiel de Sola. *American businessmen and international trade: Code book and data from a study of attitudes and communications.* Glencoe, IL: The Free Press, 1960.

Bauer, Raymond A.; Pool, Ithiel de Sola. Monograph. *The effects of audiences on communicators.* Cambridge, MA: Harvard Graduate School of Business Administration and Massachusetts Institute of Technology Center for International Studies, 1960.

Pool, Ithiel de Sola. "Content analysis for intelligence purposes." Review of Alexander L. George, *Propaganda analysis: A study of inferences made from Nazi propaganda in World War II. World Politics* 12, no. 3 (April 1960): 478–85.

Pool, Ithiel de Sola. "Free discussion and public taste." Testimony presented at Public Hearings held by the Federal Communications Commission on December 11, 1959. *Public Opinion Quarterly* 24 (Spring 1960): 19–23.

Pool, Ithiel de Sola. "Public opinion and the control of armaments." *Daedalus* (Fall 1960): 984–99.

Pool, Ithiel de Sola. "Cold war modeling." *Proceedings of the Military Operations Research Symposia (MORS)* 1, no. 1 (Fall 1961): 3–17.

Pool, Ithiel de Sola. *Communication and values in relation to war and peace.* New York: Institute for International Order, 1961.

Pool, Ithiel de Sola. "On escalation and deterrence." Ditto. Cambridge, Massachusetts, August 1961, Center for International Studies, Massachusetts Institute of Technology.

Pool, Ithiel de Sola. "The problems of international communication." In *The challenge of the 60s*, edited by Palo Alto Unified School District, pp. 39–49. Palo Alto, CA: 1960.

Pool, Ithiel de Sola. "Public opinion and the control of armaments." In *Arms control, disarmament, and national security*, edited by Brennan, Donald G., pp. 333–46. New York: George Braziller, 1961.

Pool, Ithiel de Sola. *Science and public policy*. Cambridge, MA: Massachusetts Institute of Technology Industrial Liaison Program, 1961.

Pool, Ithiel de Sola; Abelson, Robert P. "The Simulmatics project." *Public Opinion Quarterly* 25, no. 2 (Summer 1961): 167–83.

Pool, Ithiel de Sola. "Comment. In the 'new political science' reexamined: A symposium." *Social Research* 29, no. 2 (Summer 1962): 127–130.

Pool, Ithiel de Sola [Basil Boothroyd]. [A spoof of Media/Mix Simulation]. *Punch*, 19 September 1962.

Pool, Ithiel de Sola; Abt, Clark C. "The constraint of public attitudes." In *Limited strategic war*, edited by Knorr, Klaus; Read, Thornton, pp. 199–240. New York: Praeger, 1962.

Pool, Ithiel de Sola; Adler, Barbara. "Educational television: Is anyone watching?" *Journal of Social Issues* 18, no. 2 (1962): 50–60.

Bauer, Raymond A.; Pool, Ithiel de Sola; Dexter, Lewis A. *American business and public policy: The politics of foreign trade*, first edition. New York: Atherton Press of Prentice-Hall, 1963. Second edition with a new introduction. Chicago: Aldine Atherton, 1972.

Pool, Ithiel de Sola. "The effect of communication on voting behavior." In *The science of human communication*, edited by Schramm, Wilbur, pp. 128–38. New York: Basic Books, 1963.

Pool, Ithiel de Sola. "The formal requirements of a science." In *The conceptual framework for a science of marketing*, edited by Huegy, Harvey W., pp. 11–26. Urbana: University of Illinois Press, 1963.

Pool, Ithiel de Sola. "The mass media and politics in the modernization process." In *Conference on communications and political development*, edited by Pye, Lucian W., pp. 234–53. Princeton, NJ: Princeton University Press, 1963.

Pool, Ithiel de Sola; Adler, Barbara. Mimeo. *The out-of-classroom audience of WGBH: A study of motivation in viewing*. Research report. Title VII Project no. 083, grant no. 7-19-025. Cambridge, MA: Center for International Studies, Massachusetts Institute of Technology, 1963.

Schramm, Wilbur; Lyle, Jack; Pool, Ithiel de Sola. *The people look at educational television*. Stanford, CA: Stanford University Press, 1963.

Pool, Ithiel de Sola. "The role of communication in the process of modernization and technological change." In *Industrialization and society* [Proceedings], edited by Hoselitz, Bert F.; Moore, Wilbert E., pp. 279–93. Paris: UNESCO-Mouton, 1963.

Pool, Ithiel de Sola; Bernstein, Alex. "The simulation of human behavior—a primer and some possible applications." *American Behavioral Scientist* 6, no. 9 (May 1963): 83–85.

Pool, Ithiel de Sola, and others. *Social science research and national security*. A Report Prepared by the Research Group in Psychology and the Social Sciences. Office of Naval Research Contract No. 1354(08). Task Number NR 170-379. Washington, DC, March 1963, Smithsonian Institution.

Pool, Ithiel de Sola. "Some implications of the volume." Chapter 1 In *Social science research and national security*, edited by Pool, Ithiel de Sola, and others, 1–25. Washington, DC: Smithsonian Institution, 1963.

Pool, Ithiel de Sola. "Use of Available Sample Surveys in Comparative Research," *Social Sciences Information*. Paris: International Social Council, 1963.

Abelson, Robert; Pool, Ithiel de Sola; Popkin, Samuel. *Candidates, issues and strategies: A computer simulation of the 1960 Presidential election*. Cambridge, MA: MIT Press, 1964.

Pool, Ithiel de Sola. "Definitions of "International Exchange Programs," Media of Information," "Reciprocal Trade Act," "Stereotype," and "Straw Vote." In *Dictionary of political science*, edited by Dummer, Joseph, pp. 263, 343–44, 444, 501, 504. New York: Philosophical Library, 1964.

Pool, Ithiel de Sola. "The head of the company: Conceptions of role and identity." *Behavioral Science* 9, no. 2 (April 1964): 147–55.

Pool, Ithiel de Sola. "The mass media and their interpersonal social functions in the process of modernization." In *People, society and mass communications*, edited by Dexter, Lewis Anthony; White, David Manning, pp. 429–43. New York: The Free Press, 1964.

Pool, Ithiel de Sola. "The monster that isn't: The computer's true role in politics." *Chicago Sun-Times*, 13 September 1964, p. 3.

Pool, Ithiel de Sola. "Simulating social systems." *International Science and Technology*, no. 27 (March 1964): 62–70.

Kessler, A. R.; Pool, Ithiel de Sola. "Crisiscom: A computer simulation of human information processing during a crisis." *IEEE Transactions on Systems Science and Cybernetics* 1, no. 1 (November 1965): 52–58.

Kessler, Allan R.; Pool, Ithiel de Sola. "Crisiscom: A computer simulation of perception and decision making during a crisis." *IEEE International Convention Record, part 6*: 175–80, 1965.

Pool, Ithiel de Sola, Abelson, Robert P.; Popkin, Samuel L. *Candidates, issues, and strategies: A computer simulation of the 1960 and 1964 Elections*. Cambridge, MA: MIT Press, 1965.

Pool, Ithiel de Sola. "Comments." In *The Soviet Union, arms control and disarmament: background materials on Soviet attitudes*, edited by Fischer,

George, pp. 94–96, 101, 109, 163. New York: School of International Affairs, Columbia University, 1965.

Pool, Ithiel de Sola. "Comments on the Project Harbor controversy." *Science and Citizen* 7, no. 9 (August 1965): 26–27.

Pool, Ithiel de Sola. "Effects of cross-national contact on national and international images." In *International behavior: A social psychological analysis*, edited by Kelman, Herbert C., pp. 106–29. New York: Holt, Rinehart and Winston, 1965.

Pool, Ithiel de Sola. "The Functions of Mass Media in International Exchange" in *UNESCO handbook of international exchanges*. Paris: UNESCO, 1965.

Pool, Ithiel de Sola; Kessler, Allan. "The Kaiser, the Tsar, and the computer: Information processing in a crisis." *American Behavioral Scientist* 8, no. 9 (May 1965): 31–39.

Pool, Ithiel de Sola. "Mass communication and political science." In *A Seminar on communications research findings and their implications for school-community relations programs*, edited by Kindred, Lesley W.; Fehr, George N., pp. 133–50. Philadelphia, PA: College of Education, Temple University, 1965.

Pool, Ithiel de Sola; Abelson, Robert P.; Popkin, Samuel. "A postscript on the 1964 election." *American Behavioral Scientist* 8, no. 9 (May 1965): 39–44.

Pool, Ithiel de Sola. "Public opinion." Draft prepared for *Encyclopedia Brittanica*. 1965. Unpublished.

Pool, Ithiel de Sola. "The social environment for sustained technological growth." In *Patents and progress: The sources and impact of advanced technology*, edited by Alderson, Wroe; Terpstra, Vern; Shapiro, Stanley J., pp. 19–34. Homewood, IL: R. Irwin Inc., 1965.

Pool, Ithiel de Sola; Griffith, William; Pye, Lucian; Wood, Robert. "Standing firm against Communism." Letter. *The New York Times* , 11 July 1965.

Pool, Ithiel de Sola; Kramer, John F.; Selesnick, Herbert L. "Who is listening: Evaluating audiences." *Proceedings of the American Statistical Association, Business and Economic Statistics Section*: 43–49. 1965.

Pool, Ithiel de Sola. "The changing Soviet Union: The mass media as catalyst." Excerpts from: "Opportunities for Change: Communications With the U.S.S.R." Address, Department of Communications in Education, New York University School of Education, Workshop on Communications With the Peoples of the U.S.S.R. Sponsored by Radio Liberty Committee, New York, November 19, 1965. *Current* 67 (January 1966): 12–17.

Pool, Ithiel de Sola. "Communications and development." Chapter 7 In *Modernization: The dynamics of growth*, edited by Weiner, Myron, pp. 98–109. New York: Basic Books, 1966.

Pool, Ithiel de Sola. "The public." Mimeo. Paper prepared for delivery at the 1966 Annual Meeting of the American Political Science Association, New York, September 6–10. Cambridge, MA, 1966.

Pool, Ithiel de Sola with Hollander, Gayle and Rogers, Rosemarie. "Communication Media (Soviet Aspect)" for *The Soviet system and democratic society: A comparative encyclopedia*. Herder, 1967. (Draft)

Pool, Ithiel de Sola. "Computer simulation of total societies." In *The study of total societies*, edited by Klausner, Samuel Z., pp. 45–65. Garden City, NY: Doubleday & Company, Inc., 1967.

Pool, Ithiel de Sola, ed. *Contemporary political science: Toward empirical theory*. New York: McGraw Hill Book Co., 1967. Reprinted 1970. Published in Japanese by Keiso Shobo in 1973: translated by Hideo Uchiyama, Wataru Omori, Kazuo Ishikawa and Kenichi Nagata.

Pool, Ithiel de Sola. "The international system in the next half century." *Daedalus* 96, no. 3 (Summer 1967): 930–935.

Pool, Ithiel de Sola. "The necessity for social scientists doing research for governments." Paper originally presented to the 7th Annual Convention of the International Studies Association, Wayne State University, May 6, 1966. In *The rise and fall of Project Camelot: Studies in the relationship between social science and practical politics*, edited by Horowitz, Irving L., pp. 267–80. Cambridge, MA: MIT Press, 1967.

Pool, Ithiel de Sola. "Political alternatives to the Viet Cong." *Asian Survey* 7, no. 8 (August 1967): 555–566.

Pool, Ithiel de Sola. "The public and the polity." In *Contemporary political science: toward empirical theory*, edited by Pool, Ithiel de Sola, pp. 22–52. New York: McGraw Hill, 1967.

Pool, Ithiel de Sola. "Attitude research on the rocks: Summary comments." In *Attitude research on the rocks*, edited by Adlers, L.; Crespi, I. pp. 243–60. American Marketing Association, 1968.

Pool, Ithiel de Sola, et al. *The behavioral sciences and the federal government*. Report of the Advisory Committee on Government Programs in the Behavioral Sciences. Publication no. 1680. Washington, DC: National Research Council, National Academy of Sciences, 1968.

Pool, Ithiel de Sola. "Behavioral technology: Man will win more control over his destiny." Chapter 7 In *Toward the year 2018*, edited by Foreign Policy Association, pp. 87–96. New York: Cowles Publishers, 1968.

Pool, Ithiel de Sola. "Commentary." In *No more Vietnams*, edited by Pfeffer, Richard, pp. 203–8, 213–14. New York: Harper and Row, 1968.

Pool, Ithiel de Sola. "The international system in the next half century." Originally published in *Daedalus* 96 (1967): 930–35. In *Toward the year 2000: Work in progress*, edited by Bell, Daniel, pp. 318–23. Boston, MA: Houghton Mifflin, 1968.

Pool, Ithiel de Sola; Yarmolinsky, Adam et al. "No More Vietnams?" *The Atlantic Monthly* (November 1968): 99–116.

Pool, Ithiel de Sola, McIntosh, Stuart; Griffel, David. "On the design of computer-based information systems." *Social Science Information* 8, no. 5 (October 1968): 69–118. Research report of the same title, Urban Information Task Force of the MIT Urban Systems Summer Study on the ADMINS Project in the Center for International Studies, 1968.

Pool, Ithiel de Sola. "Political communication." In *International encyclopedia of the social sciences*, edited by Sills, David, volume 3, pp. 90–96. New York: Macmillan-Free Press, 1968.

Pool, Ithiel de Sola. "Political information systems." Paper prepared for the OECD Working Symposium on Long-Range Forecasting and Planning, October 28–31, 1968, Cambridge, MA: Massachusetts Institute of Technology, Center for International Studies.

Pool, Ithiel de Sola. "Social trends." *Science and Technology* no. 76 (April 1968): 87–101.

Pool, Ithiel de Sola. *Trends in public opinion about violence: 1937–1968. A report to the National Commission on the Causes and Prevention of Violence*. Cambridge, MA: Simulmatics Corporation., 1968. Mimeograph.

Pool, Ithiel de Sola. "Village violence and pacification in Viet Nam." Edumund J. James Lecture on Government. Delivered February 29, 1968. *University of Illinois Bulletin* 65, no. 133 (1 July 1968): 3–19.

Pool, Ithiel de Sola. "Village violence and international violence." *Peace Research Society Papers* 9 (1968): 87–94.

Pool, Ithiel de Sola. "The coming revolution in the study of man." In *Tomorrow's world: Challenges to U. S. diplomacy*, edited by Foreign Policy Association. *Headline Series* 189 (June 1969).

Pool, Ithiel de Sola. "Content analysis and the intelligence function in politics." Chapter 9 In *Personality and social science in the twentieth century: Essays in honor of Harold D. Lasswell*, edited by Rogow, Arnold A., pp. 197–223. Chicago, IL: University of Chicago Press, 1969.

Pool, Ithiel de Sola. "Deterrence as an influence process." In *Theory and research on the causes of war*, edited by Pruitt, Dean G.; Snyder, Richard C., pp. 189–96. Englewood Cliffs, NJ: Prentice-Hall, 1969.

Pool, Ithiel de Sola; Angell, Jr., George W. "The development of a basic social science course for undergraduate students in the natural sciences and engineering." Report to the Department of Health, Education and Welfare. Contract OE-5-10-086. Cambridge, MA: Department of Political Science, Massachusetts Institute of Technology, 1969. Mimeograph.

Pool, Ithiel de Sola. "Further thoughts on rural pacification and insurgency." Paper originally presented at the June 3–4, 1968 Conference of the Peace Research Society, Cambridge, MA. Also published in vol. 9, *Papers of the Peace Research Society (International)*. In *Vietnam: Some basic issues and alternatives*, edited by Isard, Walter, pp. 23–35. Cambridge, MA: Schenkman, 1969.

Pool, Ithiel de Sola. "Planning for the future: An optimal health information system." Chapter 7 In *Problems and perspectives in the design of a community health information system*, edited by Bauer, Katherine G., pp. 1–

28. Cambridge, MA: Joint Center for Urban Studies of MIT and Harvard University, 1969.

Pool, Ithiel de Sola. "Political information systems." Published version of the paper, "The Computer in Social Science Research," prepared for the MIT-TUB Joint Summer Conference, "The Computer and the University," July 23, 1968. In *Perspectives of planning*, edited by Jantsch, Eric, pp. 305–25. Paris: OECD, 1969.

Pool, Ithiel de Sola. "Political science." Report sponsored by the National Academy of Sciences and the Social Science Research Council. In *Behavioral and social sciences survey*, edited by Eulau, Heinz; March, James. 1969.

Pool, Ithiel de Sola. "Comparison of a human game and a computer simulation." *Political and Social Simulation* 1, no. 4 (January 1970).

Pool, Ithiel de Sola. "The paradox of nonviolent war in Vietnam." *Life Magazine*, 4 July 1970, 2.

Pool, Ithiel de Sola; Lasswell, Harold D.; Lerner, Daniel . *The prestige press: A comparative study of political symbols*. A reprinting, with new introductory material, of four volumes originally published by Stanford University Press: *The comparative study of symbols: An introduction*; *The 'prestige papers': A survey of their editorials*; *Symbols of democracy*; *Symbols of internationalism*. Cambridge, MA: MIT Press, 1970.

Pool, Ithiel de Sola. "Public opinion in Czechoslovakia." *Public Opinion Quarterly* 34, no. 1 (Spring 1970): 10–25.

Pool, Ithiel de Sola. "The social environment for sustained technological growth." In *The science of managing organized technology*, edited by Cetron, M. J.; Goldhar, Joel D., vol. 1, pp. 269–82. New York: Gordon & Breach, Science Publishers, 1970.

Pool, Ithiel de Sola. "Some facts about values." *PS* 3, no. 2 (Spring 1970): 102–6.

Pool, Ithiel de Sola, Stone, Philip; Szalai, Alexander. Monograph. *Communications, computers and automation for development*. United Nations. New York: United Nations Institute for Training and Research. UNITAR Research Reports, vol. 6. 1971.

Pool, Ithiel de Sola; Kessler, A. "Der Kaiser, der Zar und der computer: Informationsverarbietung wahrend einer krise." In *Simulations internationaler progresse*, edited by Kern, Lucian; Ronsch, Horst-Dieter. Westdeutscher Verlag Opladen, 1971. Translation of Pool and Kessler (1965).

Pool, Ithiel de Sola. "Discussion and Afterward." Transcript of a roundtable discussion held May 22, 1969, with an afterword. In *Dissent, power and confrontation*, edited by Klein, Alexander, pp. 177–234, passim. New York: McGraw-Hill, 1971

Pool, Ithiel de Sola. "Factors contributing towards modernization and socioeconomic performance: Communication." In *Approaches to the science of socio-economic development*, edited by Lengyel, Peter L., pp. 191–205. Paris: UNESCO, 1971.

Pool, Ithiel de Sola. "Foreword." In *Communications and national integration in Communist China by Alan P. L. Liu*, pp. ix–xvi. Michigan Studies on China. Berkeley: University of California Press, 1971.

Pool, Ithiel de Sola. "The impotence of power." In *Dissent, power and confrontation*, edited by Klein, Alexander. New York: McGraw Hill, 1971.

Pool, Ithiel de Sola, McIntosh, Stuart; Griffel, David. "Information systems and social knowledge." In *Information technology in a democracy*, edited by Westin, Alan F., pp. 241–49. Cambridge, MA: Harvard University Press, 1971. Based on a paper by the same authors, "On the Design of Computer-Based Information Systems" issued at the Massachusetts Institute of Technology, 1968.

Pool, Ithiel de Sola. "Communications in the national decision-making process." In *Computers, communications and the public interest*, edited by Martin Greenberger. Baltimore, MD: Johns Hopkins University Press, 1971.

Pool, Ithiel de Sola. "Technology and human communication." In *Essays on modernization of underdeveloped countries*, edited by Desai, A. R. Bombay, India: Thacker and Company, Ltd., 1971. Also: Vol. 1, pp. 514–22. New York: Humanities Press, 1972.

Pool, Ithiel de Sola. *Reprints of publications on Vietnam, 1966–1970*. MIT printing. May, 1971.

Pool, Ithiel de Sola et al. *Television and growing up: The impact of television violence*. Report of the Surgeon General's Scientific Advisory Committee on Television and Social Behavior. 6 vols. Washington, DC: U. S. Department of Health, Education, and Welfare, 1971.

Pool, Ithiel de Sola. "What will be new in the new politics?" In *The political image merchants: Strategies in the new politics*, edited by Hiebert, Ray; Jones, Robert; Lotito, Ernest; Lorenz, John, pp. 240–72. Washington, DC: Acropolis Books, 1971.

Pool, Ithiel de Sola. "Response to Vietnam survey." *The New Leader*, 29 May 1972, p. 6.

Pool, Ithiel de Sola. "International intelligence and domestic politics." Chapter 19 In *Surveillance and espionage in a free society*, edited by Blum, Richard H., pp. 272–97. New York: Praeger, 1972.

Pool, Ithiel de Sola. "Plural society in the Southwest: A comparative perspective." Proceedings of a conference sponsored by the Weatherhead Foundation. In *Plural society in the Southwest*, edited by Spicer, Edward H.; Thompson, Raymond H., pp. 321–38. New York: Interbook, Inc., 1972.

Pool, Ithiel de Sola. "Prospects for on-demand media" with Charles Murray and Kenneth Dobb. Cambridge, MA: Center for Space Research, MIT, May 30, 1972.

Pool, Ithiel de Sola. "Telecommunications and education at MIT: A report preparatory to a proposal" with Edwin Diamond, E. Lovell Dyett, John Ward and Carroll G. Bowen. March 1973.

Pool, Ithiel de Sola. Statement to Subcommittee on Communications of the Senate Commerce Committee, *Hearings on reports of the Surgeon General's Scientific Advisory Committee on Television and Social Behavior*. March 21, 1972.

Pool, Ithiel de Sola et al. *A free and responsive press. The Twentieth Century Fund task force report for a national news council.* New York: Twentieth Century Fund, 1973.

Pool, Ithiel de Sola. "Citizen feedback in political philosophy." In *Talking back: Citizen feedback and cable television*, edited by Pool, Ithiel de Sola, pp. 237–46. Cambridge, MA: MIT Press, 1973.

Pool, Ithiel de Sola. "Communication in totalitarian societies." Chapter 14 In *Handbook of communication*, edited by Pool, Ithiel de Sola and others, pp. 462–511. Chicago: Rand McNally, 1973.

Pool, Ithiel de Sola. "Communication systems." Chapter 1 In *Handbook of communication*, edited by Pool, Ithiel de Sola and others, pp. 3–26. Chicago: Rand McNally, 1973.

Pool, Ithiel de Sola, Schramm, Wilbur; with others, eds. *Handbook of communication.* Chicago, IL: Rand McNally, 1973.

Pool, Ithiel de Sola. "Inquiries beyond Watergate." *Society/Transaction* 10, no. 6 (September/October 1973): 24–26.

Pool, Ithiel de Sola. "Massenmedien und politik in modernisurungsprezt." In *MassenCommunikationsforschung 2: Konsumtion*, edited by Prokop, Dieter. Frankfurt: Fisher Tasekenbuch Verlag, 1973.

Pool, Ithiel de Sola. "Newsmen and statesmen: Adversaries or cronies?" In *Aspen notebook on government and the media*, edited by Rivers, William L.; Nyhan, Michael J., pp. 12–29, 49. New York: Praeger, 1973.

Pool, Ithiel de Sola; Alexander, Herbert E. "Politics in a wired nation." In *Talking back: Citizen feedback and cable technology*, edited by Pool, Ithiel de Sola, pp. 64–102. Cambridge, MA: MIT Press, 1973.

Pool, Ithiel de Sola. "Public Opinion." Chapter 25 in *Handbook of Communication,* edited by Pool, Ithiel de Sola and others, pp. 779–835. Chicago: Rand McNally, 1973.

Pool, Ithiel de Sola. For Voice of America: "The Soviet audience for foreign broadcasts." Simulation Reports 1-5, Research Program on Communications Policy. Report 1: "The Soviet audience for foreign broadcasts"; Report 2: "The Soviet audience for foreign broadcasts in non-Russian regions and languages"; Report 3: "The Soviet audience for domestic media"; Report 4: "Methodology"; Report 5: "Trends and variations in Soviet audiences." Cambridge, MA: MIT Research Program on Communications Policy, 1973.

Pool, Ithiel de Sola. "The satellite broadcast controversy." Working Paper for Communications Policy Conference, Aspen, Colorado, August 23–25, 1973. With J. Ruina, Abraham Chayes and Carroll G. Bowen. Report to NSF. June 15, 1973.

Pool, Ithiel de Sola, ed. *Talking back: Citizen feedback and cable technology.* Cambridge, MA: MIT Press, 1973.

Pool, Ithiel de Sola. "Focus on communications policy." *Vidura* 11, no. 3 (June 1974).

Pool, Ithiel de Sola. "The geopolitics of Israel's survival: An exchange of views." *The New Leader* 57, no. 3 (4 February 1974): 10–11.

Pool, Ithiel de Sola; Scharfenberger, Gilbert E.; Griffel, David M.; Kessler, Allan R. "Inventory of survey questions about the interests of the American public." Prepared for the Markle Foundation. Cambridge, MA: MIT Center for International Studies, 1974.

Pool, Ithiel de Sola. "The rise of communications policy research." *Journal of Communications* 24, no. 2 (Spring 1974): 31–42.

Pool, Ithiel de Sola. "Communication and a Big Ocean." *The Bulletin of the Institute for Communication Research.* Keio University, Tokyo, No. 5, 1975, 1–18.

Pool, Ithiel de Sola. "Direct broadcast satellites and cultural integrity." *Society/Transaction* 12, no. 6 (September/October 1975): 47–56.

Pool, Ithiel de Sola. "The international aspects of computer telecommunication." Conference on Computer Telecommunications Policy, OECD, Paris, France. February 4, 1975.

Pool, Ithiel de Sola. "International communications services." *Journal of the American Society for Information Science* 26, no. 1 (January/February 1975).

Pool, Ithiel de Sola; Corte, A. B. "International data communication capabilities and information revolution." *Proceedings of the American Society for Information Science* 12 (1975): 1–2.

Pool, Ithiel de Sola. "A proposal for a new international technology transfer institute." *World Future Society Bulletin* 9, no. 3 (May/June 1975).

Pool, Ithiel de Sola. "Technology and confusion: The satellite broadcast controversy in the UN." Prepared for *Foreign Affairs* (March 1975), xerox, unpublished. Cambridge, MA: Center for International Studies, Massachusetts Institute of Technology. February 10, 1975.

Pool, Ithiel de Sola. "Commentary." In *Global challenge to the U. S.*, edited by Markel, Lester; March, Audrey, pp. 189, 199, 206. Cranbury, NJ: Associated University Presses, Inc., 1976.

Pool, Ithiel de Sola. Book review essay. "Government and the media." *American Political Science Review* 70, no. 4 (December 1976): 1234–41.

Pool, Ithiel de Sola. "International aspects of computer communications." *Telecommunications Policy* 1, no. 1 (December 1976): 33–51.

Pool, Ithiel de Sola. "International policy dimensions: Background report." Paper presented at the OECD Conference on Computer Telecommunications Policy, February 4–6, 1975. OECD Informatics Studies, 11, pp. 281–308. Paris: OECD, 1976.

Pool, Ithiel de Sola, Friedman, Elliott H.; Warren, Colin John. "Low cost data and text communication for the less developed countries: A study with special reference to the needs of the international agricultural research centers." A study completed for the U.S. Agency for International Development. Cambridge, MA: Massachusetts Institute of Technology: Research Program on Communications Policy in the Center for Policy Alternatives; Center for International Studies; Center for Advanced Engineering Study, Electronic Systems Laboratory, 1976.

Pool, Ithiel de Sola. "Why don't people vote?" *TV Guide*, 23 October 1976, pp. 4–6.

Pool, Ithiel de Sola. "The changing flow of television." 1977, typescript.

Pool, Ithiel de Sola. "The communications/transportation tradeoff." *Policy Studies Journal* 6, no. 1 (Autumn 1977): 74–83. Also published in *Current issues in transportation policy*, edited by Altshuler, Alan, pp. 181–92. Lexington, MA: D.C. Heath, 1979.

Pool, Ithiel de Sola, Decker, Craig; Dizard, Stephen; Israel, Kay; Rubin, Pamela; Weinstein, Barry. "Foresight and hindsight: The case of the telephone." Chapter 6 In *The social impact of the telephone*, edited by Pool, Ithiel de Sola, pp. 127–57. Cambridge, MA: MIT Press, 1977.

Pool, Ithiel de Sola. "The influence of international communication on development." In *Perspectives in communication policy and planning*, edited by Rahim, Syad A.; Middleton, J., pp. 101–19. Honolulu, HI: East-West Center, 1977.

Pool, Ithiel de Sola. "Introduction." In *Revolutionary ideology and Chinese reality: Dissonance under Mao*, edited by Paul J. Hiniker, pp. 9–11. Beverly Hills, CA: Sage Publications, 1977.

Pool, Ithiel de Sola, Bauer, Raymond A.; Dexter, Lewis A. "The job of the Congressman." In *American politics, policies and priorities*, edited by Shank, A., 1977.

Pool, Ithiel de Sola. "The role and future of telecommunications in the economies of industrial civilization." *Journees D'Etudes—Sciences Humaines et Telecommunications*, 1977.

Pool, Ithiel de Sola. "Scarcity, abundance, and the right to communicate." In *Evolving perspectives on the right to communicate*, edited by Harms, L. S.; Richstad, Jim, pp. 175–89. Honolulu, HI: East-West Center, 1977.

Pool, Ithiel de Sola. "The social effects of the telephone." In *The telephone's first century and beyond: essays on the occasion of the 100th anniversary of telephone communication by Arthur C. Clarke* [et al.]. New York: Published in cooperation with the American Telephone & Telegraph Co. by Thomas Y. Cromwell Co., 1977.

Pool, Ithiel de Sola, ed. *The social impact of the telephone*. Cambridge, MA: MIT Press, 1977.

Pool, Ithiel de Sola. "Technological advances and the future of international broadcasting." *Studies of Broadcasting* 13 (March 1977).

Pool, Ithiel de Sola. "Technology and policy in the information age." In *Communication research: A half-century appraisal*, edited by Lerner, Daniel; Nelson, Lyle M., pp. 261–79. Honolulu: University of Hawaii Press, 1977.

Pool, Ithiel de Sola, Iwao, Sumiko. "Violence in television and social stability." *HBF [Hasa Bunku Foundation] Newsletter* (November 1977).

Pool, Ithiel de Sola. "Was failure inevitable? Some concluding perspectives." In *The lessons of Vietnam*, edited by Thompson, W. Scott; Frizell, Donaldson D. New York: Crane Russek, Inc., 1977.

Pool, Ithiel de Sola. "The art of the social science soothsayer." Chapter 2 In *Forecasting in international relations: Theory, methods, problems, prospects*, edited by Choucri, Nazli; Robinson, Thomas W., pp. 23–34. San Francisco, CA: W.H. Freeman, 1978.

Pool, Ithiel de Sola; Kochen, Manfred. "Contacts and influence." *Social Networks: An International Journal of Structural Analysis* 1, no. 1 (August 1978): 5–51. Reprinted in Manfred Kochen (ed.), *The small world: A volume of recent research advance commemorating Ithiel de Sola Pool, Stanley Milgram, Theodore Newcomb* (Norwood, NJ: Ablex Publishing Corp., 1989), pp. 3–51.

Pool, Ithiel de Sola. "Development of communication in the future: Perspectives." In *Communication in human activity*, edited by Adkins, Bruce M. Honda International Symposium, 1978.

Pool, Ithiel de Sola. "From Gutenberg to electronics: Implications for the first amendment." *The Key Reporter* 43, no. 3 (Spring 1978): 2–4, back cover.

Pool, Ithiel de Sola, Solomon, R. "International telecommunications and the requirements for international cooperation." Paper prepared for an OECD conference, July, 1978.

Pool, Ithiel de Sola. "The future prospects of international telecommunications policy." Monograph. In English and Japanese, 1–37. Tokyo: Kokusai Denshin Denwa Company, Ltd., 1978.

Pool, Ithiel de Sola. "Prospects for collaborative research." In *Information societies: Comparing the Japanese and American experiences*, edited by Edelstein, Alex S.; Bowes, John E.; Harsel, Sheldon M., pp. 265–272. Seattle: International Communications Center, University of Washington, 1978.

Pool, Ithiel de Sola. "Role des telecommunications dans l'avenir des pays industrialises." In *Les reseaux pensants: Telecommunications et societe*, edited by Giraud, Alain; Missaka, Jean-Louis; Wolton, Dominique, pp. 169–78. Paris: Masson, 1978.

Pool, Ithiel de Sola. "Scratches on social science: Images, symbols and stereotypes." In *The mixing of peoples: Problems of identity and ethnicity*, edited by Rotberg, Robert I., pp. 27–39. Stamford, CT: Greylock Publishers, 1978.

Pool, Ithiel de Sola. "Telecommunications for development: An addendum." *Telecommunications Policy* 2, no. 1 (March 1978): 68–70.

Pool, Ithiel de Sola. "Advantages and limitations of modern communications technology." Paper prepared for UNESCO, 1979.

Pool, Ithiel de Sola; Knox, Owen. "American telephone system development: The keys to success." Paper prepared for Conference on Science and Decision in Paris, February, 1979. Cambridge, MA: CNRS, Massachusetts Institute of Technology, 1979.

Pool, Ithiel de Sola. "The communications/transportation tradeoff." *Current Issues in Transportation Policy*, edited by Altshuler, Alan, pp. 181–92. Lexington, MA: D.C. Heath, 1979. Also published in *Policy Studies Journal*, 1977.

Pool, Ithiel de Sola. "Computers and communications." A sub-section of a report . In *Science and technology: A five-year outlook. A report from the National Academy of Sciences for the National Science Foundation, April, 1979*, 236–52. San Francisco, CA: W. H. Freeman, 1979.

Pool, Ithiel de Sola. "Direct satellite broadcasts and the integrity of national cultures." In *National sovereignty and international communication*, edited by Nordenstreng, Kaarle; Schiller, Herbert I. Norwood, NJ: Ablex Publishing Company, 1979.

Pool, Ithiel de Sola. "The first amendment and information policy." Address to the Information Industry Association Annual Meeting, October 28, 1979. Distributed by the Information Services Group of the New York Times Company. New York: New York Times Company, 1979.

Pool, Ithiel de Sola. "Foreword." To *The politics of international standards: France and the color tv war*, by Rhonda Crane, pp. xi–xii. Norwood, NJ: Ablex, 1979.

Pool, Ithiel de Sola. "The implications of expanding communications delivery systems." Published version of a paper given to the Canadian American Seminar in 1977. Institute for Canadian American Studies (ed.) *Accountability and responsibility in North American communication systems: future perspectives*. Ontario: Institute for Canadian American Studies, 1979.

Pool, Ithiel de Sola. "Innovation in the quaternary sector." *Apres-Demain* (July 1979).

Pool, Ithiel de Sola. "The network or the networks? Telecommunication in the USA." *Traverse*. 1979.

Pool, Ithiel de Sola; Solomon, Richard. "Problems in the regulation of transborder data flows." A shortened version, for OECD, of "The Regulation of Transborder Data Flows" in *Telecommunications Policy* for September, 1979.

Pool, Ithiel de Sola. "Protecting human subjects of research: Analysis of proposed amendments to HEW policy." *PS* 12, no. 4 (Fall 1979): 452–55.

Pool, Ithiel de Sola; Solomon, Richard J. "The regulation of transborder data flows." *Telecommunications Policy* 3, no. 3 (September 1979): 176–91.

Pool, Ithiel de Sola. "Scarcity, abundance and the right to communicate." *Worldview* (November 1979).

Pool, Ithiel de Sola. "The social meaning of the network." Paper prepared for the Edison Centennial Symposium in San Francisco, April 2, 1979.

Pool, Ithiel de Sola. "Society and computers: Effects upon the balance of social forces." *Man and Society—Automated Information Processing*, edited by Lawson Jr., Harold W., pp. 95–97. Discovery Symposium. Stockholm: Royal Swedish Academy of Engineering Sciences, 1979.

Pool, Ithiel de Sola. "Technology and change in modern communications." Paper prepared for the International Commission for the Study of Communication Problems, February 14, 1979. UNESCO, 1979.

Pool, Ithiel de Sola. "The Problems of WARC." *Journal of Communication* 29, no. 1 (Winter 1979): 187–96.

Pool, Ithiel de Sola. "Bridging the gap between content analysis and survey research." *Computerstrategien fur die Kommunikationsanalyse*, edited by Mochmann, Ekkehard, pp. 245–48. Frankfurt: Campus-Verlag, 1980.

Pool, Ithiel de Sola. "Censoring research." *Transaction/Society* 18, no. 1 (November/December 1980): 39–40.

Pool, Ithiel de Sola. "Commentary on 'Human Subjects.'" *Technology Review* (November/December 1980).

Pool, Ithiel de Sola. "Comments and observations." A Report from the Kettering Foundation. In *Polling on the issues*, edited by Cantril, Albert H., pp. 46–49. Cabin John, MD: Seven Locks Press, 1980.

Pool, Ithiel de Sola. "Communications for productivity." *Leaders Magazine* (30 April 1980).

Pool, Ithiel de Sola. "Communications technology and land use." Contribution to the special issues *Changing cities: A challenge to planning* edited by Pierre Lacoute. *Annals of the American Academy of Political and Social Science* 451 (September 1980): 1–12.

Pool, Ithiel de Sola. "Future trends in telecommunications development." *Journal of the Association of Engineers and Architects in Israel*, pp. 81–92, 1980.

Pool, Ithiel de Sola. "The governance of broadcasting: Government, the audience, and social groups." *Development Digest* 23, no. 2 (April 1980).

Pool, Ithiel de Sola; Solomon, R. J. "Intellectual property and transborder data flows." *Stanford Journal of International Law* 16 (Summer 1980): 113–39.

Pool, Ithiel de Sola. "The language of politics: General trends in content." In *Propaganda and communication in world history: A pluralizing world in formation*, edited by Lasswell, Harold D.; Lerner, Daniel; Speier, Hans, vol. 3, pp. 171–90. Honolulu: University Press of Hawaii, 1980.

Pool, Ithiel de Sola. "The new censorship of social research." *The Public Interest* 59 (Spring 1980): 57–66.

Pool, Ithiel de Sola. "The new structure of international communication: The role of research." Paper prepared for the Congress of the International Association for Mass Communication Research, Caracas, Venezuela, August 25–29, 1980.

Pool, Ithiel de Sola . "The productivity of information." *Intermedia (UK)* (July 1980): 29.

Pool, Ithiel de Sola. "Protecting human subjects of research: Proposed amendments to HEW policy response." *PS* 13, no. 2 (1980): 203–4.

Pool, Ithiel de Sola. "Regulations out-of-hand?" *Freedom at Issue* 55 (March/April 1980).

Pool, Ithiel de Sola. "Technological consequences of the NIIO." *Journal of the World Association for Christian Communication* 27 (April 1980).

Pool, Ithiel de Sola. "Technological consequences of the new information order." *Media Development* 27, no. 4 (1980).

Pool Ithiel de Sola. "Technology and change in modern communications." *Technology Review* 83, no. 2 (November/December 1980): 65–70, 75. Based on a report prepared for UNESCO's McBride Commission on the New World Information Order.

Pool, Ithiel de Sola, Solomon, R. J. "Transborder data flows: Requirements for international co-operation." *Information Computer Communications Policy*, edited by Organization for Economic Co-operation and Development, 1980.

Pool, Ithiel de Sola. "Will enquiry be regulated?" *Regulation Magazine* (March 1980).

Iwao, Sumiko, Pool, Ithiel de Sola; Hagiwara, Shigeru. "Japanese and U. S. Media: Some cross-cultural insights into tv violence." *Journal of Communication* 31, no. 2 (Spring 1981): 28-36.

Pool, Ithiel de Sola. "Approaches to intelligence and social science." Chapter 3 In *Intelligence policy and the national security*, edited by Pfaltzgraff, Jr., Robert L.; Ra'anan, Uri; Milberg, Warren H., pp. 37–45. Hamden, CT: Archon Press, 1981.

Pool, Ithiel de Sola. "Communication and integrated planning." *Media Asia* 8, no. 3 (Summer 1981): 152–55.

Pool, Ithiel de Sola. "Extended speech and sounds." Chapter VII In *Contact: Human communication and its history*, edited by Williams, Raymond, pp. 169–82. London: Thames and Hudson, 1981.

Pool, Ithiel de Sola. "The future role of telecommunications in the Pacific." *Computer Networks and ISDN Systems* 5, no. 3 (May 1981): 197–203.

Pool, Ithiel de Sola. "HHS wants unwonted assurance." Letter. *PS* 14, no. 4 (1981): 724.

Pool, Ithiel de Sola. "How powerful is big business?" A review of Charles Lindblom, *Politics and markets*. In *Does big business rule America?*, edited by Hessen, Robert, pp. 23–34. Washington, DC: Ethics and Public Policy Center, 1981.

Pool, Ithiel de Sola. "Human subjects regulations on the social sciences." *Annals of the New York Academy of Sciences* 403 (26 May 1981): 101–10.

Pool, Ithiel de Sola. "The illness of the mass media: Is it terminal?" *Communication* (January 1981): 20–29.

Pool, Ithiel de Sola. "International aspects of telecommunications policy." Chapter 7 In *Telecommunications and productivity*, edited by Moss, Mitchell L., pp. 156–67. Reading, MA: Addison-Wesley Publishing Co., 1981.

Pool, Ithiel de Sola. "International communication and free speech." *Freedom at Issue* 62 (Sept./Oct. 1981).

Pool, Ithiel de Sola. Interview. *Hihon Keisai Shimbun (Tokyo)*, 12 July 1981.

Pool, Ithiel de Sola. "The new technologies: Promise of abundant channels at lower cost." *What's news*, edited by Abel, Elie, pp. 81–96. San Francisco, CA: Institute for Contemporary Studies, 1981.

Pool, Ithiel de Sola, Schiller, Herbert I. "Perspectives on communications research: An exchange." *Journal of Communication* 31, no. 3 (Summer 1981): 15–23.

Pool, Ithiel de Sola, Sirbu, Marvin. "Prospects for audio broadcast technology." Paper prepared for the Center for Public Resources, New York, July, 1981.

Parta, R. Eugene, Klensin, John C.; Pool, Ithiel de Sola. "The shortwave audience in the USSR: Methods for improving the estimates." *Communication Research* 9, no. 4 (October 1982): 581–606.

Pool, Ithiel de Sola. "Controversy: Pluralism and communications technologies." Centro Internacional de Estudios Superiores de Comunicacion Para America Latina, Ecuador. *Chasqui* (October 1982).

Pool, Ithiel de Sola. "The culture of electronic print." *Daedalus* 111, no. 4 (Fall 1982): 17–31.

Pool, Ithiel de Sola. "Government regulation in the communications system." In *The communications revolution in politics*, edited by Benjamin, Gerald. *Proceedings of the Academy of Political Science* 34, no. 4, (1982): 121–30.

Pool, Ithiel de Sola. "Interplay of Japanese and US communications policy." In *Report on the International Investigatory Conference on Communications Policy*, pp. 146–52. Tokyo, 1982.

Pool, Ithiel de Sola. "The possibility of tv culture." Interview in Japanese. *The world from now on*, edited by Hironaka, Wakako, pp. 201–24. Tokyo: Sochisha Publishing Co., 1982.

Pool, Ithiel de Sola; Sirbu, Marvin; Solomon, Richard. "Tariff policy and capital formation in telecommunications." In *Evoluzione dele telecommunicazio negli anni 80*, edited by TECNETRA, pp. 125–64. Sarin, 1982.

Solomon, Richard; Pool, Ithiel de Sola. "Audio broadcast technology—prospects in the USA." *Telecommunications Policy* 6, no. 1 (March 1982): 2–20.

Pool, Ithiel de Sola; Steven, Peter M. "Appropriate telecommunications for rural development." In *Telecommunications in the year 2000: National and international perspectives*, edited by Singh, Indu B., pp. 150–57. Norwood, NJ: Ablex Publishing Co., 1983.

Pool, Ithiel de Sola. "Cellular telephony: Its social significance." *Technology Review* (August 1983).

Pool, Ithiel de Sola. "Changing technology—its social impact." In *Man and technology: The social and cultural challenge of modern technology*, edited by Adkins, Bruce M., pp. 108–13. Honda Foundation Discovery Series. Cambridge: Cambridge Information and Research Service Ltd., 1983. Distributed in the U. S. by Westview Press, Boulder, CO.

Pool, Ithiel de Sola. "Comments on 'The future of telecommunications regulation'" In *Telecommunications regulation today and tomorrow*, edited by Noam, Eli M., pp. 67–71. New York: Harcourt Brace Jovanovich, 1983.

Pool, Ithiel de Sola. "Communications technology and development." *UNESCO Courier* 36, no. 3 (March 1983): 26–29.

Pool, Ithiel de Sola. "Development of communication in the future perspective." Honda Foundation. In *The human use of human ideas: Discoveries project and eco-technology*, edited by Aida, Shuhei, pp. 225–38. New York: Pergamon Press, 1983.

Pool, Ithiel de Sola. *Forecasting the telephone: A retrospective technology assessment of the telephone*. Norwood, NJ: Ablex Publishing Company, 1983.

Pool, Ithiel de Sola. "Guiding the technologies of freedom." *Intermedia* 11, no. 6 (November 1983): 32.

Pool, Ithiel de Sola; Iwao, Sumiko. "International understanding via tv programmes: The case of Shogun." *Keio Communication Review* 4 (March 1983).

Pool, Ithiel de Sola. "My say." *Publishers Weekly*, 1 July 1983, p. 99.

Pool, Ithiel de Sola. "Predicting the market for cellular telephone." *Technology Review* (October 1983).

Pool, Ithiel de Sola. "Section IV, Competition and Universal Service to Users," Jackson-Wye Conference, Aspen, May 31, 1983.

Pool, Ithiel de Sola. "Some further thoughts on the technologies of freedom." *International Institute of Communications* (November 1983).

Pool, Ithiel de Sola. *Technologies of freedom*. Cambridge, MA: Harvard University Press, 1983.

Pool, Ithiel de Sola. "Telecommunications today and tomorrow." *Law and Business* (February 1983).

Pool, Ithiel de Sola. *Topic*, no. 146 (July 1983).

Pool, Ithiel de Sola. "Tracking the flow of information." *Science* 221, no. 4611 (12 August 1983): 609–613.

Pool, Ithiel de Sola. "Transborder data flows for developing countries." *Konnichiwa* 50 (Fall 1983).

Pool, Ithiel de Sola. "What ferment? A challenge for empirical research." *Journal of Communication* 33, no. 3 (Winter 1983): 258–61.

Pool, Ithiel de Sola. "Whither software copyright." Paper prepared for the Conference on Critical Issues for National Computerization Policy at the Communications Institute, East-West Center, Honolulu, Hawaii. July 31, 1983. Cambridge, MA: Research Program on Communications Policy, Massachusetts Institute of Technology , 1983.

Pool, Ithiel de Sola. "Will mobile telephones move?" *Technology Review* 86, no. 6 (November/December 1983): 59–60.

Pool, Ithiel de sola. "Wrap-up and reflections." Institute of Politics, John F. Kennedy School of Government. In *Television and the Presidential elections*, edited by Linsky, Martin, pp. 113–17. Lexington, MA: D.C. Heath, 1983.

Ward, John E.; Pool, Ithiel de Sola; Solomon, Richard J. Final report LIDS-FR-1296E. USIA Contract IA-20076-23. Revised 25 April, 1983. *Executive summary. A study of future directions for the Voice of America in the changing world of international broadcasting.* Cambridge, MA: Laboratory for Information and Decision Systems, Massachusetts Institute of Technology, 1983.

Pool, Ithiel de Sola. "Academic practices, freedoms, and the new technologies." American Association for Higher Education, pp. 19–24. *Current Issues in Higher Education, 1983–84*, vol. 1. 1983.

Pool, Ithiel de Sola. "Comment." In *Disconnecting Bell—the impact of the AT&T divestiture*, edited by Shooshan III, Harry M., pp. 112–31. New York: Pergamon Press, 1984.

Pool, Ithiel de Sola, Inose, H.; Takasake, N.; Hurwitz, Roger. *Communications flows: A census in the United States and Japan.* Tokyo: University of Tokyo Press, 1984.

Pool, Ithiel de Sola. "Looking down the road of technological change." In Crossroads. *Proceedings of the first national conference of the Library and Information Technology Association.* September 17–21, 1983. Baltimore, Maryland., edited by Gorman, Michael, pp. 16–22. Library and Information Technology Series No. 1. Chicago: American Library Association, 1984.

Pool, Ithiel de Sola. "User interfaces." *Information Society* 2, no. 3–4 (May 1984).

Pool, Ithiel de Sola. "Who needs the bandwidth?" Text of a speech. Paper prepared for the Optical Society, New Orleans, January 23, 1984.

Pool, Ithiel de Sola, Neuman, Russell. "The flow of communication into the home." In *Media audience and social structure*, edited by Ball-Rokeach, Sandra; Cantor, Muriel G., pp. 71–86. Beverly Hills, CA: Sage Publications, 1986.

Pool, Ithiel de Sola. "Speech in an electronic age." In *To govern a changing society: Constitutionalism and the challenge of new technology*, edited by Peck, Robert S., pp. 31–43. Washington, DC: Smithsonian Institution Press, 1990.

Pool, Ithiel de Sola. *Technologies without boundaries: On telecommuncations in a global age*, edited by Noam, Eli M. Cambridge, MA: Harvard University Press, 1990.
Pool, Ithiel de Sola. "The shrinking island." Mimeo. [Undated]

Index